Houghton
Mifflin
Harcourt

Geometry
Volume 2

TIMOTHY D. KANOLD

EDWARD B. BURGER

JULI K. DIXON

MATTHEW R. LARSON

STEVEN J. LEINWAND

© Houghton Mifflin Harcourt Publishing Company • Cover/Title Page (Lagoon Bridge, Boston, MA) Sean Pavone/Shutterstock; (Potato Field, ID) alexmisu/Shutterstock; (Pineapple Fountain, Charleston, SC ClimberJAK/Shutterstock; (Observatory, Tucson, AZ) John A. Davis/Shutterstock.

Printed in the U.S.A.

ISBN 978-0-544-38580-1

8 9 10   1026   24 23 22 21 20 19 18 17 16

4500606308   D E F G H

Authors

Timothy D. Kanold, Ph.D., is an award-winning international educator, author, and consultant. He is a former superintendent and director of mathematics and science at Adlai E. Stevenson High School District 125 in Lincolnshire, Illinois. He is a past president of the National Council of Supervisors of Mathematics (NCSM) and the Council for the Presidential Awardees of Mathematics (CPAM). He has served on several writing and leadership commissions for NCTM during the past decade. He presents motivational professional development seminars with a focus on developing professional learning communities (PLC's) to improve the teaching, assessing, and learning of students. He has recently authored nationally recognized articles, books, and textbooks for mathematics education and school leadership, including *What Every Principal Needs to Know about the Teaching and Learning of Mathematics*.

Edward B. Burger, Ph.D., is the President of Southwestern University, a former Francis Christopher Oakley Third Century Professor of Mathematics at Williams College, and a former vice provost at Baylor University. He has authored or coauthored more than sixty- five articles, books, and video series; delivered over five hundred addresses and workshops throughout the world; and made more than fifty radio and television appearances. He is a Fellow of the American Mathematical Society as well as having earned many national honors, including the Robert Foster Cherry Award for Great Teaching in 2010. In 2012, Microsoft Education named him a "Global Hero in Education."

Juli K. Dixon, Ph.D., is a Professor of Mathematics Education at the University of Central Florida. She has taught mathematics in urban schools at the elementary, middle, secondary, and post-secondary levels. She is an active researcher and speaker with numerous publications and conference presentations. Key areas of focus are deepening teachers' content knowledge and communicating and justifying mathematical ideas. She is a past chair of the NCTM Student Explorations in Mathematics Editorial Panel and member of the Board of Directors for the Association of Mathematics Teacher Educators.

Matthew R. Larson, Ph.D., is the K-12 mathematics curriculum specialist for the Lincoln Public Schools and served on the Board of Directors for the National Council of Teachers of Mathematics from 2010 to 2013. He is a past chair of NCTM's Research Committee and was a member of NCTM's Task Force on Linking Research and Practice. He is the author of several books on implementing the Common Core Standards for Mathematics. He has taught mathematics at the secondary and college levels and held an appointment as an honorary visiting associate professor at Teachers College, Columbia University.

Steven J. Leinwand is a Principal Research Analyst at the American Institutes for Research (AIR) in Washington, D.C., and has over 30 years in leadership positions in mathematics education. He is past president of the National Council of Supervisors of Mathematics and served on the NCTM Board of Directors. He is the author of numerous articles, books, and textbooks and has made countless presentations with topics including student achievement, reasoning, effective assessment, and successful implementation of standards.

Performance Task Consultant

STEM Consultants
Science, Technology, Engineering, and Mathematics

Reviewers

Similarity

Similarity and Transformations

MODULE 12 Using Similar Triangles

UNIT 5 Trigonometry

Volume 2

MODULE 13

Trigonometry with Right Triangles

MODULE 14

Trigonometry with All Triangles

Properties of Circles

 MODULE 15

Angles and Segments in Circles

Real-World Video 777
Are You Ready? 778

 MODULE 16

Arc Length and Sector Area

Real-World Video 849
Are You Ready? 850

MODULE 17

Equations of Circles and Parabolas

Measurement and Modeling in Two and Three Dimensions

MODULE 18

Volume Formulas

MODULE 19

Visualizing Solids

MODULE 20

Modeling and Problem Solving

Probability

MODULE 21 — Introduction to Probability

MODULE 22 — Conditional Probability and Independence of Events

MODULE 23

Probability and Decision Making

Similarity

MATH IN CAREERS

Special Effects Engineer Special effects engineers make movies come to life. With the use of math and some creative camera angles, special effects engineers can make big things appear small and vice versa.

If you're interested in a career as a special effects engineer, you should study these mathematical subjects:
- Algebra
- Geometry
- Trigonometry

Research other careers that require the use of engineering to understand real-world scenarios. See the related Career Activity at the end of this unit.

Reading Start-Up

Vocabulary

Review Words

✔ betweenness (*intermediación*)

✔ collinearity (*colinealidad*)

✔ congruent (*congruente*)

✔ orientation (*orientación*)

✔ parallel (*paralelo*)

✔ reflection (*reflejo*)

✔ rotation (*rotación*)

✔ transformation (*transformación*)

✔ translation (*traslación*)

Preview Words

center of dilation (*centro de la dilatación*)

dilation (*dilatación*)

geometric mean (*media geométrica*)

indirect measurement (*medición indirecta*)

scale factor (*factor de escala*)

similar (*similar*)

similarity transformation (*transformación de semejanza*)

Visualize Vocabulary

Use the ✔ words to complete the main idea web. Write the review words in the squares and include definitions.

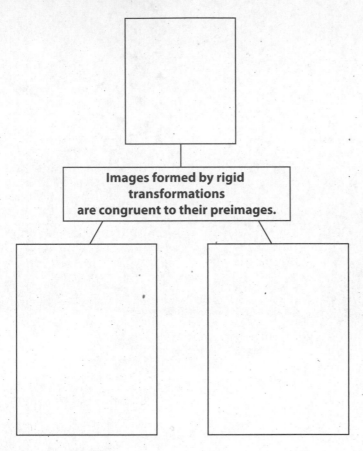

Images formed by rigid transformations are congruent to their preimages.

Understand Vocabulary

Complete the sentences using the preview words.

1. The image formed by a(n) _____ has the same shape as its pre-image.

2. The _____ indicates the ratio of the lengths of corresponding sides of two similar figures.

3. In the proportion $\frac{a}{x} = \frac{x}{b}$, x is called the _____.

Active Reading

Double-Door Fold Create a Double-Door Fold prior to starting the unit. Write characteristics of congruency under one flap. Fill out the other flap with corresponding characteristics of similarity so that the two topics can be compared more easily.

Similarity and Transformations

Essential Question: How can you use similarity and transformations to solve real-world problems?

REAL WORLD VIDEO
Check out how properties of similarity and transformations can be used to create scale models of large, real-world structures like monuments.

MODULE PERFORMANCE TASK PREVIEW

Modeling the Washington Monument

In this module, you will be challenged to create a plan for a scale model of the Washington Monument. How can you use similarity and dilations to help you produce an accurate model? Let's find out.

Are(YOU)Ready?

Complete these exercises to review skills you will need for this module.

Properties of Dilations

Example 1   Stretch $\triangle ABC$ with points $A(1, 2)$, $B(3, 2)$, and $C(3, -1)$ horizontally and vertically by a factor of 4.

$(x, y) \rightarrow (4x, 4y)$ Write the transformation rule.

$A'(4, 8)$, $B'(12, 8)$, $C'(12, -4)$ Use the transformation to write each transformed point.

Describe the transformation.

1. Stretch $\triangle DEF$ with points $D(-2, 1)$, $E(-1, -1)$, and $F(-2, -2)$ horizontally and vertically by a factor of -3.

_____

2. Is the stretch a rigid motion?

_____

3. Is it true that $\triangle DEF \cong \triangle D'E'F'$?

_____

Similar Figures

Example 2   Transform $\triangle ABC$ with points $A(3, 4)$, $B(-1, 6)$, and $C(0, 1)$ by shifting it 2 units to the right and 1 unit up.

$(x, y) \rightarrow (x + 2, y + 1)$ Write the transformation rule.

$A'(5, 5)$, $B'(1, 7)$, $C'(2, 2)$ Write each transformed point.

Describe the transformation shown in the graph.

4. Write the rule used to transform $\triangle ABC$.

_____

5. Describe in words the transformation shown in the figure.

_____

_____

_____

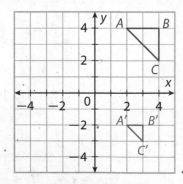

11.2 Proving Figures are Similar Using Transformations

Essential Question: How can similarity transformations be used to show two figures are similar?

🧭 Explore   Confirming Similarity

A **similarity transformation** is a transformation in which an image has the same shape as its pre-image. Similarity transformations include reflections, translations, rotations, and dilations. Two plane figures are **similar** if and only if one figure can be mapped to the other through one or more similarity transformations.

A grid shows a map of the city park. Use tracing paper to confirm that the park elements are similar.

(A) Trace patio *EFHG*. Turn the paper so that patio *EFHG* is mapped onto patio *LMON*. Describe the transformation. What does this confirm about the patios?

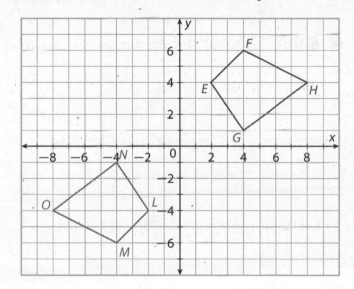

_____

(B) Trace statues *ABCDEF* and *JKLMNO*. Fold the paper so that statue *ABCDEF* is mapped onto statue *JKLMNO*. Describe the transformation. What does this confirm about the statues?

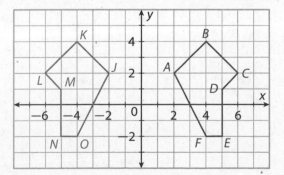

_____

_____

(C) Describe the transformation you can use to map vertices of garden *RST* to corresponding vertices of garden *DEF*. What does this confirm about the gardens?

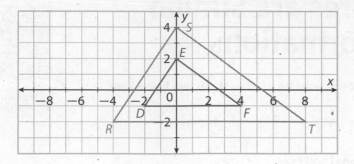

Reflect

1. Look back at all the steps. Were any of the images congruent to the pre-images? If so, what types of similarity transformations were performed with these figures? What does this tell you about the relationship between similar and congruent figures?

_____

_____

_____

2. If two figures are similar, can you conclude that corresponding angles are congruent? Why or why not?

_____

_____

🔧 Explain 1 Determining If Figures are Similar

You can represent dilations using the coordinate notation $(x, y) \rightarrow (kx, ky)$, where k is the scale factor and the center of dilation is the origin. If $0 < k < 1$, the dilation is a reduction. If $k > 1$, the dilation is an enlargement.

Example 1 **Determine whether the two figures are similar using similarity transformations. Explain.**

(A) △*RST* and △*XYZ*

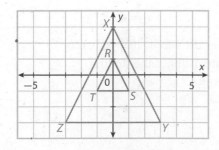

To map △*RST* onto △*XYZ*, there must be some factor k that dilates △*RST*.

Pre-image	Image
$R(0, 1)$	$X(0, 3)$
$S(1, -1)$	$Y(3, -3)$
$T(-1, -1)$	$Z(-3, -3)$

You can see that each coordinate of the pre-image is multiplied by 3 to get the image, so this is a dilation with scale factor 3. Therefore, $\triangle RST$ can be mapped onto $\triangle XYZ$ by a dilation with center at the origin, which is represented by the coordinate notation $(x, y) \rightarrow (3x, 3y)$. A dilation is a similarity transformation, so $\triangle RST$ is similar to $\triangle XYZ$.

(B) *PQRS and WXYZ*

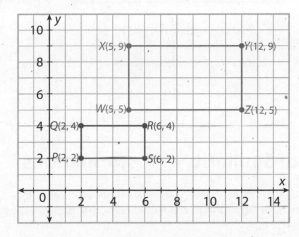

To map *PQRS* onto *WXYZ*, there must be some factor k that enlarges *PQRS*.

Pre-image	Image
$P(2, 2)$	
$Q(2, 4)$	$X(5, 9)$
	$Z(12, 5)$

Find each distance: $PQ = 2$, $QR = \boxed{}$, $WX = \boxed{}$, and ____ = 7

If $kPQ = WX$, then $k = 2$. However. $2QR = / \neq XY$.

No value of k can be determined that will map *PQRS* to *WXYZ*.

So, the figures are/are not similar.

Your Turn

Determine whether the two figures are similar using similarity transformations. Explain.

3.   *LMNO* and *GHJK*

4. $\triangle JKL$ and $\triangle MNP$

5. $CDEF$ and $TUVF$

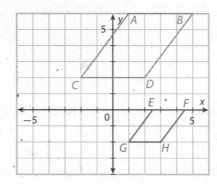

🎸 **Explain 2** **Finding a Sequence of Similarity Transformations**

In order for two figures to be similar, there has to be some sequence of similarity transformations that maps one figure to the other. Sometimes there will be a single similarity transformation in the sequence. Sometimes you must identify more than one transformation to describe a mapping.

Example 2 Find a sequence of similarity transformations that maps the first figure to the second figure. Write the coordinate notation for each transformation.

(A) $ABDC$ to $EFHG$

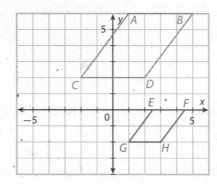

Since $EFHG$ is smaller than $ABDC$, the scale factor k of the dilation must be between 0 and 1. The length of $\overline{AB}$ is 4 and the length of $\overline{EF}$ is 2; therefore, the scale factor is $\frac{1}{2}$. Write the new coordinates after the dilation:

Original Coordinates	$A(1, 6)$	$B(5, 6)$	$C(-2, 2)$	$D(2, 2)$
Coordinates after dilation $k = \frac{1}{2}$	$A'\left(\frac{1}{2}, 3\right)$	$B'\left(\frac{5}{2}, 3\right)$	$C'(-1, 1)$	$D'(1, 1)$

A translation right 2 units and down 3 units completes the mapping.

Coordinates after dilation	$A'\left(\frac{1}{2}, 3\right)$	$B'\left(\frac{5}{2}, 3\right)$	$C'(-1, 1)$	$D'(1, 1)$
Coordinates after translation $(x + 2, y - 3)$	$E\left(\frac{5}{2}, 0\right)$	$F\left(\frac{9}{2}, 0\right)$	$G(1, -2)$	$H(3, -2)$

The coordinates after translation are the same as the coordinates of $EFGH$, so you can map $ABDC$ to $EFHG$ by the dilation $(x, y) \rightarrow \left(\frac{1}{2}x, \frac{1}{2}y\right)$ followed by a translation $(x, y) \rightarrow (x + 2, y - 3)$.

B △JKL to △PQR

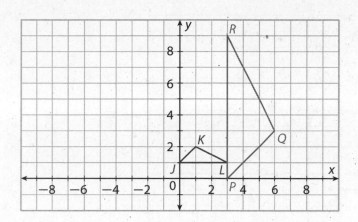

You can map △JKL to △PQR with a reflection across the x-axis followed by a _____ followed by a

[ ]° counterclockwise rotation about the origin.

Reflection: $(x, y) \rightarrow (x, -y)$ _____ : $(x, y) \rightarrow ($ [ ] $)$ [ ]° counterclockwise rotation:
$(x, y) \rightarrow ($ [ ] $)$

Reflect

6. Using the figure in Example 3A, describe a single dilation that maps *ABDC* to *EFHG*.

_____

_____

7. Using the figure in Example 3B, describe a different sequence of transformations that will map △JKL to △PQR.

_____

Your Turn

For each pair of similar figures, find a sequence of similarity transformations that maps one figure to the other. Use coordinate notation to describe the transformations.

8. *PQRS* to *TUVW*

9. △*ABC* to △*DEF*

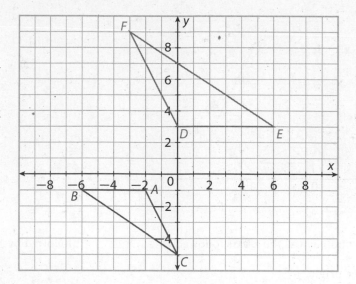

10. Describe a sequence of similarity transformations that maps *JKLMN* to *VWXYZ*.

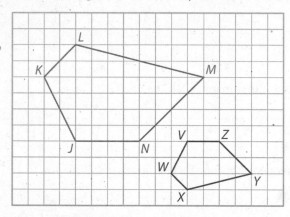

⊘ Explain 3 **Proving All Circles Are Similar**

You can use the definition of similarity to prove theorems about figures.

Circle Similarity Theorem
All circles are similar.

Example 3 **Prove the Circle Similarity Theorem.**

Given: Circle *C* with center *C* and radius *r*.
Circle *D* with center *D* and radius *s*.

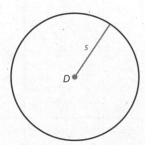

Prove: Circle *C* is similar to circle *D*.

To prove similarity, you must show that there is a sequence of similarity transformations that maps circle *C* to circle *D*.

(A) Start by transforming circle C with a _____ along the vector $\vec{CD}$.

Through this _____, the image of point C is _____.

Let the image of circle C be circle C'. The center of circle C' coincides with point _____.

(B) Transform circle C' with the dilation with center of dilation _____ and scale factor $\frac{s}{r}$.

Circle C' is made up of all the points at distance _____ from point _____.

After the dilation, the image of circle C' will consist of all the points at distance _____ from point D.

These are the same points that form circle _____. Therefore, the _____ followed by the dilation

maps circle C to circle _____. Because _____ and dilations are _____,

you can conclude that circle C is _____ to circle _____.

Reflect

11. Can you show that circle C and circle D are similar through another sequence of similarity transformations? Explain.

_____

_____

12. Discussion Is it possible that circle C and circle D are congruent? If so, does the proof of the similarity of the circles still work? Explain.

_____

_____

Elaborate

13. Translations, reflections, and rotations are rigid motions. What unique characteristic keeps dilations from being considered a rigid motion?

_____

_____

_____

14. Essential Question Check-In Two squares in the coordinate plane have horizontal and vertical sides. Explain how they are similar using similarity transformations.

_____

_____

Personal Math Trainer

• Online Homework
• Hints and Help
• Extra Practice

In Exercises 1–4, determine if the two figures are similar using similarity transformations. Explain.

1. *EFGH* and *ABCD*

2. △*PQR* and △*STU*

3. *JKLMN* and *JPQRS*

4. △*UVW* and △*GHI*

For the pair of similar figures in each of Exercises 5–10, find a sequence of similarity transformations that maps one figure to the other. Provide the coordinate notation for each transformation.

5. Map △*ABC* to △*PQR*.

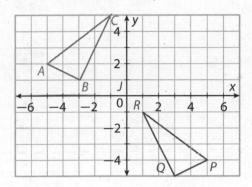

6. Map *ABCD* to *EFGH*.

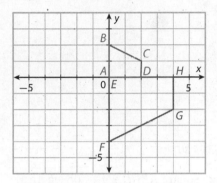

7. Map △*CED* to △*CBA*.

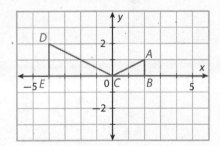

8. Map *ABCDE* to *JKLMN*.

9. Map *ABCD* to *JKLM*.

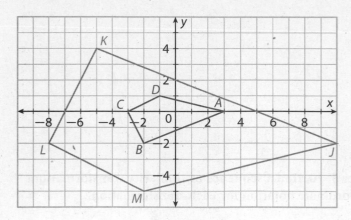

10. Map △*JKL* to △*PQR*

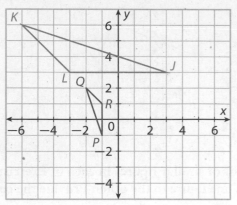

Complete the proof.

11. Given: Square *ABCD* with side length *x*.
Square *EFGH* with side length *y*.

Prove: Square *ABCD* is similar to square *EFGH*.

12. Given: Equilateral $\triangle JKL$ with side length j.
Equilateral $\triangle PQR$ with side length p

Prove: $\triangle JKL$ is similar to $\triangle PQR$.

13. Given: $\triangle ABC$ with $AB = c$, $BC = a$, $AC = b$
$\triangle XYZ$ with $YZ = x$, $XY = \frac{cx}{a}$, $XZ = \frac{bx}{a}$

Prove: $\triangle ABC$ is similar to $\triangle XYZ$.

14. The dimensions of a standard tennis court are 36 feet × 78 feet with a net that is 3 feet high in the center. The court is modified for players aged 10 and under such that the dimensions are 27 feet × 60 feet, and the same net is used. Use similarity to determine if the modified court is similar to the standard court.

15. **Represent Real-World Problems** A scuba flag is used to indicate there is a diver below. In North America, scuba flags are red with a white stripe from the upper left corner to the lower right corner. Justify the triangles formed on the scuba flag are similar triangles.

16. The most common picture size is 4 inches ×6 inches. Other common pictures sizes (in inches) are 5 × 7, 8 × 10, 9 × 12, 11 × 14, 14 × 18, and 16 × 20.

    a. Are any of these picture sizes similar? Explain using similarity transformations.

    b. What does your conclusion indicate about resizing pictures?

17. Nicole wants to know the height of the snow sculpture but it is too tall to measure. Nicole measured the shadow of the snow sculpture's highest point to be 10 feet long. At the same time of day Nicole's shadow was 40 inches long. If Nicole is 5 feet tall, what is the height of the snow sculpture?

18. Which of the following is a dilation?

    A. $(x, y) \rightarrow (x, 3y)$

    B. $(x, y) \rightarrow (3x, -y)$

    C. $(x, y) \rightarrow (3x, 3y)$

    D. $(x, y) \rightarrow (x, y - 3)$

    E. $(x, y) \rightarrow (x - 3, y - 3)$

19. What is not preserved under dilation? Select all that apply.

    A. Angle measure

    B. Betweenness

    C. Collinearity

    D. Distance

    E. Proportionality

20. **Analyze Relationships** Consider the transformations below.

   I. Translation   **II.** Reflection   **III.** Rotation   **IV.** Dilation

   a. Which transformations preserve distance?

   b. Which transformations preserve angle measure?

   c. Use your knowledge of rigid transformations to compare and contrast congruency and similarity.

Justify Reasoning For Exercises 21–23, use the figure shown. Determine whether the given assumptions are enough to prove that the two triangles are similar. Write the correct correspondence of the vertices. If the two triangles must be similar, describe a sequence of similarity transformations that maps one triangle to the other. If the triangles are not necessarily similar, explain why.

21. The lengths AX, BX, CX, and DX satisfy the equation $\frac{AX}{BX} = \frac{DX}{CX}$.

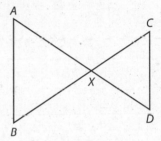

22. Lines AB and CD are parallel.

23. $\angle XAB$ is congruent to $\angle XCD$.

Lesson Performance Task

Answer the following questions about the dartboard pictured here.

1. Are the circles similar? Explain, using the concept of a dilation in your explanation.

2. You throw a dart and it sticks in a random location on the board. What is the probability that it sticks in Circle A? Circle B? Circle C? Circle D? Explain how you found your answers.

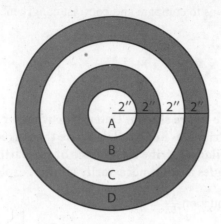

11.3 Corresponding Parts of Similar Figures

Essential Question: If you know two figures are similar, what can you determine about measures of corresponding angles and lengths?

Resource Locker

⊘ Explore **Connecting Angles and Sides of Figures**

You know that if figures are similar, the side lengths are proportional and the angle measures are equal. If you have two figures with proportional side lengths and congruent angles, can you conclude that they are similar?

Ⓐ Consider the graph of *ABCD* and *KLMN*.

Are corresponding angles congruent? Yes/No

Measure the angles.

$m\angle A =$ _____ $m\angle K =$ _____

$m\angle B =$ _____ $m\angle L =$ _____

$m\angle C =$ _____ $m\angle M =$ _____

$m\angle D =$ _____ $m\angle N =$ _____

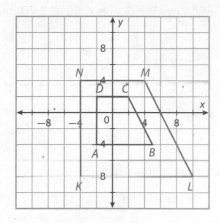

Ⓑ Are the ratios of corresponding side lengths equal? Yes/No

$$\frac{AB}{KL} = \frac{\Box}{\Box} \qquad \frac{BC}{LM} = \frac{\Box}{\Box} \qquad \frac{CD}{MN} = \frac{\Box}{\Box} \qquad \frac{AD}{KN} = \frac{\Box}{\Box}$$

Ⓒ Are the figures similar? Describe how you know using similarity transformations.

_____

_____

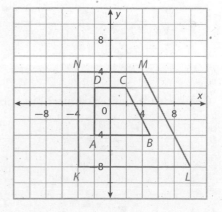

Ⓓ Consider the graph of *ABCD* and *EFGH*.

Are corresponding angles congruent? Yes/No Explain.

_____

_____

Ⓔ Are the ratios of corresponding side lengths equal? Yes/No

$\dfrac{AB}{EF} = \dfrac{\Box}{\Box}$ $\dfrac{BC}{FG} = \dfrac{\Box}{\Box}$ $\dfrac{CD}{GH} = \dfrac{\Box}{\Box}$ $\dfrac{AD}{EH} = \dfrac{\Box}{\Box}$

Ⓕ Are the figures similar? Describe how you know using similarity transformations.

_____

_____

Ⓖ Consider the graph of *PQRS* and *WXYZ*.

Are corresponding angles congruent? Yes/No

Measure the angles.

m∠*P* = _____   m∠*W* = _____

m∠*Q* = _____   m∠*X* = _____

m∠*R* = _____   m∠*Y* = _____

m∠*S* = _____   m∠*Z* = _____

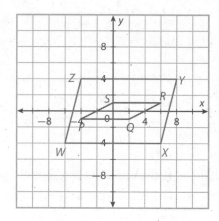

Ⓗ Are the ratios of corresponding side lengths equal? Yes/No

$\dfrac{PQ}{WX} = \dfrac{\Box}{\Box}$ $\dfrac{QR}{XY} = \dfrac{\Box}{\Box}$ $\dfrac{RS}{YZ} = \dfrac{\Box}{\Box}$ $\dfrac{PS}{WZ} = \dfrac{\Box}{\Box}$

Ⓘ Are the figures similar? Describe how you know using similarity transformations.

_____

_____

_____

1. If two figures have the same number of sides and the corresponding angles are congruent, does this mean that a pair of corresponding sides are either congruent or proportional?

_____

_____

2. If two figures have a center of dilation, is a corresponding pair of sides necessarily proportional?

_____

_____

3. If two figures have a correspondence of proportional sides, do the figures necessarily have a center of dilation?

_____

_____

⚘ Explain 1   Justifying Properties of Similar Figures Using Transformations

Two figures that can be mapped to each other by similarity transformations (dilations and rigid motions) are similar. Similar figures have certain properties.

Properties of Similar Figures

Corresponding angles of similar figures are congruent.

Corresponding sides of similar figures are proportional.

If $\triangle ABC \sim \triangle XYZ$, then

$\angle A \cong \angle X \quad \angle B \cong \angle Y \quad \angle C \cong \angle Z$

$\dfrac{AB}{XY} = \dfrac{BC}{YZ} = \dfrac{AC}{XZ}$

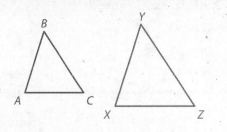

To show that two figures with all pairs of corresponding sides having equal ratio k and all pairs of corresponding angles congruent are similar, you can use similarity transformations.

Dilate one figure using k. The dilated figure is congruent to the second figure by the definition of congruence. So, there is a sequence of rigid motions (which are also similarity transformations) that maps one to the other.

Example 1   Identify properties of similar figures.

Ⓐ Figure $EFGH$ maps to figure $RSTU$ by a similarity transformation. Write a proportion that contains EF and RU. List any angles that must be congruent to $\angle G$ or congruent to $\angle U$.

$\dfrac{EF}{RS} = \dfrac{EH}{RU} \qquad \angle T$ is congruent to $\angle G$, and $\angle H$ is congruent to $\angle U$.

Ⓑ Figure $JKLMN$ maps to figure $TUVWX$ by a similarity transformation. Write a proportion that contains TX and LM. List any angles that must be congruent to $\angle V$ or congruent to $\angle K$.

$\dfrac{\boxed{}}{TX} = \dfrac{LM}{\boxed{}} \qquad \angle\_\_\_\_$ is congruent to $\angle V$, and $\angle\_\_\_\_$ is congruent to $\angle K$.

4. If you know two figures are similar, what angle or side measurements must you know to find the dilation used in the transformations mapping one figure to another?

_____

Your Turn

5. Triangles $\triangle PQR$ and $\triangle LMN$ are similar. If $QR = 6$ and $MN = 9$, what similarity transformation (in coordinate notation) maps $\triangle PQR$ to $\triangle LMN$?

6. **Error Analysis** Triangles $\triangle DEF$ and $\triangle UVW$ are similar. $\dfrac{DE}{UV} = \dfrac{VW}{EF}$ Is the statement true?

⚙ Explain 2 Applying Properties of Similar Figures

The properties of similar figures can be used to find the measures of corresponding parts.

Example 2 Given that the figures are similar, find the values of x and y.

Find the value of x.

$\angle C \cong \angle R$, so $m\angle C = m\angle R$

$4x + 27 = 95$

$4x = 68$

$x = 17$

Find the value of y.

$\dfrac{AB}{PS} = \dfrac{AD}{PQ}$

$\dfrac{4y}{10} = \dfrac{3y - 5}{5}$

$\dfrac{4y}{10} \cdot 10 = \dfrac{3y - 5}{5} \cdot 10$

$4y = 6y - 10$

$y = 5$

Find the value of x.

$m\angle LMN = m\angle XYZ$

_____ = _____

_____ = _____

_____ = _____

Find the value of y.

$\dfrac{JK}{VW} = \dfrac{\quad}{\quad}$

$= $

_____ = _____

_____

_____

_____

7. Discussion What are some things you need to be careful about when solving problems involving finding the values of variables in similar figures?

_____

_____

_____

_____

Use the diagram, in which △ABE ~ △ACD.

8. Find the value of x.

9. Find the value of y.

Elaborate

10. Consider two similar triangles △ABC and △A′B′C′. If both m∠A′ = m∠C and m∠B′ = m∠A, what can you conclude about triangle △ABC? Explain your reasoning.

_____

_____

_____

11. Rectangle JKLM maps to rectangle RSTU by the transformation $(x, y) \rightarrow (4x, 4y)$. If the perimeter of RSTU is x, what is the perimeter of JKLM in terms of x?

_____

_____

12. Essential Question Check-In If two figures are similar, what can we conclude about their corresponding parts?

_____

_____

☆ Evaluate: Homework and Practice

In the figures, are corresponding angles congruent? Are corresponding sides proportional? Are the figures similar? Describe how you know using similarity transformations.

1.

2.

3.

4.

5. Figure *ABCD* is similar to figure *MNKL*. Write a proportion that contains *BC* and *KL*.

6. △*DEF* is similar to △*STU*. Write a proportion that contains *ST* and *SU*.

7. △*XYZ* is similar to △*XVW*. Write the congruence statements that must be true.

8. △*MNP* is similar to △*HJK*, and both triangles are isosceles. If $m\angle P > 90°$, name all angles that are congruent to ∠*H*.

9. *CDEF* maps to *JKLM* with the transformations $(x, y) \rightarrow (5x, 5y) \rightarrow (x - 4, y - 4)$. What is the value of $\frac{EF}{LM}$?

10. △*PQR* maps to △*VWX* with the transformation $(x, y) \rightarrow (x + 3, y - 1) \rightarrow (2x, 2y)$. If $WX = 12$, what does *QR* equal?

11. $\triangle QRS$ maps to $\triangle XYZ$ with the transformation $(x, y) \rightarrow (6x, 6y)$. If $QS = 7$, what is the length of XZ?

12. Algebra Two similar figures are similar based on the transformation $(x, y) \rightarrow (12x, 3a^2y)$. What is/are the value(s) of a?

13. Algebra $\triangle PQR$ is similar to $\triangle XYZ$. If $PQ = n + 2$, $QR = n - 2$, and $XY = n^2 - 4$, what is the value of YZ, in terms of n?

14. Which transformations will not produce similar figures? Select all that apply and explain your choices.

A. $(x, y) \rightarrow (x - 4, y) \rightarrow (-x, -y) \rightarrow (8x, 8y)$

B. $(x, y) \rightarrow (x + 1, y + 1) \rightarrow (3x, 2y) \rightarrow (-x, -y)$

C. $(x, y) \rightarrow (5x, 5y) \rightarrow (x, -y) \rightarrow (x + 3, y - 3)$

D. $(x, y) \rightarrow (x, 2y) \rightarrow (x + 6, y - 2) \rightarrow (2x, y)$

E. $(x, y) \rightarrow (x, 3y) \rightarrow (2x, y) \rightarrow (x - 3, y - 2)$

15. The figures in the picture are similar to each other. Find the value of x.

16. In the diagram, $\triangle NPQ \sim \triangle NLM$ and $PL = 5$.

a. Find the value of x.

b. Find the lengths NP and NL.

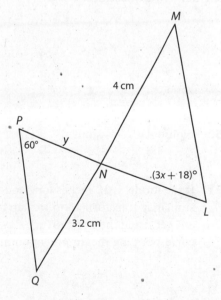

17. $\triangle CDE$ maps to $\triangle STU$ with the transformations
$(x, y) \rightarrow (x - 2, y - 2) \rightarrow (3x, 3y) \rightarrow (x, -y)$.
If $CD = a + 1$, $DE = 2a - 1$, $ST = 2b + 3$, and $TU = b + 6$, find the values of a and b.

18. If a sequence of transformations contains the transformation (ax, by), with $a \neq b$, could the pre-image and image represent congruent figures? Could they represent similar, non-congruent figures? Justify your answers with examples.

19. Is any pair of equilateral triangles similar to each other? Why or why not?

20. Figure $CDEF$ is similar to figure $KLMN$. Which statements are false? Select all that apply and explain why.

A. $\dfrac{CD}{KL} = \dfrac{EF}{MN}$ **B.** $\dfrac{CF}{KN} = \dfrac{EF}{MN}$ **C.** $\dfrac{DE}{LM} = \dfrac{CF}{KN}$ **D.** $\dfrac{LM}{DE} = \dfrac{KL}{CD}$ **E.** $\dfrac{LM}{DE} = \dfrac{KN}{CD}$

Consider this model of a train locomotive when answering the next two questions.

21. If the model is 18 inches long and the actual locomotive is 72 feet long, what is the similarity transformation to map from the model to the actual locomotive? Express the answer using the notation $x \rightarrow ax$, where x is a measurement on the model and ax is the corresponding measurement on the actual locomotive.

22. If the diameter of the front wheels on the locomotive is 4 feet, what is the diameter of the front wheels on the model? Express the answer in inches.

Use the following graph to answer the next two problems.

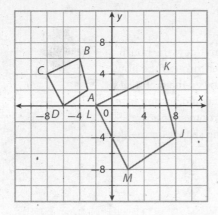

23. Specify a sequence of two transformations that will map *ABCD* onto *JKLM*.

24. Find the value of $\dfrac{AC + BD}{JL + KM}$.

25. Counterexamples Consider the statement "All rectangles are similar." Is this statement true or false? If true, explain why. If false, provide a counterexample.

26. Justify Reasoning If *ABCD* is similar to *KLMN* and *MNKL*, what special type of quadrilateral is *KLMN*? Justify your reasoning.

27. Critique Reasoning Consider the statement "If △*PQR* is similar to △*QPR*, then △*PQR* is similar to △*RPQ*." Explain whether or not this statement is true.

Lesson Performance Task

You've hired an architect to design your dream house and now the house has been built. Before moving in, you've decided to wander through the house with a tape measure to see how well the builders have followed the architect's floor plan. Describe in as much detail as you can how you could accomplish your goal. Then discuss how you can decide whether the room shapes and other features of the house are similar to the corresponding shapes on the floor plan.

11.4 AA Similarity of Triangles

Essential Question: How can you show that two triangles are similar?

Resource
Locker

⊘ Explore   **Exploring Angle-Angle Similarity for Triangles**

Two triangles are similar when their corresponding sides are proportional and their corresponding angles are congruent. There are several shortcuts for proving triangles are similar.

Ⓐ Draw a triangle and label it $\triangle ABC$. Elsewhere on your page, draw a segment longer than $\overline{AB}$ and label the endpoints D and E.

Ⓑ Copy $\angle CAB$ and $\angle ABC$ to points D and E, respectively. Extend the rays of your copied angles, if necessary, and label their intersection point F. You have constructed $\triangle DEF$.

Ⓒ You constructed angles D and E to be congruent to angles A and B, respectively. Therefore, angles C and F must also be _____ because of the _____Theorem.

Ⓓ Check the proportionality of the corresponding sides.

$$\frac{AB}{DE} = \frac{\boxed{}}{\boxed{}} = \boxed{} \qquad \frac{AC}{DF} = \frac{\boxed{}}{\boxed{}} = \boxed{} \qquad \frac{BC}{EF} = \frac{\boxed{}}{\boxed{}} = \boxed{}$$

Since the ratios are _____ the sides of the triangles are _____.

Reflect

1. **Discussion** Compare your results with your classmates. What conjecture can you make about two triangles that have two corresponding congruent angles?

_____

_____

🔘 Explain 1 Proving Angle-Angle Triangle Similarity

The Explore suggests the following theorem for determining whether two triangles are similar.

> ### Angle-Angle (AA) Triangle Similarity Theorem
>
> If two angles of one triangle are congruent to two angles of another triangle, then the two triangles are similar.

Example 1 Prove the Angle-Angle Triangle Similarity Theorem.

Given: $\angle A \cong \angle X$ and $\angle B \cong \angle Y$

Prove: $\triangle ABC \sim \triangle XYZ$

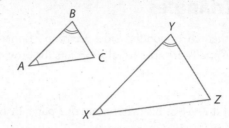

① Apply a dilation to $\triangle ABC$ with scale factor $k = \dfrac{XY}{AB}$. Let the image of $\triangle ABC$ be $\triangle A'B'C$.

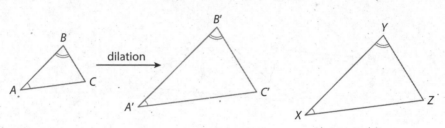

$\triangle A'B'C$ is similar to $\triangle ABC$, and $\angle A' \cong$ _____ and $\angle B' \cong$ _____

because _____.

Also, $A'B' = k \cdot AB =$ _____.

② It is given that $\angle A \cong \angle X$ and $\angle B \cong \angle Y$

By the Transitive Property of Congruence, $\angle A' \cong$ _____ and $\angle B' \cong$ _____.

So, $\triangle A'B'C' \cong \triangle XYZ$ by _____.

This means there is a sequence of rigid motions that maps $\triangle A'B'C'$ to $\triangle YYZ$.

The dilation followed by this sequence of rigid motions shows that there is a sequence of similarity transformations that maps $\triangle ABC$ to $\triangle XYZ$. Therefore, $\triangle ABC \sim \triangle XYZ$.

Reflect

2. **Discussion** Compare and contrast the AA Similarity Theorem with the ASA Congruence Theorem.

_____

_____

_____

_____

3. In $\triangle JKL$, $m\angle J = 40°$ and $m\angle K = 55°$. In $\triangle MNP$, $m\angle M = 40°$ and $m\angle P = 85°$. A student concludes that the triangles are not similar. Do you agree or disagree? Why?

_____

_____

🔗 Explain 2   Applying Angle-Angle Similarity

Architects and contractors use the properties of similar figures to find any unknown dimensions, like the proper height of a triangular roof. They can use a bevel angle tool to check that the angles of construction are congruent to the angles in their plans.

Example 2   Find the indicated length, if possible.

(A)   *BE*

First, determine whether $\triangle ABC \sim \triangle DBE$.

By the Alternate Interior Angles Theorem, $\angle A \cong \angle D$ and $\angle C \cong \angle E$, so $\triangle ABC \sim \triangle DBE$ by the AA Triangle Similarity Theorem.

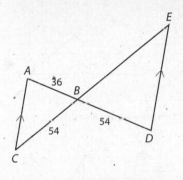

Find *BE* by solving a proportion.

$$\frac{BD}{BA} = \frac{BE}{BC}$$

$$\frac{54}{36} = \frac{BE}{54}$$

$$\frac{54}{36} \cdot 54 = \frac{BE}{54} \cdot 54$$

$$BE = 81$$

(B)   *RT*

Check whether $\triangle RSV \sim \triangle RTU$:

It is given in the diagram that $\angle \boxed{} \cong \angle \boxed{}$. $\angle R$ is shared by both triangles,

so $\angle R \cong \angle R$ by the _____ Property of Congruence.

So, by the _____, $\triangle RST \sim \triangle RTU$.

Find *RT* by solving a proportion.

$$\cdot \frac{RT}{RS} = \frac{TU}{SV}$$

$$\frac{RT}{\boxed{}} = \frac{\boxed{}}{\boxed{}}$$

$$RT = \boxed{}$$

4. In Example 2*A*, is there another way you can set up the proportion to solve for *BE*?

_____

5. Discussion When asked to solve for *y*, a student sets up the proportion as shown. Explain why the proportion is wrong. How should you adjust the proportion so that it will give the correct result?

$$\frac{y}{8} = \frac{14}{10}$$

_____

_____

_____

6. A builder was given a design plan for a triangular roof as shown. Explain how he knows that △*AED* ∼ △*ACB*. Then find *AB*.

7. Find *PQ*, if possible.

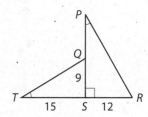

⚙ Explain 3 Applying SSS and SAS Triangle Similarity

In addition to Angle-Angle Triangle Similarity, there are two additional shortcuts for proving two triangles are similar.

Side-Side-Side (SSS) Triangle Similarity Theorem

If the three sides of one triangle are proportional to the corresponding sides of another triangle, then the triangles are similar.

Side-Angle-Side (SAS) Triangle Similarity Theorem

If two sides of one triangle are proportional to the corresponding sides of another triangle and their included angles are congruent, then the triangles are similar.

Example 3 Determine whether the given triangles are similar. Justify your answer.

 A

You are given two pairs of corresponding side lengths and one pair of congruent corresponding angles, so try using SAS.

Check that the ratios of corresponding sides are equal.

$$\frac{MN}{MR} = \frac{4}{6} = \frac{2}{3} \qquad\qquad \frac{MP}{MQ} = \frac{8}{8+4} = \frac{8}{12} = \frac{2}{3}$$

Check that the included angles are congruent: $\angle NMP \cong \angle QMR$ is given in the diagram.

Therefore $\triangle NMP \sim \triangle RMQ$ by the SAS Triangle Similarity Theorem.

B

You are given _____ pairs of corresponding side lengths and _____ congruent corresponding angles, so try using _____.

Check that the ratios of corresponding sides are equal.

$$\frac{LM}{GH} = \frac{\boxed{}}{\boxed{}} = \frac{\boxed{}}{\boxed{}} \qquad \frac{MN}{} = \frac{\boxed{}}{\boxed{}} = \frac{\boxed{}}{\boxed{}} \qquad \frac{}{} = \frac{\boxed{}}{\boxed{}} = \frac{\boxed{}}{\boxed{}}$$

Therefore $\triangle\ \boxed{} \sim \triangle\ \boxed{}$ by _____.

Since you are given all three pairs of sides, you don't need to check for congruent angles.

Reflect

8. Are all isosceles right triangles similar? Explain why or why not.

_____

_____

_____

9. Why isn't Angle-Side-Angle (ASA) used to prove two triangles similar?

_____

_____

If possible, determine whether the given triangles are similar. Justify your answer.

10.

11.

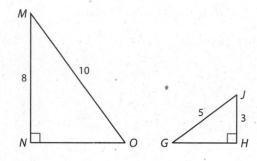

💬 Elaborate

12. Is triangle similarity transitive? If you know $\triangle ABC \sim \triangle DEF$ and $\triangle DEF \sim \triangle GHJ$, is $\triangle ABC \sim \triangle GHJ$? Explain.

_____

_____

_____

13. The AA Similarity Theorem applies to triangles. Is there an AAA Similarity Theorem for quadrilaterals? Use your geometry software to test your conjecture or create a counterexample.

_____

_____

_____

14. Essential Question Check-In How can you prove triangles are similar?

_____

_____

_____

_____

_____

Show that the triangles are similar by measuring the lengths of their sides and comparing the ratios of the corresponding sides.

1.

$\dfrac{DE}{AB} = \dfrac{}{} = \boxed{}$

$\dfrac{DF}{AC} = \dfrac{}{} = \boxed{}$

$\dfrac{EF}{BC} = \dfrac{}{} = \boxed{}$

2.

$\dfrac{AB}{DE} = \dfrac{}{} = \boxed{}$

$\dfrac{AC}{DF} = \dfrac{}{} = \boxed{}$

$\dfrac{BC}{EF} = \dfrac{}{} = \boxed{}$

Determine whether the two triangles are similar. If they are similar, write the similarity statement.

3.

4.

Determine whether the two triangles are similar. If they are similar, write the similarity statement.

5.

6.

Explain how you know whether the triangles are similar. If possible, find the indicated length.

7. *AC*

8. *AD*

9. *QR*

10. Find *BD*.

Show whether or not each pair of triangles are similar, if possible. Justify your answer, and write a similarity statement when the triangles are similar.

11.

12.

13.

14.

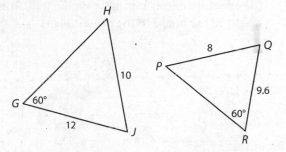

15. Explain the Error A student analyzes the two triangles shown below. Explain the error that the student makes.

$\frac{AB}{EF} = \frac{5.5}{4.8} = 1.15$, and $\frac{BC}{DF} = \frac{6}{6} = 1$

Because the two ratios are not equal, the two triangles are not similar.

16. Algebra Find all possible values of x for which these two triangles are similar.

17. Multi-Step Identify two similar triangles in the figure, and explain why they are similar. Then find AB:

18. The picture shows a person taking a pinhole photograph of himself. Light entering the opening reflects his image on the wall, forming similar triangles. What is the height of the image to the nearest inch?

15 in.

4 ft 6 in.

5 ft 5 in.

H.O.T. Focus on Higher Order Thinking

19. Analyze Relationships Prove the SAS Triangle Similarity Theorem.

Given: $\dfrac{XY}{AB} = \dfrac{XZ}{AC}$ and $\angle A \cong \angle X$

Prove: $\triangle ABC \sim \triangle XYZ$

20. Analyze Relationships Prove the SSS Triangle Similarity Theorem.

Given: $\dfrac{XY}{AB} = \dfrac{XZ}{AC} = \dfrac{YZ}{BC}$

Prove: $\triangle ABC \sim \triangle XYZ$

(Hint: The main steps of the proof are similar to those of the proof of the AA Triangle Similarity Theorem.)

21. Communicate Mathematical Ideas A student is asked to find point X on $\overleftrightarrow{BC}$ such that $\triangle ABC \sim \triangle XBA$ and XB is as small as possible. The student does so by constructing a perpendicular line to $\overleftrightarrow{AC}$ at point A, and then labeling X as the intersection of the perpendicular line with $\overleftrightarrow{BC}$. Explain why this procedure generates the similar triangle that the student was requested to construct.

22. Make a Conjecture Builders and architects use scale models to help them design and build new buildings. An architecture student builds a model of an office building in which the height of the model is $\frac{1}{400}$ of the height of the actual building, while the width and length of the model are each $\frac{1}{200}$ of the corresponding dimensions of the actual building. The model includes several triangles. Describe how a triangle in this model could be similar to the corresponding triangle in the actual building, then describe how a triangle in this model might not be similar to the corresponding triangle in the actual building. Use a similarity theorem to support each answer.

Lesson Performance Task

The figure shows a camera obscura and the object being "photographed." Answer the following questions about the figure:

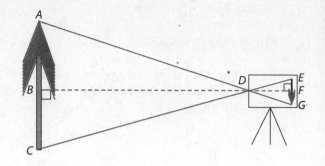

1. Explain how the image of the object would be affected if the camera were moved closer to the object. How would that limit the height of objects that could be photographed?

2. How do you know that △ADC is similar to △GDE?

3. Write a proportion you could use to find the height of the pine tree.

4. $DF = 12$ in., $EG = 8$ in., $BD = 96$ ft. How tall is the pine tree?

Similarity and Transformations

Essential Question: How can you use similarity and transformations to solve real-world problems?

KEY EXAMPLE *(Lesson 11.1)*

Determine the center of dilation and the scale factor of the dilation.

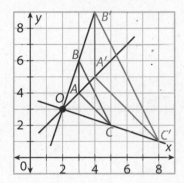

Draw a line through A and A'. Draw a line through B and B'. Draw a line through C and C'.

The three lines intersect at point $O(2, 3)$.

Find the distance from point O to points A and A'.

$$d_A = \sqrt{(2-3)^2 + (3-4)^2} = \sqrt{2}$$ Find the distance to point **A**.

$$d_{A'} = \sqrt{(2-4)^2 + (3-5)^2} = 2\sqrt{2}$$ Find the distance to point **A'**.

The distance from point O to point A' is twice the distance from point O to point A. The scale factor of dilation is 2 to 1.

KEY EXAMPLE *(Lesson 11.3)*

$\triangle ABCD$ maps to $\triangle EFGH$ by a similarity transformation. Write a proportion that contains $\overline{BC}$ and $\overline{EH}$. Then list any angles that are congruent to $\angle D$ or $\angle E$.

Corresponding sides of similar figures are proportional.

$\overline{BC} \cong \overline{FG}$ and $\overline{EH} \cong \overline{AD}$, so $\dfrac{BC}{FG} = \dfrac{AD}{EH}$.

Corresponding angles of similar figures are congruent.

$\angle D \cong \angle H$ and $\angle E \cong \angle A$.

Key Vocabulary

center of dilation *(centro de dilatación)*

dilation *(dilatación)*

scale factor *(factor de escala)*

Side-Side-Side Similarity *(Similitud Lado-Lado-Lado)*

Side-Angle-Side Similarity *(Similitud Lado-Ángulo-Lado)*

similar *(semejantes)*

similarity transformation *(transformación de semejanza)*

623

(Lesson 11.4)

Determine whether △*ABC* and △*DEF* are similar. If so, justify by SSS Similarity or SAS Similarity.

Check that the ratios of the lengths of corresponding sides are equal.

$\dfrac{3}{4}$

$\dfrac{6}{8} = \dfrac{3}{4}$

$\dfrac{7.5}{10} = \dfrac{3}{4}$

Since all the ratios of the lengths of corresponding sides are equal, the triangles are similar by SSS Similarity.

EXERCISES

Determine the following for the dilation. *(Lesson 11.1)*

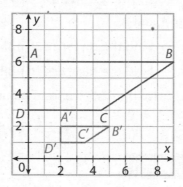

1. center _____

2. scale factor _____

Determine whether the two figures are similar using similarity transformations.
(Lesson 11.2)

3. △ABC to △DEF _____

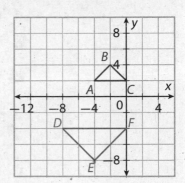

4. △ABCD to △EFGH _____

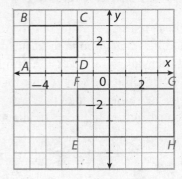

△ABC maps to △DEF by a similarity transformation. *(Lesson 11.3)*

5. Write a proportion that contains AB and EF. _____

6. Write a proportion that contains BC and DF. _____

7. List any angles that are congruent to ∠A or ∠E. _____

Determine whether △ABC and △DEF are similar. If so, justify by SSS or SAS.
(Lesson 11.4)

8. _____

9. _____

Designing a Model of the Washington Monument

Your challenge is to design a scale model of the Washington Monument that would be small enough to fit inside your classroom. Here are some key dimensions of the Washington Monument for you to consider in determining the scale factor for your model. (Note that the color of the stone changes part way up the monument because of a halt in construction between 1854 and 1877.)

Key Dimension	Measurement
Total height	555 ft 5 in.
Height to top of trapezoidal side	500 ft
Width at base	55 ft 1 in.
Width at top of trapezoidal side	34 ft 5 in.
Height at which stone color changes	151 ft

What scale factor will you use for your model? What are the key dimensions of your model?

Begin by making some notes in the space below about your strategy for designing the model. Then use your own paper to complete the task. Present your plan using diagrams, words, and/or numbers.

(Ready) to Go On?

11.1–11.4 Similarity and Transformations

Answer each problem about the image. *(Lesson 11.1)*

1. Are the two shapes similar? _____

2. Find the scale factor k. _____

3. Find the center of dilation. _____

4. Compare k to the ratio $\dfrac{\text{area } \triangle A'D'C'}{\text{area } \triangle ADC}$.

_____

Determine which of the following transformations are dilations. *(Lesson 11.1)*

5. $(x, y) \rightarrow (4x, 4y)$

_____

6. $(x, y) \rightarrow (-x, 3y)$

_____

7. $(x, y) \rightarrow (x - 2, y - 2)$

_____

8. $(x, y) \rightarrow \left(\dfrac{1}{3}x, \dfrac{1}{3}y\right)$

_____

Find the missing length. *(Lesson 11.3)*

9. $\triangle XYZ$ maps to $\triangle MNO$ with the transformation $(x, y) \rightarrow (7x, 7y)$. If $XY = 3$, what is the length of MN?

_____

Find the appropriate statements about the triangles. *(Lesson 11.4)*

10. $\triangle ABC$ is similar to $\triangle RTS$. Write a proportion that contains AC and RT. Also write the angle congruence statements that must be true.

ESSENTIAL QUESTION

11. How can you determine whether a shape is similar to another shape?

Assessment Readiness

1. Consider each transformation. Does the transformation preserve distance? Select Yes or No for A–C.

   A. Dilations   ○ Yes   ○ No

   B. Reflections   ○ Yes   ○ No

   C. Rotations   ○ Yes   ○ No

2. $\triangle MNO$ maps to $\triangle RST$ with the transformation $(x, y) \rightarrow \left(\frac{1}{3}x, \frac{1}{3}y\right)$. Choose True or False for each statement.

   A. If $RT = 3$, $MO = 9$.   ○ True   ○ False

   B. If $RT = 12$, $MO = 4$.   ○ True   ○ False

   C. If $RT = 9$, $MO = 27$.   ○ True   ○ False

3. Determine if the following pair of triangles are similar. If so, explain how. Note that $\overline{AC} \parallel \overline{BD}$.

4. If $\triangle ABC$ is similar to $\triangle XYZ$ and $\triangle YZX$, what special type of triangle is $\triangle ABC$? Justify your reasoning.

Using Similar Triangles

Essential Question: How can you use similar triangles to solve real-world problems?

REAL WORLD VIDEO
Check out how properties of similar triangles can be used to determine real-world areas of geographic regions like the Bermuda Triangle.

MODULE PERFORMANCE TASK PREVIEW

How Large Is the Bermuda Triangle?

In this module, you will be asked to determine the area of the Bermuda Triangle from a map. How can indirect measurement and the properties of similar triangles help you find the answer? Let's get started on solving this "mystery" of the Bermuda Triangle!

Complete these exercises to review skills you will need for this module.

Scale Factor and Scale Drawings

Example 1

Determine the length of the side $\overline{A'B'}$ given $AB = 4$, $BC = 3$, and $B'C' = 6$.

The image of $\triangle ABC$ is created as a result of a scale drawing, so the transformation is a dilation.

$2BC = B'C'$, so $2AB = A'B'$.

$A'B' = 2(4) = 8$

• Online Homework
• Hints and Help
• Extra Practice

Give the side length in $\triangle RST$.

1. ST, given $RT = 5$, $R'T' = 15$, and $S'T' = 18$ _____

Similar Figures

Example 2

The figures $PQRS$ and $KLMN$ are similar. Determine the angle in figure $KLMN$ that is congruent to $\angle Q$ and find its measure if m$\angle Q = 45°$.

$\angle Q \cong \angle L$ **Corresponding angles of similar figures are congruent.**

m$\angle Q = $ m$\angle L = 45°$ **Definition of congruency of angle.**

Give each angle measure.

2. m$\angle A$, given $\triangle ABC \cong \triangle DEF$ and m$\angle D = 67°$ _____

3. m$\angle E$, given $\triangle PQR \cong \triangle DEF$, m$\angle R = 13°$, and m$\angle D = 67°$ _____

The Pythagorean Theorem

Example 3

A right triangle $\triangle ABC$ has side lengths $AB = 3$ and $BC = 4$. Find the length of the hypotenuse $\overline{AC}$.

$\triangle ABC$ is a right triangle, so the Pythagorean Theorem can be used.

$AC = \sqrt{(AB)^2 + (BC)^2}$ **Write the Pythagorean Theorem.**

$AC = \sqrt{3^2 + 4^2} = \sqrt{9 + 16}$ **Substitute and simplify.**

$AC = 5$ **Simplify.**

Find the side length for each right triangle.

4. DE, given $DF = 5$, $EF = 12$, and $\overline{DE}$ is the hypotenuse _____

5. BC, given $AB = 15$, $AC = 17$, and $\overline{AC}$ is the hypotenuse _____

12.1 Triangle Proportionality Theorem

Essential Question: When a line parallel to one side of a triangle intersects the other two sides, how does it divide those sides?

⊘ Explore Constructing Similar Triangles

In the following activity you will see one way to construct a triangle similar to a given triangle.

Ⓐ Do your work for Steps A–C in the space provided. Draw a triangle.
Label it *ABC* as shown.

Ⓑ Select a point on $\overline{AB}$. Label it *E*.

Ⓒ Construct an angle with vertex *E* that is congruent to ∠*B*. Label the point where the side of the angle you constructed intersects $\overline{AC}$ as *F*.

Ⓓ Why are $\overleftrightarrow{EF}$ and $\overline{BC}$ parallel?

_____

_____

Ⓔ Use a ruler to measure $\overline{AE}$, $\overline{EB}$, $\overline{AF}$, and $\overline{FC}$. Then compare the ratios $\frac{AE}{EB}$ and $\frac{AF}{FC}$.

_____

_____

1. **Discussion** How can you show that $\triangle AEF \sim \triangle ABC$? Explain.

_____

_____

_____

_____

2. What do you know about the ratios $\frac{AE}{AB}$ and $\frac{AF}{AC}$? Explain.

_____

_____

3. **Make a Conjecture** Use your answer to Step E to make a conjecture about the line segments produced when a line parallel to one side of a triangle intersects the other two sides.

_____

_____

🔎 Explain 1   Proving the Triangle Proportionality Theorem

As you saw in the Explore, when a line parallel to one side of a triangle intersects the other two sides of the triangle, the lengths of the segments are proportional.

Triangle Proportionality Theorem		
Theorem	**Hypothesis**	**Conclusion**
If a line parallel to a side of a triangle intersects the other two sides, then it divides those sides proportionally.	A E F B C $\overline{EF} \parallel \overline{BC}$	$\dfrac{AE}{EB} = \dfrac{AF}{FC}$

Example 1   Prove the Triangle Proportionality Theorem

(A)   Given: $\overleftrightarrow{EF} \parallel \overline{BC}$

Prove: $\dfrac{AE}{EB} = \dfrac{AF}{FC}$

Step 1 Show that $\triangle AEF \sim \triangle ABC$.

Because $\overleftrightarrow{EF} \parallel \overline{BC}$, you can conclude that $\angle 1 \cong \angle 2$ and

$\angle 3 \cong \angle 4$ by the _____ Theorem.

So, $\triangle AEF \sim \triangle ABC$ by the _____.

Step 2 Use the fact that corresponding sides of similar triangles are proportional to prove that $\frac{AE}{EB} = \frac{AF}{FC}$.

$\dfrac{AB}{AE} =$		Corresponding sides are proportional.
$\dfrac{AE + EB}{AE} =$		Segment Addition Postulate
$1 + \dfrac{EB}{AB} =$		Use the property that $\frac{a+b}{c} = \frac{a}{c} + \frac{b}{c}$.
$\dfrac{EB}{AE} =$		Subtract 1 from both sides.
$\dfrac{AE}{EB} =$		Take the reciprocal of both sides.

Reflect

4. Explain how you conclude that $\triangle AEF \sim \triangle ABC$ without using $\angle 3$ and $\angle 4$.

_____

_____

 Explain 2 ## Applying the Triangle Proportionality Theorem

Example 2 **Find the length of each segment.**

(A) $\overline{CY}$

It is given that $\overline{XY} \parallel \overline{BC}$ so $\frac{AX}{XB} = \frac{AY}{YC}$ by the Triangle Proportionality Theorem.

Substitute 9 for AX, 4 for XB, and 10 for AY.

Then solve for CY.

$$\frac{9}{4} = \frac{10}{CY}$$

Take the reciprocal of both sides.

$$\frac{4}{9} = \frac{CY}{10}$$

Next, multiply both sides by 10.

$$10\left(\frac{4}{9}\right) = \left(\frac{CY}{10}\right)10 \qquad \rightarrow \qquad \frac{40}{9} = CY, \text{ or } 4\frac{4}{9} = CY$$

(B) Find PN.

It is given that $\overline{PQ} \parallel \overline{LM}$, so $\frac{NQ}{QM} = $ _____ by the

Triangle Proportionality Theorem.

Substitute _____ for NQ, _____ for QM, and 3 for _____.

$$\frac{5}{2} = \frac{NP}{3}$$

Multiply both sides by ____: $\boxed{}\left(\dfrac{5}{2}\right) = \boxed{}\left(\dfrac{NP}{3}\right) \rightarrow$ _____ $= NP$

Find the length of each segment.

5. $\overline{DG}$

6. $\overline{RN}$

 Explain 3 # Proving the Converse of the Triangle Proportionality Theorem

The converse of the Triangle Proportionality Theorem is also true.

Converse of the Triangle Proportionality Theorem		
Theorem	**Hypothesis**	**Conclusion**
If a line divides two sides of a triangle proportionally, then it is parallel to the third side.	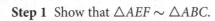 $\dfrac{AE}{EB} = \dfrac{AF}{FC}$	$\overleftrightarrow{EF} \parallel \overline{BC}$

Example 3 **Prove the Converse of the Triangle Proportionality Theorem**

(A) Given: $\dfrac{AE}{EB} = \dfrac{AF}{FC}$

Prove: $\overleftrightarrow{EF} \parallel \overline{BC}$

Step 1 Show that $\triangle AEF \sim \triangle ABC$.

It is given that $\dfrac{AE}{EB} = \dfrac{AF}{FC}$, and taking the reciprocal

of both sides shows that _____. Now add 1 to

both sides by adding $\dfrac{AE}{AE}$ to the left side and $\dfrac{AF}{AF}$ to the right side.

This gives _____.

Adding and using the Segment Addition Postulate gives _____.

Since $\angle A \cong \angle A$, $\triangle AEF \sim \triangle ABC$ by the _____ Theorem.

Step 2 Use corresponding angles of similar triangles to show that $\overleftrightarrow{EF} \parallel \overline{BC}$.

$\angle AEF \cong \angle$ _____ and are corresponding angles.

So, $\overleftrightarrow{EF} \parallel \overline{BC}$ by the _____ Theorem.

7. **Critique Reasoning** A student states that $\overline{UV}$ must be parallel to $\overline{ST}$. Do you agree? Why or why not?

🔧 **Explain 4** ## Applying the Converse of the Triangle Proportionality Theorem

You can use the Converse of the Triangle Proportionality Theorem to verify that a line is parallel to a side of a triangle.

Example 4 Verify that the line segments are parallel.

Ⓐ $\overline{MN}$ and $\overline{KL}$

$$\frac{JM}{MK} = \frac{42}{21} = 2 \qquad\qquad \frac{JN}{NL} = \frac{30}{15} = 2$$

Since $\frac{JM}{MK} = \frac{JN}{NL}$, $\overline{MN} \parallel \overline{KL}$ by the Converse of the

Triangle Proportionality Theorem.

Ⓑ $\overline{DE}$ and $\overline{AB}$ (Given that $AC = 36$ cm, and $BC = 27$ cm)

$AD = AC - DC = 36 - 20 = 16$

$BE = BC - \square = \square - \square = \square$

$\dfrac{CD}{DA} = \dfrac{\square}{\square} = \dfrac{\square}{\square} \qquad\qquad \dfrac{CE}{EB} = \dfrac{\square}{\square} = \square$

Since $\dfrac{CD}{DA} = \underline{\quad}$, $\overline{DE} \parallel \overline{AB}$ by the _____ Theorem.

8. **Communicate Mathematical Ideas** In $\triangle ABC$, in the example, what is the value of $\frac{AB}{DE}$? Explain how you know.

9. Verify that $\overline{TU}$ and $\overline{RS}$ are parallel.

10. In $\triangle ABC$, $\overline{XY} \parallel \overline{BC}$. Use what you know about similarity and proportionality to identify as many different proportions as possible.

_____

11. **Discussion** What theorems, properties, or strategies are common to the proof of the Triangle Proportionality Theorem and the proof of Converse of the Triangle Proportionality Theorem?

_____

_____

_____

12. **Essential Question Check-In** Suppose a line parallel to side $\overline{BC}$ of $\triangle ABC$ intersects sides $\overline{AB}$ and $\overline{AC}$ at points X and Y, respectively, and $\frac{AX}{XB} = 1$. What do you know about X and Y? Explain.

_____

_____

_____

_____

⭐ Evaluate: Homework and Practice

- Online Homework
- Hints and Help
- Extra Practice

1. Copy the triangle ABC that you drew for the Explore activity. Construct a line $\overleftrightarrow{FG}$ parallel to $\overline{AB}$ using the same method you used in the Explore activity.

2. $\overline{ZY} \parallel \overleftrightarrow{MN}$. Write a paragraph proof to show that $\frac{XM}{MZ} = \frac{XN}{NY}$.

Find the length of each segment.

3. $\overline{KL}$

4. $\overline{XZ}$

5. $\overline{VM}$

Verify that the given segments are parallel.

6. $\overline{AB}$ and $\overline{CD}$

7. $\overline{MN}$ and $\overline{QR}$

8. $\overline{WX}$ and $\overline{DE}$

9. Use the Converse of the Triangle Proportionality Theorem to identify parallel lines in the figure.

10. On the map, 1st Street and 2nd Street are parallel. What is the distance from City Hall to 2nd Street along Cedar Road?

11. On the map, 5th Avenue, 6th Avenue, and 7th Avenue are parallel. What is the length of Main Street between 5th Avenue and 6th Avenue?

12. Multi-Step The storage unit has horizontal siding that is parallel to the base.

  a. Find LM.

  b. Find GM.

  c. Find MN to the nearest tenth of a foot.

  d. Make a Conjecture Write the ratios $\frac{LM}{MN}$ and $\frac{HJ}{JK}$ as decimals to the nearest hundredth and compare them. Make a conjecture about the relationship between parallel lines $\overleftrightarrow{LD}$, $\overleftrightarrow{ME}$, and $\overleftrightarrow{NF}$ and transversals $\overleftrightarrow{GN}$ and $\overleftrightarrow{GK}$.

13. A corollary to the Converse of the Triangle Proportionality Theorem states that if three or more parallel lines intersect two transversals, then they divide the transversals proportionally. Complete the proof of the corollary.

Given: Parallel lines $\overleftrightarrow{AB} \parallel \overleftrightarrow{CD}$, $\overleftrightarrow{CD} \parallel \overleftrightarrow{EF}$

Prove: $\frac{AC}{CE} = \frac{BX}{XE}$, $\frac{BX}{XE} = \frac{BD}{DF}$, $\frac{AC}{CE} = \frac{BD}{DF}$

Statements	Reasons
1. $\overleftrightarrow{AB} \parallel \overleftrightarrow{CD}$, $\overleftrightarrow{CD} \parallel \overleftrightarrow{AF}$	1. Given
2. Draw $\overleftrightarrow{EB}$ intersecting $\overleftrightarrow{CD}$ at X.	2. Two points _____
3. $\frac{AC}{CE} = \frac{BX}{XE}$	3. _____
4. $\frac{BX}{XE} = \frac{BD}{DF}$	4. _____
5. $\frac{AC}{CE} = \frac{BD}{DF}$	5. _____ Property of Equality

14. Suppose that $LM = 24$. Use the Triangle Proportionality Theorem to find PM.

15. Which of the given measures allow you to conclude that $\overline{UV} \parallel \overline{ST}$? Select all that apply.

A. $SR = 12, TR = 9$

B. $SR = 16, TR = 20$

C. $SR = 35, TR = 28$

D. $SR = 50, TR = 48$

E. $SR = 25, TR = 20$

16. Algebra For what value of x is $\overline{GF} \parallel \overline{HJ}$?

17. Communicate Mathematical Ideas John used $\triangle ABC$ to write a proof of the Centroid Theorem. He began by drawing medians $\overline{AK}$ and $\overline{CL}$, intersecting at Z. Next he drew midsegments $\overline{LM}$ and $\overline{NP}$, both parallel to median $\overline{AK}$.

Given: $\triangle ABC$ with medians $\overline{AK}$ and $\overline{CL}$, and midsegments $\overline{LM}$ and $\overline{NP}$

Prove: Z is located $\frac{2}{3}$ of the distance from each vertex of $\triangle ABC$ to the midpoint of the opposite side.

a. Complete each statement to justify the first part of John's proof.

By the definition of _____, $MK = \frac{1}{2}BK$. By the definition

of _____, $BK = KC$. So, by _____, $MK = \frac{1}{2}KC$, or $\frac{KC}{MK} = 2$.

Consider $\triangle LMC$. $\overline{LM} \parallel \overline{AK}$ (and therefore $\overline{LM} \parallel \overline{ZK}$), so $\frac{ZC}{LZ} = \frac{KC}{MK}$ by the

_____ Theorem, and $ZC = 2LZ$. Because

$LC = 3LZ$, $\frac{ZC}{LC} = \frac{2LZ}{3LZ} = \frac{2}{3}$, and Z is located $\frac{2}{3}$ of the distance from vertex C of $\triangle ABC$ to the midpoint of the opposite side.

b. Explain how John can complete his proof.

18. Persevere in Problem Solving Given $\triangle ABC$ with $FC = 5$, you want to find BF. First, find the value that y must have for the Triangle Proportionality Theorem to apply. Then describe more than one way to find BF, and find BF.

Lesson Performance Task

Shown here is a triangular striped sail, together with some of its dimensions. In the diagram, segments BJ, CI, and DH are all parallel to segment EG. Find each of the following:

1. AJ

2. CD

3. HG

4. GF

5. the perimeter of $\triangle AEF$

6. the area of $\triangle AEF$

7. the number of sails you could make for $10,000 if the sail material costs $30 per square yard

12.2 Subdividing a Segment in a Given Ratio

Essential Question: How do you find the point on a directed line segment that partitions the given segment in a given ratio?

⊘ Explore **Partitioning a Segment in a One-Dimensional Coordinate System**

It takes just one number to specify an exact location on a number line. For this reason, a number line is sometimes called a one-dimensional coordinate system. The mile markers on a straight stretch of a highway turn that part of the highway into a one-dimensional coordinate system.

On a straight highway, the exit for Arthur Avenue is at mile marker 14. The exit for Collingwood Road is at mile marker 44. The state highway administration plans to put an exit for Briar Street at a point that is $\frac{2}{3}$ of the distance from Arthur Avenue to Collingwood Road. Follow these steps to determine where the new exit should be placed.

(A) Mark Arthur Avenue (point *A*) and Collingwood Road (point *C*) on the number line.

(B) What is the distance from Arthur Avenue to Collingwood Road? Explain.

_____

(C) How far will the Briar Street exit be from Arthur Avenue? Explain.

_____

(D) What is the mile marker number for the Briar Street exit? Why?

_____

(E) Plot and label the Briar Street exit (point *B*) on the number line.

_____

(F) The highway administration also plans to put an exit for Dakota Lane at a point that divides the highway from Arthur Avenue to Collingwood Road in a ratio of 2 to 3. What is the mile marker number for Dakota Lane? Why? (*Hint*: Let the distance from Arthur Avenue to Dakota Lane be $2x$ and let the distance from Dakota Lane to Collingwood Road be $3x$.)

_____

_____

_____

(G) Plot and label the Dakota Lane exit (point D) on the number line.

_____

Reflect

1. How can you tell that the location at which you plotted point B is reasonable?

_____

_____

2. Would your answer in Step F be different if the exit for Dakota Lane divided the highway from Arthur Avenue to Collingwood Road in a ratio of 3 to 2? Explain.

_____

_____

🔧 Explain 1 Partitioning a Segment in a Two-Dimensional Coordinate System

A *directed line segment* is a segment between two points A and B with a specified direction, from A to B or from B to A. To partition a directed line segment is to divide it into two segments with a given ratio.

Example 1 **Find the coordinates of the point P that divides the directed line segment from A to B in the given ratio.**

(A) $A(-8, -7)$, $B(8, 5)$; 3 to 1

Step 1 Write a ratio that expresses the distance of point P along the segment from A to B.

Point P is $\dfrac{3}{3+1} = \dfrac{3}{4}$ of the distance from A to B.

Step 2 Find the run and the rise of the directed line segment.

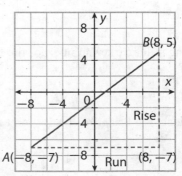

$\text{run} = 8 - (-8) = 16$

$\text{rise} = 5 - (-7) = 12$

Step 3 Point P is $\frac{3}{4}$ of the distance from point A to point B, so find $\frac{3}{4}$ of both the rise and the run.

$\frac{3}{4}$ of run $= \frac{3}{4}(16) = 12$ $\qquad\qquad$ $\frac{3}{4}$ of rise $= \frac{3}{4}(12) = 9$

Step 4 To find the coordinates of point P, add the values from Step 3 to the coordinates of point A.

x-coordinate of point $P = -8 + 12 = 4$

y-coordinate of point $P = -7 + 9 = 2$

The coordinates of point P are $(4, 2)$.

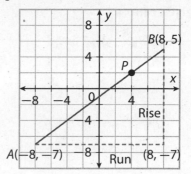

B $A(-4, 4)$, $B(2, 1)$; 1 to 2

Step 1 Write a ratio that expresses the distance of point P along the segment from A to B.

Point P is $\dfrac{\boxed{}}{\boxed{} + \boxed{}} = \dfrac{\boxed{}}{\boxed{}}$ of the distance from A to B.

Step 2 Graph the directed line segment. Find the rise and the run of the directed line segment.

run $= 2 - (-4) = 6$

rise $= \boxed{} - \boxed{} = \boxed{}$

Step 3 Point P is $\dfrac{\boxed{}}{\boxed{}}$ of the distance from point A to point B.

$\dfrac{\boxed{}}{\boxed{}}$ of run $= \dfrac{\boxed{}}{\boxed{}}(6) = \boxed{}$ $\qquad\qquad$ $\dfrac{\boxed{}}{\boxed{}}$ of run $= \dfrac{\boxed{}}{\boxed{}}\left(\boxed{}\right) = \boxed{}$

Step 4 To find the coordinates of point P, add the values from Step 3 to the coordinates of point A.

x-coordinate of point $P = -4 + \boxed{} = \boxed{}$ $\qquad$ y-coordinate of point $P = 4 + \boxed{} = \boxed{}$

The coordinates of point P are $\left(\boxed{}, \boxed{}\right)$. Plot point P on the above graph.

Reflect

3. In Part A, show how you can use the Distance Formula to check that point P partitions the directed line segment in the correct ratio.

_____

_____

4. **Discussion** What can you conclude about a point that partitions a segment in the ratio 1 to 1? How can you find the coordinates of such a point?

_____

Find the coordinates of the point *P* that divides the directed line segment from *A* to *B* in the given ratio.

5. $A(-6, 5)$, $B(2, -3)$; 5 to 3

6. $A(4, 2)$, $B(-6, -13)$; 3 to 2

✪ Explain 2   Constructing a Partition of a Segment

Example 2 Given the directed line segment from *A* to *B*, construct the point *P* that divides the segment in the given ratio from *A* to *B*.

(A) 2 to 1 $A \bullet\text{————————————}\bullet B$

Step 1 Use a straightedge to draw $\overrightarrow{AC}$. The exact measure of the angle is not important, but the construction is easiest for angles from about 30° to 60°.

Step 2 Place the compass point on *A* and draw an arc through $\overrightarrow{AC}$. Label the intersection *D*. Using the same compass setting, draw an arc centered on *D* and label the intersection *E*. Using the same compass setting, draw an arc centered on *E* and label the intersection *F*.

Step 3 Use the straightedge to connect points *B* and *F*. Construct an angle congruent to ∠*AFB* with *D* as its vertex. Construct an angle congruent to ∠*AFB* with *E* as its vertex.

Step 4 The construction partitions $\overline{AB}$ into 3 equal parts. Label point *P* at the point that divides the segment in the ratio 2 to 1 from *A* to *B*.

Step 1 Use a straightedge to draw $\overrightarrow{AC}$.

Step 2 Place the compass point on A and draw an arc through $\overrightarrow{AC}$. Label the intersection D. Using the same compass setting, draw an arc centered on D and label the intersection E. Using the same compass setting, draw an arc centered on E and label the intersection F. Using the same compass setting, draw an arc centered on F and label the intersection G.

Step 3 Use the straightedge to connect points B and G. Construct angles congruent to $\angle AGB$ with D, E, and F as the vertices.

Step 4 The construction partitions $\overline{AB}$ into ⬜ equal parts. Label point P at the point that divides the segment in the ratio ⬜ to ⬜ from A to B.

Reflect

7. In Part A, why is $\overline{EP}$ is parallel to $\overline{FB}$?

_____

_____

8. How can you use the Triangle Proportionality Theorem to explain why this construction method works?

_____

_____

_____

Your Turn

Given the directed line segment from A to B, construct the point P that divides the segment in the given ratio from A to B.

9. 1 to 2

10. 3 to 2

11. How is a one-dimensional coordinate system similar to a two-dimensional coordinate system? How is it different?

_____

_____

_____

_____

12. Is finding a point that is $\frac{4}{5}$ of the distance from point A to point B the same as finding a point that divides $\overline{AB}$ in the ratio 4 to 5? Explain.

_____

_____

_____

13. **Essential Question Check-In** What are some different ways to divide a segment in the ratio 2 to 1?

_____

_____

_____

_____

_____

_____

☆ Evaluate: Homework and Practice

Personal Math Trainer

• Online Homework
• Hints and Help
• Extra Practice

A choreographer uses a number line to position dancers for a ballet. Dancers A and B have coordinates 5 and 23, respectively. In Exercises 1–4, find the coordinate for each of the following dancers based on the given locations.

1. Dancer C stands at a point that is $\frac{5}{6}$ of the distance from Dancer A to Dancer B.

2. Dancer D stands at a point that is $\frac{1}{3}$ of the distance from Dancer A to Dancer B.

3. Dancer *E* stands at a point that divides the line segment from Dancer *A* to Dancer *B* in a ratio of 2 to 1.

4. Dancer *F* stands at a point that divides the line segment from Dancer *A* to Dancer *B* in a ratio of 1 to 5.

Find the coordinates of the point *P* that divides the directed line segment from *A* to *B* in the given ratio.

5. $A(-3, -2)$, $B(12, 3)$; 3 to 2

6. $A(-1, 5)$, $B(7, -3)$; 7 to 1

7. $A(-1, 4)$, $(B-9, 0)$; 1 to 3

8. $A(7, -3)$, $B(-7, 4)$; 3 to 4

Given the directed line segment from *A* to *B*, construct the point *P* that divides the segment in the given ratio from *A* to *B*.

9. 3 to 1

10. 2 to 3

Given the directed line segment from A to B, construct the point P that divides the segment in the given ratio from A to B.

11. 1 to 4

12. 4 to 1

Find the coordinate of the point P that divides each directed line segment in the given ratio.

13. from *J* to *M*; 1 to 9

14. from *K* to *L*; 1 to 1

15. from *N* to *K*; 3 to 5

16. from *K* to *J*; 7 to 11

17. Communicate Mathematical Ideas Leon constructed a point *P* that divides the directed segment from *A* to *B* in the ratio 2 to 1. Chelsea constructed a point *Q* that divides the directed segment from *B* to *A* in the ratio 1 to 2. How are points *P* and *Q* related? Explain.

18. City planners use a number line to place landmarks along a new street. Each unit of the number line represents 100 feet. A fountain F is located at coordinate -3 and a plaza P is located at coordinate 21. The city planners place two benches along the street at points that divide the segment from F to P in the ratios 1 to 2 and 3 to 1. What is the distance between the benches?

19. The course for a marathon includes a straight segment from city hall to the main library. The planning committee wants to put water stations along this part of the course so that the stations divide the segment into three equal parts. Find the coordinates of the points at the which the water stations should be placed.

20. Multi-Step Carlos is driving on a straight section of highway from Ashford to Lincoln. Ashford is at mile marker 433 and Lincoln is at mile marker 553. A rest stop is located along the highway $\frac{2}{3}$ of the distance from Ashford to Lincoln. Assuming Carlos drives at a constant rate of 60 miles per hour, how long will it take him to drive from Ashford to the rest stop?

21. The directed segment from J to K is shown in the figure.

Points divide the segment from J to K in the each of the following ratios. Which points have integer coordinates? Select all that apply

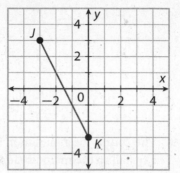

A. 1 to 1

B. 2 to 1

C. 2 to 3

D. 1 to 3

E. 1 to 2

22. **Critique Reasoning** Jeffrey was given a directed line segment and was asked to use a compass and straightedge to construct the point that divides the segment in the ratio 4 to 2. He said he would have to draw a ray and then construct 6 congruent segments along the ray. Tamara said it is not necessary to construct 6 congruent segments along the ray. Do you agree? If so, explain Tamara's shortcut. If not, explain why not.

23. **Explain the Error** Point A has coordinate -9 and point B has coordinate 9. A student was asked to find the coordinate of the point P that is $\frac{2}{3}$ of the distance from A to B. The student said the coordinate of point P is -3.

   a. Without doing any calculations, how can you tell that the student made an error?

   b. What error do you think the student made?

24. **Analyze Relationships** Point P divides the directed segment from A to B in the ratio 3 to 2. The coordinates of point A are $(-4, -2)$ and the coordinates of point P are $(2, 1)$. Find the coordinates of point B.

25. **Critical Thinking** $\overline{RS}$ passes through $R(-3, 1)$ and $S(4, 3)$. Find a point P on $\overline{RS}$ such that the ratio of RP to SP is 5 to 4. Is there more than one possibility? Explain.

Lesson Performance Task

In this lesson you will subdivide line segments in given ratios. The diagram shows a line segment divided into two parts in such a way that the longer part divided by the shorter part equals the entire length divided by the longer part:

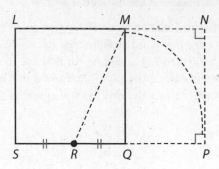

$$\frac{a}{b} = \frac{a+b}{a}$$

Each of these ratios is called the Golden Ratio. To find the point on a line segment that divides the segment this way, study this figure:

In the figure, $LMQS$ is a square. $\frac{LN}{LM}$ equals the Golden Ratio (the entire segment length divided by the longer part).

1. Describe how, starting with line segment $\overline{LM}$, you can find the location of point N.

2. Letting LM equal 1, find $\frac{LN}{LM} = \frac{LN}{1} = LN$, the Golden Ratio. Describe your method.

12.3 Using Proportional Relationships

Essential Question: How can you use similar triangles to solve problems?

Resource
Locker

🧭 **Explore**   **Exploring Indirect Measurement**

In this Explore, you will consider how to find heights, lengths, or distances that are too great to be measured directly, that is, with measuring tools like rulers. **Indirect measurement** involves using the properties of similar triangles to measure such heights or distances.

(A) During the day sunlight creates shadows, as shown in the figure below. The dashed segment represents the ray of sunlight. What kind of triangle is formed by the flagpole, its shadow, and the ray of sunlight?

_____

(B) Suppose the sun is shining, and you are standing near a flagpole, but out of its shadow. You will cast a shadow as well. You can assume that the rays of the sun are parallel. What do you know about the two triangles formed? Explain your reasoning.

_____
_____
_____
_____

(C) In the diagram, what heights or lengths do you already know?

_____

(D) What heights or lengths can be measured directly?

_____

1. How could you use similar triangles to measure the height of the flagpole indirectly?

_____

_____

_____

⚓ Explain 1 Finding an Unknown Height

Example 1 **Find the indicated dimension using the measurements shown in the figure and the properties of similar triangles.**

(A) In order to find the height of a palm tree, you measure the tree's shadow and, at the same time of day, you measure the shadow cast by a meter stick that you hold at a right angle to the ground. Find the height h of the tree.

Because $\overline{ZX} \parallel \overline{CA}$, $\angle Z \cong \angle C$. All right angles are congruent, so $\angle Y \cong \angle B$. So $\triangle XYZ \cong \triangle ABC$.

Set up proportion. $\dfrac{AB}{XY} = \dfrac{BC}{YZ}$

Substitute. $\dfrac{h}{7.2} = \dfrac{1}{1.6}$

Multiply each side by 7.2. $h = 7.2\left(\dfrac{1}{1.6}\right)$

Simplify. $h = 4.5$

The tree is 4.5 meters high.

(B) Sid is 72 inches tall. To measure a flagpole, Sid stands near the flag. Sid's friend Miranda measures the lengths of Sid's shadow and the flagpole's shadow. Find the height h of the flagpole.

The triangles are similar by the AA Triangle Similarity Theorem.

Set up proportion. $\dfrac{\text{height}}{\text{person's height}} = \dfrac{\text{shadow}}{\text{person's shadow}}$

Substitute. $\dfrac{h}{72} = \dfrac{\boxed{}}{48}$

Multiply each side by 72. $h = 72\left(\dfrac{\boxed{}}{48}\right)$

Simplify. $x = \boxed{}$

The flagpole is _____ tall.

2. In the tree example, how can you check that your answer is reasonable?

_____

_____

_____

3. Liam is 6 feet tall. To find the height of a tree, he measures his shadow and the tree's shadow. The measurements of the two shadows are shown. Find the height h of the tree.

Explain 2 Finding an Unknown Distance

In real-world situations, you may not be able to measure an object directly because there is a physical barrier separating you from the object. You can use similar triangles in these situations as well.

Example 2 Explain how to use the information in the figure to find the indicated distance.

(A) A hiker wants to find the distance d across a canyon. She locates points as described.

1. She identifies a landmark at X. She places a marker (Y) directly across the canyon from X.

2. At Y, she turns 90° away from X and walks 400 feet in a straight line. She places a marker (Z) at this location.

3. She continues walking another 600 feet, and places a marker (W) at this location.

4. She turns 90° away from the canyon and walks until the marker Z aligns with X. She places a marker (V) at this location and measures $\overline{WV}$.

$\angle VWZ \cong \angle XYZ$ (All right angles are congruent) and $\angle VZW \cong \angle XZY$ (Vertical angles are congruent). So, $\triangle VWZ \sim \triangle XYZ$ by the AA Triangle Similarity Theorem.

$\dfrac{XY}{VW} = \dfrac{YZ}{WZ}$, So $\dfrac{d}{327} = \dfrac{400}{600}$, or $\dfrac{d}{327} = \dfrac{2}{3}$

Then $d = 327\left(\dfrac{2}{3}\right) = 218$.

The distance across the canyon is 218 feet.

(B) To find the distance d across the gorge, a student identifies points as shown in the figure. Find d.

$\triangle JKL \sim \triangle NML$ by the AA Triangle Similarity Theorem.

$$\frac{JK}{NM} = \frac{KL}{\boxed{}}$$

$$\frac{d}{35} = \frac{24}{\boxed{}}$$

$$d = \boxed{} \cdot \frac{\boxed{}}{42} = \boxed{} \cdot \frac{\boxed{}}{7}$$

$$d = \frac{\boxed{}}{7}$$

$$d = \boxed{}$$

The distance across the gorge is _____.

4. In the example, why is $\angle JLK \cong \angle NLM$?

_____

5. To find the distance d across a stream, Levi located points as shown in the figure. Use the given information to find d.

💬 Elaborate

6. **Discussion** Suppose you want to help a friend prepare for solving indirect measurement problems. What topics would you suggest that your friend review?

_____

_____

_____

7. **Essential Question Check-In** You are given a figure including triangles that represent a real-world situation. What is the first step you should take to find an unknown measurement?

_____

☆ Evaluate: Homework and Practice

1. Finding distances using similar triangles is called _____.

Use similar triangles △ABC and △XYZ to find the missing height h.

2.

3.

4.

5.

Use similar triangles △EFG and △IHG to find the missing distance d.

6.

7.

8.

9.

10. To find the height h of a dinosaur in a museum, Amir placed a mirror on the ground 40 feet from its base. Then he stepped back 4 feet so that he could see the top of the dinosaur in the mirror. Amir's eyes were approximately 5 feet 6 inches above the ground. What is the height of the dinosaur?

5 ft 6 in.

⊢4 ft⊢——40 ft——⊣

11. Jenny is 5 feet 2 inches tall. To find the height h of a light pole, she measured her shadow and the pole's shadow. What is the height of the pole?

h

15.5 ft

5 ft 2 in.

7 ft 9 in.

12. A student wanted to find the height h of a statue of a pineapple in Nambour, Australia. She measured the pineapple's shadow and her own shadow. The student's height is 5 feet 4 inches. What is the height of the pineapple?

D

A

B 1 2

2 ft C E 8 ft 9 in. F

h

13. To find the height h of a flagpole, Casey measured her own shadow and the flagpole's shadow. Given that Casey's height is 5 feet 4 inches, what is the height of the flagpole?

5 ft 4 in.

3 ft

h

14 ft 3 in.

A city is planning an outdoor concert for an Independence Day celebration. To hold speakers and lights, a crew of technicians sets up a scaffold with two platforms by the stage. The first platform is 8 feet 2 inches off the ground. The second platform is 7 feet 6 inches above the first platform. The shadow of the first platform stretches 6 feet 3 inches across the ground.

14. Explain why △ABC is similar to △ADE. (*Hint*: rays of light are parallel.)

15. Find the length of the shadow of the second platform in feet and inches to the nearest inch.

16. A technician is 5 feet 8 inches tall. The technician is standing on top of the second platform. Find the length s of the shadow that is cast by the scaffold and the technician to the nearest inch.

17. To find the distance *XY* across a lake, you locate points as shown in the figure. Explain how to use this information to find *XY*.

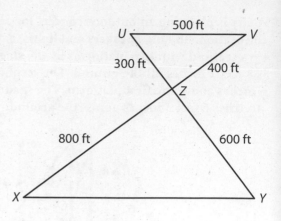

18. In order to find the height of a cliff, you stand at the bottom of the cliff, walk 60 feet from the base, and place a mirror on the ground. Then you face the cliff and step back 5 feet so that can see the top of the cliff in the mirror. Assuming your eyes are 6 feet above the ground, explain how to use this information to find the height of the cliff. (The angles marked congruent are congruent because of the nature of the reflection of light in a mirror.)

Mirror

19. To find the height of a tree, Adrian measures the tree's shadow and then his shadow. Which proportion could Adrian use to find the height of the tree? Select all that apply.

A. $\dfrac{AC}{DF} = \dfrac{BC}{EF}$

B. $\dfrac{DF}{AC} = \dfrac{EF}{BC}$

C. $\dfrac{AB}{DF} = \dfrac{BC}{EF}$

D. $\dfrac{DF}{BC} = \dfrac{EF}{AC}$

E. $\dfrac{BC}{EF} = \dfrac{AC}{DF}$

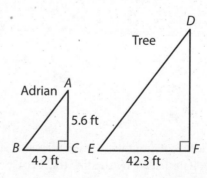

20. Critique Reasoning Jesse and Kyle are hiking. Jesse is carrying a walking stick. They spot a tall tree and use the walking stick as a vertical marker to create similar triangles and measure the tree indirectly. Later in the day they come upon a rock formation. They measure the rock formation's shadow and again want to use similar triangles to measure its height indirectly. Kyle wants to use the shadow length they measured earlier for the stick. Jesse says they should measure it again. Who do you think is right?

21. Error Analysis Andy wants to find the distance d across a river. He located points as shown in the figure and then used similar triangles to find that $d = 220.5$ feet. How can you tell without calculating that he must be wrong? Tell what you think he did wrong and correct his error.

Lesson Performance Task

Around 240 B.C., the Greek astronomer Eratosthenes was residing in Alexandria, Egypt. He believed that the Earth was spherical and conceived of an experiment to measure its circumference. At noon in the town of Syene, the sun was directly overhead. A stick stuck vertically in the ground cast no shadow. At the same moment in Alexandria, 490 miles from Syene, a vertical stick cast a shadow that veered 7.2° from the vertical.

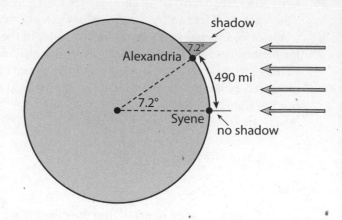

1. Refer to the diagram. Explain why Eratosthenes reasoned that the angle at the center of the Earth that intercepted a 490-mile arc measured 7.2 degrees.

2. Calculate the circumference of the Earth using Eratosthenes's figures. Explain how you got your answer.

3. Calculate the radius of the Earth using Eratosthenes's figures.

4. The accepted circumference of the Earth today is 24,901 miles. Calculate the percent error in Eratosthenes's calculations.

12.4 Similarity in Right Triangles

Essential Question: How does the altitude to the hypotenuse of a right triangle help you use similar right triangles to solve problems?

Resource Locker

🧭 Explore   Identifying Similarity in Right Triangles

Ⓐ Make two copies of the right triangle on a piece of paper and cut them out.

Ⓑ Choose one of the triangles. Fold the paper to find the altitude to the hypotenuse.

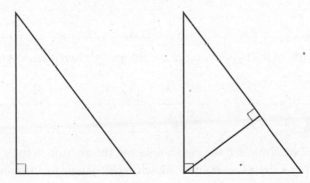

Ⓒ Cut the second triangle along the altitude. Label the triangles as shown.

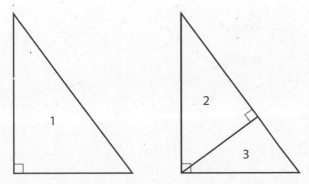

(D) Place triangle 2 on top of triangle 1. What do you notice about the angles?

_____

(E) What is true of triangles 1 and 2? How do you know?

_____

(F) Repeat Steps 1 and 2 for triangles 1 and 3. Does the same relationship hold true for triangles 1 and 3?

_____

_____

Reflect

1. How are the hypotenuses of the triangles 2 and 3 related to triangle 1?

_____

_____

2. What is the relationship between triangles 2 and 3? Explain.

_____

_____

3. When you draw the altitude to the hypotenuse of a right triangle, what kinds of figures are produced?

_____

_____

4. Suppose you draw $\triangle ABC$ such that $\angle B$ is a right angle and the altitude to the hypotenuse intersects hypotenuse $\overline{AC}$ at point P. Match each triangle to a similar triangle. Explain your reasoning.

A. $\triangle ABC$ _____ $\triangle PAB$

B. $\triangle PBC$ _____ $\triangle CAB$

C. $\triangle BAP$ _____ $\triangle BPC$

_____

_____

_____

Consider the proportion $\frac{a}{x} = \frac{x}{b}$ where two of the numbers in the proportion are the same. The number x is the *geometric mean* of a and b. The **geometric mean** of two positive numbers is the positive square root of their product. So the geometric mean of a and b is the positive number x such that $x = \sqrt{ab}$ or $x^2 = ab$.

Example 1   Find the geometric mean x of the numbers.

(A)   4 and 25

Write proportion.	$\frac{4}{x} = \frac{x}{25}$
Multiply both sides by the product of the denominators.	$25x \cdot \frac{4}{x} = 25x \cdot \frac{x}{25}$
Multiply.	$\frac{100x}{x} = \frac{25x^2}{25}$
Simplify.	$100 = x^2$
Take the square root of both sides.	$\sqrt{100} = \sqrt{x^2}$
Simplify.	$10 = x$

(B)   9 and 20

Write proportion.

$$\frac{\boxed{}}{x} = \frac{x}{20}$$

Multiply both sides by the product of the denominators.

$$20x \cdot \frac{\boxed{}}{x} = 20x \cdot \frac{x}{20}$$

Multiply.

$$\frac{\boxed{}\,x}{x} = \frac{20x^2}{20}$$

Simplify.

$$\boxed{} = x^2$$

Take the square root of both sides.

$$\sqrt{\boxed{}} = \sqrt{x^2}$$

Simplify.

$$\boxed{} = x$$

Reflect

5.   How can you show that if positive numbers a and b are such that $\frac{a}{x} = \frac{x}{b}$, then $x = \sqrt{ab}$?

_____

_____

Your Turn

Find the geometric mean of the numbers. If necessary, give the answer in simplest radical form.

6.   6 and 24

7.   5 and 12

⚙ Explain 2   Proving the Geometric Means Theorems

In the Explore activity, you discovered a theorem about right triangles and similarity.

The altitude to the hypotenuse of a right triangle forms two triangles that are similar to each other and to the original triangle.

That theorem leads to two additional theorems about right triangles. Both of the theorems involve geometric means.

Geometric Means Theorems		
Theorem	**Example**	**Diagram**
The length of the altitude to the hypotenuse of a right triangle is the geometric mean of the lengths of the segments of the hypotenuse.	$h^2 = xy$ or $h = \sqrt{xy}$	
The length of a leg of a right triangle is the geometric mean of the lengths of the hypotenuse and the segment of the hypotenuse adjacent to that leg.	$a^2 = xc$ or $a = \sqrt{xc}$ $b^2 = yc$ or $b = \sqrt{yc}$	

Example 2   **Prove the first Geometric Means Theorem.**

Given: Right triangle ABC with altitude $\overline{BD}$

Prove: $\dfrac{CD}{BD} = \dfrac{BD}{AD}$

Statements	Reasons
1. $\triangle ABC$ with altitude $\overline{BD}$	1. Given
2. $\triangle CBD \sim \triangle BAD$	2.
3. $\dfrac{CD}{BD} = \dfrac{BD}{AD}$	3.

Reflect

8. **Discussion**   How can you prove the second Geometric Means Theorem?

_____

_____

_____

_____

Explain 3 Using the Geometric Means Theorems

You can use the Geometric Means Theorems to find unknown segment lengths in a right triangle.

Example 3 Find the indicated value.

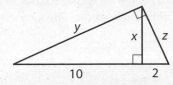

A x

Write proportion.	$\dfrac{2}{x} = \dfrac{x}{10}$
Multiply both sides by the product of the denominators.	$10x \cdot \dfrac{2}{x} = 10x \cdot \dfrac{x}{10}$
Multiply.	$\dfrac{20x}{x} = \dfrac{10x^2}{10}$
Simplify.	$20 = x^2$
Take the square root of both sides.	$\sqrt{20} = \sqrt{x^2}$
Simplify.	$2\sqrt{5} = x$

B y

Write proportion.	$\dfrac{10}{y} = \dfrac{y}{12}$
Multiply both sides by the product of the denominators.	$\boxed{}\dfrac{10}{y} = \boxed{}\dfrac{y}{12}$
Multiply.	$\dfrac{\boxed{}}{y} = \dfrac{\boxed{}}{.12}$
Simplify.	$\boxed{} = \boxed{}$
Take the square root of both sides.	$\sqrt{\boxed{}} = \sqrt{\boxed{}}$
Simplify.	$\boxed{} = y$

Reflect

9. **Discussion** How can you check your answers?

_____

Your Turn

10. Find x.

⚙ Explain 4   Proving the Pythagorean Theorem using Similarity

You have used the Pythagorean Theorem in earlier courses as well as in this one. There are many, many proofs of the Pythagorean Theorem. You will prove it now using similar right triangles.

> **The Pythagorean Theorem**
>
> In a right triangle, the square of the sum of the lengths of the legs is equal to the square of the length of the hypotenuse.

Example 4   Complete the proof of the Pythagorean Theorem.

Given: Right $\triangle ABC$

Prove: $a^2 + b^2 = c^2$

Part 1

Draw the altitude to the hypotenuse.
Label the point of intersection X.

$\angle BXC \cong \angle BCA$ because _____.

$\angle B \cong \angle B$ by _____.

So, $\triangle BXC \sim \triangle BCA$ by _____.

$\angle AXC \cong \angle ACB$ because _____.

$\angle A \cong \angle A$ by _____.

So, $\triangle AXC \sim \triangle ACB$ by _____.

Part 2

Let the lengths of the segments of the hypotenuse
be d and e, as shown in the figure.

Use the fact that corresponding sides of similar triangles are proportional
to write two proportions.

Proportion 1: $\triangle BXC \sim \triangle BCA$, so $\dfrac{a}{c} = \dfrac{\boxed{}}{a}$.

Proportion 2: $\triangle AXC \sim \triangle ACB$, so $\dfrac{b}{c} = \dfrac{\boxed{}}{b}$.

Part 3

Now perform some algebra to complete the proof as follows.

Multiply both sides of Proportion1 by ac. Write the resulting equation. _____

Multiply both sides of Proportion12 by bc. Write the resulting equation. _____

Adding the two resulting equations give this: _____

Factor the right side of the equation: _____

Finally, use the fact that $e + d =$ _____ by the Segment Addition Postulate to rewrite the equation

as _____.

Reflect

11. **Error Analysis** A student used the figure in Part 2 of the example, and wrote the following incorrect proof of the Pythagorean Theorem. Critique the student's proof. $\triangle BXC \sim \triangle BCA$ and $\triangle BCA \sim \triangle CXA$, so $\triangle BXC \sim \triangle CXA$ by transitivity of similarity. Let $CX = f$. Since corresponding sides of similar triangles are proportional, $\dfrac{e}{f} = \dfrac{f}{d}$ and $f^2 = ed$. Because $\triangle BXC \sim \triangle CXA$ and they are right triangles, $a^2 = e^2 + f^2$ and $b^2 = f^2 + d^2$.

Add the equations.	$a^2 + b^2 = e^2 + 2f^2 + d^2$
Substitute.	$= e^2 + 2ed + d^2$
Factor.	$- (e + d)^2$
Segment Addition Postulate	$= c^2$

_____

_____

_____

12. How would you explain to a friend how to find the geometric mean of two numbers?

_____

_____

_____

13. $\triangle XYZ$ is an isosceles right triangle and the right angle is $\angle Y$. Suppose the altitude to hypotenuse $\overline{XZ}$ intersects $\overline{XZ}$ at point P. Describe the relationships among triangles $\triangle XYZ$, $\triangle YPZ$ and $\triangle XPY$.

_____

_____

14. Can two different pairs of numbers have the same geometric mean? If so, give an example. If not, explain why not.

_____

_____

15. Essential Question Check-In How is the altitude to the hypotenuse of a right triangle related to the segments of the hypotenuse it creates?

_____

_____

Evaluate: Homework and Practice

• Online Homework
• Hints and Help
• Extra Practice

Write a similarity statement comparing the three triangles to each diagram.

1.

2.

3.

Find the geometric mean x of each pair of numbers. If necessary, give the answer in simplest radical form.

4.   5 and 20

5.   3 and 12

6.   8 and 13

7.   3.5 and 20

8.   1.5 and 84

9. $\frac{2}{3}$ and $\frac{27}{40}$

Find x, y, and z.

10.

11.

12.

Use the diagram to complete each equation.

13. $\dfrac{c}{e} = \dfrac{\boxed{}}{d}$

14. $\dfrac{c}{a} = \dfrac{a}{\boxed{}}$

15. $\dfrac{c+d}{b} = \dfrac{b}{\boxed{}}$

16. $\dfrac{d}{\boxed{}} = \dfrac{e}{c}$

17. $c(c+d) = \boxed{}^2$

18. $\boxed{}^2 = cd$

Find the length of the altitude to the hypotenuse under the given conditions.

19. $BC = 5$
$AC = 4$

20. $BC = 17$
$AC = 15$

21. $BC = 13$
$AC = 12$

22. Communicate Mathematical Ideas The area of a rectangle with a length of ℓ and a width of w has the same area as a square. Show that the side length of the square is the geometric mean of the length and width of the rectangle.

H.O.T.   Focus on Higher Order Thinking

23. Algebra An 8-inch-long altitude of a right triangle divides the hypotenuse into two segments. One segment is 4 times as long as the other. What are the lengths of the segments of the hypotenuse?

24. Error Analysis Cecile and Amelia both found a value for EF in $\triangle DEF$. Both students work are shown. Which student's solution is correct? What mistake did the other student make?

Cecile: $\dfrac{12}{EF} = \dfrac{EF}{8}$

So $EF^2 = 12(8) = 96$.

Then $EF = \sqrt{96} = 4\sqrt{6}$.

Amelia: $\dfrac{8}{EF} = \dfrac{EF}{4}$

So $EF^2 = 8(4) = 32$.

Then $EF = \sqrt{32} = 4\sqrt{2}$.

Lesson Performance Task

In the example at the beginning of the lesson, a $100 investment grew for one year at the rate of 50%, to $150, then fell for one year at the rate of 50%, to $75. The arithmetic mean of +50% and −50%, which is 0%, was not a good predictor of the change, for it predicted the investment would still be worth $100 after two years, not $75.

1. Find the geometric mean of $1 + 50\%$ and $1 - 50\%$. (Each 1 represents the fact that at the beginning of each year, an investment is worth 100% of itself.) Round to the nearest thousandth.

2. It is the geometric mean, not the arithmetic mean, that tells you what the interest rate would have had to have been over an entire investment period to achieve the end result. You can use your answer to Exercise 1 to check this claim. Find the value of a $100 investment after it increased or decreased at the rate you found in Exercise 1 for two years. Show your work.

3. Copy the right triangle shown here. Write the terms "Year 1 Rate", "Year 2 Rate", and "Average Rate" to show geometrically how the three investment rates relate to each other.

4. The geometric mean of n numbers is the nth root of the product of the numbers. Find what the interest rate would have had to have been over 4 years to achieve the result of a $100 investment that grew 20% in Year 1 and 30% in Year 2, then lost 20% in Year 3 and 30% in Year 4. Show your work. Round your answer to the nearest tenth of a percent.

Using Similar Triangles

Essential Question: How can you use similar triangles to solve real-world problems?

KEY EXAMPLE   (Lesson 12.1)

Find the missing length x.

$$\frac{ZU}{UX} = \frac{ZV}{VY} \qquad \text{Write a proportion.}$$

$$\frac{x}{10} = \frac{16}{9} \qquad \text{Substitute.}$$

$$x = \left(\frac{16}{9}\right)(10) \qquad \text{Multiply both sides by 10.}$$

$$x \approx 17.8 \qquad \text{Simplify.}$$

KEY EXAMPLE   (Lesson 12.2)

Given the directed line segment from A to B, construct the point P that divides the segment in the ratio 2 to 3 from A to B.

Use a straightedge to draw $\overrightarrow{AC}$.

Place a compass on point A and draw an arc through $\overrightarrow{AC}$. Label the intersection D. Continue this for intersections D through H.

Use a straightedge to connect points B and H.

Construct angles congruent to $\angle AHB$ with points D through G.

$\overline{AB}$ is partitioned into five equal parts. Label point P at the point that divides the segment in the ratio 2 to 3 from A to B.

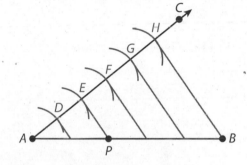

KEY EXAMPLE   (Lesson 12.3)

A 5.8-foot-tall man is standing next to a basketball hoop that casts an 11.2-foot shadow. The man's shadow is 6.5 feet long. How tall is the basketball hoop?

Let x be the height of the basketball hoop.

$$\frac{x}{11.2} = \frac{5.8}{6.5} \qquad \text{Write a proportion.}$$

$$x = \left(\frac{5.8}{6.5}\right)(11.2) \qquad \text{Multiply both sides by 11.2.}$$

$$x \approx 10$$

EXERCISES

Find the missing lengths. *(Lesson 12.1)*

1. $BG =$ _____

2. $CE =$ _____

Given the directed line segment from A to B, construct the point P that divides the segment in the ratio 3 to 1 from A to B. *(Lesson 12.2)*

Find the unknown length. *(Lesson 12.3)*

3.

4. A 5.9-foot-tall-man stands near a 12-foot statue. The man places a mirror on the ground a certain distance from the base of the statue, and then stands another 7 feet from the mirror to see the top of the statue in it. How far is the mirror from the base of the statue?

_____

5. A 45-foot flagpole casts a 22-foot shadow. At the same time of day, a woman casts a 2.7-foot shadow. How tall is the woman?

_____

Find the lengths. *(Lesson 12.4)*

6. $x =$ _____

7. $y =$ _____

8. $z =$ _____

MODULE PERFORMANCE TASK

How Large Is the Bermuda Triangle?

The boundaries of the Bermuda Triangle are not well defined, but the region is often represented as a triangle with vertices at Miami, Florida; San Juan, Puerto Rico; and Hamilton, Bermuda. The distance between Miami and San Juan is about 1,034 miles. What is the approximate area of this region? One tool that you may find helpful in solving this problem is the similar triangle shown here with angle measures labeled.

Use your own paper to complete the task. Be sure to record all your data and assumptions. Then use graphs, diagrams, words, or numbers to explain how you reached your conclusion.

12.1–12.4 Using Similar Triangles

- Online Homework
- Hints and Help
- Extra Practice

Find the missing lengths. *(Lesson 12.1)*

1.

2.

Given the directed line segment from A to B, construct the point P that divides the segment in the given ratio from A to B. *(Lesson 12.2)*

3. 3 to 4

Find the missing height. *(Lesson 12.3)*

4. The height of a street light is 25 feet. It casts a 12-foot shadow. At the same time, a man standing next to the street light casts a 3-foot shadow. How tall is the man?

ESSENTIAL QUESTION

5. How can you use similar triangles to find the missing parts of a triangle?

Assessment Readiness

SELECTED RESPONSE

1. $\triangle XYZ$ is given by the points $X(-1, -1)$, $Y(3, 5)$, and $Z(5, 1)$. Consider each of the points below. Is each point a vertex of the image under the transformation

   $(x, y) \rightarrow (x + 3, y - 2) \rightarrow \left(\frac{1}{2}x, y\right) \rightarrow (y, -x)$?

   Select Yes or No for A–C.

   A. $X'''(-3, -1)$ ○ Yes   ○ No
   B. $Y'''(3, -3)$ ○ Yes   ○ No
   C. $Z'''(-1, -4)$ ○ Yes   ○ No

2. Which of the following statements are true about the triangle at the right? Choose True or False for each statement.

   A. The value of x is 15.   ○ True   ○ False
   B. The value of y is 12.   ○ True   ○ False
   C. The value of y is 16.   ○ True   ○ False

3. $\triangle ABC$ is given by the points $A(-1, 2)$, $B(2, 5)$, and $C(4, -1)$. What is the point $\left(\frac{1}{2}, \frac{5}{2}\right)$? Explain what this means.

4. Given the directed segment from A to B, construct the point P that divides the segment in the ratio 1 to 5 from A to B. Explain your process and how it relates to similar triangles.

Assessment Readiness

- Online Homework
- Hints and Help
- Extra Practice

1. Determine whether the statements are true.

   Select True or False for each statement.

   A. Dilations preserve angle measure. ○ True ○ False

   B. Dilations preserve distance. ○ True ○ False

   C. Dilations preserve collinearity. ○ True ○ False

   D. Dilations preserve orientation. ○ True ○ False

2. Was the given transformation used to map $ABCD$ to $QRST$?

   Select Yes or No for each statement.

   A. Reflection across the y-axis ○ Yes ○ No

   B. Reflection across the x-axis ○ Yes ○ No

   C. Dilation ○ Yes ○ No

   D. Translation ○ Yes ○ No

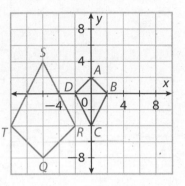

3. The vertices of quadrilateral $JKLM$ are $J(-2, 0)$, $K(-1, 2)$, $L(1, 3)$, and $M(0, 1)$. Can you use slopes and/or the distance formula to prove each statement?

   Select Yes or No for A–C.

   A. Quadrilateral $JKLM$ is a parallelogram. ○ Yes ○ No

   B. Quadrilateral $JKLM$ is a rhombus. ○ Yes ○ No

   C. Quadrilateral $JKLM$ is a rectangle. ○ Yes ○ No

4. Will the transformation produce similar figures?

   Select Yes or No for each statement.

   A. $(x, y) \rightarrow (x - 5, y + 5) \rightarrow (-x, -y) \rightarrow (3x, 3y)$ ○ Yes ○ No

   B. $(x, y) \rightarrow (3x, y + 5) \rightarrow (x, 3y) \rightarrow (x - 1, y - 1)$ ○ Yes ○ No

   C. $(x, y) \rightarrow (x, y + 5) \rightarrow (2x, y) \rightarrow (x + 5, y)$ ○ Yes ○ No

5. Is ABC similar to DEF? Select Yes or No for each statement.

   A. $A(-1, -3)$, $B(1, 3)$, $C(3, -5)$
      $D(2, -6)$, $E(3, 0)$, $F(6, -8)$ ○ Yes ○ No

   B. $A(-1, -3)$, $B(1, 3)$, $C(3, -5)$
      $D(-5, -1)$, $E(-4, 2)$, $F(-3, -2)$ ○ Yes ○ No

   C. $A(-1, -3)$, $B(1, 3)$, $C(3, -5)$
      $D(-2, -2)$, $E(2, 4)$, $F(2, -4)$ ○ Yes ○ No

6. Are the triangles similar? Select Yes or No for each pair of figures.

A.

○ Yes   ○ No

B.

○ Yes   ○ No

C.

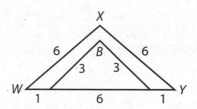

○ Yes   ○ No

7. Find the missing side lengths *PQ*, *PR*, and *TU*.

Performance Tasks

★ **8.** The map shows that A Street and B Street are parallel. Find the distance on 6th Ave between A Street and the library. Explain any theorems that come into play here.

★★ **9.** A city has a walkway between the middle school and the library that can be represented in the image given. The city decides it wants to place three trash cans, equally spaced along the walkway, to help reduce any littering. Find the coordinates of the points at which the trash cans should be placed, and then plot them on the graph.

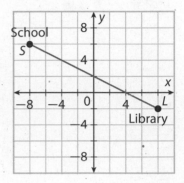

★★ **10.** A person playing table tennis can be represented by the image shown, where *A* is the point where the person hits the ball with the paddle, at a vertical distance of 152.25 cm from the floor. The height of the table is 76 cm and the net is 15.25 cm tall. Determine the path of the ball.

Special Effects Engineers A special effects engineer is helping create a movie and needs to add a shadow to a tall totem pole that is next to a 6-foot-tall man. The totem pole is 48 feet tall and is next to the man, who has a shadow that is 2.5 feet long. Create an image with the given information and then use the image to find the length of the shadow that the engineer needs to create for the totem pole.

Trigonometry

MATH IN CAREERS

Detective A detective uses clues to determine the time and place that an event has occurred. With the use of logic and math skills, a detective can pinpoint the time of day shown in a photograph, based on the position of shadows in the image.

If you're interested in a career as a detective, you should study these mathematical subjects:

- Algebra
- Geometry
- Trigonometry
- Calculus

Research other careers that require the use of forensics to understand real-world scenarios. See the related Career Activity at the end of this unit.

Reading Start-Up

Review Words

Visualize Vocabulary

Use the review words to complete the chart.

Term	Description
	A triangle with a right angle
	An angle whose measure is 90°
	The longest side of a right triangle
	The shorter sides of a right triangle
	Angles whose measures sum to 90°
	Angles whose measures sum to 180°
	A representation of the relative sizes of two or more values

Review Words

✔ complementary angles (*ángulos complementarios*)

✔ hypotenuse (*hipotenusa*)

✔ legs (*catetos*)

✔ ratio (*razón*)

✔ right angle (*ángulo recto*)

✔ right triangle (*triángulo rectángulo*)

✔ supplementary angles (*ángulos suplementarios*)

Preview Words

adjacent (*adyacente*)

cosine (*coseno*)

inverse trigonometric ratios (*razónes trigonométricas inversas*)

opposite (*opuesto*)

Pythagorean triple (*terna pitagórica*)

sine (*seno*)

tangent (*tangente*)

trigonometric ratio *razón trigonométrica*

Understand Vocabulary

Complete the sentences using the preview words.

1. In a right triangle, the side _____ to an acute angle is the leg that forms one side of the angle.

2. Sine, cosine, and tangent are examples of _____.

3. A set of positive integers a, b, and c that satisfy the equation $a^2 + b^2 = c^2$ is called a(n) _____.

Active Reading

Booklet Create a booklet at the start of the unit. During discussions of the material in class, write vocabulary that you know toward the front, vocabulary that you recognize but are unsure of toward the middle, and vocabulary that you do not know toward the back. Use the booklet as a tool for studying the vocabulary.

Trigonometry with Right Triangles

Essential Question: How can you use trigonometry with right triangles to solve real-world problems?

REAL WORLD VIDEO
Check out how right triangle trigonometry is used in real-world warehouses to minimize the space needed for items being shipped or stored.

MODULE PERFORMANCE TASK PREVIEW

How Much Shorter Are Staggered Pipe Stacks?

In this module, you will investigate how much space can be saved by stacking pipes in a staggered pattern rather than directly on top of each other. How can trigonometry help you find the answer to this problem? Get prepared to discover the "staggering" results!

Complete these exercises to review skills you will need for this module.

Angle Relationships

Example 1   Find the angle complementary to the given angle. 75°

$x + 75° = 90°$ Write as an equation.

$x = 90° - 75°$ Solve for x.

$x = 15°$

Find the complementary angle.

1. 20° _____

2. 35° _____

3. 67° _____

Find the supplementary angle.

4. 80° _____

5. 65° _____

6. 34° _____

Find the remaining angle or angles for △ABC.

7. m∠A = 50°, m∠B = 40° _____

8. m∠A = 60°, m∠C = 20° _____

9. m∠B = 70° and ∠A ≅ ∠C _____

10. ∠A ≅ ∠B ≅ ∠C _____

11. m∠B = 30° and m∠A = $\frac{1}{2}$m∠C _____

12. △ABC is similar to △DEF and m∠D = 70° and m∠F = 50° _____

13. △ABC is similar to △PQR and m∠R = 50° and ∠P ≅ ∠Q _____

14. m∠A = 45° and m∠B = m∠C _____

15. m∠B = 105° and m∠A = 2 · m∠C _____

16. m∠A = 5° and m∠B = 9 · m∠C _____

13.1 Tangent Ratio

Essential Question: How do you find the tangent ratio for an acute angle?

Resource
Locker

⊘ Explore   Investigating a Ratio in a Right Triangle

In a given a right triangle, $\triangle ABC$, with a right angle at vertex C, there are three sides. The side adjacent to $\angle A$ is the leg that forms one side of $\angle A$. The side opposite $\angle A$ is the leg that does not form a side of $\angle A$. The side that connects the adjacent and opposite legs is the hypotenuse.

(A) In $\triangle DEF$, label the legs opposite and adjacent to $\angle D$. Then measure the lengths of the legs in centimeters and record their values in the rectangles provided.

(B) What is the ratio of the opposite leg length to the adjacent leg length, rounded to the nearest hundredth?

$\dfrac{EF}{DF} \approx$ ☐ _____

(C) Using a protractor and ruler, draw right triangle $\triangle JKL$ with a right angle at vertex L and $\angle J = 40°$ so that $\triangle JKL \sim \triangle DEF$. Label the opposite and adjacent legs to $\angle J$ and include their measurements.

_____

_____

(D) What is the ratio of the opposite leg length to the adjacent leg length, rounded to the nearest hundredth?

$\dfrac{KL}{JL} \approx$ ☐

1. **Discussion** Compare your work with that of other students. Do all the triangles have the same angles? Do they all have the same side lengths? Do they all have the same leg ratios? Summarize your findings.

_____

_____

_____

2. If you repeated Steps A–D with a right triangle having a 30° angle, how would your results be similar? How would they be different?

_____

_____

_____

⏱ Explain 1 Finding the Tangent of an Angle

The ratio you calculated in the Explore section is called the *tangent* of an angle. The **tangent** of acute angle A, written tan $\angle A$, is defined as follows:

$$\tan A = \frac{\text{length of leg opposite } \angle A}{\text{length of leg adjacent to } \angle A}$$

You can use what you know about similarity to show why the tangent of an angle is constant. By the AA Similarity Theorem, given $\angle D \cong \angle J$ and also $\angle F \cong \angle L$, then $\triangle DEF \sim \triangle JKL$. This means the lengths of the sides of $\triangle JKL$ are each the same multiple, k, of the lengths of the corresponding sides of $\triangle DEF$. Substituting into the tangent equation shows that the ratio of the length of the opposite leg to the length of the adjacent leg is always the same value for a given acute angle.

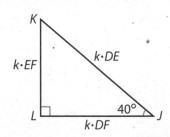

tangent defined for specified angle $\triangle DEF$ $\triangle JKL$

$$\tan 40° = \frac{\text{leg opposite } \angle 40°}{\text{leg adjacent to } \angle 40°} = \frac{EF}{DF} = \frac{KL}{JL} = \frac{k \cdot EF}{k \cdot DF} = \frac{EF}{DF}$$

Example 1 Find the tangent of each specified angle. Write each ratio as a fraction and as a decimal rounded to the nearest hundredth.

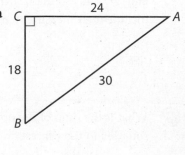

Ⓐ $\angle A$

$$\tan A = \frac{\text{length of leg opposite } \angle A}{\text{length of leg adjacent to } \angle A} = \frac{18}{24} = \frac{3}{4} = 0.75$$

Ⓑ $\angle B$

$$\tan B = \frac{\text{length of leg } \boxed{} \angle B}{\text{length of leg } \boxed{} \text{ to } \angle B} = \frac{\boxed{}}{\boxed{}} = \frac{\boxed{}}{3} \approx \boxed{}$$

3. What is the relationship between the ratios for tan *A* and tan *B*? Do you believe this relationship will be true for acute angles in other right triangles? Explain.

_____

_____

4. Why does it not make sense to ask for the value of tan *L*?

_____

_____

Your Turn

Find the tangent of each specified angle. Write each ratio as a fraction and as a decimal rounded to the nearest hundredth.

5. ∠*Q*

6. ∠*R*

⚙ Explain 2 Finding a Side Length using Tangent

When you know the length of a leg of a right triangle and the measure of one of the acute angles, you can use the tangent to find the length of the other leg. This is especially useful in real-world problems.

Example 2 **Apply the tangent ratio to find unknown lengths.**

(A) In order to meet safety guidelines, a roof contractor determines that she must place the base of her ladder 6 feet away from the house, making an angle of 76° with the ground. To the nearest tenth of a foot, how far above the ground is the eave of the roof?

Step 1 Write a tangent ratio that involves the unknown length.

$$\tan A = \frac{\text{length of leg opposite } \angle A}{\text{length of leg adjacent to } \angle A} = \frac{BC}{BA}$$

Step 2 Identify the given values and substitute into the tangent equation.

Given: $BA = 6$ ft and m∠*A* = 76°

Substitute: $\tan 76° = \frac{BC}{6}$

Step 3 Solve for the unknown leg length. Be sure the calculator is in degree mode and do not round until the final step of the solution.

Multiply each side by 6.

$$6 \cdot \tan 76° = \frac{6}{1} \cdot \frac{BC}{6}$$

Use a calculator to find $\tan 76°$.

$$6 \cdot \tan 76° = BC$$

Substitute this value in for $\tan 76°$.

$$6(4.010780934) = BC$$

Multiply. Round to the nearest tenth.

$$24.1 \approx BC$$

So, the eave of the roof is about 24.1 feet above the ground.

B. For right triangle $\triangle STU$, what is the length of the leg adjacent to $\angle S$?

Step 1 Write a tangent ratio that involves the unknown length.

$$\tan S = \frac{\text{length of leg} \quad \angle S}{\text{length of leg} \quad \text{to } \angle S} = \frac{\boxed{}}{\boxed{}}$$

Step 2 Identify the given values and substitute into the tangent equation.

Given: $TU = \boxed{}$ and $m\angle S = \boxed{}°$

Substitute: $\tan \boxed{}° = \dfrac{\boxed{}}{SU}$

Step 3 Solve for the unknown leg length.

Multiply both sides by SU, then divide both sides by 54°. $SU = \dfrac{\boxed{}}{\boxed{}°}$

Use a calculator to find 54° and substitute. $SU \approx \dfrac{\boxed{}}{\boxed{}}$

Divide. Round to the nearest tenth. $SU \approx \boxed{}$

Your Turn

7. A ladder needs to reach the second story window, which is 10 feet above the ground, and make an angle with the ground of 70°. How far out from the building does the base of the ladder need to be positioned?

⚙ Explain 3 **Finding an Angle Measure using Tangent**

In the previous section you used a given angle measure and leg measure with the tangent ratio to solve for an unknown leg. What if you are given the leg measures and want to find the measures of the acute angles? If you know the tan A, read as "tangent of $\angle A$," then you can use the **tan⁻¹ A**, read as "**inverse tangent of $\angle A$**," to find $m\angle A$. So, given an acute angle $\angle A$, if $\tan A = x$, then $\tan^{-1} x = m\angle A$.

Example 3 **Find the measure of the indicated angle. Round to the nearest degree.**

19 in.

36 in.

(A) What is m∠A?

Step 1 Write the tangent ratio for ∠A using the known values.	Step 2 Write the inverse tangent equation.	Step 3 Evaluate using a calculator and round as indicated.
$\tan A = \dfrac{19}{36}$	$\tan^{-1} \dfrac{19}{36} = m\angle A$	$m\angle A \approx 27.82409638 \approx 28°$

(B) What is m∠B?

Step 1 Write the tangent ratio for ∠B using the known values.	Step 2 Write the inverse tangent equation.	Step 3 Evaluate using a calculator and round as indicated.
$\tan B = \dfrac{\square}{\square}$	$\dfrac{\square}{\square} = m\angle B$	$m\angle B \approx \boxed{}° \approx \boxed{}°$

Your Turn

8. Find m∠J.

93

46

💬 Elaborate

9. Explain how to identify the opposite and adjacent legs of a given acute angle.

_____

_____

10. **Discussion** How does tan A change as m∠A increases? Explain the basis for the identified relationship.

_____

_____

_____

_____

11. Essential Question Check-In Compare and contrast the use of the tangent and inverse tangent ratios for solving problems.

_____

_____

_____

_____

_____

⭐ Evaluate: Homework and Practice

1. In each triangle, measure the length of the adjacent side and the opposite side of the 22° angle. Then calculate and compare the ratios.

In each right triangle, find the tangent of each angle that is not the right angle.

2.

3.

4.

5.

Let $\triangle ABC$ be a right triangle, with $m\angle C = 90°$. Given the tangent of one of the complementary angles of the triangle, find the tangent of the other angle.

6. $\tan \angle A = 1.25$ **7.** $\tan \angle B = 0.50$ **8.** $\tan \angle B = 1.0$

Use the tangent to find the unknown side length.

9. Find QR.

10. Find AC.

11. Find PQ.

12. Find DE.

13. Find AB.

14. Find PR.

Find the measure of the angle specified for each triangle. Use the inverse tangent (tan⁻¹) function of your calculator. Round your answer to the nearest degree.

15. Find $\angle A$.

16. Find $\angle R$.

17. Find $\angle B$.

Write an equation using either tan or tan⁻¹ to express the measure of the angle or side. Then solve the equation.

18. Find BC.

19. Find PQ.

20. Find $\angle A$ and $\angle C$.

21. Multi-Step Find the measure of angle D. Show your work.

22. Engineering A client wants to build a ramp that carries people to a height of 1.4 meters, as shown in the diagram. What additional information is necessary to identify the measure of angle a, the angle the ramp forms with the horizontal? After the additional measurement is made, describe how to find the measure of the angle.

1.4 m

23. Explain the Error A student uses the triangle shown to calculate a. Find and explain the student's error.

6.5   2.5
a

$a = \tan^{-1}\left(\dfrac{6.5}{2.5}\right) = \tan^{-1}(2.6)$

$a = 69.0°$

24. When $m\angle A + m\angle B = 90°$, what relationship is formed by $\tan \angle A$ and $\tan \angle B$? Select all that apply.

A. $\tan\angle A = \dfrac{1}{\tan B}$

C. $(\tan\angle A)(\tan\angle B) = 1$

B. $\tan\angle A + \tan\angle B = 1$

D. $(\tan\angle A)(\tan\angle B) = -1$

H.O.T. Focus on Higher Order Thinking

25. Analyze Relationships To travel from Pottstown to Cogsville, a man drives his car 83 miles due east on one road, and then 15 miles due north on another road. Describe the path that a bird could fly in a straight line from Pottstown to Cogsville. What angle does the line make with the two roads that the man used?

26. Critical Thinking A right triangle has only one 90° angle. Both of its other angles have measures greater than 0° and less than 90°. Why is it useful to define the tangent of 90° to equal 1, and the tangent of 0° to equal 0?

Lesson Performance Task

When they form conical piles, granular materials such as salt, gravel, and sand settle at different "angles of repose," depending on the shapes of the grains. One particular 13-foot tall cone of dry sand has a base diameter of 38.6 feet.

angle of repose

1. To the nearest tenth of a degree, what is the angle of repose of this type of dry sand?

2. A different conical pile of the same type of sand is 10 feet tall. What is the diameter of the cone's base?

3. Henley Landscaping Supply sells a type of sand with a 30° angle of repose for $32 per cubic yard. Find the cost of an 11-foot-tall cone of this type of sand. Show your work.

13.2 Sine and Cosine Ratios

Essential Question: How can you use the sine and cosine ratios, and their inverses, in calculations involving right triangles?

Resource
Locker

Ⓔ **Explore**   **Investigating Ratios in a Right Triangle**

You can use geometry software or an online tool to explore ratios of side lengths in right triangles.

Ⓐ Construct three points A, B, and C.
Construct rays $\overrightarrow{AB}$ and $\overrightarrow{AC}$. Move C so that $\angle A$ is acute.

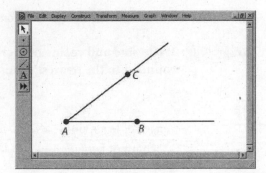

Ⓑ Construct point D on $\overline{AC}$. Construct a line through D perpendicular to $\overline{AB}$. Construct point E as the intersection of the perpendicular line and $\overline{AB}$.

Ⓒ Measure $\angle A$. Measure the side lengths DE, AE, and AD of $\triangle ADE$.

Ⓓ Calculate the ratios $\dfrac{DE}{AD}$ and $\dfrac{AE}{AD}$.

Reflect

1. Drag D along $\overrightarrow{AC}$. What happens to m$\angle A$ as D moves along $\overrightarrow{AC}$? What postulate or theorem guarantees that the different triangles formed are similar to each other?

_____

2. As you move D along $\overrightarrow{AC}$, what happens to the values of the ratios $\dfrac{DE}{AD}$ and $\dfrac{AE}{AD}$? Use the properties of similar triangles to explain this result.

_____

3. Move C. What happens to m$\angle A$? With a new value of m$\angle A$, note the values of the two ratios. What happens to the ratios if you drag D along $\overrightarrow{AC}$?

_____

_____

⚙ Explain 1   Finding the Sine and Cosine of an Angle

Trigonometric Ratios

A **trigonometric ratio** is a ratio of two sides of a right triangle. You have already seen
one trigonometric ratio, the tangent. There are two additional trigonometric ratios, the
sine and the cosine, that involve the hypotenuse of a right triangle.

The **sine** of ∠A, written sin A, is defined as follows:

$$\sin A = \frac{\text{length of leg opposite } \angle A}{\text{length of hypotenuse}} = \frac{BC}{AB}$$

The **cosine** of ∠A, written cos A, is defined as follows:

$$\cos A = \frac{\text{length of leg adjacent to } \angle A}{\text{length of hypotenuse}} = \frac{AC}{AB}$$

You can use these definitions to calculate trigonometric ratios.

Example 1   Write sine and cosine of each angle as a fraction and as a decimal
rounded to the nearest thousandth.

Ⓐ ∠D

$$\sin D = \frac{\text{length of leg opposite } \angle D}{\text{length of hypotenuse}} = \frac{EF}{DF} = \frac{8}{17} \approx 0.471$$

$$\cos D = \frac{\text{length of leg adjacent to } \angle D}{\text{length of hypotenuse}} = \frac{DE}{DF} = \frac{15}{17} \approx 0.882$$

Ⓑ ∠F

$$\sin F = \frac{\text{length of leg opposite to } \angle F}{\text{length of hypotenuse}} = \frac{DE}{DF} = \frac{\boxed{}}{\boxed{}} \approx \boxed{}$$

$$\cos F = \frac{\text{length of leg adjacent to } \angle F}{\text{length of hypotenuse}} = \frac{\boxed{}}{\boxed{}} \approx \boxed{}$$

Reflect

4.   What do you notice about the sines and cosines you found? Do you think this relationship
will be true for any pair of acute angles in a right triangle? Explain.

_____

_____

5.   In a right triangle △PQR with PR = 5, QR = 3, and m∠Q = 90°, what are the
values of sin P and cos P?

sin P = ☐

cos P = ☐

Explain 2   Using Complementary Angles

The acute angles of a right triangle are complementary. Their trigonometric ratios are related to each other as shown in the following relationship.

> ### Trigonometric Ratios of Complementary Angles
>
> If $\angle A$ and $\angle B$ are the acute angles in a right triangle, then $\sin A = \cos B$ and $\cos A = \sin B$.
>
> Therefore, if θ ("theta") is the measure of an acute angle, then $\sin \theta = \cos(90° - \theta)$ and $\cos \theta = \sin(90° - \theta)$.
>
>

You can use these relationships to write equivalent expressions.

Example 2   Write each trigonometric expression.

(A) Given that $\sin 38° \approx 0.616$, write the cosine of a complementary angle in terms of the sine of 38°. Then find the cosine of the complementary angle.

Use an expression relating trigonometric ratios of complementary angles.

$$\sin \theta = \cos(90° - \theta)$$

Substitute 38 into both sides. $\sin 38° = \cos(90° - 38°)$

Simplify. $\sin 38° = \cos 52°$

Substitute for $\sin 38°$. $0.616 \approx \cos 52°$

So, the cosine of the complementary angle is about 0.616.

(B) Given that $\cos 60° = 0.5$, write the sine of a complementary angle in terms of the cosine of 60°. Then find the sine of the complementary angle.

Use an expression relating trigonometric ratios of complementary angles.

$$\cos \theta = \sin(90° - \theta)$$

Substitute ☐ into both sides. $\cos \boxed{}° = \sin\left(90° - \boxed{}°\right)$

Simplify the right side. $\cos \boxed{}° = \sin \boxed{}°$

Substitute for the cosine of ☐°. $\boxed{} = \sin \boxed{}°$

So, the sine of the complementary angle is 0.5.

6. What can you conclude about the sine and cosine of 45°? Explain.

_____

_____

7. **Discussion** Is it possible for the sine or cosine of an acute angle to equal 1? Explain.

_____

_____

Your Turn

Write each trigonometric expression.

8. Given that $\cos 73° \approx 0.292$, write the sine of a complementary angle.

9. Given that $\sin 45° \approx 0.707$, write the cosine of a complementary angle.

⊘ Explain 3 Finding Side Lengths using Sine and Cosine

You can use sine and cosine to solve real-world problems.

Example 3 A 12-ft ramp is installed alongside some steps to provide wheelchair access to a library. The ramp makes an angle of 11° with the ground. Find each dimension, to the nearest tenth of a foot.

Ⓐ Find the height x of the wall.

Use the definition of sine.

$$\sin A = \frac{\text{length of leg opposite } \angle A}{\text{length of hypotenuse}} = \frac{AB}{AC}$$

Substitute 11° for A, x for BC, and 12 for AC.

$$\sin 11° = \frac{x}{12}$$

Multiply both sides by 12.

$$12\sin 11° = x$$

Use a calculator to evaluate the expression.

$$x \approx 2.3$$

So, the height of the wall is about 2.3 feet.

Ⓑ Find the distance y that the ramp extends in front of the wall.

Use the definition of cosine.
$$\cos A = \frac{\text{length of leg adjacent to } \angle A}{\text{length of hypotenuse}} = \frac{AB}{AC}$$

Substitute ☐° for A, y for AB, and ☐ for AC. $\cos$ ☐° $= \dfrac{y}{\boxed{}}$

Multiply both sides by ☐.   ☐ $\cos$ ☐° $= y$

Use a calculator to evaluate the expression. $y \approx$ ☐

So, the ramp extends in front of the wall about ☐ feet.

Reflect

10. Could you find the height of the wall using the cosine? Explain.

_____

_____

Your Turn

11. Suppose a new regulation states that the maximum angle of a ramp for wheelchairs is 8°. At least how long must the new ramp be? Round to the nearest tenth of a foot.

🖊 Explain 4   Finding Angle Measures using Sine and Cosine

In the triangle, $\sin A = \dfrac{5}{10} = \dfrac{1}{2}$. However, you already know that $\sin 30° = \dfrac{1}{2}$. So you can conclude that $m\angle A = 30°$,

and write $\sin^{-1}\left(\dfrac{1}{2}\right) = 30°$.

Extending this idea, the **inverse trigonometric ratios** for sine and cosine are defined as follows:

Given an acute angle, $\angle A$,

- if $\sin A = x$, then $\sin^{-1} x = m\angle A$, read as "inverse sine of x"
- if $\cos A = x$, then $\cos^{-1} x = m\angle A$, read as "inverse cosine of x"

You can use a calculator to evaluate inverse trigonometric expressions.

Example 4 Find the acute angle measures in $\triangle PQR$, to the nearest degree.

(A) Write a trigonometric ratio for $\angle R$.

Since the lengths of the hypotenuse and the opposite leg are given,

use the sine ratio.

$$\sin R = \frac{PQ}{PR}$$

Substitute 7 for PQ and 13 for PR.

$$\sin R = \frac{7}{13}$$

(B) Write and evaluate an inverse trigonometric ratio to find $m\angle R$ and $m\angle P$.

Start with the trigonometric ratio for $\angle R$.

$\sin R = \boxed{}$

Use the definition of the inverse sine ratio.

$m\angle R = \sin^{-1}\boxed{}$

Use a calculator to evaluate the inverse sine ratio.

$m\angle R = \boxed{}°$

Write a cosine ratio for $\angle P$.

$\cos P = \frac{PQ}{PR}$

Substitute $\boxed{}$ for PQ and $\boxed{}$ for PR.

$\cos P = \boxed{}$

Use the definition of the inverse cosine ratio.

$m\angle P = \cos^{-1}\boxed{}$

Use a calculator to evaluate the inverse cosine ratio.

$m\angle P = \boxed{}°$

Reflect

12. How else could you have determined $m\angle P$?

_____

Your Turn

Find the acute angle measures in $\triangle XYZ$, to the nearest degree.

13. $m\angle Y$

14. $m\angle Z$

Elaborate

15. How are the sine and cosine ratios for an acute angle of a right triangle defined?

_____

16. How are the inverse sine and cosine ratios for an acute angle of a right triangle defined?

_____

_____

_____

_____

17. Essential Question Check-In How do you find an unknown angle measure in a right triangle?

_____

_____

☆ Evaluate: Homework and Practice

- Online Homework
- Hints and Help
- Extra Practice

Write each trigonometric expression. Round trigonometric ratios to the nearest thousandth.

1. Given that sin 60° ≈ 0.866, write the cosine of a complementary angle.

2. Given that cos 26° ≈ 0.899, write the sine of a complementary angle.

Write each trigonometric ratio as a fraction and as a decimal, rounded (if necessary) to the nearest thousandth.

3. sin A

4. cos A

5. cos B

6. sin D

7. cos F

8. sin F

Find the unknown length x in each right triangle, to the nearest tenth.

9.

10.

11.

12.

Find each acute angle measure, to the nearest degree.

13. m∠P

14. m∠Q

15. m∠U

16. m∠W

17. Use the property that corresponding sides of similar triangles are proportional to explain why the trigonometric ratio sin A is the same when calculated in $\triangle ADE$ as in $\triangle ABC$.

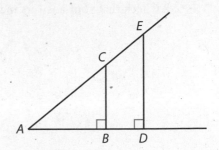

18. Technology The specifications for a laptop computer describe its screen as measuring 15.6 in. However, this is actually the length of a diagonal of the rectangular screen, as represented in the figure. How wide is the screen horizontally, to the nearest tenth of an inch?

19. Building Sharla's bedroom is directly under the roof of her house. Given the dimensions shown, how high is the ceiling at its highest point, to the nearest tenth of a foot?

20. Zoology You can sometimes see an eagle gliding with its wings flexed in a characteristic double-vee shape. Each wing can be modeled as two right triangles as shown in the figure. Find the measure of the angle in the middle of the wing, $\angle DHG$ to the nearest degree.

21. Algebra Find a pair of acute angles that satisfy the equation $\sin(3x + 9) = \cos(x + 5)$. Check that your answers make sense.

22. Multi-Step Reginald is planning to fence his back yard. Every side of the yard except for the side along the house is to be fenced, and fencing costs $3.50/yd. How much will the fencing cost?

23. Architecture The sides of One World Trade Center in New York City form eight isosceles triangles, four of which are 200 ft long at their base BC. The length AC of each sloping side is approximately 1185 ft.

Find the measure of the apex angle BAC of each isosceles triangle, to the nearest tenth of a degree. (*Hint:* Use the midpoint D of $\overline{BC}$ to create two right triangles.)

24. **Explain the Error** Melissa has calculated the length of $\overline{XZ}$ in $\triangle XYZ$. Explain why Melissa's answer must be incorrect, and identify and correct her error.

Melissa's solution:

$$\cos X = \frac{XZ}{XY}$$

$$XZ = \frac{XY}{\cos X}$$

$$XZ = 27 \cos 42° \approx 20.1$$

25. **Communicate Mathematical Ideas** Explain why the sine and cosine of an acute angle are always between 0 and 1.

26. **Look for a Pattern** In $\triangle ABC$, the hypotenuse $\overline{AB}$ has a length of 1. Use the Pythagorean Theorem to explore the relationship between the squares of the sine and cosine of $\angle A$, written $\sin^2 A$ and $\cos^2 A$. Could you derive this relationship using a right triangle without any lengths specified? Explain.

27. **Justify Reasoning** Use the Triangle Proportionality Theorem to explain why the trigonometric ratio $\cos A$ is the same when calculated in $\triangle ADE$ as in $\triangle ABC$.

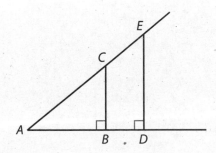

Lesson Performance Task

As light passes from a vacuum into another medium, it is *refracted*—that is, its direction changes. The ratio of the sine of the angle of the incoming *incident* ray, *I*, to the sine of the angle of the outgoing *refracted* ray, *r*, is called the *index of refraction*:

$n = \frac{\sin I}{\sin r}$. where *n* is the index of refraction.

This relationship is important in many fields, including gemology, the study of precious stones. A gemologist can place an unidentified gem into an instrument called a refractometer, direct an incident ray of light at a particular angle into the stone, measure the angle of the refracted ray, and calculate the index of refraction. Because the indices of refraction of thousands of gems are known, the gemologist can then identify the gem.

1. Identify the gem, given these angles obtained from a refractometer:

   a. $I = 71°, r = 29°$

   b. $I = 51°, r = 34°$

   c. $I = 45°, r = 17°$

2. A thin slice of sapphire is placed in a refractometer. The angle of the incident ray is 56°. Find the angle of the refracted ray to the nearest degree.

3. An incident ray of light struck a slice of serpentine. The resulting angle of refraction measured 21°. Find the angle of incidence to the nearest degree.

4. Describe the error(s) in a student's solution and explain why they were error(s):

$n = \dfrac{\sin I}{\sin r}$

$= \dfrac{\sin 51°}{\sin 34°}$

$= \dfrac{51°}{34°}$

$= 1.5 \rightarrow$ coral

Gem	Index of Refraction
Hematite	2.94
Diamond	2.42
Zircon	1.95
Azurite	1.85
Sapphire	1.77
Tourmaline	1.62
Serpentine	1.56
Coral	1.49
Opal	1.39

13.3 Special Right Triangles

Essential Question: What do you know about the side lengths and the trigonometric ratios in special right triangles?

⊘ Explore 1 Investigating an Isosceles Right Triangle

Discover relationships that always apply in an isosceles right triangle.

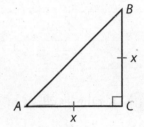

(A) The figure shows an isosceles right triangle. Identify the base angles, and use the fact that they are complementary to write an equation relating their measures.

_____

(B) Use the Isosceles Triangle Theorem to write a different equation relating the base angle measures.

_____

(C) What must the measures of the base angles be? Why?

_____

_____

(D) Use the Pythagorean Theorem to find the length of the hypotenuse in terms of the length of each leg, x.

_____

_____

Reflect

1. Is it true that if you know one side length of an isosceles right triangle, then you know all the side lengths? Explain.

_____

_____

_____

2. **What if?** Suppose you draw the perpendicular from C to $\overline{AB}$. Explain how to find the length of $\overline{CD}$.

_____

_____

_____

⊘ Explore 2 Investigating Another Special Right Triangle

Discover relationships that always apply in a right triangle formed as half of an equilateral triangle.

Ⓐ △ABD is an equilateral triangle and $\overline{BC}$ is a perpendicular from B to $\overline{AD}$. Determine all three angle measures in △ABC.

_____

_____

Ⓑ Explain why △ABC ≅ △DBC.

_____

_____

_____

_____

Ⓒ Let the length of $\overline{AC}$ be x. What is the length of $\overline{AB}$, and why?

_____

_____

_____

Ⓓ Using the Pythagorean Theorem, find the length of $\overline{BC}$.

_____

Reflect

3. What is the numerical ratio of the side lengths in a right triangle with acute angles that measure 30° and 60°? Explain.

_____

_____

4. **Explain the Error** A student has drawn a right triangle with a 60° angle and a hypotenuse of 6. He has labeled the other side lengths as shown. Explain how you can tell at a glance that he has made an error and how to correct it.

_____

_____

_____

🔑 Explain 1   Applying Relationships in Special Right Triangles

The right triangles you explored are sometimes called 45°–45°–90° and 30°–60°–90° triangles. In a 45°–45°–90° triangle, the hypotenuse is $\sqrt{2}$ times as long as each leg. In a 30°–60°–90° triangle, the hypotenuse is twice as long as the shorter leg and the longer leg is $\sqrt{3}$ times as long as the shorter leg. You can use these relationships to find side lengths in these special types of right triangles.

Example 1   **Find the unknown side lengths in each right triangle.**

(A)   Find the unknown side lengths in $\triangle ABC$.

The hypotenuse is $\sqrt{2}$ times
as long as each leg. $AB = AC\sqrt{2} = BC\sqrt{2}$

Substitute 10 for AB. $10 = AC\sqrt{2} = BC\sqrt{2}$

Multiply by $\sqrt{2}$. $10\sqrt{2} = 2AC = 2BC$

Divide by 2. $5\sqrt{2} = AC = BC$

(B)   In right $\triangle DEF$, m$\angle D = 30°$ and m$\angle E = 60°$. The shorter leg measures $5\sqrt{3}$. Find the remaining side lengths.

The hypotenuse is twice as long as the shorter leg. $DE = 2\ \boxed{}$

Substitute $\boxed{}$ for $\boxed{}$. $DE = 2\ \boxed{}$

Simplify. $DE = \boxed{}$

The longer leg is $\sqrt{3}$ times as long as the shorter leg. $\boxed{} = \boxed{}\ \sqrt{3}$

Substitute $\boxed{}$ for $\boxed{}$. $\boxed{} = \boxed{}\ \sqrt{3}$

Simplify. $\boxed{} = \boxed{}$

Find the unknown side lengths in each right triangle.

5.

6.

🖉 Explain 2 Trigonometric Ratios of Special Right Triangles

You can use the relationships you found in special right triangles to find trigonometric ratios for the angles 45°, 30°, and 60°.

Example 2 For each triangle, find the unknown side lengths and trigonometric ratios for the angles.

(A) **A 45°—45°—90° triangle with a leg length of 1**

Step 1

Since the lengths of the sides opposite the 45° angles are congruent, they are both 1. The length of the hypotenuse is $\sqrt{2}$ times as long as each leg, so it is $1(\sqrt{2})$, or $\sqrt{2}$.

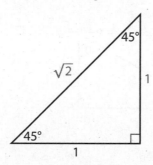

Step 2

Use the triangle to find the trigonometric ratios for 45°. Write each ratio as a simplified fraction.

Angle	Sine = $\dfrac{\text{opp}}{\text{hyp}}$	Cosine = $\dfrac{\text{adj}}{\text{hyp}}$	Tangent = $\dfrac{\text{opp}}{\text{adj}}$
45°	$\dfrac{\sqrt{2}}{2}$	$\dfrac{\sqrt{2}}{2}$	1

Step 1

The hypotenuse is _____ as long as the _____ leg,

so the length of the hypotenuse is _____.

The longer leg is _____ times as long as the _____ leg,

so the length of the longer leg is _____.

Step 2

Use the triangle to complete the table. Write each ratio as a simplified fraction.

Angle	Sine $= \dfrac{opp}{hyp}$	Cosine $= \dfrac{adj}{hyp}$	Tangent $= \dfrac{opp}{adj}$
30°			
60°			

Reflect

7. Write any patterns or relationships you see in the tables in Part A and Part B as equations. Why do these patterns or relationships make sense?

_____

_____

8. For which acute angle measure θ, is $\tan\theta$ less than 1? equal to 1? greater than 1?

_____

Your Turn

Find the unknown side lengths and trigonometric ratios for the 45° angles.

9.

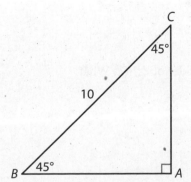

⚙ Explain 3　Investigating Pythagorean Triples

Pythagorean Triples

A **Pythagorean triple** is a set of positive integers a, b, and c that satisfy the equation $a^2 + b^2 = c^2$. This means that a, b, and c are the legs and hypotenuse of a right triangle. Right triangles that have non-integer sides will not form Pythagorean triples.

Examples of Pythagorean triples include 3, 4, and 5; 5, 12, and 13; 7, 24, and 25; and 8, 15, and 17.

Example 3　Use Pythagorean triples to find side lengths in right triangles.

Ⓐ　Verify that the side lengths 3, 4, and 5; 5, 12, and 13; 7, 24, and 25; and 8, 15, and 17 are Pythagorean triples.

_____

_____

The numbers in Step A are not the only Pythagorean triples. In the following steps you will discover that multiples of known Pythagorean triples are also Pythagorean triples.

Ⓑ　In right triangles DEF and JKL, a, b, and c form a Pythagorean triple, and k is a positive integer greater than 1. Explain how the two triangles are related.

$\triangle DEF$ is similar to _____ by the _____
because the corresponding sides are proportional. Complete the ratios to verify Side-Side-Side (SSS) Triangle Similarity.

$a : \underline{\quad} : c = \underline{\quad} : \underline{\quad} : \underline{\quad}$

Ⓒ　You can use the Pythagorean Theorem to compare the lengths of the sides of $\triangle JKL$. What must be true of the set of numbers ka, kb, and kc?

$$\left(ka^2\right) + \left(kb^2\right) = \underline{\quad\quad} + k^2 b^2$$

$$= k^2 \underline{\quad\quad\quad}$$

$$= k^2(c^2) = \underline{\quad\quad}$$

The set of numbers ka, kb, and kc form a _____.

10. Suppose you are given a right triangle with two side lengths. What would have to be true for you to use a Pythagorean triple to find the remaining side length?

_____

_____

_____

_____

Your Turn

Use Pythagorean triples to find the unknown side length.

11.

12. In $\triangle XYZ$, the hypotenuse $\overline{XY}$ has length 68, and the shorter leg $\overline{XZ}$ has length 32.

💬 Elaborate

13. Describe the type of problems involving special right triangles you can solve.

_____

_____

_____

14. How can you use Pythagorean triples to solve right triangles?

_____

_____

_____

_____

_____

15. Discussion How many Pythagorean triples are there?

_____

_____

16. Essential Question Check-In What is the ratio of the length of the hypotenuse to the length of the shorter leg in any 30°-60°-90° triangle?

_____

- Online Homework
- Hints and Help
- Extra Practice

For each triangle, state whether the side lengths shown are possible. Explain why or why not.

1.

6    $6\sqrt{3}$

60°

$3\sqrt{3}$

2.

$3\sqrt{3}$ 45°

$3\sqrt{3}$ $3\sqrt{6}$

3.

12    $8\sqrt{3}$

30°

$4\sqrt{3}$

4.

6    $2\sqrt{3}$

45°

$2\sqrt{3}$

Find the unknown side lengths in each right triangle.

5.

A   45°

18   *B*

C

6.

L   30°

9

J   60°   *K*

7. Right triangle *UVW* has acute angles *U* measuring 30° and *W* measuring 60°. Hypotenuse $\overline{UW}$ measures 12. (You may want to draw the triangle in your answer.)

8. Right triangle *PQR* has acute angles *P* and *Q* measuring 45°. Leg $\overline{PR}$ measures $5\sqrt{10}$. (You may want to draw the triangle in your answer.)

Use trigonometric ratios to solve each right triangle.

9.

10.

11. Right △*KLM* with m∠*J* = 45°, leg *JK* = $4\sqrt{3}$

12. Right △*PQR* with m∠*Q* = 30°, leg *QR* = 15

For each right triangle, find the unknown side length using a Pythagorean triple. If it is not possible, state why.

13.

14.

15. In right $\triangle PQR$, the legs have lengths $PQ = 9$ and $QR = 21$.

16. In right $\triangle XYZ$, the hypotenuse $\overline{XY}$ has length 35, and the shorter leg $\overline{YZ}$ has length 21.

17. Solve for x.

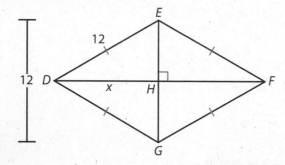

18. **Represent Real-World Problems** A baseball "diamond" actually forms a square, each side measuring 30 yards. How far, to the nearest yard, must the third baseman throw the ball to reach first base?

19. In a right triangle, the longer leg is exactly $\sqrt{3}$ times the length of the shorter leg. Use the inverse tangent trigonometric ratio to prove that the acute angles of the triangle measure 30° and 60°.

Algebra Find the value of x in each right triangle.

20.

21.

22. Explain the Error Charlene is trying to find the unknown sides of a right triangle with a 30° acute angle, whose hypotenuse measures $12\sqrt{2}$. Identify, explain, and correct Charlene's error.

23. Represent Real-World Problems Honeycomb blinds form a string of almost-regular hexagons when viewed end-on. Approximately how much material, to the nearest ten square centimeters, is needed for each 3.2-cm deep cell of a honeycomb blind that is 125 cm wide? (*Hint: Draw a picture.* A regular hexagon can be divided into 6 equilateral triangles.)

24. Which of these pairs of numbers are two out of three integer-valued side lengths of a right triangle? *(Hint: for positive integers a, b, c, and k, ka, kb,* and *kc* are side lengths of a right triangle if and only if *a, b,* and *c* are side lengths of a right triangle.)

A. 15, 18   ○ True   ○ False

B. 15, 30   ○ True   ○ False

C. 15, 51   ○ True   ○ False

D. 16, 20   ○ True   ○ False

E. 16, 24   ○ True   ○ False

25. Communicate Mathematical Ideas Is it possible for the three side lengths of a right triangle to be odd integers? Explain.

26. Make a Conjecture Use spreadsheet software to investigate this question: are there sets of positive integers a, b, and c such that $a^3 + b^3 = c^3$? You may choose to begin with these formulas:

	A	B	C	D
1	1	=A1+1	=A1^3+B1^3	=C1^(1/3)
2	=A1	=B1+1	=A2^3+B2^3	=C2^(1/3)

Lesson Performance Task

Kate and her dog are longtime flying disc players. Kate has decided to start a small business making circles of soft material that dogs can catch without injuring their teeth. Since she also likes math, she's decided to see whether she can apply Pythagorean principles to her designs. She used the Pythagorean triple 3-4-5 for the dimensions of her first three designs.

$r = 3$ in. $\quad$ $r = 4$ in. $\quad$ $r = 5$ in.
small $\qquad$ medium $\qquad$ large

1. Is it true that the (small area) + (medium area) = (large area)? Explain.

2. If the circles had radii based on the Pythagorean triple 5—12—13, would the above equation be true? Explain.

3. Three of Kate's circles have radii of a, b, and c, where a, b, and c form a Pythagorean triple $(a^2 + b^2 = c^2)$. Show that the sum of the areas of the small and medium circles equals the area of the large circle.

4. Kate has decided to go into the beach ball business. Sticking to her Pythagorean principles, she starts with three spherical beach balls--a small ball with radius 3 in., a medium ball with radius 4 in., and a large ball with radius 5 in. Is it true that (small volume) + (medium volume) = (large volume)? Show your work.

5. Explain the discrepancy between your results in Exercises 3 and 4.

13.4 Problem Solving with Trigonometry

Essential Question: How can you solve a right triangle?

⊘ Explore Deriving an Area Formula

You can use trigonometry to find the area of a triangle without knowing its height.

Ⓐ Suppose you draw an altitude $\overline{AD}$ to side $\overline{BC}$ of $\triangle ABC$. Then write an equation using a trigonometric ratio in terms of $\angle C$, the height h of $\triangle ABC$, and the length of one of its sides.

Ⓑ Solve your equation from Step A for h.

Ⓒ Complete this formula for the area of $\triangle ABC$ in terms of h and

another of its side lengths: Area $= \dfrac{1}{2}\boxed{}$

Ⓓ Substitute your expression for h from Step B into your formula from Step C.

Reflect

1. Does the area formula you found work if $\angle C$ is a right angle? Explain.

_____

_____

2. Suppose you used a trigonometric ratio in terms of $\angle B$, h, and a different side length. How would this change your findings? What does this tell you about the choice of sides and included angle?

Explain 1   Using the Area Formula

Area Formula for a Triangle in Terms of its Side Lengths

The area of $\triangle ABC$ with sides a, b, and c can be found using the lengths of two of its sides and the sine of the included angle: Area $= \frac{1}{2}bc \sin A$, Area $= \frac{1}{2}ac \sin B$, or Area $= \frac{1}{2}ab \sin C$.

You can use any form of the area formula to find the area of a triangle, given two side lengths and the measure of the included angle.

Example 1   Find the area of each triangle to the nearest tenth.

Let the known side lengths be a and b. $a = 3.2$ m and $b = 4.7$ m

Let the known angle be $\angle C$.   m $\angle C = 142°$

Substitute in the formula Area $= \frac{1}{2}ab \sin C$.   Area $= \frac{1}{2}(3.2)(4.7)\sin 142°$

Evaluate, rounding to the nearest tenth.   Area ≈ 4.6 m^2

Ⓑ In △DEF, DE = 9 in., DF = 13 in., and m∠D = 57°.

Sketch △DEF and check that ∠D is the included angle.

Write the area formula in terms of △DEF.   Area = $\frac{1}{2}$ (DE) $\boxed{}$ sin $\boxed{}$

Substitute in the area formula.   Area = $\frac{1}{2}$ $\boxed{}$ $\boxed{}$ sin $\boxed{}$ °

Evaluate, rounding to the nearest tenth.   Area ≈ $\boxed{}$ in.²

Your Turn

Find the area of each triangle to the nearest tenth.

3.

12 mm
34°
15 mm

4. In △PQR, PQ = 3 cm, QR = 6 cm, and m∠Q = 108°.

R
6 cm
P
108°
Q
3 cm

🔑 Explain 2   Solving a Right Triangle

Solving a right triangle means finding the lengths of all its sides and the measures of all its angles. To solve a right triangle you need to know two side lengths or one side length and an acute angle measure. Based on the given information, choose among trigonometric ratios, inverse trigonometric ratios, and the Pythagorean Theorem to help you solve the right triangle.

A shelf extends perpendicularly 7 in. from a wall. You want to place a 9-in. brace under the shelf, as shown. To the nearest tenth of an inch, how far below the shelf will the brace be attached to the wall? To the nearest degree, what angle will the brace make with the shelf and with the wall?

Ⓐ Find BC.

Use the Pythagorean Theorem to find the length of the third side.

$$AC^2 + BC^2 = AB^2$$

Substitute 7 for AC and 9 for AB.

$$7^2 + BC^2 = 9^2$$

Find the squares.

$$49 + BC^2 = 81$$

Subtract 49 from both sides.

$$BC^2 = 32$$

Find the square root and root.

$$BC \approx 5.7$$

Ⓑ Find $m\angle A$ and $m\angle B$.

Use an inverse trigonometric ratio to find $m\angle A$. You know the lengths of the adjacent side and the hypotenuse, so use the cosine ratio.

Write a cosine ratio for $\angle A$. $\cos A = \boxed{}$

Write an inverse cosine ratio. $m\angle A = \cos^{-1}\left(\boxed{}\right)$

Evaluate the inverse cosine ratio and round. $m\angle A \approx \boxed{}^{\circ}$

$\angle \boxed{}$ and $\angle B$ are complementary. $m\angle\boxed{} + m\angle B = 90^{\circ}$

Substitute $\boxed{}^{\circ}$ for $m\angle\boxed{}$. $\boxed{}^{\circ} + m\angle B \approx 90^{\circ}$

Subtract $\boxed{}^{\circ}$ from both sides. $m\angle B \approx \boxed{}^{\circ}$

Reflect

5. Is it possible to find $m\angle B$ before you find $m\angle A$? Explain.

A building casts a 33-m shadow when the Sun is at an angle of 27° to the vertical. How tall is the building, to the nearest meter? How far is it from the top of the building to the tip of the shadow? What angle does a ray from the Sun along the edge of the shadow make with the ground?

6. Use a trigonometric ratio to find the distance *EF*.

7. Use another trigonometric ratio to find the distance *DF*.

8. Use the fact that acute angles of a right triangle are complementary to find m∠*D*.

⚙ Explain 3   Solving a Right Triangle in the Coordinate Plane

You can use the distance formula as well as trigonometric tools to solve right triangles in the coordinate plane.

Example 3   Solve each triangle.

Ⓐ Triangle *ABC* has vertices *A*(−3, 3), *B*(−3, −1), and *C*(4, −1). Find the side lengths to the nearest hundredth and the angle measures to the nearest degree.

Plot points *A*, *B*, and *C*, and draw △*ABC*.

Find the side lengths: *AB* = 4, *BC* = 7

Use the distance formula to find the length of $\overline{AC}$.

$$AC = \sqrt{\left(4 - (-3)\right)^2 + (-1 - 3)^2} = \sqrt{65} \approx 8.06$$

Find the angle measures: $\overline{AB} \perp \overline{BC}$, so m∠*B* = 90°.

Use an inverse tangent ratio to find

$$m\angle C = \tan^{-1}\!\left(\frac{AB}{BC}\right) = \tan^{-1}\!\left(\frac{4}{7}\right) \approx 30°.$$

∠*A* and ∠*C* are complementary, so m∠*A* ≈ 90° − 30° = 60°.

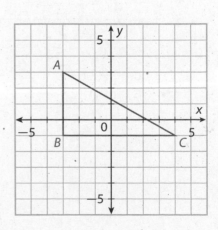

Ⓑ Triangle *DEF* has vertices $D(-4, 3)$, $E(3, 4)$, and $F(0, 0)$. Find the side lengths to the nearest hundredth and the angle measures to the nearest degree.

Plot points *D*, *E*, and *F*, and draw △*DEF*.

∠*F* appears to be a right angle. To check, find the slope

of $\overline{DF}$: $\dfrac{\boxed{} - 3}{0 - \boxed{}} = \dfrac{\boxed{}}{\boxed{}} = \boxed{}$;

slope of $\overline{\boxed{}}$: $\dfrac{\boxed{} - \boxed{}}{\boxed{} - 3} = \dfrac{\boxed{}}{\boxed{}} = \dfrac{\boxed{}}{\boxed{}}$;

so m∠*F* = $\boxed{}$°.

Find the side lengths using the distance formula:

$$DE = \sqrt{\left(3 - \boxed{}\right)^2 + \left(\boxed{} - 3\right)^2} = \sqrt{\boxed{}} = \boxed{}\sqrt{\boxed{}} \approx \boxed{},$$

$$DF = \sqrt{\left(\boxed{} - \boxed{}\right)^2 + \left(\boxed{} - 3\right)^2} = \sqrt{\boxed{}} = \boxed{},$$

$$\boxed{} = \sqrt{\left(\boxed{} - \boxed{}\right)^2 + \left(\boxed{} - 4\right)^2} = \sqrt{\boxed{}} = \boxed{}$$

Use an inverse sine ratio to find m∠*D*.

$$m\angle D = \sin^{-1}\left(\dfrac{EF}{\boxed{}}\right) = \sin^{-1}\left(\dfrac{\boxed{}}{\boxed{}}\right) = \boxed{}^\circ$$

∠*D* and ∠$\boxed{}$ are complementary, so m∠$\boxed{}$ = 90° − $\boxed{}$° = $\boxed{}$°.

Reflect

9. How does the given information determine which inverse trigonometric ratio you should use to determine an acute angle measure?

_____

_____

_____

10. Triangle *JKL* has vertices *J*(3, 5), *K*(−3, 2), and *L*(5, 1). Find the side lengths to the nearest hundredth and the angle measures to the nearest degree.

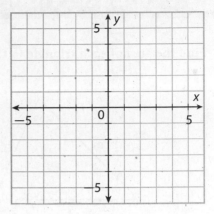

💬 Elaborate

11. Would you use the area formula you determined in this lesson for a right triangle? Explain.

_____

_____

12. Discussion How does the process of solving a right triangle change when its vertices are located in the coordinate plane?

_____

_____

_____

13. Essential Question Check-In How do you find the unknown angle measures in a right triangle?

_____

_____

_____

• Online Homework
• Hints and Help
• Extra Practice

Find the area of each triangle to the nearest tenth.

1.

62°

4.1 cm   3.2 cm

2. In △PQR, PR = 23 mm, QR = 39 mm, and m∠R = 163°.

Solve each right triangle. Round lengths to the nearest tenth and angles to the nearest degree.

3.

A

3.1 cm

C   2.7 cm   B

4.

F

D 56° E

26 m

5. Right △PQR with $\overline{PQ} \perp \overline{PR}$, QR = 47 mm, and m∠Q = 52°

Solve each triangle. Find the side lengths to the nearest hundredth and the angle measures to the nearest degree.

6. Triangle *ABC* with vertices *A*(−4, 4), *B*(3, 4), and *C*(3, −2)

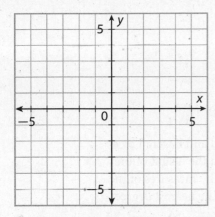

7. Triangle *JKL* with vertices *J*(−3, 1), *K*(−1, 4), and *L*(6, −5)

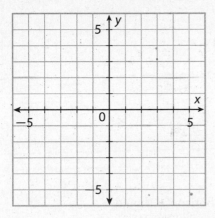

8. Triangle *PQR* with vertices *P*(5, 5), *Q*(−5, 3), and *R*(−4, −2)

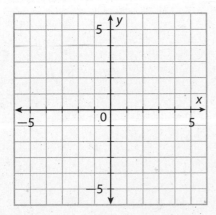

9. **Surveying** A plot of land is in the shape of a triangle, as shown. Find the area of the plot, to the nearest hundred square yards.

10. **History** A drawbridge at the entrance to an ancient castle is raised and lowered by a pair of chains. The figure represents the drawbridge when flat. Find the height of the suspension point of the chain, to the nearest tenth of a meter, and the measures of the acute angles the chain makes with the wall and the drawbridge, to the nearest degree.

11. **Building** For safety, the angle a wheelchair ramp makes with the horizontal should be no more than 3.5°. What is the maximum height of a ramp of length 30 ft? What distance along the ground would this ramp cover? Round to the nearest tenth of a foot.

12. Multi-Step The figure shows an origami crane as well as a stage of its construction. The area of each wing is shown by the shaded part of the figure, which is symmetric about its vertical center line. Use the information in the figure to find the total wing area of the crane, to the nearest tenth of a square inch.

13. Right triangle $\triangle XYZ$ has vertices $X(1, 4)$ and $Y(2, -3)$. The vertex Z has positive integer coordinates, and $XZ = 5$. Find the coordinates of Z and solve $\triangle XYZ$; give exact answers.

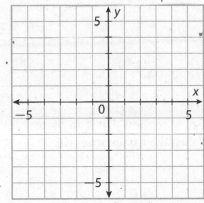

14. Critique Reasoning Shania and Pedro are discussing whether it is always possible to solve a right triangle, given enough information, without using the Pythagorean Theorem. Pedro says that it is always possible, but Shania thinks that when two side lengths and no angle measures are given, the Pythagorean Theorem is needed. Who is correct, and why?

15. Design The logo shown is symmetrical about one of its diagonals. Find the angle measures in △CAE, to the nearest degree. (*Hint:* First find an angle in △ABC, △CDE or △AEF) Then, find the area of △CAE, without first finding the areas of the other triangles.

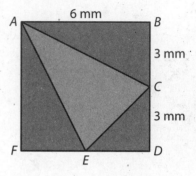

16. Use the area formula for obtuse ∠B in the diagram to show that if an acute angle and an obtuse angle are supplementary, then their sines are equal.

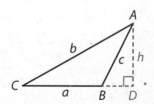

17. **Communicate Mathematical Ideas** The HL Congruence
Theorem states that for right triangles *ABC* and *DEF* such that
∠*A* and ∠*D* are right angles, $\overline{BC} \cong \overline{EF}$, and $\overline{AB} \cong \overline{DE}$,
△*ABC* ≅ △*DEF*.

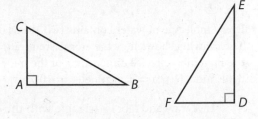

Explain, without formal proof, how solving a right triangle
with given leg lengths, or with a given side length and acute
angle measure, shows that right triangles with both legs
congruent, or with corresponding sides and angles congruent,
must be congruent.

18. **Persevere in Problem Solving** Find the perimeter and area of
△*ABC*, as exact numbers. Then, find the measures of all the angles
to the nearest degree.

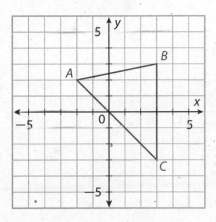

19. **Analyze Relationships** Find the area of the triangle using two different
formulas, and deduce an expression for sin2θ.

Lesson Performance Task

Every molecule of water contains two atoms of hydrogen and one atom of oxygen. The drawing shows how the atoms are arranged in a molecule of water, along with the incredibly precise dimensions of the molecule that physicists have been able to determine. (1 pm = 1 picometer = 10^{-12}m)

1. Draw and label a triangle with the dimensions shown.

2. Find the area of the triangle in square centimeters. Show your work.

3. Find the distance between the hydrogen atoms in centimeters. Explain your method.

Trigonometry with Right Triangles

Essential Question: How can you use trigonometry with right triangles to solve real-world problems?

KEY EXAMPLE (Lesson 13.1)

Find the tangent of angle A.

$\tan A = \dfrac{\text{length of leg opposite } \angle A}{\text{length of leg adjacent to } \angle A}$ Definition of tangent

$\tan A = \dfrac{60}{11} \approx 5.45$ Substitute and simplify

KEY EXAMPLE (Lesson 13.2)

Find the sine and cosine of angle A.

$\sin A = \dfrac{\text{length of leg opposite } \angle A}{\text{length of hypotenuse}}$ Definition of sine

$\sin A = \dfrac{60}{61} \approx .98$ Simplify.

$\cos A = \dfrac{\text{length of leg adjacent to } \angle A}{\text{length of hypotenuse}}$ Definition of cosine

$\cos A = \dfrac{11}{61} \approx .18$ Simplify.

KEY EXAMPLE (Lesson 13.3)

Given an isosceles right triangle *DEF* with m$\angle F$ = 90° and *DE* = 7, find the length of the other two sides.

$DE = DF\sqrt{2}$ Apply the relationship of 45°-45°-90° triangles.

$7 = DF\sqrt{2}$ Substitute.

$\dfrac{7}{\sqrt{2}} = DF$ Simplify.

$DF = EF = \dfrac{7}{\sqrt{2}} = \dfrac{7\sqrt{2}}{2}$ Apply properties of isosceles triangles.

EXERCISES

Given a right triangle $\triangle XYZ$ where $\angle Z$ is a right angle, $XY = 53$, $YZ = 28$, and $XZ = 45$, find the following rounded to the nearest hundredth. *(Lessons 13.1, 13.2)*

1. $\sin X$ _____

2. $\cos X$ _____

3. $\tan X$ _____

Find the lengths of the other two sides of the following triangle. Find exact answers in order of least to greatest. *(Lesson 13.3)*

4. 30°-60°-90° triangle with a hypotenuse of length 14 _____

Find the area of the following triangle, rounded to the nearest tenth. *(Lesson 13.4)*

5. triangle $\triangle ABC$, where m$\angle C = 127°$, $AC = 5$, and $BC = 9$ _____

MODULE PERFORMANCE TASK

How Much Shorter Are Staggered Pipe Stacks?

How much space can be saved by stacking pipe in a staggered pattern? The illustration shows you the difference between layers of pipe stacked directly on top of each other (left) and in a staggered pattern (right). Suppose you have pipes that are 2 inches in diameter. How much shorter will a staggered stack of 10 layers be than a non-staggered stack with the same number of layers? In general, how much shorter are n layers of staggered pipe?

Start by listing in the space below how you plan to tackle the problem. Then use your own paper to complete the task. Be sure to write down all your data and assumptions. Then use numbers, graphs, diagrams, or algebraic equations to explain how you reached your conclusion.

13.1–13.4 Trigonometry with Right Triangles

- Online Homework
- Hints and Help
- Extra Practice

Solve the problem. *(Lesson 13.1)*

1. A painter is placing a ladder to reach the third story window, which is 20 feet above the ground and makes an angle with the ground of 70°. How far out from the building does the base of the ladder need to be positioned?

2. Given the value of $\cos 30° = \dfrac{\sqrt{3}}{2}$, write the sine of a complementary angle. Use an expression relating trigonometric ratios of complementary angles. *(Lesson 13.2)*

Find the area of the regular polygon. *(Lesson 13.3)*

3. What is the area of a regular hexagon with a distance from its center to a vertex of 1 cm? (Hint: A regular hexagon can be divided into six equilateral triangles.)

ESSENTIAL QUESTION

4. How would you go about finding the area of a regular pentagon given the distance from its center to the vertices?

Assessment Readiness

1. Julia is standing 2 feet away from a lamppost. She casts a shadow of 5 feet and the light makes a 20° angle relative to the ground from the top of her shadow. Consider each expression. Does the expression give you the height of the lamppost?

   Select Yes or No for A–C.

   A. 7 sin20° ○ Yes ○ No

   B. 7 tan20° ○ Yes ○ No

   C. 7 tan70° ○ Yes ○ No

2. A right triangle has two sides with lengths 10 and 10. Choose True or False for each statement.

   A. The triangle has two angles that measure 45° each. ○ True ○ False

   B. The triangle is equilateral. ○ True ○ False

   C. The length of the third side is $10\sqrt{2}$. ○ True ○ False

3. The measure of angle 1 is 125° and the measure of angle 2 is 55°. State two different relationships that can be used to prove $m\angle 3 = 125°$.

4. For the rhombus, specify how to find its area using the four congruent right triangles with variable angle θ.

Trigonometry with All Triangles

Essential Question: How can you use triangle trigonometry to solve real-world problems?

REAL WORLD VIDEO
Air traffic controllers must understand trigonometry and other mathematics to make rapid judgments about the positions of aircraft and the distances between them.

MODULE PERFORMANCE TASK PREVIEW

Controlling the Air

You've probably seen photos of air traffic controllers studying green-tinted screens covered with blinking blips. Their job is to analyze the positions of every plane in the airspace near the airport and see to it that the planes land safely. In this module, you'll learn to solve triangles of the type air traffic controllers encounter. Then you'll apply what you've learned to find the distance between two planes approaching an airport.

Are (YOU) Ready?

Complete these exercises to review skills you will need for this module.

• Online Homework
• Hints and Help
• Extra Practice

Similar Triangles

Example 1

In $\triangle PRK$, $PK = 34$, $RK = 50$, and m$\angle K = 74°$. Why is this triangle similar to $\triangle ABC$? What is the similarity statement?

$PK = 34 = 2AB$ (Side),

m$\angle K = 74° = $ m$\angle A$ (Angle), and $RK = 50 = 2AC$ (Side). So, $\triangle ABC \sim \triangle KPR$ by $SAS\triangle\sim$.

Complete each similarity statement and name the theorem that supports it.

1. Given: In $\triangle MNT$, $MN = 8.5$, $TM = 13$, and $TN = 12.5$.

    $\triangle ABC \sim$ _____ by _____

2. Given: In $\triangle ZQE$, m$\angle E = 67°$, $ZQ = 4$, and m$\angle Q = 39°$.

    $\triangle ABC \sim$ _____ by _____

Proportional Relationships

Example 2

Given: $\triangle PQR \sim \triangle NCL$, $PQ = 15$, $QR = 12$, $PR = 18$, and $CL = 15$.

What is NL?

$\dfrac{CL}{QR} = \dfrac{NL}{PR}$ Write a proportion.

$\dfrac{15}{12} = \dfrac{NL}{18}$ Substitute.

$NL = 22.5$ Solve.

Solve, given that $\triangle RST \sim \triangle FGH$, $RT = 9$, $ST = 6$, $FG = 7.5$, and $FH = 13.5$.

3. Find RS.

_____

4. Find GH.

_____

Multi-Step Equations

Example 3

Solve $4x + 15 = 1$ for x.

$4x + 15 - 15 = 1 - 15$ Subtract 15 from both sides.

      $4x = -14$ Combine like terms.

       $x = -3.5$ Divide.

Solve each equation.

5. $2r - 5 = -9$

6. $\dfrac{4m - 5}{3} = -7$

7. $9.9 - 4.2k = 3k - 0.9$

14.1 Law of Sines

Essential Question: How can you use trigonometric ratios to find side lengths and angle measures of non-right triangles?

⊘ Explore   Use an Area Formula to Derive the Law of Sines

Recall that the area of a triangle can be found using the sine of one of the angles.

$$\text{Area} = \frac{1}{2}b \cdot c \cdot \sin(A)$$

You can write variations of this formula using different angles and sides from the same triangle.

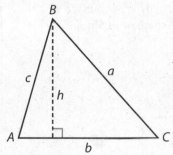

(A) Rewrite the area formula using side length a as the base of the triangle and $\angle C$.

(B) Rewrite the area formula using side length c as the base of the triangle and $\angle B$.

(C) What do all three formulas have in common?

_____

(D) Why is this statement true?

$$\frac{1}{2}b \cdot c \cdot \sin(A) = \frac{1}{2}a \cdot b \cdot \sin(C) = \frac{1}{2}c \cdot a \cdot \sin(B)$$

_____

(E) Multiply each area by the expression $\frac{2}{abc}$. Write an equivalent statement.

_____

1. In the case of a right triangle, where C is the right angle, what happens to the area formula?

_____

2. **Discussion** In all three cases of the area formula you explored, what is the relationship between the angle and the two side lengths in the area formula?

_____

🎯 Explain 1 Applying the Law of Sines

The results of the Explore activity are summarized in the Law of Sines.

Law of Sines

Given: $\triangle ABC$

$$\frac{\sin(A)}{a} = \frac{\sin(B)}{b} = \frac{\sin(C)}{c}$$

The Law of Sines allows you to find the unknown measures for a given triangle, as long as you know either of the following:

1. Two angle measures and any side length—angle-angle-side (AAS) or angle-side-angle (ASA) information

2. Two side lengths and the measure of an angle that is not between them—side-side-angle (SSA) information

Example 1   **Find all the unknown measures using the given triangle. Round to the nearest tenth.**

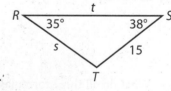

(A) **Step 1** Find the third angle measure.

$m\angle R + m\angle S + m\angle T = 180°$ Triangle Sum Theorem

$35° + 38° + m\angle T = 180°$ Substitute the known angle measures.

$m\angle T = 107°$ Solve for the measure of $\angle T$.

Step 2 Find the unknown side lengths. Set up proportions using the Law of Sines and solve for the unknown.

$$\frac{\sin(T)}{t} = \frac{\sin(R)}{r}$$ Law of Sines $$\frac{\sin(S)}{s} = \frac{\sin(R)}{r}$$

$$\frac{\sin(107°)}{t} = \frac{\sin(35°)}{15}$$ Substitute. $$\frac{\sin(38°)}{s} = \frac{\sin(35°)}{15}$$

$$t = \frac{15 \cdot \sin(107°)}{\sin(35°)}$$ Solve for the unknown. $$s = \frac{15 \cdot (\sin38°)}{\sin(35°)}$$

$$t \approx 25$$ Evaluate. $$s \approx 16.1$$

Ⓑ **Step 1** Find the third angle measure.

$$m\angle R + m\angle S + m\angle T = 180°$$ Triangle Sum Theorem

$$\boxed{}° + \boxed{}° + m\angle T = 180°$$ Substitute the known angle measures.

$$m\angle T = \boxed{}°$$ Solve for the measure of $\angle T$.

Step 2 Find the unknown side lengths. Set up proportions using the Law of Sines and solve for the unknown.

$$\frac{\sin(T)}{t} = \frac{\sin(R)}{r}$$ Law of Sines

$$\frac{\sin\left(\boxed{}°\right)}{t} = \frac{\sin\left(\boxed{}°\right)}{\boxed{}}$$ Substitute.

$$t = \frac{\boxed{} \cdot \sin\left(\boxed{}°\right)}{\sin\left(\boxed{}°\right)}$$ Solve for the unknown.

$$t \approx \boxed{}$$ Evaluate.

$$\frac{\sin(S)}{s} = \frac{\sin(R)}{r}$$

$$\frac{\sin\left(\boxed{}°\right)}{s} = \frac{\sin\left(\boxed{}°\right)}{\boxed{}}$$

$$s = \frac{\boxed{} \cdot \sin\left(\boxed{}°\right)}{\sin\left(\boxed{}°\right)}$$

$$s \approx \boxed{}$$

Reflect

3. Suppose that you are given $m\angle A$. To find c, what other measures do you need to know?

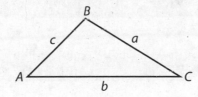

_____

Find all the unknown measures using the given triangle. Round to the nearest tenth.

4.

5.

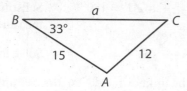

⚙ Explain 2   Evaluating Triangles When SSA is Known Information

When you use the Law of Sines to solve a triangle for which you know side-side-angle (SSA) information, zero, one, or two triangles may be possible. For this reason, SSA is called the ambiguous case.

Example 2 **Design** Each triangular wing of a model airplane has one side that joins the wing to the airplane. The other sides have lengths $b = 18$ in. and $a = 15$ in. The side with length b meets the airplane at an angle A with a measure of $30°$, and meets the side with length a at point C. Find each measure.

(A) Find $m\angle B$.

Step 1 Determine the number of possible triangles. Find h.

$\sin(30°) = \dfrac{h}{18}$, so $h = 18 \cdot \sin(30°) = 9$

Because $h < a < b$, two triangles are possible.

Step 2 Determine $m\angle B_1$ and $m\angle B_2$.

$\dfrac{\sin(A)}{a} = \dfrac{\sin(B)}{b}$ Law of Sines

$\dfrac{\sin(30°)}{15} = \dfrac{\sin(B)}{18}$ Substitute.

$\sin(B) = \dfrac{18 \cdot \sin(30°)}{15}$ Solve for $\sin(B)$.

Let $\angle B_1$ be the acute angle with the given sine, and let $\angle B_2$ be the obtuse angle. Use the inverse sine function on your calculator to determine the measures of the angles.

$m\angle B_1 = \sin^{-1}\left(\dfrac{18 \cdot \sin(30°)}{15}\right) \approx 36.9°$ and $m\angle B_2 = 180° - 36.9° = 143.1°$

(B) Determine $m\angle C$ and length c.

Solve for $m\angle C_1$.

$\boxed{}° + 30° + m\angle C_1 = 180°$

$m\angle C_1 = \boxed{}°$

Solve for $m\angle C_2$.

$\boxed{}° + 30° + m\angle C_2 = 180°$

$m\angle C_2 = \boxed{}°$

$\dfrac{\sin(A)}{a} = \dfrac{\sin(C_1)}{c_1}$ Law of Sines $\dfrac{\sin(A)}{a} = \dfrac{\sin(C_2)}{c_2}$

$\dfrac{\sin\left(\boxed{}°\right)}{\boxed{}} = \dfrac{\sin\left(\boxed{}°\right)}{c_1}$ Substitute. $\dfrac{\sin\left(\boxed{}°\right)}{\boxed{}} = \dfrac{\sin\left(\boxed{}°\right)}{c_2}$

$c_1 = \dfrac{\boxed{} \cdot \sin\left(\boxed{}°\right)}{\sin\left(\boxed{}°\right)}$ Solve for the unknown. $c_2 = \dfrac{\boxed{} \cdot \sin\left(\boxed{}°\right)}{\sin\left(\boxed{}°\right)}$

$c_1 \approx \boxed{}$ in.   Evaluate. $c_2 \approx \boxed{}$ in.

In Exercises 6 and 7, suppose that for the model airplane in the Example, $a = 21$ in., $b = 18$ in., and m$\angle A = 25°$.

18 in.

C

25°

A

6. How many triangles are possible with this configuration? Explain.

_____

7. Find the unknown measurements. Round to the nearest tenth.

💬 Elaborate

8. If the base angles of a triangle are congruent, use the Law of Sines to show the triangle is isosceles.

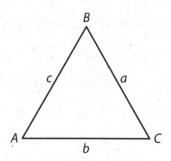

9. Show that when $h = a$, $\angle C$ is a right angle.

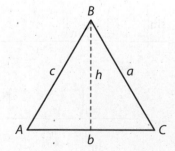

10. Essential Question Check-In Given the measures of △*ABC*, describe a method for finding any of the altitudes of the triangle.

- Online Homework
- Hints and Help
- Extra Practice

Find the area of each triangle. Round to the nearest tenth.

1.

2.

3.

4.

5.

6.

7. What is the area of an isosceles triangle with congruent side lengths *x* and included angle *θ*?

8. What is the area of an equilateral triangle of side length *x*?

Find all the unknown measurements using the Law of Sines.

9.

10.

11.

12.

13.

14.

Design A model airplane designer wants to design wings of the given dimensions. Determine the number of different triangles that can be formed. Then find all the unknown measurements. Round values to the nearest tenth.

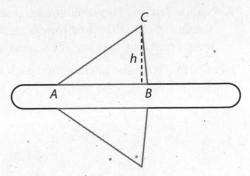

15. $a = 7$ m, $b = 9$ m, $m\angle A = 55°$

16. $a = 12$ m, $b = 4$ m, $m\angle A = 120°$

17. $a = 9$ m, $b = 10$ m, $m\angle A = 35°$

18. $a = 7$ m, $b = 5$ m, $m\angle A = 45°$

19. Space Travel Two radio towers that are 50 miles apart track a satellite in orbit. The first tower's signal makes a 76° angle between the ground and satellite. The second tower forms an 80.5° angle.

a. How far is the satellite from each tower?

b. How could you determine how far above Earth the satellite is? What is the satellite's altitude?

20. Biology The dorsal fin of a shark forms an obtuse triangle with these measurements. Find the missing measurements and determine if another triangle can be formed.

21. Navigation As a ship approaches the dock, it forms a 70° angle between the dock and lighthouse. At the lighthouse, an 80° angle is formed between the dock and the ship. How far is the ship from the dock?

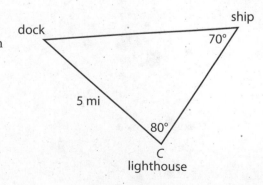

22. For the given triangle, match each altitude with its equivalent expression.

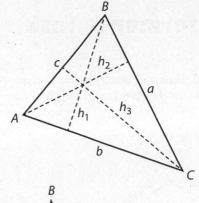

A. h_1 _____ $a \cdot \sin(B)$

B. h_2 _____ $c \cdot \sin(A)$

C. h_3 _____ $b \cdot \sin(C)$

H.O.T. **Focus on Higher Order Thinking**

Use the diagram, in which $\triangle ABC \sim \triangle DEF$.

23. To find the missing measurements for either triangle using the Law of Sines, what must you do first?

24. Find the missing measurements for $\triangle ABC$.

25. Find the missing measurements for $\triangle DEF$.

26. **Surveying** Two surveyors are at the same altitude and are 10 miles apart on opposite sides of a mountain. They each measure the angle relative to the ground and the top of the mountain. Use the given diagram to indirectly measure the height of the mountain.

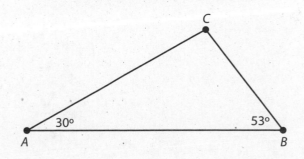

Lesson Performance Task

In the middle of town, State and Elm streets meet at an angle of 40°. A triangular pocket park between the streets stretches 100 yards along State Street and 53.2 yards along Elm Street.

a. Find the area of the pocket park using the given dimensions.

b. If the total distance around the pocket park is 221.6 yards, find ∠S, the angle that West Avenue makes with State Street, to the nearest degree.

c. Suppose West Avenue makes angles of 55° with State Street and 80° with Elm Street. The distance from State to Elm along West Avenue is 40 yards. Find the distance from West Avenue to Elm Street along State Street.

14.2 Law of Cosines

Essential Question: How can you use the Law of Cosines to find measures of any triangle?

⊘ Explore Deriving the Law of Cosines

You learned to solve triangle problems by using the Law of Sines. However, the Law of Sines cannot be used to solve triangles for which side-angle-side (SAS) or side-side-side (SSS) information is given. Instead, you must use the Law of Cosines.

To derive the Law of Cosines, draw $\triangle ABC$ with altitude $\overline{BD}$. If x represents the length of $\overline{AD}$, the length of $\overline{DC}$ is $b - x$.

Ⓐ Use the Pythagorean Theorem to write a relationship for the side lengths of $\triangle BCD$ and for the side lengths of $\triangle ABD$.

Ⓑ Notice that c^2 is equal to a sum of terms in the equation for a^2. Substitute c^2 for those terms.

Ⓒ In $\triangle ABD$, $\cos A = \frac{x}{c}$. Solve for x. Then substitute into the equation you wrote for a^2.

$\cos A = \frac{x}{c}$, or $x = $ _____.

$a^2 = b^2 - $ _____ $+ c^2$

Reflect

1. The equation you wrote in Step D is the Law of Cosines, which is usually written as $a^2 = b^2 + c^2 - 2bc\cos A$. Write formulas using $\cos B$ or $\cos C$ to describe the same relationships in this triangle.

🔑 Explain 1   Using the Law of Cosines

To find the missing side length of a right triangle, you can use the Pythagorean Theorem. To find a missing side length of a general triangle, you can use the Law of Cosines.

> ### Law of Cosines
>
> For $\triangle ABC$, the Law of Cosines states that
>
> $a^2 = b^2 + c^2 - 2bc\cos A$
>
> $b^2 = a^2 + c^2 - 2ac\cos B$
>
> $c^2 = a^2 + b^2 - 2ab\cos C$

Example 1   Solve $\triangle ABC$. Round to the nearest tenth.

(A)   **Step 1** Find the length of the third side.

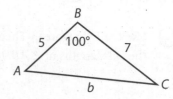

$b^2 = a^2 + c^2 - 2ac\cos B$	Law of Cosines
$b^2 = 7^2 + 5^2 - 2(7)(5)\cos 100°$	Substitute.
$b^2 \approx 86.2$	Evaluate.
$b \approx 9.3$	Solve for a positive value of b.

Step 2 Find an angle measure.

$\dfrac{\sin A}{a} = \dfrac{\sin B}{b}$	Law of Sines
$\dfrac{\sin A}{7} = \dfrac{\sin 100°}{9.3}$	Substitute.
$\sin A = \dfrac{7\sin 100°}{9.3}$	Solve for $\sin A$.
$m\angle A = \sin^{-1}\left(\dfrac{7\sin 100°}{9.3}\right) \approx 47.8°$	Solve for $m\angle A$.

Step 3 Find the third angle measure.

$$47.8° + 100° + m\angle C = 180°$$
$$m\angle C = 32.2°$$

(B)   **Step 1** Find the measure of the largest angle, $\angle C$.

	Law of Cosines
$^2 =$ $^2 +$ ____$^2 - 2$____cos$C$	Substitute.
$\cos C \approx$ _____	Solve for $\cos C$.
$m\angle C \approx \cos^{-1}($ _____$) \approx$ _____	Solve for $m\angle C$.

Step 2 Find another angle measure.

$b^2 = a^2 + c^2 - 2ac \cos B$ _____

$\underline{\quad}^2 = \underline{\quad}^2 + \underline{\quad}^2 - 2(\underline{\quad})(\underline{\quad})\cos B$ Substitute.

$\cos B \approx$ _____   Solve for _____.

$m\angle B \approx \cos^{-1}(\underline{\qquad}) \approx \underline{\quad}$ Solve for _____.

Step 3 Find the third angle measure.

$m\angle A + \underline{\quad} + \underline{\quad} = 180°$ _____

$\qquad\qquad m\angle A = \underline{\quad}$ Solve for $m\angle A$.

Reflect

2. Suppose a student used the Law of Sines to solve this triangle. Determine whether the measurements are correct. Explain.

Your Turn

Solve $\triangle ABC$. Round to the nearest tenth.

3. $b = 23, c = 18, m\angle A = 173°$

4. $a = 35, b = 42, c = 50.3$

⚙ Explain 2 Problem Solving Using the Law of Cosines

You now know many triangle relationships that you can use to solve real-world problems.

Example 2

A coast guard patrol boat and a fishing boat leave a dock at the same time at the courses shown. The patrol boat travels at a speed of 12 nautical miles per hour (12 knots), and the fishing boat travels at a speed of 5 knots. After 3 hours, the fishing boat sends a distress signal picked up by the patrol boat. If the fishing boat does not drift, how long will it take the patrol boat to reach it at a speed of 12 knots?

Step 1 Understand the Problem

The answer will be the number of hours that the patrol boat needs to reach the fishing boat.

List the important information:

- The patrol boat's speed is 12 knots. Its direction is 15° east of north.
- The fishing boat's speed is 5 knots. Its direction is 130° east of north.
- The boats travel for 3 hours before the distress call is given.

Step 2 Make a Plan

Determine the angle between the boats' courses and the distance that each boat travels in 3 hours. Use this information to draw and label a diagram.

Then use the Law of Cosines to find the distance d between the boats at the time of the distress call. Finally, determine how long it will take the patrol boat to travel this distance.

Step 3 Draw and Label a Diagram

- The angle between the boats' courses is $130° - 15° = 115°$. In 3 hours, the patrol boat travels $3(12) = 36$ nautical miles and the fishing boat travels $3(5) = 15$ nautical miles.
- Find the distance d between the boats.

$d^2 = p^2 + f^2 - 2pf\cos D$	Law of Cosines
$d^2 = 15^2 + 36^2 - 2(15)(36)\cos 115°$	Substitute.
$d^2 \approx 1,977.4$	Evaluate.
$d \approx 44.5$	Solve for the positive value of d.

- Determine the number of hours.
  The patrol boat must travel about 44.5 nautical miles to reach the fishing boat. At a speed of 12 nautical miles per hour, it will take the patrol boat $\frac{44.5}{12} \approx 3.7$ hours to reach the fishing boat.

Step 4 Look Back

To reach the fishing boat, the patrol boat will have to travel a greater distance than it did during the first 3 hours of its trip. Therefore, it makes sense that it will take the patrol boat longer than 3 hours to reach the fishing boat. An answer of 3.7 hours seems reasonable.

5. If Lucas hikes at an average of 2.5 miles per hour, how long will it take him to travel from the cave to the waterfall? Round to the nearest tenth of an hour.

6. A pilot is flying from Houston to Oklahoma City. To avoid a thunderstorm, the pilot flies 28° off of the direct route for a distance of 175 miles. He then makes a turn and flies straight on to Oklahoma City. To the nearest mile, how much farther than the direct route was the route taken by the pilot?

Elaborate

7. Explain why you cannot solve a triangle if you are given only angle-angle-angle information.

_____

_____

8. When using the Law of Cosines, $a^2 = b^2 + c^2 - 2bc\cos A$, you can take the square root of both sides to find the value of a. Explain why the negative square root is not used when considering the answer.

_____

9. **Essential Question Check-In** Copy and complete the graphic organizer. List the types of triangles that can be solved by using each law. Consider the following types of triangles: ASA, AAS, SAS, SSA, and SSS.

Draw and label the diagram you would use to derive the given form of the Law of Cosines.

1. $b^2 = a^2 + c^2 - 2ac\cos B$

2. $c^2 = a^2 + b^2 - 2ab\cos C$

3. What information do you need to be able to use the Law of Cosines to solve a triangle?

Solve each triangle. Round to the nearest tenth.

4.

5.

6.

7.

8.

9.

Solve △ABC. Round to the nearest tenth.

10. m∠A = 120°, b = 16, c = 20

11. m∠B = 78°, a = 6; c = 4

12. m∠C = 96°, a = 13, b = 9

13. a = 14, b = 9, c = 10

14. a = 5, b = 8, c = 6

15. a = 30, b = 26, c = 35

16. A triangular hiking trail is being planned. At an average walking speed of 2 m/s, how many minutes will it take a hiker to make a complete circuit around the trail? Round to the nearest minute.

410 m

100°

200 m

17. An ecologist is studying a pair of zebras fitted with radio-transmitter collars. One zebra is 1.4 miles from the ecologist, and the other is 3.5 miles from the ecologist. To the nearest tenth of a mile, how far apart are the two zebras?

1.4 mi   93°   3.5 mi

18. Critical Thinking Find the length of $\overline{AE}$.

19. Which is the approximate measure of $\angle K$ in the triangle shown?

A. $-30°$ D. $45°$

B. $-45°$ E. $54°$

C. $30°$ F. $60°$

20. Critical Thinking Use the Law of Cosines to explain why $c^2 = a^2 + b^2$ for $\triangle ABC$, where $\angle C$ is a right angle.

21. A graphic artist is asked to draw a triangular logo with sides measuring 15 cm, 18 cm, and 20 cm. If she draws the triangle correctly, what will be the measures of its angles to the nearest degree?

22. Represent Real-World Problem Two performers hang by their knees from trapezes, as shown.

a. To the nearest degree, what acute angles *A* and *B* must the ropes of each trapeze make with the horizontal if the performer on the left is to grab the wrists of the performer on the right and pull her away from her trapeze?

b. Later, the performer on the left grabs the trapeze of the performer on the right and lets go of his trapeze. To the nearest degree, what angles *A* and *B* must the ropes of each trapeze make with the horizontal for this trick to work?

23. Barrington Crater in Arizona was produced by the impact of a meteorite. Based on the measurements shown, what is the diameter *d* of Barrington Crater to the nearest tenth of a kilometer?

24. Analyze Relationships What are the angle measures of an isosceles triangle whose base is half as long as its congruent legs? Round to the nearest tenth.

25. Explain the Error Abby uses the Law of Cosines to find m∠A when $a = 2$, $b = 3$, $c = 5$. The answer she gets is 0°. Did she make an error? Explain.

Lesson Performance Task

Standing on a small bluff overlooking a local pond, Clay wants to calculate the width of the pond.

a. From point C, Clay walks the distances CA and CB. Then he measures the angle between these line segments. What is the distance to the nearest meter from A to B?

b. From another point F, Clay measures 20 meters to D and 50 meters to E. Reece says that last summer this area dried out so much that he could walk the 49 meters from D to E. What is the measure of $\angle F$?

c. Reece tells Clay that when the area defined by $\triangle DEF$ dries out, it becomes covered with native grasses and plants. What is the area of this section?

Trigonometry with All Triangles

Essential Question: How can you use triangle trigonometry to solve real-world problems?

Key Vocabulary

cosine *(coseno)*

sine *(seno)*

trigonometric ratio
(razón trigonométrica)

KEY EXAMPLE   (Lesson 14.1)

Find the area of the triangle. Round to the nearest tenth.

$$\text{area} = \frac{1}{2}\,ac\,\sin B \qquad \textit{Write the area formula.}$$

$$= \frac{1}{2}\,(5)(12)\,\sin 128° \qquad \textit{Substitute the known values.}$$

$$\approx 23.6 \qquad \textit{Use a calculator to evaluate the expression.}$$

The area of the triangle is about 23.6 cm².

KEY EXAMPLE   (Lesson 14.1)

Solve the triangle. Round to the nearest tenth.

$$m\angle F = 180° - (102° + 44°) = 34° \qquad \textit{Triangle Sum Theorem}$$

$$\frac{\sin D}{d} = \frac{\sin F}{f} \qquad \textit{Law of Sines}$$

$$\frac{\sin 102°}{d} = \frac{\sin 34°}{21} \qquad \textit{Substitute.}$$

$$d = \frac{21\sin 102°}{\sin 34°} \approx 36.7 \qquad \textit{Solve for d and e.}$$

$$\frac{\sin E}{e} = \frac{\sin F}{f}$$

$$\frac{\sin 44°}{e} = \frac{\sin 34°}{21}$$

$$e = \frac{21\sin 44°}{\sin 34°} \approx 26.1$$

KEY EXAMPLE   (Lesson 14.2)

Find *a*. Round to the nearest tenth.

$$a^2 = b^2 + c^2 - 2bc\cos A \qquad \textit{Law of Cosines}$$

$$a^2 = 20^2 + 15^2 - 2(20)(15)\cos 32° \qquad \textit{Substitute.}$$

$$a^2 \approx 116.2 \qquad \textit{Use a calculator to simplify.}$$

$$a \approx 10.8 \qquad \textit{Solve for the positive value of a.}$$

EXERCISES

Find the area of each triangle. Round to the nearest tenth. *(Lesson 14.1)*

1.

Solve each triangle. Round to the nearest tenth. *(Lesson 14.1)*

2.

3.

Solve each triangle. Round to the nearest tenth. *(Lesson 14.2)*

4.

5.

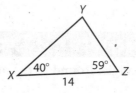

MODULE PERFORMANCE TASK

Controlling the Air

It's a busy day in the airspace above Metropolitan Airport and the traffic controllers in the tower below have their hands full. Right now there's a passenger jet that's located at a bearing of 45° east of north and 22 miles from the airport. A private plane is located 34° east of north and 14 miles from the airport. The planes are at the same altitude. How far apart are they?

Start by listing in the space below the information you will need to solve the problem. Then use your own paper to work on the task. Then use numbers, words, or algebra to explain how you reached your conclusion.

to Go On?

14.1–14.2 Trigonometry with All Triangles

Solve. Round answers to the nearest tenth. *(Lesson 14.1)*

1. The sides of a triangle measure 31 inches, 23 inches, and 17 inches. What is the area of the triangle?

2. The sides of a triangle measure 11 centimeters, 13 centimeters, and 15 centimeters. What are the measures of the angles of the triangles?

3. A triangle has two sides measuring 10 inches and 16 inches. The angle opposite the 16-inch side measures 70.3°. Solve the triangle.

4. One of the base angles of an isosceles triangle measures 72°. The base of the triangle measures 11 centimeters. What is the perimeter of the triangle?

5. Tony is standing at sea level. From his location, the angle of elevation of the top of Blue Mountain is 23°. Staying at sea level, he walks 200 yards toward the mountain. The angle of elevation of the top is now 27°. Find the height of Blue Mountain.

ESSENTIAL QUESTION

6. How can you use trigonometric ratios to find a side length in a non-right triangle?

Assessment Readiness

1. You know the two legs of a right triangle. You also know the measure of one of the acute angles of the triangle. Could you use the given law or theorem to find the length of the hypotenuse? Select Yes or No for A–C.

   A. Law of Sines   ◯ Yes   ◯ No

   B. Law of Cosines   ◯ Yes   ◯ No

   C. Pythagorean Theorem   ◯ Yes   ◯ No

2. Consider each statement about finding the measurements of triangles. Choose True or False for each statement.

   A. If you know the measures of the three angles of a triangle, you can find the lengths of the sides.   ◯ True   ◯ False

   B. If you know the lengths of the three sides of a triangle, you can find the measures of the angles.   ◯ True   ◯ False

   C. If you know the measures of the two sides of a triangle and the measure of an angle not included between the two sides, you can solve the triangle.   ◯ True   ◯ False

3. In the figure, O is the center of the circle and G and H are points on the circle. What is the circumference of the circle? Round your answer to the nearest tenth. Explain how you found the answer.

4. In solving triangle ABC, Dawn found that the cosine of $\angle B$ and the sine of $\angle A$ were both negative. What conclusions can she draw about her solution? Why?

Assessment Readiness

1. Given $\triangle JKL$ where $\angle K$ is a right angle, determine which measurements will produce $m\angle J$ to be greater than 45°.

   Select Yes or No for each pair of sides.

   A. $KL = 27, JK = 23$ ⚪ Yes   ⚪ No

   B. $KL = 15, JK = 32$ ⚪ Yes   ⚪ No

   C. $KL = 10, JK = 10$ ⚪ Yes   ⚪ No

2. Using the image provided, which of the following equations could be used to find x?

   Select Yes or No for each equation.

   A. $\sin 40 = \dfrac{x}{13}$ ⚪ Yes   ⚪ No

   B. $\tan 40 = \dfrac{x}{7}$ ⚪ Yes   ⚪ No

   C. $\cos 40 = \dfrac{13}{x}$ ⚪ Yes   ⚪ No

3. Which of the following statements are true?

   Select True or False for each statement.

   A. When given an angle and the opposite leg, you should use cosine to find the measure of the adjacent leg.   ⚪ True   ⚪ False

   B. The values of sine and cosine are always between 0 and 1.   ⚪ True   ⚪ False

   C. Use the inverse sine ratio when you know the length of the leg opposite the required angle and the length of the hypotenuse.   ⚪ True   ⚪ False

4. The following points are graphed on the coordinate plane: $A(-3, 5)$, $B(4, 1)$, and $C(-1, 1)$. Does the given point make $ABCD$ a trapezoid?

   Select Yes or No for ordered pairs A–C.

   A. $D(-2, 3)$ ⚪ Yes   ⚪ No

   B. $D(3, 3)$ ⚪ Yes   ⚪ No

   C. $D(-3, 6)$ ⚪ Yes   ⚪ No

5. Which of the relationships are true?

Select True or False for each statement.

A. $\sin 90° = \cos 90° = \dfrac{1}{2}$ ○ True   ○ False

B. $\sin 45° = \cos 45° = \dfrac{\sqrt{2}}{2}$ ○ True   ○ False

C. $\sin 60° = \cos 30° = \dfrac{\sqrt{3}}{2}$ ○ True   ○ False

D. $\tan \theta < 1$ for $\theta \leq 45°$ ○ True   ○ False

6. Is the triangle a Pythagorean triple?

Select Yes or No for each set of numbers.

A. $3 - 4 - 5$ ○ Yes   ○ No

B. $11 - 12 - 13$ ○ Yes   ○ No

C. $9 - 24 - 25$ ○ Yes   ○ No

7. Is $\triangle DEF$ a right triangle?

Select True or False for each statement.

A. $D(0, 2), E(-2, 5), F(5, 5)$ ○ True   ○ False

B. $D(-1, 0), E(-1, -7), F(0, 3)$ ○ True   ○ False

C. $D(-8, 8), E(-10, -2), F(0, -4)$ ○ True   ○ False

8. The plans for a new house include a wall with two triangular windows, $\triangle ABC$ and $\triangle A'B'C'$. The vertices of $\triangle ABC$ are $A(-4, 1)$, $B(-1, 1)$, and $C(-1, 5)$. The vertices of $\triangle A'B'C'$ are $A'(-1, -5)$, $B'(-1, -2)$, and $C'(-5, -2)$. The architect wants to give a sequence of rigid motions that maps $\triangle ABC$ to $\triangle A'B'C'$. Provide verbal descriptions and algebraic rules for the appropriate sequence of rigid motions.

9. Find the side lengths to the nearest hundredth and the angle measures to the nearest degree.

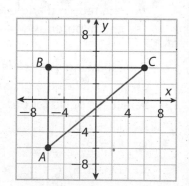

Performance Tasks

★10. A painter is using a ladder to help reach the top of a house. If the house is 12 feet tall and the angle of the ladder needs to be at an angle of at least 60° and no greater than 75° to be safe, how far away should the painter place the ladder from the house? Show your work.

★★11. Gerta and Jeremy are talking on their two-way hand-held radios, which have a range of 35 miles. Gerta is sitting in her car on the side of the road as Jeremy drives past. He continues along the straight road for 28 miles, and then makes a right turn onto a straight road, turning through an angle of 100°. How many miles can Jeremy drive along this second road until he is out of range of Gerta's radio? Show your work.

★★12. Sam is planning to fence his backyard. Every side of the yard except for the side along the house is to be fenced, and fencing costs $3/yd and can only be bought in whole yards. (Note that m∠NPM = 28°, and the side of his yard opposite the house measures 35 yd.) How much will the fencing cost? Explain how you found your answer.

A detective knows what time of day it is based on the angle at which the sun is hitting a man. Suppose a detective is looking at a photograph of a 6-foot-tall man with a shadow that is 3.5 feet long. Find the angle at which the sun was hitting the ground.

Properties of Circles

MATH IN CAREERS

Astronomer An astronomer uses advanced technology and mathematics to study outer space. Astronomers apply mathematics to study the positions, movement, and energy of celestial objects.

If you're interested in a career as an astronomer, you should study these mathematical subjects:

- Algebra
- Geometry
- Trigonometry
- Calculus

Research other careers that require the use of physics to understand real-world scenarios. See the related Career Activity at the end of this unit.

Reading Start-Up

Vocabulary

Review Words

✔ area (*área*)

✔ circumference (*circunferencia*)

✔ diameter (*diámetro*)

✔ perpendicular (*perpendicular*)

✔ radius (*radio*)

✔ vertical angles (*ángulos verticales*)

Preview Words

adjacent arcs (*arcos adyacentes*)

arc (*arco*)

arc length (*longitud de arco*)

central angle (*ángulo central*)

chord (*acorde*)

circumscribed (*circunscrito*)

inscribed angle (*ángulo apuntado*)

point of tangency (*punto de tangencia*)

radian measure (*radianes*)

secant (*secante*)

sector (*sector*)

semicircle (*semicírculo*)

tangent (*tangente*)

Visualize Vocabulary

Use the ✔ words to complete the sequence diagram.

Given the _____ of a circle → Divide by 2 to get the _____.

Square the result. → Multiply by π to find the_____ of the circle.

Understand Vocabulary

Complete the sentences using the preview words.

1. An angle with a vertex on a circle formed by two rays that intersect other points on the circle is called a(n) _____.

2. A radius of a circle is perpendicular to a tangent line at _____.

3. A _____ of a circle is a line segment with both endpoints on the circle.

Active Reading

Four-Corner Fold Create a Four-Corner Fold with flaps for segments, angles, arcs, and sectors. Add relevant vocabulary terms while reading the modules. Emphasize using the written words when discussing these topics with teachers and classmates.

Angles and Segments in Circles

Essential Question: How can you use angles and segments in circles to solve real-world problems?

REAL WORLD VIDEO
Check out how package designers make use of the mathematics of angles and segments to design efficient and attractive packages and containers.

MODULE PERFORMANCE TASK PREVIEW

How Many Marbles Will Fit?

In this module, you will be challenged to determine the size of the largest marble that can fit into a triangular package. How can an understanding of segment and angle relationships in circles help you to solve this problem? Don't "lose your marbles" before you get a chance to find out!

Are (YOU) Ready?

Complete these exercises to review skills you will need for this module.

Angle Relationships

Example 1 Find m∠ABD given that m∠CBE = 40° and the angles are formed by the intersection of the lines $\overleftrightarrow{AC}$ and $\overleftrightarrow{DE}$ at point m.

• Online Homework
• Hints and Help
• Extra Practice

When two lines intersect, they form two pairs of vertical angles at their intersection. Note that ∠ABD and ∠CBE are vertical angles and ∠DBC and ∠ABE are vertical angles.

∠ABD ≅ ∠CBE   Theorem: Vertical Angles are Congruent

m∠ABD = m∠CBE = 40°   Definition of congruence of angles

Find the measure of the complementary or supplementary angle.

1. Complementary to 40° _____

2. Complementary to 67° _____

3. Supplementary to 80° _____

4. Supplementary to 65° _____

Use the image to find the angles or their measures assuming $\overleftrightarrow{CD}$ is parallel to $\overleftrightarrow{EF}$.

5. All angles congruent to ∠APD

_____

6. m∠BPD when m∠BQE = 165°

_____

7. m∠APG when m∠DPG = 55° and m∠BPC = 110°

_____

8. All angles congruent to ∠GPC

_____

Determine whether the lines $\overleftrightarrow{CD}$ and $\overleftrightarrow{EF}$ in the image are parallel for the given angle measures.

9. m∠BPG = 135°, m∠GPC = 95°, and m∠BQF = 110°

_____

10. m∠BPD = 35°, m∠APG = 115°, and m∠EQA = 35°

_____

15.1 Central Angles and Inscribed Angles

Essential Question: How can you determine the measures of central angles and inscribed angles of a circle?

⊘ Explore Investigating Central Angles and Inscribed Angles

A **chord** is a segment whose endpoints lie on a circle.

A **central angle** is an angle with measure less than or equal to 180° whose vertex lies at the center of a circle.

An **inscribed angle** is an angle whose vertex lies on a circle and whose sides contain chords of the circle.

The diagram shows two examples of an inscribed angle and the corresponding central angle.

Chords
$\overline{AB}$ and $\overline{BD}$
Central Angle
∠ACD
Inscribed Angle
∠ABD

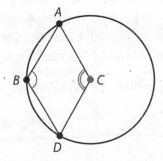

Ⓐ Use a compass to draw a circle. Label the center C.

Ⓑ Use a straightedge to draw an acute inscribed angle on your circle from Step A. Label the angle as ∠DEF.

Ⓒ Use a straightedge to draw the corresponding central angle, ∠DCF.

Ⓓ Use a protractor to measure the inscribed angle and the central angle. Record the measure of the inscribed angle, the measure of the central angle, and the measure of 360° minus the central angle. List your results in the table.

Angle Measure	Circle C	Circle 2	Circle 3	Circle 4	Circle 5	Circle 6	Circle 7
m∠DEF							
m∠DCF							
360° − m∠DCF							

(E) Repeat Steps A-D six more times. Examine a variety of inscribed angles (two more acute, one right, and three obtuse). Record your results in the table in Step D.

1. Examine the values in the first and second rows of the table. Is there a mathematical relationship that exists for some or all of the values? Make a conjecture that summarizes your observation.

_____

_____

2. Examine the values in the first and third rows of the table. Is there a mathematical relationship that exists for some or all of the values? Make a conjecture that summarizes your observation.

_____

_____

_____

🔑 Explain 1 Understanding Arcs and Arc Measure

An **arc** is a continuous portion of a circle consisting of two points (called the endpoints of the arc) and all the points on the circle between them.

Arc	Measure	Figure
A **minor arc** is an arc whose points are on or in the interior of a corresponding central angle.	The measure of a minor arc is equal to the measure of the central angle. $m\widehat{AB} = m\angle ACB$	
A **major arc** is an arc whose points are on or in the exterior of a corresponding central angle.	The measure of a major arc is equal to 360° minus the measure of the central angle. $m\widehat{ADB} = 360° - m\angle ACB$	
A **semicircle** is an arc whose endpoints are the endpoints of a diameter.	The measure of a semicircle is 180°.	

Adjacent arcs are arcs of the same circle that intersect in exactly one point. $\overarc{DE}$ and $\overarc{EF}$ are adjacent arcs.

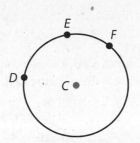

Arc Addition Postulate

The measure of an arc formed by two adjacent arcs is the sum of the measures of the two arcs.

$$m\overarc{ADB} = m\overarc{AD} + m\overarc{DB}$$

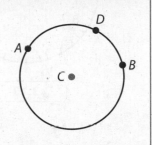

Example 1

(A) If $m\angle BCD = 18°$ and $m\overarc{EF} = 33°$, determine $m\overarc{ABD}$ using the appropriate theorems and postulates. $\overleftrightarrow{AF}$ and $\overleftrightarrow{BE}$ intersect at Point C.

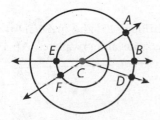

If $m\overarc{EF} = 33°$, then $m\angle ECF = 33°$. If $m\angle ECF = 33°$, then $m\angle ACB = 33°$ by the Vertical Angles Theorem. If $m\angle ACB = 33°$ and $m\angle BCD = 18°$, then $m\overarc{AB} = 33°$ and $m\overarc{BD} = 18°$. By the Arc Addition Postulate, $m\overarc{ABD} = m\overarc{AB} + m\overarc{BD}$, and so $m\overarc{ABD} = 51°$.

(B) If $m\overarc{JK} = 27°$, determine $m\overarc{NP}$ using the appropriate theorems and postulates. $\overleftrightarrow{MK}$ and $\overleftrightarrow{NJ}$ intersect at Point C.

If $m\overarc{JK} = 27°$, then $m\angle JCK = 27°$. If $m\angle JCK = 27°$, then

$m\angle \boxed{} = 27°$ by the _____.

If $m\angle MCN = 27°$ and $m\angle MCP = \boxed{}°$, then $m\overarc{MN} = 27°$

and $m\overarc{MNP} = \boxed{}°$. By the _____,

$m\overarc{MNP} = m\overarc{MN} + m\overarc{NP}$, and so $m\overarc{NP} = m\boxed{} - m\overarc{MN} = \boxed{}°$

3. The minute hand of a clock sweeps out an arc as time moves forward. From 3:10 p.m. to 3:30 p.m., what is the measure of this arc? Explain your reasoning.

3:10   3:30

_____

_____

Your Turn

4. If $m\widehat{EF} = 45°$ and $m\angle ACD = 56°$, determine $m\widehat{BD}$ using the appropriate theorems and postulates. $\overleftrightarrow{AE}$, $\overleftrightarrow{BF}$, and $\overleftrightarrow{DC}$ intersect at Point C.

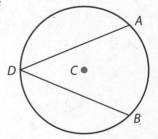

_____

_____

_____

🖋 Explain 2 **Using the Inscribed Angle Theorem**

In the Explore you looked at the relationship between central angles and inscribed angles. Those results, combined with the definitions of arc measure, lead to the following theorem about inscribed angles and their *intercepted arcs*. An **intercepted arc** consists of endpoints that lie on the sides of an inscribed angle and all the points of the circle between them.

Inscribed Angle Theorem

The measure of an inscribed angle is equal to half the measure of its intercepted arc.

$m\angle ADB = \frac{1}{2}\, m\widehat{AB}$

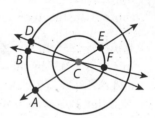

Example 2 Use the Inscribed Angle Theorem to find inscribed angle measures.

(A) Determine $m\widehat{DE}$, $m\widehat{BD}$, $m\angle DAB$, and $m\angle ADE$ using the appropriate theorems and postulates.

By the Inscribed Angle Theorem, $m\angle DAE = \frac{1}{2}m\widehat{DE}$, and so

$m\widehat{DE} = 2 \times 54° = 108°$. By the Arc Addition Postulate,

$m\widehat{BD} = m\widehat{BE} + m\widehat{ED} = 18° + 108° = 126°$. By the Inscribed Angle

Theorem, $m\angle DAB = \frac{1}{2}m\widehat{BD} = \frac{1}{2} \times 126° = 63°$. Note that $\widehat{ABE}$ is a

semicircle, and so $m\widehat{ABE} = 180°$. By the Inscribed Angle Theorem,

$m\angle ADE = \frac{1}{2}m\widehat{ABE} = \frac{1}{2} \times 180° = 90°$.

(B) Determine $m\widehat{WX}$, $m\widehat{XZ}$, $m\angle XWZ$, and $m\angle WXZ$ using the appropriate theorems and postulates.

By the Inscribed Angle Theorem, $m\angle WZX = \boxed{} m\widehat{WX}$,

and so $m\widehat{WX} = 2 \times 9° = \boxed{}$. Note that $\widehat{WXZ}$ is a _____ and,

therefore, $m\widehat{WXZ} = 180°$. By the _____,

$m\widehat{WXZ} = m\widehat{WX} + m\widehat{XZ}$ and then $m\widehat{XZ} = 180° - 18° = \boxed{}$

By the _____, $m\angle XWZ = \frac{1}{2}m\widehat{XZ} = \frac{1}{2} \times 162° = 81°$.

Note that $\boxed{}$ is a semicircle, and so $m\widehat{WYZ} = \boxed{}$. By the Inscribed

Angle Theorem, $m\angle WXZ = \frac{1}{2}m\boxed{} = \frac{1}{2} \times \boxed{} = \boxed{}$.

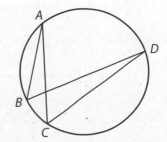

Reflect

5. **Discussion** Explain an alternative method for determining $m\angle XZ$ in Example 2B.

_____

_____

_____

6. **Justify Reasoning** How does the measure of $\angle ABD$ compare to the measure of $\angle ACD$? Explain your reasoning.

_____

_____

_____

7. If m∠EDF = 15°, determine m∠ABE using the appropriate theorems and postulates.

⊘ Explain 3 Investigating Inscribed Angles on Diameters

You can examine angles that are inscribed in a semicircle.

Example 3 Construct and analyze an angle inscribed in a semicircle.

Ⓐ Use a compass to draw a circle with center *C*. Use a straightedge to draw a diameter of the circle. Label the diameter $\overline{DF}$.

Ⓑ Use a straightedge to draw an inscribed angle ∠DEF on your circle from Step A whose sides contain the endpoints of the diameter.

Ⓒ Use a protractor to determine the measure of ∠DEF (to the nearest degree). Record the results in the table.

Angle Measure	Circle C	Circle 2	Circle 3	Circle 4
m∠DEF				

Ⓓ Repeat the process three more times. Make sure to vary the size of the circle, and the location of the vertex of the inscribed angle. Record the results in the table in Step C.

Ⓔ Examine the results, and make a conjecture about the measure of an angle inscribed in a semicircle.

_____

Ⓕ How can does the Inscribed Angle Theorem justify your conjecture?

_____

_____

_____

Inscribed Angle of a Diameter Theorem

The endpoints of a diameter lie on an inscribed angle if and only if the inscribed angle is a right angle.

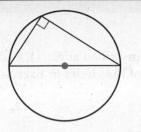

Reflect

8. A right angle is inscribed in a circle. If the endpoints of its intercepted arc are connected by a segment, must the segment pass through the center of the circle?

_____

_____

💬 Elaborate

9. An equilateral triangle is inscribed in a circle. How does the relationship between the measures of the inscribed angles and intercepted arcs help determine the measure of each angle of the triangle?

_____

_____

_____

_____

10. **Essential Question Check-In** What is the relationship between inscribed angles and central angles in a circle?

_____

_____

_____

Identify the chord(s), inscribed angle(s), and central angle(s) in the figure. The center of the circles in Exercises 1, 2, and 4 is *C*.

1.

Chord(s): _____

InscribedAngle(s): _____

Central Angle(s): _____

2.

Chord(s): _____

Inscribed Angle(s): _____

Central Angle(s): _____

_____

3.

Chord(s): _____

Inscribed Angle(s):

_____

Central Angle(s): _____

4.

Chord(s): _____

Inscribed Angle(s): _____

Central Angle(s): _____

_____

In circle C, m$\widehat{DE}$ = 84°. Find each measure.

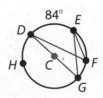

5. m∠*DGE*

6. m∠*EFD*

The center of the circle is A. **Find each measure using the appropriate theorems and postulates.**

7. m$\overset{\frown}{CE}$

8. m$\overset{\frown}{DF}$

9. m$\overset{\frown}{BEC}$

Find each measure using the appropriate theorems and postulates. m$\overset{\frown}{AC}$ = 116°

10. m$\overset{\frown}{BC}$

11. m$\overset{\frown}{AD}$

The center of the circle is C. **Find each measure using the appropriate theorems and postulates.** m$\overset{\frown}{LM}$ = 70° **and** m$\overset{\frown}{NP}$ = 60°.

12. m∠MNP

13. m∠LMN

The center of the circle is O. Find each arc or angle measure using the appropriate theorems and postulates.

14. m∠BDE

15. m$\widehat{ABD}$

16. m$\widehat{ED}$

17. m∠DBE

Represent Real-World Problems The circle graph shows how a typical household spends money on energy. Use the graph to find the measure of each arc.

18. m$\widehat{PQ}$

19. m$\widehat{UPT}$

20. Communicate Mathematical Ideas A carpenter's square is a tool that is used to draw right angles. Suppose you are building a toy car and you have four small circles of wood that will serve as the wheels. You need to drill a hole in the center of each wheel for the axle. Explain how you can use the carpenter's square to find the center of each wheel.

Carpenter's square

21. Choose the expressions that are equivalent to m∠AOB. Select all that apply.

A. $\frac{1}{2}$m∠ACB

B. m∠ACB

C. 2m∠ACB

D. m$\widehat{AB}$

E. m∠DOE

F. m∠DFE

G. 2m∠DFE

H. m$\widehat{DE}$

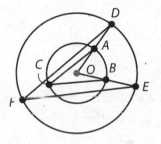

22. Analyze Relationships Draw arrows to connect the concepts shown in the boxes. Then explain how the terms shown in the concept map are related.

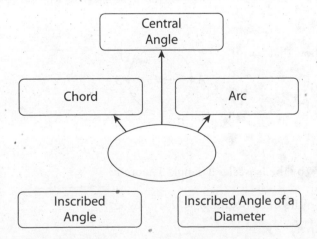

23. In circle E, the measures of $\angle DEC$, $\angle CEB$, and $\angle BEA$ are in the ratio 3:4:5. Find $m\widehat{AC}$.

24. Explain the Error The center of the circle is G. Below is a student's work to find the value of x. Explain the error and find the correct value of x.

$\overline{AD}$ is a diameter, so $m\widehat{ACD} = 180°$.

Since $m\widehat{ACD} = m\widehat{AB} + m\widehat{BC} + m\widehat{CD}$, $m\widehat{AB} + m\widehat{BC} + m\widehat{CD} = 180°$.

$5x + 90 + 15x = 180$

$20x = 90$

$x = 4.5$

25. Multi-Step An inscribed angle with a diameter as a side has measure $x°$. If the ratio of $m\widehat{AD}$ to $m\widehat{DB}$ is 1:4, what is $m\widehat{DB}$?

26. Justify Reasoning To prove the Inscribed Angle Theorem you need to prove three cases. In Case 1, the center of the circle is on a side of the inscribed angle. In Case 2, the center the circle is in the interior of the inscribed angle. In Case 3, the center the circle is in the exterior of the inscribed angle.

a. Fill in the blanks in the proof for Case 1 to show that $m\angle DAB = \frac{1}{2} m\widehat{DB}$.

Given: $\angle DAB$ is inscribed in circle C.

Prove: $m\angle DAB = \frac{1}{2}m\widehat{DB}$

Proof: Let $m\angle A = x°$. Draw $\overline{DC}$.

$\triangle ADC$ is _____. So $m\angle A = m\angle$ ⬚ by the Isosceles Triangle Theorem.

Then ⬚ $= 2x°$ by the Exterior Angle Theorem. So, $m\widehat{DB} =$ ⬚ by the definition of the measure of an arc of a circle.

Since $m\widehat{DB} =$ ⬚ and $m\angle DAB =$ ⬚, $m\angle DAB = \frac{1}{2}\widehat{DB}$.

b. Draw and label a diagram for Case 2. Then use a paragraph proof to prove that the inscribed angle is one-half the intercepted arc.

c. Draw and label a diagram for Case 3. Then use a paragraph proof to prove that the inscribed angle is one-half the intercepted arc.

Lesson Performance Task

Diana arrives late at the theater for a play. Her ticket entitles her to sit anywhere in Circle G. She had hoped to sit in Seat *D*, which she thought would give her the widest viewing angle of the stage. But Seat *D* is taken, as are all the other nearby seats in Circle G. The seating chart for the theater is shown.

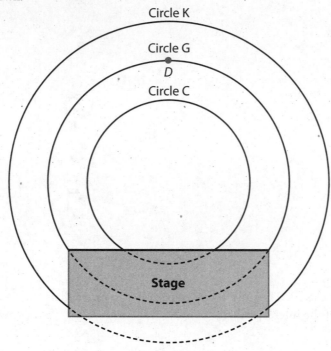

Identify two other spots where Diana can sit that will give her the same viewing angle she would have had in Seat *D*. Explain how you know how your points would provide the same viewing angle, and support your claim by showing the viewing angles on the drawing.

15.2 Angles in Inscribed Quadrilaterals

Essential Question: What can you conclude about the angles of a quadrilateral inscribed in a circle?

⊘ Explore Investigating Inscribed Quadrilaterals

There is a relationship among the angles of a quadrilateral that is inscribed in a circle. You can use a protractor and compass to explore the angle measures of a quadrilateral inscribed in a circle.

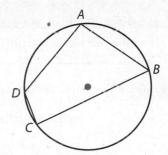

(A) Measure the four angles of quadrilateral *ABCD* and record their values to the nearest degree on the diagram.

(B) Find the sums of the indicated angles.

$m\angle DAB + m\angle ABC =$ ____ ° $m\angle ABC + m\angle BCD =$ ____ °

$m\angle DAB + m\angle BCD =$ ____ ° $m\angle ABC + m\angle CDA =$ ____ °

$m\angle DAB + m\angle CDA =$ ____ ° $m\angle BCD + m\angle CDA =$ ____ °

(C) Use a compass to draw a circle with a diameter greater than the circle in Step A. Plot points *E, F, G,* and *H* consecutively around the circumference of the circle so that the center of the circle is not inside quadrilateral *EFGH*. Use a straightedge to connect each pair of consecutive points to draw quadrilateral *EFGH*.

(D) Measure the four angles of *EFGH* to the nearest degree and record their values on your diagram.

(E) Find the sums of the indicated angles.

$m\angle HEF + m\angle EFG =$ ____ ° $m\angle EFG + m\angle FGH =$ ____ °

$m\angle HEF + m\angle FGH =$ ____ ° $m\angle EFG + m\angle GHE =$ ____ °

$m\angle HEF + m\angle GHE =$ ____ ° $m\angle FGH + m\angle GHE =$ ____ °

Reflect

1. **Discussion** Compare your work with that of other students. What conclusions can you make about the angles of a quadrilateral inscribed in a circle?

   _____

   _____

2. Based on your observations, does it matter if the center of the circle is inside or outside the inscribed quadrilateral for the relationship between the angles to hold? Explain.

   _____

   _____

🔧 Explain 1 Proving the Inscribed Quadrilateral Theorem

The result from the Explore can be formalized in the Inscribed Quadrilateral Theorem.

> **Inscribed Quadrilateral Theorem**
>
> If a quadrilateral is inscribed in a circle, then its opposite angles are supplementary.

Example 1 Prove the Inscribed Quadrilateral Theorem.

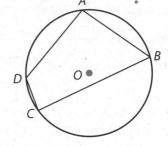

Given: Quadrilateral $ABCD$ is inscribed in circle O.

Prove: $\angle A$ and $\angle C$ are supplementary.
$\angle B$ and $\angle D$ are supplementary.

Step 1 The union of $\overset{\frown}{BCD}$ and $\overset{\frown}{DAB}$ is circle O.

Therefore, $m\overset{\frown}{BCD} + m\overset{\frown}{DAB} = \boxed{}°$

Step 2 $\angle A$ is an inscribed angle and its intercepted arc is $\boxed{}$.

$\angle\boxed{}$ is an inscribed angle and its intercepted arc is $\overset{\frown}{DAB}$.

By the Inscribed Angle Theorem, $m\angle A = \dfrac{\boxed{}}{\boxed{}} \; m\boxed{}$ and

$m\angle C = \dfrac{\boxed{}}{\boxed{}} \; m\boxed{}$.

Step 3 So, $m\angle A + m\angle C = \boxed{}$ Substitution Property of Equality

$= \boxed{}$ Distributive Property

$= \boxed{}$ Substitution Property of Equality

$= \boxed{}$ Simplify.

So, $\angle A$ and $\angle C$ are supplementary, by the definition of supplementary. Similar reasoning shows that $\angle B$ and $\angle D$ are also supplementary.

The converse of the Inscribed Quadrilateral Theorem is also true. That is, if the opposite angles of a quadrilateral are supplementary, it can be inscribed in a circle. Taken together, these statements can be stated as the following biconditional statement. A quadrilateral can be inscribed in a circle *if and only if* its opposite angles are supplementary.

Reflect

3. What must be true about a parallelogram that is inscribed in a circle? Explain.

_____

_____

_____

_____

4. Quadrilateral *PQRS* is inscribed in a circle and $m\angle P = 57°$. Is it possible to find the measure of some or all of the other angles? Explain.

_____

_____

_____

 Explain 2 **Applying the Inscribed Quadrilateral Theorem**

Example 2 Find the angle measures of each inscribed quadrilateral.

(A) *PQRS*

Find the value of *y*.

$$m\angle P + m\angle R = 180° \qquad \text{*PQRS* is inscribed in a circle.}$$

$$(5y + 3) + (15y + 17) = 180 \qquad \text{Substitute.}$$

$$20y + 20 = 180 \qquad \text{Simplify.}$$

$$y = 8 \qquad \text{Solve for } y.$$

Find the measure of each angle.

$$m\angle P = 5(8) + 3 = 43° \qquad \text{Substitute the value of } y \text{ into each angle expression and evaluate.}$$

$$m\angle R = 15(8) + 17 = 137°$$

$$m\angle Q = 8^2 + 53 = 117°$$

$$m\angle S + m\angle Q = 180° \qquad \text{Definition of supplementary}$$

$$m\angle S + 117° = 180° \qquad \text{Substitute.}$$

$$m\angle S = 63° \qquad \text{Subtract 117 from both sides.}$$

So, $m\angle P = 43°$, $m\angle R = 137°$, $m\angle Q = 117°$, and $m\angle S = 63°$.

B *JKLM*

Find the value of *x*.

$$m\angle J + m\angle \boxed{} = \boxed{}^\circ \qquad \text{\textit{JKLM} is inscribed in a circle.}$$

$$\left(\boxed{} + \boxed{}\right) + \left(\boxed{} - \boxed{}\right) = \boxed{} \qquad \text{Substitute.}$$

$$\boxed{}\,x + \boxed{} = \boxed{} \qquad \text{Simplify.}$$

$$\boxed{}\,x = \boxed{} \qquad \text{Subtract 24 from both sides.}$$

$$x = \boxed{} \qquad \text{Divide both sides by 13.}$$

Find the measure of each angle.

$$m\angle J = 39 + 7\left(\boxed{}\right) = \boxed{}^\circ \qquad \text{Substitute the value of \textit{x} into each angle expression and evaluate.}$$

$$m\angle L = 6\left(\boxed{}\right) - 15 = \boxed{}^\circ$$

$$m\angle K = \frac{20\left(\boxed{}\right)}{3} = \boxed{}^\circ$$

$$m\angle M + m\angle \boxed{} = \boxed{}^\circ \qquad \text{Definition of supplementary}$$

$$m\angle M + \boxed{}^\circ = \boxed{}^\circ \qquad \text{Substitute.}$$

$$m\angle M = \boxed{}^\circ \qquad \text{Subtract 80 from both sides.}$$

So, $m\angle J = \boxed{}^\circ$, $m\angle L = \boxed{}^\circ$, $m\angle K = \boxed{}^\circ$, and $m\angle M = \boxed{}^\circ$.

Your Turn

5. Find the measure of each angle of inscribed quadrilateral *TUVW*.

✏️ Explain 3   Constructing an Inscribed Square

Many designs are based on a square inscribed in a circle. Follow the steps to construct rectangle *ACBD* inscribed in a circle. Then show *ACBD* is a square.

Example 3   **Construct an inscribed square.**

Step 1   Use your compass to draw a circle. Mark the center, *O*. Draw diameter $\overline{AB}$ using a straightedge.

Step 2   Use your compass to construct the perpendicular bisector of $\overline{AB}$. Label the points where the bisector intersects the circle as *C* and *D*.

Step 3   Use your straightedge to draw $\overline{AC}$, $\overline{CB}$, $\overline{BD}$, and $\overline{DA}$.

Step 4   To show that *ACBD* is a square, you need to show that it has 4 _____ sides and 4 _____ angles.

Step 5   Complete the two-column proof to prove that *ACBD* has four congruent sides.

Statements	Reasons
$\overline{OA} \cong \boxed{} \cong \boxed{} \cong \boxed{}$	Radii of the circle *O*
$m\angle AOC = m\angle COB = m\angle \boxed{} = m\angle \boxed{} = \boxed{}°$	$\overline{CD}$ is the perpendicular bisector of $\overline{AB}$.
$\triangle AOC \cong \triangle COB \cong \triangle BOD \cong \triangle DOA$	
$\overline{AC} \cong \overline{CB} \cong \overline{BD} \cong \overline{DA}$	

Use the diagram to complete the paragraph proof in Steps 6 and 7 that *ACBD* has four right angles.

Step 6   Since $\triangle AOC \cong \triangle COB$, then $\angle 1 \cong \angle \boxed{}$ by CPCTC. By reasoning similar to

that in the previous proof, it can be shown that $\triangle BOC \cong \triangle COB$. Therefore,

by the Transitive Property of Congruence, $\triangle AOC \cong \triangle \boxed{}$, and $\angle 1 \cong \angle 4$ by

CPCTC. Also by the Transitive Property of Congruence, $\angle \boxed{} \cong \angle 4$. Similar

arguments show that $\angle 1 \cong \angle \boxed{}$, $\angle 5 \cong \angle \boxed{}$, and $\angle 7 \cong \angle \boxed{}$.

Step 7 The sum of all the angle measures in a triangle is _____°, so $m\angle 1 + m\angle 2 + m\angle \boxed{} = 180°$.

Since $m\angle AOC = \boxed{}°$, $m\angle 1 + m\angle 2 + 90° = 180°$. This means that $m\angle 1 + m\angle 2 = \boxed{}°$.

Since $m\angle 1 = m\angle 2$, it can be concluded that $m\angle 1 = m\angle 2 = \boxed{}°$. By similar reasoning, it is

shown that the measure of each of the congruent numbered angles is $\boxed{}°$. Therefore, the measure

of each of the four angles of quadrilateral $ACBD$ is the _____ of the measures of two of the adjacent

numbered angles, which is _____°.

Reflect

6. How could reflections be used to construct an inscribed square?

_____

_____

_____

Your Turn

7. Finish the quilt block pattern by inscribing a square in the circle. Shade in your square.

⊙ Elaborate

8. **Critique Reasoning** Marcus said he thought some information was missing from one of his homework problems because it was impossible to answer the question based on the given information. The question and his work are shown. Critique Marcus's work and reasoning.

<u>Homework Problem</u>

Find the measures of the angles of quadrialatral *ABCD*, which can be inscribed in a circle.

Marcus's Work
$x - 2 + 6z - 1 + 2x - 28 + 10z + 5 = 360$
$3x + 16z - 26 = 360$
$3x + 16z = 386$
Cannot solve for two
different variables!

_____

_____

_____

_____

_____

_____

_____

9. What must be true about a rhombus that is inscribed in a circle? Explain.

_____

_____

_____

_____

10. Essential Question Check-In Can all types of quadrilaterals be inscribed in a circle? Explain.

_____

_____

_____

_____

☆ Evaluate: Homework and Practice

You use geometry software to inscribe quadrilaterals *ABCD* and *GHIJ* in a circle as shown in the figures. You then measure the angle at each vertex.

- Online Homework
- Hints and Help
- Extra Practice

Use the figure for Exercises 1–2.

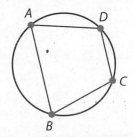

Use the figure for Exercises 3–4.

1. Suppose you drag the vertices of ∠A and ∠C to new positions on the circle and then measure ∠A and ∠C again. Does the relationship between ∠A and ∠C change? Explain.

3. Suppose m∠HIJ = 65° and that m∠H = m∠J. Can you find the measures of all the angles? Explain.

2. Suppose you know that m∠B is 74°. Is m∠D = 74°? Explain.

4. Justify Reasoning You have found that m∠H = m∠J, but then you drag the vertex of ∠H so that m∠H changes. Is the statement m∠H = m∠J still true? Justify your reasoning.

Use the figure for Exercises 5–6. Find each measure using the appropriate theorems and postulates.

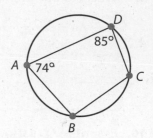

5. m∠B

6. m$\overset{\frown}{DAB}$

7. *GHIJ* is a quadrilateral. If m∠HIJ + m∠HGJ = 180° and m∠H + m∠J = 180°, could the points *G, H, I,* and *J* points of a circle? Explain.

8. *LMNP* is a quadrilateral inscribed in a circle. If m∠L = m∠N, is $\overline{MP}$ a diameter of the circle? Explain.

9. Rafael was asked to construct a square inscribed in a circle. He drew a circle and a diameter of the circle. Describe how to complete his construction. Then, complete the construction.

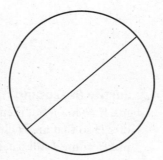

Multi-Step Find the angle measures of each inscribed quadrilateral.

10.

$(5x + 20)°$
$10x°$
$(7x - 8)°$

11.

$(4z - 10)°$
$(6z - 5)°$
$(10 + 5z)°$

12.

$(z - 59)°$
$\left[\dfrac{z}{2}\right]°$
$\left[\dfrac{z}{4} + 30\right]°$

13.

$(15y - 4)°$
$(6x - 14)°$
$(14 + 4x)°$
$(12y - 5)°$

14. Critical Thinking Haruki is designing a fountain that consists of a square pool inscribed in a circular base represented by circle O. He wants to construct the square so that one of its vertices is point X. Construct the square and then explain your method.

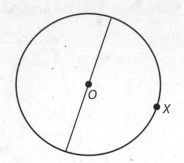

For each quadrilateral, tell whether it can be inscribed in a circle. If so, describe a method for doing so using a compass and straightedge. If not, explain why not.

15. a parallelogram that is not a rectangle

16. a kite with two right angles

17. Represent Real-World Problems Lisa has not yet learned how to stop on ice skates, so she just skates straight across the circular rink until she reaches a wall. If she starts at P, turns 75° at Q, and turns 100° at R, find how many degrees she must turn at S to go back to her starting point.

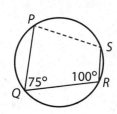

18. In the diagram, C is the center of the circle and ∠YXZ is inscribed in the circle. Classify each statement.

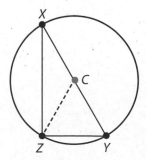

   a. $\overline{CX} \cong \overline{CY}$ True/False/Cannot be determined

   b. $\overline{CZ} \cong \overline{XY}$ True/False/Cannot be determined

   c. △CXZ is isosceles.   True/False/Cannot be determined

   d. △CYZ is equilateral.   True/False/Cannot be determined

   e. $\overline{XY}$ is a diameter of circle C.   True/False/Cannot be determined

19. Multi-Step In the diagram, m$\widehat{JKL}$ = 198° and m$\widehat{KLM}$ = 216°. Find the measures of the angles of quadrilateral *JKLM*.

20. Critical Thinking Explain how you can construct a regular octagon inscribed in a circle.

21. Represent Real-World Problems A patio tile design is constructed from a square inscribed in a circle. The circle has radius $5\sqrt{2}$ feet.

a. Find the area of the square.

b. Find the area of the shaded region outside the square.

Lesson Performance Task

Here are some facts about the baseball field shown here:

- *ABCD* is the baseball "diamond," a square measuring 90 feet on a side.
- Points *A*, *B*, *E*, *H* are collinear.
- The distance from third base (Point *B*) to the left field fence (Point *E*) equals the distance from first base (point *D*) to the right field fence (Point *G*).

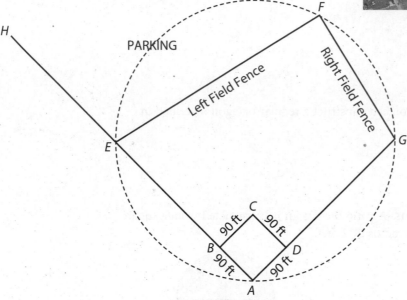

a. Is $\overset{\frown}{EA}$ congruent to $\overset{\frown}{AG}$? Explain why or why not.

b. Find m∠*F*. Explain your reasoning.

c. Identify an angle congruent to ∠*HEF*. Explain your reasoning.

15.3 Tangents and Circumscribed Angles

Essential Question: What are the key theorems about tangents to a circle?

⊘ Explore   Investigating the Tangent-Radius Theorem

A **tangent** is a line in the same plane as a circle that intersects the circle in exactly one point. The point where a tangent and a circle intersect is the **point of tangency**.

In the figure, the line is tangent to circle C, and point P is the point of tangency. You can use a compass and straightedge to construct a circle and a line tangent to it.

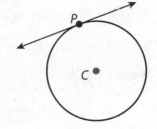

(A) Use a compass to draw a circle. Label the center C.

(B) Mark a point P on the circle. Using a straightedge, draw a tangent to the circle through point P. Mark a point Q at a different position on the tangent line.

(C) Use a straightedge to draw the radius $\overline{CP}$.

(D) Use a protractor to measure $\angle CPQ$. Record the result in the table. Repeat the process two more times. Make sure to vary the size of the circle and the location of the point of tangency.

	Circle 1	Circle 2	Circle 3
Measure of $\angle CPQ$	☐	☐	☐

Reflect

1. **Make a Conjecture** Examine the values in the table. Make a conjecture about the relationship between a tangent line and the radius to the point of tangency.

_____

2. **Discussion** Describe any possible inaccuracies related to the tools you used in this Explore.

_____

_____

Explain 1 Proving the Tangent-Radius Theorem

The Explore illustrates the Tangent-Radius Theorem.

> **Tangent-Radius Theorem**
>
> If a line is tangent to a circle, then it is perpendicular to a radius drawn to the point of tangency.

Example 1 Complete the proof of the Tangent–Radius Theorem.

Given: Line m is tangent to circle C at point P.

Prove: $\overline{CP} \perp m$

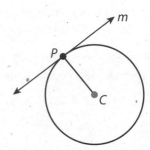

(A) Use an indirect proof. Assume that $\overline{CP}$ is not perpendicular to line m. There must be a point Q on line m such that $\overline{CQ} \perp m$.

If $\overline{CQ} \perp m$, then $\triangle CQP$ is a _____ triangle, and $CP > CQ$ because

_____ is the_____ of the right triangle.

(B) Since line m is a tangent line, it can intersect circle C at only point _____, and all other points

of line m are in the _____ of the circle.

(C) This means point Q is in the _____ of the circle. You can conclude that $CP < CQ$ because

_____ is a _____ of circle C.

(D) This contradicts the initial assumption that a point Q exists such that $\overline{CQ} \perp m$, because that meant that $CP > CQ$. Therefore, the assumption

is _____ and _____ must be perpendicular to line m.

Reflect

3. Both lines in the figure are tangent to the circle, and $\overline{AB}$ is a diameter. What can you conclude about the tangent lines?

_____

_____

The converse of the Tangent-Radius Theorem is also true. You will be asked to prove this theorem as an exercise.

Converse of the Tangent-Radius Theorem

If a line is perpendicular to a radius of a circle at a point on the circle, then it is tangent to the circle at that point on the circle.

⚙ Explain 2 Constructing Tangents to a Circle

From a point outside a circle, two tangent lines can be drawn to the circle.

Example 2 **Use the steps to construct two tangent lines from a point outside a circle.**

Ⓐ Use a compass to draw a circle. Label the center C.

Ⓑ Mark a point X outside the circle and use a straightedge to draw $\overline{CX}$.

Ⓒ Use a compass and straightedge to construct the midpoint of $\overline{CX}$ and label the midpoint M.

Ⓓ Use a compass to construct a circle with center M and radius CM.

Ⓔ Label the points of intersection of circle C and circle M as A and B. Use a straightedge to draw $\overleftrightarrow{XA}$ and $\overleftrightarrow{XB}$. Both lines are tangent to circle C.

Reflect

4. How can you justify that $\overleftrightarrow{XA}$ (or $\overleftrightarrow{XB}$) is a tangent line? (Hint: Draw $\overline{CA}$ on the diagram.)

_____

_____

_____

_____

5. Draw $\overline{CA}$ and $\overline{CB}$ on the diagram. Consider quadrilateral $CAXB$. State any conclusions you can reach about the measures of the angles of $CAXB$.

_____

_____

_____

_____

🔑 Explain 3   Proving the Circumscribed Angle Theorem

A **circumscribed angle** is an angle formed by two rays from a common endpoint that are tangent to a circle.

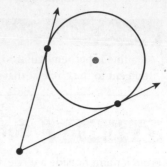

Circumscribed Angle Theorem

A circumscribed angle of a circle and its associated central angle are supplementary.

Example 3   **Prove the Circumscribed Angle Theorem.**

Given: $\angle AXB$ is a circumscribed angle of circle C.

Prove: $\angle AXB$ and $\angle ACB$ are supplementary.

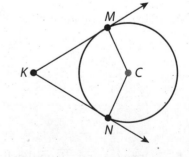

Since $\angle AXB$ is a circumscribed angle of circle C, $\overline{XA}$ and $\overline{XB}$ are

_____ to the circle. Therefore, $\angle XAC$ and $\angle XBC$ are

_____ by the _____.

In quadrilateral $XACB$, the sum of the measures of its four angles is _____.

Since $m\angle XAC + m\angle XBC = \boxed{}$, this means $m\angle AXB + m\angle ACB = 360° - 180° = \boxed{}$.

So, $\angle AXB$ and $\angle ACB$ are supplementary by the _____.

Reflect

6. Is it possible for quadrilateral $AXBC$ to be a parallelogram? If so, what type of parallelogram must it be? If not, why not?

_____

💬 Elaborate

7. $\overrightarrow{KM}$ and $\overrightarrow{KN}$ are tangent to circle C. Explain how to show that $\overline{KM} \cong \overline{KN}$, using congruent triangles.

_____

_____

_____

_____

8. **Essential Question Check-In** What are the key theorems regarding tangent lines to a circle?

_____

_____

_____

• Online Homework
• Hints and Help
• Extra Practice

Use the figure for Exercises 1–2. You use geometry software to construct a tangent to circle *O* at point *X* on the circle, as shown in the diagram.

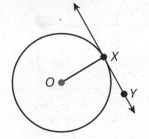

1. What do you expect to be the measure of ∠*OXY*? Explain.

2. Suppose you drag point *X* so that is in a different position on the circle. Does the measure of ∠*OXY* change? Explain.

3. Make a Conjecture You use geometry software to construct circle *A*, diameters $\overline{AB}$ and $\overline{AD}$, and lines *m* and *n* which are tangent to circle *A* at points *D* and *B*, respectively. Make a conjecture about the relationship of the two tangents. Explain your conjecture.

4. In the figure, $\overline{RQ}$ is tangent to circle *P* at point *Q*. What is m∠*PRQ*? Explain your reasoning.

5. Represent Real-World Problems The International Space Station orbits Earth at an altitude of about 240 miles. In the diagram, the Space Station is at point *E*. The radius of Earth is approximately 3960 miles. To the nearest ten miles, what is *EH*, the distance from the space station to the horizon?

3960 mi

Multi-Step Find the length of each radius. Identify the point of tangency, and write the equation of the tangent line at that point.

6.

7.

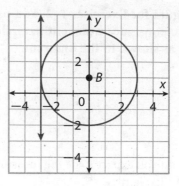

8. In the figure, $QS = 5$, $RT = 12$, and $\overleftrightarrow{RT}$ is tangent to radius $\overline{QR}$ with the point of tangency at R. Find QT.

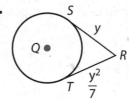

The segments in each figure are tangent to the circle at the points shown. Find each length.

9.

10.

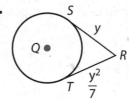

11. Justify Reasoning Suppose you construct a figure with $\overline{PR}$ tangent to circle Q at R and $\overline{PS}$ tangent to circle Q at S. Make a conjecture about $\angle P$ and $\angle Q$. Justify your reasoning.

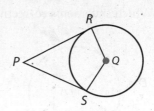

12. $\overline{PR}$ is tangent to circle Q at R and $\overline{PS}$ is tangent to circle Q at S. Find $m\angle Q$.

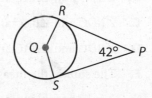

13. $\overline{PR}$ is tangent to circle Q at R and $\overline{PS}$ is tangent to circle Q at S. Find $m\angle P$.

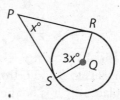

$\overline{PA}$ **is tangent to circle O at A and** $\overline{PB}$ **is tangent to circle O at B, and** $m\angle P = 56°$. **Use the figure to find each measure.**

14. $m\angle AOB$

15. $m\angle OGF$

16. Which statements correctly relate ∠*BDC* and ∠*BAC*? Select all that apply.

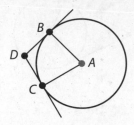

  A. ∠*BDC* and ∠*BAC* are complementary.

  B. ∠*BDC* and ∠*BAC* are supplementary.

  C. ∠*BDC* and ∠*BAC* are congruent.

  D. ∠*BDC* and ∠*BAC* are right angles.

  E. The sum of the measures of ∠*BDC* and ∠*BAC* is 180°.

  F. It is impossible to determine a relationship between ∠*BDC* and ∠*BAC*.

17. Critical Thinking Given a circle with diameter $\overline{BC}$, is it possible to construct tangents to *B* and *C* from an external point *X*? If so, make a construction. If not, explain why it is not possible.

$\overrightarrow{KJ}$ is tangent to circle *C* at *J*, $\overrightarrow{KL}$ is tangent to circle *C* at *L*, and m$\overarc{ML}$ = **138°**.

18. Find m∠*M*.

19. Find m$\overarc{MJ}$.

20. **Justify Reasoning** Prove the converse of the Tangent-Radius Theorem.
    Given: Line m is in the plane of circle C, P is a point of circle C, and $\overline{CP} \perp m$
    Prove: m is tangent to circle C at P.

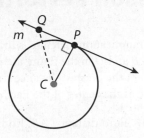

21. **Draw Conclusions** A grapic designer created a preliminary sketch for
    a company logo. In the figure, $\overleftrightarrow{BC}$ and $\overleftrightarrow{CD}$ are tangent to circle A and
    $BC > BA$. What type of quadrilateral is figure $ABCD$ that she created?
    Explain.

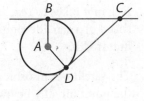

22. **Explain the Error** In the given figure, $\overleftrightarrow{QP}$ and $\overleftrightarrow{QR}$ are tangents.
    A student was asked to find m$\angle PSR$. Critique the student's work and
    correct any errors.

    Since $\angle PQR$ is a circumscribed angle, $\angle PQR$ and $\angle PCR$ are supplementary.
    So m$\angle PCR = 110°$. Since $\angle PSR \cong \angle PQR$, m$\angle PCR = 110°$.

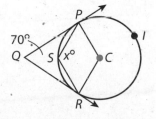

23. Given circle O and points B and C, construct
    a triangle that is circumscribed around the circle.

Lesson Performance Task

A communications satellite is in a synchronous orbit 22,000 miles above Earth's surface. Points B and D in the figure are points of tangency of the satellite signal with the Earth. They represent the greatest distance from the satellite at which the signal can be received directly. Point C is the center of the Earth.

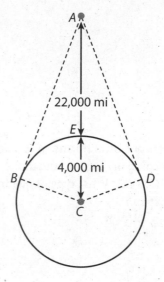

1. Find distance AB. Round to the nearest mile. Explain your reasoning.

2. $m\angle BAC = 9°$. If the circumference of the circle represents the Earth's equator, what percent of the Earth's equator is within range of the satellite's signal? Explain your reasoning.

3. How much longer does it take a satellite signal to reach point B than it takes to reach point E? Use 186,000 mi/sec as the speed of a satellite signal. Round your answer to the nearest hundredth.

4. The satellite is in orbit above the Earth's equator. Along with the point directly below it on the Earth's surface, the satellite makes one complete revolution every 24 hours. How fast must it travel to complete a revolution in that time? You can use the formula $C = 2\pi r$ to find the circumference of the orbit. Round your answer to the nearest whole number.

15.4 Segment Relationships in Circles

Essential Question: What are the relationships between the segments in circles?

⊘ Explore   Exploring Segment Length Relationships in Circles

Any segment connecting two points on a circle is a chord. In some cases, two chords drawn inside the same circle will intersect, creating four segments. In the following activity, you will look for a pattern in how these segments are related and form a conjecture.

(A) Using geometry software or a compass and straightedge, construct circle A with two chords $\overline{CD}$ and $\overline{EF}$ that intersect inside the circle. Label the intersection point G.

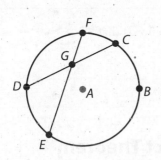

Circle 1

(B) Repeat your construction with two more circles. Vary the size of the circles and where you put the intersecting chords inside them.

Circle 2

Circle 3

(C) Fill in the chart with the lengths of the segments measured to the nearest millimeter and calculate their products.

	DG	GC	EG	GF	DG · GC	EG · GF
Circle 1	___	___	___	___	___	___
Circle 2	___	___	___	___	___	___
Circle 3	___	___	___	___	___	___

(D) Look for a pattern among the measurements and calculations of the segments. From the table, it appears that _____ will always equal _____.

Reflect

1. **Discussion** Compare your results with those of your classmates. What do you notice?

_____

_____

2. What conjecture can you make about the products of the segments of two chords that intersect inside a circle?

Conjecture: _____

_____

⚙ Explain 1   Applying the Chord-Chord Product Theorem

In the Explore, you discovered a pattern in the relationship between the parts of two chords that intersect inside a circle. In this Example, you will apply the following theorem to solve problems.

Chord-Chord Product Theorem

If two chords intersect inside a circle, then the products of the lengths of the segments of the chords are equal.

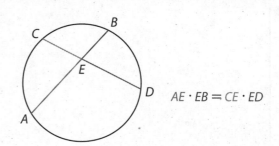

$AE \cdot EB = CE \cdot ED$

Example 1 Find the value of *x* and the length of each chord.

 A Set up an equation according to the Chord-Chord Product Theorem and solve for *x*.

$$CE \cdot ED = AE \cdot EB$$

$$6(2) = 3(x)$$

$$12 = 3x$$

$$4 = x$$

Add the segment lengths to find the length of each chord.

$$CD = CE + ED = 6 + 2 = 8$$

$$AB = AE + EB = 4 + 3 = 7$$

 B Set up an equation according to the Chord-Chord Product Theorem and solve for *x*:

$$HG \cdot GJ = KG \cdot GI$$

$$\boxed{}\left(\boxed{}\right) = \boxed{}\left(\boxed{}\right)$$

$$\boxed{} = 6x$$

$$\boxed{} = x$$

Add the segment lengths together to find the lengths of each chord:

$$HJ = HG + GJ = \boxed{} + 8 = \boxed{}$$

$$KI = \boxed{} + GI = 6 + \boxed{} = \boxed{}$$

Your Turn

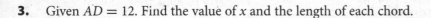

3. Given $AD = 12$. Find the value of *x* and the length of each chord.

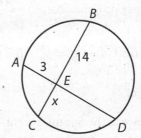

🔵 Explain 2 Proving the Secant-Secant Product Theorem

A **secant** is any line that intersects a circle at exactly two points. A **secant segment** is part of a secant line with at least one point on the circle. A secant segment that lies in the exterior of the circle with one point on the circle is called an **external secant segment**. Secant segments drawn from the same point in the exterior of a circle maintain a certain relationship that can be stated as a theorem.

Secant-Secant Product Theorem

If two secants intersect in the exterior of a circle, then the product of the lengths of one secant segment and its external segment equals the product of the lengths of the other secant segment and its external segment.

$AE \cdot BE = CE \cdot DE$

Example 2 Use similar triangles to prove the Secant-Secant Product Theorem.

Step 1 Identify the segments in the diagram. The whole secant segments in this diagram are _____ and _____.

The external secant segments in this diagram are _____ and _____.

Step 2

Given the diagram as shown, prove that $AE \cdot BE = CE \cdot DE$.

Prove: $AE \cdot BE = CE \cdot DE$

Proof: Draw auxiliary line segments $\overline{AD}$ and $\overline{CB}$. $\angle EAD$ and $\angle ECB$ both intercept _____, so $\angle$ [□] $\cong \angle$ [□] . $\angle E \cong \angle E$ by the _____ Property. Thus, $\triangle EAD \sim \triangle ECB$ by

the _____. Therefore, corresponding sides

are proportional, so $\dfrac{AE}{[□]} = \dfrac{[□]}{BE}$. By the _____ Property of Equality,

$BE(CE) \cdot \frac{AE}{CE} = \frac{DE}{BE} \cdot BE(CE)$, and thus $AE \cdot BE = CE \cdot DE$.

Reflect

4. Rewrite the Secant-Secant Theorem in your own words. Use a diagram or shortcut notation to help you remember what it means.

_____

_____

5. **Discussion:** Suppose that two secants are drawn so that they intersect on the circle. Can you determine anything about the lengths of the segments formed? Explain.

_____

_____

Explain 3   Applying the Secant-Secant Product Theorem

You can use the Secant-Secant Product Theorem to find unknown measures of secants and secant segments by setting up an equation.

Example 3   Find the value of x and the length of each secant segment.

(A)   Set up an equation according to the Secant-Secant Product Theorem and solve for x.

$$AC \cdot AB = AE \cdot AD$$

$$(5 + x)(5) = (12)(6)$$

$$5x + 25 = 72$$

$$5x = 47$$

$$x = 9.4$$

Add the segments together to find the lengths of each secant segment.

$$AC = 5 + 9.4 = 14.4; \; AE = 6 + 6 = 12$$

(B)   Set up an equation according to the Secant-Secant Product Theorem and solve for x.

$$UP \cdot TP = SP \cdot RP$$

$$\left(\boxed{}\right)(7) = \left(\boxed{}\right)(6)$$

$$\boxed{}x + \boxed{} = \boxed{}$$

$$\boxed{}x = \boxed{}$$

$$x = \boxed{}$$

Add the segments together to find the lengths of each secant segment.

$$UP = 7 + \boxed{} = \boxed{}; \; SP = 8 + 6 = 14$$

Your Turn

Find the value of x and the length of each secant segment.

6.

7.

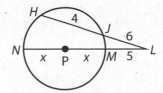

⚙ Explain 4 Applying the Secant-Tangent Product Theorem

A similar theorem applies when both a secant segment and tangent segment are drawn to a circle from the same exterior point. A **tangent segment** is a segment of a tangent line with exactly one endpoint on the circle.

Secant-Tangent Product Theorem

If a secant and a tangent intersect in the exterior of a circle, then the product of the lengths of the secant segment and its external segment equals the length of the tangent segment squared.

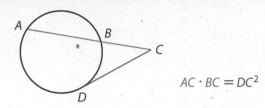

$$AC \cdot BC = DC^2$$

Example 4 Find the value of x.

Ⓐ Given the diameter of the Earth as 8,000 miles, a satellite's orbit is 6,400 miles above the Earth. Its range, shown by $\overline{SP}$, is a tangent segment.

Set up an equation according to the Secant-Tangent Product Theorem and solve for x:

$$SA \cdot SE = SP^2$$

$$(8000 + 6400)(6400) = x^2$$

$$(14400)(6400) = x^2$$

$$92{,}160{,}000 = x^2$$

$$\pm 9600 = x$$

Since distance must be positive, the value of x must be 9600 miles.

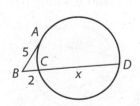

Ⓑ Set up an equation according to the Secant-Tangent Product Theorem and solve for x:

$$BD \cdot BC = BA^2$$

$$\left(\boxed{}\right)(2) = 5^2$$

$$\boxed{}\,x + \boxed{} = \boxed{}$$

$$\boxed{}\,x = \boxed{}$$

$$x = \boxed{}$$

8. Compare and contrast the Secant-Secant Product Theorem with the Secant-Tangent Product Theorem.

_____

_____

_____

Your Turn

Find the value of x.

9. On a bird-watching trip, you travel along a path tangent to a circular pond to a lookout station that faces a hawk's nest. Given the measurements in the diagram on your bird-watching map, how far is the nest from the lookout station?

10.

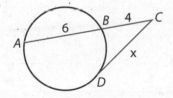

11. How is solving for y in the following diagram different from Example 3?

_____

_____

_____

_____

_____

12. A circle is constructed with two secant segments that intersect outside the circle. If both external secant segments are equal, is it reasonable to conclude that both secant segments are equal? Explain.

_____

_____

_____

_____

_____

13. Essential Question Check-In How are the theorems in this lesson related?

_____

_____

_____

_____

_____

Use the figure for Exercises 1–2.

Suppose you use geometry software to construct two chords $\overline{RS}$ and $\overline{TU}$ that intersect inside a circle at V.

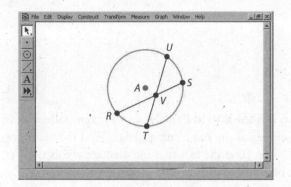

1. If you measured $\overline{RV}$, $\overline{VS}$, $\overline{TV}$, and $\overline{VU}$, what would be true about the relationship between their lengths?

2. Suppose you drag the points around the circle and examine the changes in the measurements. Would your answer to Exercise 1 change? Explain.

Use the figure for Exercises 3–4.

Suppose you use geometry software to construct two secants $\overleftrightarrow{DC}$ and $\overrightarrow{BE}$ that intersect outside a circle at F.

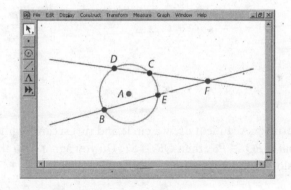

3. If you measured $\overline{DF}$, $\overline{CF}$, $\overline{BF}$, and $\overline{EF}$, what would be true about the relationship between their lengths?

4. Suppose you drag F and examine the changes in the measurements. Would your answer to Exercise 3 change? Explain.

Find the value of the variable and the length of each chord.

5.

6.

7. M is the midpoint of $\overline{PQ}$, The diameter of circle O is 13 in. and $RM = 4$ in.

   a. Find PM.

   b. Find PQ.

8. **Representing a Real-World Problem** A broken pottery shard found at archaeological dig has a curved edge. Find the diameter of the original plate. (Use the fact that the diameter $\overline{PR}$ is the perpendicular bisector of chord $\overline{AB}$.)

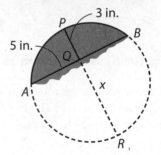

9. **Critique Reasoning** A student drew a circle and two secant segments. He concluded that if $\overline{PQ} \cong \overline{PS}$, then $\overline{QR} \cong \overline{ST}$. Do you agree with the student's conclusion? Why or why not?

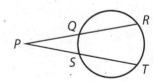

Find the value of the variable and the length of each secant segment.

10.

11.

12. Find the value of x.

Find the value of the variable.

13.

14.

15.

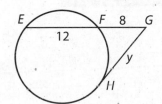

16. Tangent $\overleftrightarrow{PF}$ and secants $\overleftrightarrow{PD}$ and $\overleftrightarrow{PB}$ are drawn to circle A. Determine whether each of the following relationships is true or false. Select the correct answer for each lettered part.

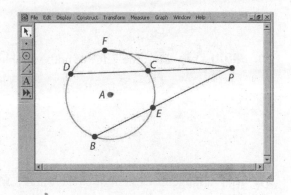

a. $PB \cdot EB = PD \cdot DC$ ○ True   ○ False

b. $PE \cdot EB = PC \cdot DC$ ○ True   ○ False

c. $PB \cdot PE = PF^2$ ○ True   ○ False

d. $PB \cdot DC = PD \cdot EB$ ○ True   ○ False

e. $PB \cdot PE = PD \cdot PC$ ○ True   ○ False

f. $PB \cdot PE = PF \cdot PC$ ○ True   ○ False

17. Which of these is closest to the length of tangent segment $\overline{PQ}$?

A. 6.9   B. 9.2

C. 9.9   D. 10.6

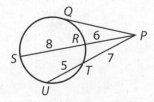

18. Explain the Error Below is a student's work to find the value of x. Explain the error and find the correct value of x.

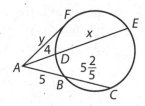

$$AB \cdot BC = DC^2$$

$$6(4) = x^2$$

$$x^2 = 24$$

$$x = \pm\sqrt{24} = \pm 2\sqrt{6}$$

19. Represent Real-World Problems Molokini is a small, crescent-shaped island $2\frac{1}{2}$ miles from the Maui, Hawaii, coast. It is all that remains of an extinct volcano. To approximate the diameter of the mouth of the volcano, a geologist used a diagram like the one shown. The geologist assumed that the mouth of the volcano was a circle. What was the approximate diameter of the volcano's mouth to the nearest ten feet?

20. Multi-step Find the value of both variables in the figure.

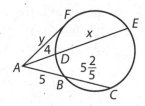

21. $\overline{KL}$ is a tangent segment of circle N and $\overline{KM}$ and $\overline{LM}$ are secants of the circle. Find the value of x.

22. **Justify Reasoning** Prove the Chord-Chord Product Theorem

    · Given: Chords $\overline{AB}$ and $\overline{CD}$ intersect at point E.

    · Prove: $AE \cdot EB = CE \cdot ED$ (*Hint*: Draw $\overline{AC}$ and $\overline{BD}$.)

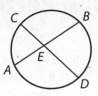

23. **Justify Reasoning** $\overline{PQ}$ is a tangent segment of a circle with radius 4 in. Q lies on the circle, and $PQ = 6$ in. Make a sketch and find the distance from P to the circle. Round to the nearest tenth of an inch. Explain your reasoning.

24. **Justify Reasoning** The circle in the diagram has radius c. Use this diagram and the Chord-Chord Product Theorem to prove the Pythagorean Theorem.

25. **Critical Thinking** The radius of circle A is 4. $CD = 4$, and $\overline{CB}$ is a tangent segment. Describe two different methods you can use to find BC.

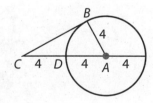

Lesson Performance Task

The figure shows the basic design of a Wankel rotary engine. The triangle is equilateral, with sides measuring 10 inches. An arc on each side of the triangle has as its center the vertex on the opposite side of the triangle. In the figure, the arc *ADB* is an arc of a circle with its center at *C*.

a. Use the sketch of the engine. What is the measure of each arc along the side of the triangle?

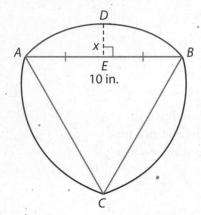

b. Use the relationships in an equilateral triangle to find the value of *x*. Explain.

c. Use the Chord-Chord Product Theorem to find the value of *x*. Explain.

15.5 Angle Relationships in Circles

Essential Question: What are the relationships between angles formed by lines that intersect a circle?

Resource
Locker

⊘ Explore   Exploring Angle Measures in Circles

The sundial is one of many instruments that use angles created in circles for practical applications, such as telling time.

In this lesson, you will observe the relationships between angles created by various line segments and their intercepted arcs.

Ⓐ Using geometry software, construct a circle with two secants $\overleftrightarrow{CD}$ and $\overleftrightarrow{EF}$ that intersect inside the circle at G, as shown in the figure.

Ⓑ Create two new points H and I that are on the circle as shown. These will be used to measure the arcs. Hide B if desired.

Ⓒ Measure $\angle DGF$ formed by the secant lines, and measure $\overarc{CHE}$ and $\overarc{DIF}$. Record angle and arc measurements in the first column of the table.

m∠DGF				
m$\overarc{CHE}$				
m$\overarc{DIF}$				
Sum of Arc Measures				

Ⓓ Drag F around the circle and record the changes in measures in the table in Part C. Try to create acute, right, and obtuse angles. Be sure to keep H between C and E and I between D and F for accurate arc measurement. Move them if necessary.

1. Can you make a conjecture about the relationship between the angle measure and the two arc measures?

_____

2. Using the same circle you created in step A, drag points around the circle so that the intersection is outside the circle, as shown. Measure $\angle FGC$ formed by the secant lines and measure $\widearc{CIF}$ and $\widearc{DHE}$. Drag points around the circle and observe the changes in measures. Record some measures in the table.

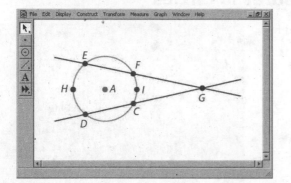

m∠FGC			
m$\widearc{CIF}$			
m$\widearc{DHE}$			
Difference of Arc Measures			

What is similar and different about the relationships between the angle measure and the arc measures when the secants intersect outside the circle?

_____

_____

_____

⚙ Explain 1 Proving the Intersecting Chords Angle Measure Theorem

In the Explore section, you discovered the effects that line segments, such as chords and secants, have on angle measures and their intercepted arcs. These relationships can be stated as theorems, with the first one about chords.

The Intersecting Chords Angle Measure Theorem
If two secants or chords intersect in the interior of a circle, then the measure of each angle formed is half the sum of the measures of its intercepted arcs.   Chords $\overline{AD}$ and $\overline{BC}$ intersect at E. $m\angle 1 = \frac{1}{2}\left(m\widearc{AB} + m\widearc{CD}\right)$ 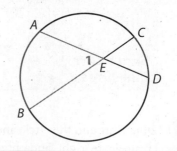

Example 1

Example 1 **Prove the Intersecting Chords Angle Measure Theorem**

Given: $\overline{AD}$ and $\overline{BC}$ intersect at E.

Prove: $m\angle 1 = \frac{1}{2}\left(m\widehat{AB} + m\widehat{CD}\right)$

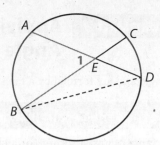

Statements	Reasons
1. $\overline{AD}$ and $\overline{BC}$ intersect at E.	1. Given
2. Draw $\overline{BD}$.	2. Through any two points, there is exactly one line.
3. $m\angle 1 = m\angle EDB + m\angle EBD$	3.
4. $m\angle EDB = \frac{1}{2} m\widehat{AB}$, $m\angle EBD = \frac{1}{2} m\widehat{CD}$	4.
5. $m\angle 1 = \frac{1}{2}m\widehat{AB} + \frac{1}{2}m\boxed{}$	5. Substitution Property
6.	6.

Reflect

3. **Discusssion** Explain how an auxiliary segment and the Exterior Angle Theorem are used in the proof of the Intersecting Chords Angle Measure Theorem.

_____

_____

_____

_____

Your Turn

Find each unknown measure.

4. $m\angle MPK$

5. $m\widehat{PR}$

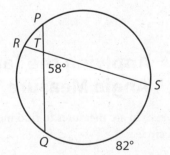

Applying the Tangent-Secant Interior Angle Measure Theorem

The angle and arc formed by a tangent and secant intersecting *on* a circle also have a special relationship.

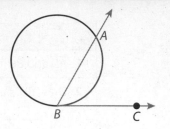

> **The Tangent-Secant Interior Angle Measure Theorem**
>
> If a tangent and a secant (or a chord) intersect on a circle at the point of tangency, then the measure of the angle formed is half the measure of its intercepted arc.
>
> Tangent $\vec{BC}$ and secant $\vec{BA}$ intersect at B.
>
> $$m\angle ABC = \frac{1}{2}\, m\widehat{AB}$$

Example 2 Find each unknown measure.

Ⓐ $m\angle BCD$

$m\angle BCD = \frac{1}{2}m\widehat{BC}$

$\qquad = \frac{1}{2}(142°)$

$\qquad = 71°$

Ⓑ $m\widehat{ABC}$

$m\angle ACD = \frac{1}{2}\left(m\widehat{ABC}\right)$

$\boxed{} = \frac{1}{2}\left(m\widehat{ABC}\right)$

$\boxed{} = m\widehat{ABC}$

Your Turn

Find the measure.

6. $m\widehat{PN}$

7. $m\angle MNP$

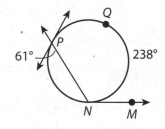

Applying the Tangent-Secant Exterior Angle Measure Theorem

You can use the *difference* in arc measures to find measures of angles formed by tangents and secants intersecting *outside* a circle.

The Tangent-Secant Exterior Angle Measure Theorem

If a tangent and a secant, two tangents, or two secants intersect in the exterior of a circle, then the measure of the angle formed is half the difference of the measures of its intercepted arcs.

  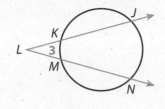

$$m\angle 1 = \tfrac{1}{2}\left(m\,\widehat{AD} - m\,\widehat{BD}\right) \qquad m\angle 2 = \tfrac{1}{2}\left(m\,\widehat{EHG} - m\,\widehat{EG}\right) \qquad m\angle 3 = \tfrac{1}{2}\left(m\,\widehat{JN} - m\,\widehat{KM}\right)$$

Example 3   Find the value of x.

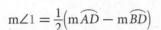

$$m\angle L = \tfrac{1}{2}\left(m\,\widehat{JN} - m\,\widehat{KM}\right)$$
$$25° = \tfrac{1}{2}\left(83° - x°\right)$$
$$50 = 83 - x$$
$$-33 = -x$$
$$33 = x$$

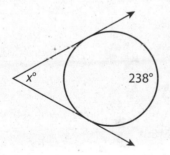

$$x° = \tfrac{1}{2}\left(238° - \left(360° - \boxed{}\right)\right)$$
$$x = \tfrac{1}{2}\left(\left(238 - \boxed{}\right)\right)$$
$$x = \tfrac{1}{2}\left(\boxed{}\right)$$
$$x = \boxed{}$$

Your Turn

Find the value of x.

8.

9. The superior oblique and inferior oblique are two muscles that help control eye movement. They intersect behind the eye to create an angle, as shown. If $m\widehat{AEB} = 225°$, what is $m\angle ACB$?

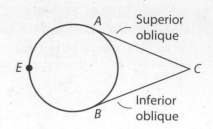

⚙ Explain 4   Understanding Angle Relationships in Circles

You can summarize angle relationships in circles by looking at where the vertex of the angle lies: on the circle, inside the circle, or outside the circle.

	Angle Relationships in Circles	
Vertex of the Angle	**Measure of Angle**	**Diagrams**
On a circle	Half the measure of its intercepted arc	120° 200° $m\angle 1 = 60°$ $m\angle 2 = 100°$
Inside a circle	Half the sum of the measures of its intercepted arcs	44° 1 86° $m\angle 1 = \frac{1}{2}(44° + 86°)$ $= 65°$
Outside a circle	Half the difference of the measures of its intercepted arcs	1 78° 202° 2 45° 125° $m\angle 1 = \frac{1}{2}(202° - 78°)$ $m\angle 2 = \frac{1}{2}(125° - 45°)$ $= 62°$ $= 40°$

Example 4 Find the unknown arc measures.

150°

B   F
64° A 50°
C   D E

(A) Find m$\widehat{FD}$.

$$m\angle E = \frac{1}{2}\left(m\widehat{BF} - m\widehat{FD}\right)$$

$$50° = \frac{1}{2}\left(150° - m\widehat{FD}\right)$$

$$100° = \left(50° - m\widehat{FD}\right)$$

$$-50° = -m\widehat{FD}$$

$$50° = m\widehat{FD}$$

(B) Find m$\widehat{CD}$.

$$m\widehat{CD} = \boxed{} - \left(m\widehat{BC} + m\widehat{BF} + m\widehat{FD}\right)$$

$$= \boxed{} - \left(64° + \boxed{} + \boxed{}\right)$$

$$= \boxed{} - \boxed{}$$

$$= \boxed{}$$

Your Turn

10. Find m$\widehat{KN}$.

86°
J   P
48° Q
     79°
M
K
L
N

Elaborate

11. Complete the graphic organizer that shows the relationship between the angle measurement and the location of its vertex.

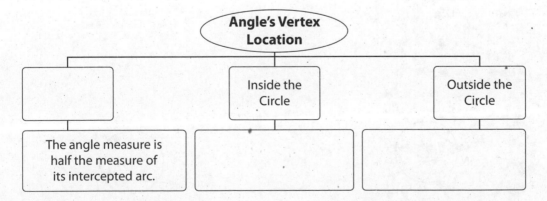

Angle's Vertex Location

| | Inside the Circle | Outside the Circle |

The angle measure is half the measure of its intercepted arc.

12. **Essential Question Check-In** What is similar about all the relationships between angle measures and their intercepted arcs?

• Online Homework
• Hints and Help
• Extra Practice

Use the figure for Exercises 1–2.

Suppose you use geometry software to construct a secant $\overleftrightarrow{CE}$ and tangent $\overleftrightarrow{CD}$ that intersect on a circle at point C.

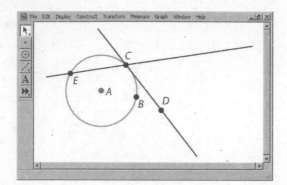

1. Suppose you measure $\angle DCE$ and you measure $\overparen{CBE}$. Then you drag the points around the circle and measure the angle and arc three more times. What would you expect to find each time? Which theorem from the lesson would you be demonstrating?

2. When the measure of the intercepted arc is 180°, what is the measure of the angle? What does that tell you about the secant?

Find each measure.

3. $m\angle QPR$

4. $m\angle ABC$

5. $m\angle MKJ$

6. $m\angle NPK$

Find each measure. Use the figure for Exercises 7–8.

7. m∠*BCD*

8. m∠*ABC*

Find each measure. Use the figure for Exercises 9–10.

9. m∠*XZW*

10. m∠*YXZ*

Find the value of x.

11.

12.

13.

14. Represent Real-World Problems Stonehenge is a circular arrangement of massive stones near Salisbury, England. A viewer at *V* observes the monument from a point where two of the stones *A* and *B* are aligned with stones at the endpoints of a diameter of the circular shape. Given that m$\widehat{AB}$ = 48°, what is m∠*AVB*?

15. Multi-Step Find each measure.

   a. Find m$\widehat{PN}$.

   b. Use your answer to part a to find m$\widehat{KN}$.

16. Multi-Step Find each measure.

   a. Find m$\widehat{DE}$.

   b. Use your answer to part a to find m∠*F*.

$\overleftrightarrow{MS} \parallel \overleftrightarrow{PQ}$ and m∠PNS = 50°. **Find each measure.**

17. m$\overparen{PR}$

18. m$\overparen{LP}$

19. Represent Real-World Problems A satellite orbits Mars. When it reaches S it is about 12,000 km above the planet. What is x°, the measure of the arc that is visible to a camera in the satellite?

20. Use the circle with center J. Match each angle or arc on the left with its measure on the right. Indicate a match by writing the letter for the angle or arc on the line in front of the corresponding measure.

A. ∠BAE   _____ 41°

B. ∠ACD   _____ 180°

C. $\overparen{AF}$ _____ 101°

D. ∠AED   _____ 90°

E. $\overparen{ADE}$ _____ 60°

21. Use the Plan for Proof to write a proof for one case of the Tangent-Secant Exterior Angle Measure Theorem.

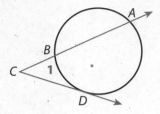

Given: Tangent $\overrightarrow{CD}$ and secant $\overrightarrow{CA}$

Prove: $m\angle ACD = \frac{1}{2}\left(m\widehat{AD} - m\widehat{BD}\right)$

Plan: Draw auxiliary line segment $\overline{BD}$. Use the Exterior Angle Theorem to show that $m\angle ACD = m\angle ABD - m\angle BDC$. Then use the Inscribed Angle Theorem and the Tangent-Secant Interior Angle Measure Theorem.

22. Justify Reasoning Write a proof that the figure shown is a square.

Given: $\overline{YZ}$ and $\overline{WZ}$ are tangent to circle X, $m\widehat{WY} = 90°$

Prove: $WXYZ$ is a square.

23. Justify Reasoning Prove the Tangent-Secant Interior Angle Theorem.

Given: Tangent $\overrightarrow{BC}$ and secant $\overrightarrow{BA}$

Prove: $m\angle ABC = \frac{1}{2}m\widehat{AB}$

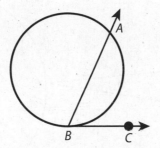

$\left(Hint:\right.$ Consider two cases, one where $\overline{AB}$ is a diameter and one where $\overline{AB}$ is not a diameter.$\left.\right)$

24. Critical Thinking Suppose two secants intersect in the exterior of a circle as shown. Which is greater, $m\angle 1$ or $m\angle 2$? Justify your answer.

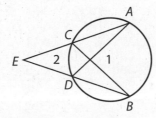

Lesson Performance Task

The diameter of the Moon is about 2160 miles. From Earth, the portion of the Moon's surface that an observer can see is from a circumscribed angle of approximately 0.5°.

a. Find the measure of $\widehat{ADC}$. Explain how you found the measure.

b. What fraction of the circumference of the Moon is represented by $\widehat{ADC}$?

c. Find the length of $\widehat{ADC}$. You can use the formula $C = 2\pi r$ to find the circumference of the Moon.

Angles and Segments in Circles

Essential Question: How can you use angles and segments in circles to solve real-world problems?

KEY EXAMPLE   (Lesson 15.1)

Determine $m\widehat{DE}$, $m\widehat{BD}$, $m\widehat{DAB}$, and $m\angle ADE$.

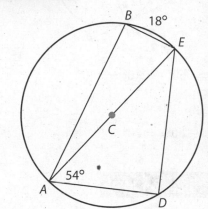

Since chord AE passes through the center of the circle at C, the chord AE is a diameter of the circle. $\widehat{ABE}$ is then a semicircle, and $m\widehat{ABE} = 180°$.

But $m\angle ADE = \frac{1}{2}m\widehat{ABE} = 90°$. $\triangle ADE$ is a right triangle with $m\angle AED = 36°$.

Also, $m\angle DAE = \frac{1}{2}m\widehat{DE}$, which implies that $m\widehat{DE} = 2m\angle DAE = 108°$. Since $m\widehat{BD} = m\widehat{BE} + m\widehat{DE}$, $m\widehat{BD} = 18° + 108° = 126°$. Finally, $m\angle DAB = \frac{1}{2}m\widehat{BD} = 63°$.

KEY EXAMPLE   (Lesson 15.2)

Determine the angles J, K, L, and M in the given quadrilateral.

$(40 + 8x) + (5x - 16) = 180$.
$24 + 13x = 180$.
$13x = 156$. $x = 12$.

$m\angle J = 40 + 8x = 40 + 8(12)$
     $= 136°$

$m\angle L = 5x - 16 = 5(12) - 16$
     $= 60 - 16 = 44°$

$m\angle K = \dfrac{20(12)}{4} = 60°$. $m\angle M + m\angle K = 180°$.

$m\angle M = 180° - 60° = 120°$

Key Vocabulary

chord *(cuerda)*

central angle *(ángulo central)*

inscribed angle *(ángulo inscrito)*

arc *(arco)*

minor arc *(arco menor)*

major arc *(arco principal)*

semicircle *(semicírculo)*

adjacent arcs *(arcos adyacentes)*

Inscribed Angle Theorem *(teorema del ángulo inscrito)*

Inscribed Quadrilateral Theorem *(teorema del ángulo inscrito)*

tangent *(tangent)*

point of tangency *(punto de tangencia)*

Tangent-Radius Theorem *(teorema de la tangente radio)*

Chord-Chord Product Theorem *(teorema del producto de la cuerda de la cuerda)*

secant *(secante)*

secant segment *(segmente secante)*

external secant segment *(segmento externo secante)*

Secant-Secant Theorem *(Teorema de la secante-secante)*

tangent segment *(segmento tangente)*

Intersecting Chords Angle Measure Theorem *(teorema de medida de ángulo de intersección acordes)*

Tangent-Secant Interior Angle Measure Theorem *(teorema de la medida de ángulo interior tangente-secante)*

Tangent-Secant Exterior Angle Measure Theorem *(teorema de la medida de ángulo exterior tangente-secante)*

Two tangent lines are drawn to a circle from point K intersecting the circle at points M and N. If $\widehat{mMPN} = 210°$, what is $m\angle MKN$?

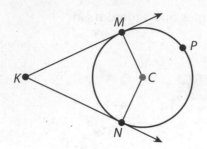

If $\widehat{mMPN} = 210°$, then $\widehat{mMN} = 360° - 210° = 150°$.

$m\angle MKN = \frac{1}{2}\left(\widehat{mMPN} - \widehat{mMN}\right)$

$m\angle MKN = \frac{1}{2}(210° - 150°) = \frac{1}{2}(60°) = 30°$

A tangent and a secant are drawn to a circle from the external point B. The point of tangency is at point A, and the secant intersects the circle at points C and D. Find x.

From the Secant-Tangent Product Theorem, we can say that $BD \cdot BC = AB^2$. So $(2 + x) \cdot 2 = 8^2$.

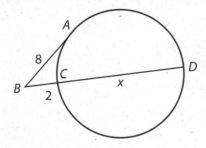

So $4 + 2x = 64$. $2x = 60$ and $x = 30$.

Two chords intersect the interior of a circle at point T. Find $\widehat{mPR}$.

By the Intersecting Chords Angle Measure Theorem we can say the following:

$m\angle QTS = \frac{1}{2}\left(\widehat{mQS} + \widehat{mPR}\right)$

$60° = \frac{1}{2}\left(80° + \widehat{mPR}\right)$

$120° = \left(80° + \widehat{mPR}\right)$

$120° - 80° = \widehat{mPR}$

$40° = \widehat{mPR}$

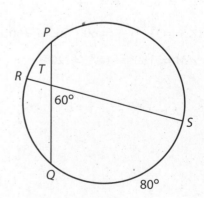

EXERCISES

Use the Inscribed Angle Theorem. *(Lesson 15.1)*

1. Find the measure of the intercepted arc for an inscribed angle of 50°.

Use the Inscribed Quadrilateral Theorem. *(Lesson 15.2)*

2. If one angle of a quadrilateral inscribed in a circle is 50°, what is the measure of its opposite angle?

Use the Circumscribed Angle Theorem. *(Lesson 15.3)*

3. Two tangents are drawn from an external point *A* to a circle. If one of the intercepted arcs on the circle is 120°, what must be the measure of the other intercepted arc?

Use the Chord-Chord Product Theorem. *(Lesson 15.4)*

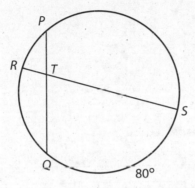

4. Given $RT = 2$, $TS = 6$, and $PT = 3$. Find TQ

Use the Tangent-Secant Exterior Angle Measure Theorem. *(Lesson 15.5)*

5. Find m∠L in the diagram given the m$\widehat{KM}$ and m$\widehat{JN}$.

How Many Marbles Will Fit?

Consider a package of marbles in the shape of a triangular prism. The cross-section of the package is an equilateral triangle with a side length of 1.5 inches, and the length of the package is 10 inches. What is the diameter of the largest marble that will fit inside the package? How many such marbles can fit within the package?

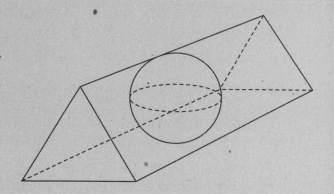

Start by listing in the space below how you plan to tackle the problem. Then use your own paper to complete the task. Be sure to write down all your data and assumptions. Then use words, numbers, diagrams, or algebra to explain how you reached your conclusion.

(Ready) to Go On?

15.1–15.5 Angles and Segments in Circles

- Online Homework
- Hints and Help
- Extra Practice

1. If m∠BCD = 20° and m$\overparen{EF}$ = 34°, determine m$\overparen{ABD}$ using the appropriate theorems and postulates. *(Lesson 15.1)*

   If m$\overparen{EF}$ = 34°, then m∠ECF = _____ . If m∠ECF = 34°,

   then m∠ACB = _____ by the _____

   Theorem. If m∠ACB = 34° and m∠BCD = 20°, then

   m$\overparen{AB}$ = _____ and _____ . By the

   _____ , m$\overparen{ABD}$ = m$\overparen{AB}$ + m$\overparen{BD}$, and

   so m$\overparen{ABD}$ = _____ .

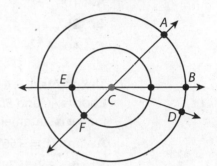

2. Find the measures of each angle in the inscribed quadrilateral. *(Lesson 15.2)*

Fill in the proper conclusions based on known theorems and relationships. *(Lesson 15.5)*

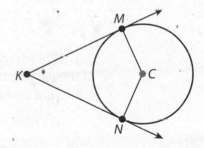

3. Using the given figure where $\overline{KM}$ and $\overline{KN}$ are tangent to the circle at M and N respectively, what can you say about the following?

   a. What angles are right angles? _____

   b. Suppose that m∠MKN = 80°. What is m∠MCN?

ESSENTIAL QUESTION

4. What are the major theorems that allow you to determine the relationships between angles formed by lines that intersect a circle?

Assessment Readiness

SELECTED RESPONSE

1. An angle of 20° is inscribed in a circle. Could the given value be the measure of the arc intercepted by this angle?
   Select Yes or No for A–C.

   A. 10° ○ Yes ○ No
   B. 20° ○ Yes ○ No
   C. 40° ○ Yes ○ No

2. The points A, B, C, and D are taken in order on the circumference of a circle. Chords AC and BD intersect at point E. m$\widehat{AB} = 76°$ and m$\widehat{CD} = 80°$. Choose True or False for each statement.

   A. m$\widehat{ABC} = 156°$ ○ True ○ False
   B. m$\angle AEB = 78°$ ○ True ○ False
   C. m$\angle AED = 72°$ ○ True ○ False

3. Line F bisects $\angle ABC$, $\angle ABF = 6x$, and $\angle FBC = 2x + 60$. Choose True or False for each statement.

   A. m$\angle FBC = 45°$ ○ True ○ False
   B. m$\angle ABC = 180°$ ○ True ○ False
   C. $\angle ABF$ is a right angle. ○ True ○ False

4. If two chords intersect inside a circle, then what do you know about the products of the lengths of the segments of the chords? How can you determine whether two circles are similar?

5. $\triangle ABC$ is inscribed in a circle such that vertices A and B lie on a diameter of the circle. If the length of the diameter of the circle is 13 and the length of chord BC is 5, find side AC.

Arc Length and Sector Area

Essential Question: How can the arc length and sector area of a circle be used to solve real-world problems?

REAL WORLD VIDEO
Check out how you can use sector areas to help you order wisely the next time you're buying pizza.

MODULE PERFORMANCE TASK PREVIEW
What's the Better Deal on Pizza?

In this module, you will use geometry to figure out which pizza order gets you more pizza for your money. How can calculating sector area help you to solve this problem? Let's find out.

Are (YOU) Ready?

Complete these exercises to review skills you will need for this module.

• Online Homework
• Hints and Help
• Extra Practice

Area of a Circle

Example 1   Find the area of a circle with radius equal to 5.

$$A = \pi r^2$$ Write the equation for the area of a circle of radius *r*.
$$A = \pi(5)^2$$ Substitute the radius.
$$A = 25\pi$$ Simplify.

Find each area.

1. A circle with radius 3 _____

2. A circle with radius 6 _____

3. A circle with radius 2π _____

4. A circle with radius $\frac{5}{\pi}$ _____

Circumference

Example 2   Find the circumference of a circle with radius equal to 6.

$$C = 2\pi r$$ Write the equation for the circumference of a circle with radius *r*.
$$C = 2\pi(6)$$ Substitute the radius.
$$C = 12\pi$$ Simplify.

Find each circumference.

5. A circle with radius 4

    _____

6. A circle with radius 3π

    _____

7. A circle with diameter 2

    _____

8. A circle with diameter $\frac{6}{\pi}$

    _____

Quadratic Functions

Example 3   Write *x* in terms of *y*. $10yx^2 = 60$

$$10yx^2 = 60$$ Write the equation.
$$yx^2 = 6$$ Divide both sides by 10.
$$x^2 = \frac{6}{y}$$ Divide both sides by *y*.
$$x = \sqrt{\frac{6}{y}}, x = -\sqrt{\frac{6}{y}}$$ Find the square root and its negative.

Solve each equation for *x*.

9. $4x^2 + 8x + 4 = 100$

    _____

10. $5y^2x^2 = 125$

    _____

16.1 Justifying Circumference and Area of a Circle

Essential Question: How can you justify and use the formulas for the circumference and area of a circle?

Resource Locker

⊘ Explore Justifying the Circumference Formula

To find the circumference of a given circle, consider a regular polygon that is inscribed in the circle. As you increase the number of sides of the polygon, the perimeter of the polygon gets closer to the circumference of the circle.

| Inscribed pentagon | Inscribed hexagon | Inscribed octagon |

Let circle O be a circle with center O and radius r. Inscribe a regular n–gon in circle O and draw radii from O to the vertices of the n-gon.

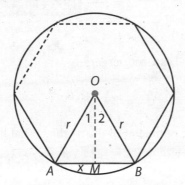

Let $\overline{AB}$ be one side of the n-gon. Draw $\overline{OM}$, the segment from O to the midpoint of $\overline{AB}$.

(A) Then $\triangle AOM \cong \triangle BOM$ by _____.

(B) So, $\angle 1 \cong \angle 2$ by _____.

(C) There are n triangles, all congruent to $\triangle AOB$, that surround point O and fill the n-gon.

Therefore, $m\angle AOB =$ ☐ and $m\angle 1 =$ ☐.

Ⓓ Since $\angle OMA \cong \angle OMB$ by CPCTC, and $\angle OMA$ and $\angle OMB$ form a linear pair, these angles are supplementary and must have measures of 90°. So $\triangle AOM$ and $\triangle BOM$ are right triangles.

In $\triangle AOM$, $\sin\angle 1 = \dfrac{\text{length of opposite leg}}{\text{length of hypotenuse}} = \dfrac{x}{r}$.

So, $x = r\sin\angle 1$ and substituting the expression for m$\angle 1$ from above gives

$x = r\sin$ ☐ .

Ⓔ Now express the perimeter of the n-gon in terms of r.

The length of $\overline{AB}$ is $2x$, because_____.

This means the perimeter of the n-gon in terms of x is _____.

Substitute the expression for x found in Step D.

The perimeter of the n-gon in terms of r is _____.

Ⓕ Your expression for the perimeter of the n–gon should include the factor $n\sin\left(\dfrac{180°}{n}\right)$. What happens to this factor as n gets larger?

Use your calculator to do the following.

- Enter the expression $x\sin\left(\dfrac{180}{x}\right)$ as Y_1.
- Go to the Table Setup menu and enter the values shown.
- View a table for the function.
- Use arrow keys to scroll down.

What happens to the value of $x\sin\left(\dfrac{180°}{x}\right)$ as x gets larger?

_____

Ⓖ Look at the expression you wrote for the perimeter of the n–gon. What happens to the value of this expression, as n gets larger?

_____

Reflect

1. When n is very large, does the perimeter of the n-gon ever equal the circumference of the circle? Why or why not?

_____

_____

2. How does the above argument justify the formula $C = 2\pi r$?

_____

_____

🎸 Explain 1 Applying the Circumference Formula

Example 1 Find the circumference indicated.

(A) A Ferris wheel has a diameter of 40 feet. What is its circumference? Use 3.14 for π.

Diameter $= 2r$

$40 = 2r$

$20 = r$

Use the formula $C = 2\pi r$ to find the circumference.

$C = 2\pi r$

$C = 2\pi(20)$

$C = 2(3.14)(20)$

$C \approx 125.6$

The circumference is about 125.6 feet.

(B) A pottery wheel has a diameter of 2 feet. What is its circumference? Use 3.14 for π.

The diameter is 2 feet, so the radius in inches is $r = \boxed{}$.

$C = 2\pi r$

$C = \boxed{} \cdot \boxed{} \cdot \boxed{}$

$C \approx \boxed{}$ in.

Reflect

3. **Discussion** Suppose you double the radius of a circle. How does the circumference of this larger circle compare with the circumference of the smaller circle? Explain.

_____

_____

Your Turn

4. The circumference of a tree is 20 feet. What is its diameter? Round to the nearest tenth of a foot. Use 3.14 for π.

5. The circumference of a circular fountain is 32 feet. What is its diameter? Round to the nearest tenth of a foot. Use 3.14 for π.

⚙ Explain 2 Justifying the Area Formula

To find the area of a given circle, consider a regular polygon that is inscribed in the circle. As you increase the number of sides of the polygon, the area of the polygon gets closer to the area of the circle.

Inscribed
pentagon

Inscribed
hexagon

Inscribed
octagon

Let circle O be a circle with center O and radius r. Inscribe a regular n–gon in circle O and draw radii from O to the vertices of the n-gon.

Let $\overline{AB}$ be one side of the n–gon. Draw $\overline{OM}$, the segment from O to the midpoint of $\overline{AB}$.

We know that $\overline{OM}$ is perpendicular to $\overline{AB}$ because triangle AOM is congruent to triangle BOM.

Let the length of $\overline{OM}$ be h.

Example 2 Justify the formula for the area of a circle.

(A) There are n triangles, all congruent to $\triangle AOB$, that surround point O and fill the n-gon.

Therefore, the measure of $\angle AOB$ is $\dfrac{360°}{n}$, and the measure of $\angle 1$ is $\dfrac{180°}{n}$.

We know that $x = r\sin\left(\dfrac{180°}{n}\right)$. Write a similar expression for h. _____

(B) The area of $\triangle AOB$ is $\dfrac{1}{2}(2x)(h) = xh = r\sin\left(\dfrac{180°}{n}\right)h$.

Substitute your value for h to get area $\triangle AOB =$ _____.

(C) There are n of these triangles, so the area of the n-gon is _____.

(D) Your expression for the area of the n–gon includes the factor $n\sin\left(\dfrac{180°}{n}\right)\cos\left(\dfrac{180°}{n}\right)$. What happens to this expression as n gets larger?

Use your graphing calculator to do the following.

- Enter the expression $x\sin\left(\dfrac{180°}{x}\right)\cos\left(\dfrac{180°}{x}\right)$ as Y_1.
- View a table for the function.
- Use arrow keys to scroll down.

What happens to the value of $x\sin\left(\dfrac{180°}{x}\right)\cos\left(\dfrac{180°}{x}\right)$ as x gets larger? _____

(E) Look at the expression you wrote for the area of the n–gon. What happens to the value of this expression as n gets larger? _____.

6. When n is very large, does the area of the n-gon ever equal the area of the circle? Why or why not?

_____

7. How does the above argument justify the formula $A = \pi r^2$?

_____

_____

⚙ Explain 3 Applying the Area Formula

Example 3 Find the area indicated.

(A) A rectangular piece of cloth is 3 ft by 6 ft. What is the area of the largest circle that can be cut from the cloth? Round the nearest square inch.

The diameter of the largest circle is 3 feet, or 36 inches. The radius of the circle is 18 inches.

$A = \pi r^2$

$A = \pi(18)^2$

$A = 324\pi$

$A \approx 1,017.9 \text{ in}^2$

So, the area is about 1,018 square inches.

(B) A slice of a circular pizza measures 9 inches in length. What is the area of the entire pizza? Use 3.14 for π.

The 9-in. side of the pizza is also the length of the _____ of the circle. So, $r = \boxed{}$.

$A = \pi r^2$

$A = \pi \boxed{}^2$

$A = \boxed{}\,\pi \approx \boxed{}$

To the nearest square inch, the area of the pizza is _____.

8. Suppose the slice of pizza represents $\frac{1}{6}$ of the whole pizza. Does this affect your answer to Example 3B? What additional information can you determine with this fact?

_____

_____

9. A circular swimming pool has a diameter of 18 feet. To the nearest square foot, what is the smallest amount of material needed to cover the surface of the pool? Use 3.14 for π.

10. If the radius of a circle is doubled, is the area doubled? Explain.

_____

_____

11. Essential Question Check-In How do you justify and use the formula for the circumference of a circle?

_____

_____

_____

_____

☆ Evaluate: Homework and Practice

- Online Homework
- Hints and Help
- Extra Practice

1. Which inscribed figure has a perimeter closer to the circumference of a circle, a regular polygon with 20 sides or a regular polygon with 40 sides? Explain.

Find the circumference of each circle with the given radius or diameter. Round to the nearest tenth. Use 3.14 for π.

2. $r = 9$ cm

3. $r = 24$ in.

4. $d = 14.2$ mm

5. A basketball rim has a radius of 9 inches. Find the circumference of the rim. Round to the nearest tenth. Use 3.14 for π.

6. The diameter of a circular swimming pool is 12 feet. Find its circumference. Use 3.14 for π.

7. The diameter of the U.S. Capitol Building's dome is 96 feet at its widest point. Find its circumference. Use 3.14 for π.

Find the area of each circle with the given radius or diameter. Use 3.14 for π.

8. $r = 7$ yd

9. $d = 5$ m

10. $d = 16$ ft

11. A drum has a diameter of 10 inches. Find the area of the top of the drum. Use 3.14 for π.

12. The circumference of a quarter is about 76 mm. What is the area? Round to the nearest tenth.

Algebra Find the area of the circle with the given circumference *C*. Use 3.14 for π.

13. $C = 31.4$ ft

14. $C = 21.98$ ft

15. $C = 69.08$ ft

16. A Ferris wheel has a diameter of 56 ft. How far will a rider travel during a 4-minute ride if the wheel rotates once every 20 seconds? Use $\frac{22}{7}$ for π.

17. A giant water lily pad is shaped like a circle with a diameter of up to 5 feet. Find the circumference and area of the pad. Round to the nearest tenth.

18. A pizza parlor offers pizzas with diameters of 8 in., 10 in., and 12 in. Find the area of each size pizza. Round to the nearest tenth. If the pizzas cost $9, $12, and $18 respectively, which is the better buy?

19. Critical Thinking Which do you think would seat more people, a 4 ft by 6 ft rectangular table or a circular table with a diameter of 6 ft? How many people would you sit at each table? Explain your reasoning.

20. You can estimate a tree's age in years by using the formula $a = \frac{r}{w}$, where r is the tree's radius without bark and w is the average thickness of the tree's rings. The circumference of a white oak tree is 100 inches. The bark is 0.5 in. thick, and the average thickness of a ring is 0.2 in. Estimate the tree's age and the area enclosed by the outer circumference of the widest ring.

21. Multi-Step A circular track for a model train has a diameter of 8.5 feet. The train moves around the track at a constant speed of 0.7 ft/s.

a. To the nearest foot, how far does the train travel when it goes completely around the track 10 times?

b. To the nearest minute, how long does it take the train to go completely around the track 10 times?

22. The Parthenon is a Greek temple dating to about 445 BCE. The temple features 46 Doric columns, which are roughly cylindrical. The circumference of each column at the base is about 5.65 meters. What is the approximate diameter of each column? Round to the nearest tenth.

23. Explain the Error A circle has a diameter of 2π in. Which calculation of the area is incorrect? Explain.

A The circumference is 2π in., so the diameter is 2 in. The area is $A = \pi(2^2) = 4\pi$ in^2.

B The circumference is 2π in., so the radius is 1 in. The area is $A = \pi(1^2) = \pi$ in^2.

24. Write About It The center of each circle in the figure lies on the number line. Describe the relationship between the circumference of the largest circle and the circumferences of the four smaller circles.

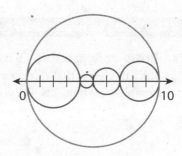

25. Find the diameter of a data storage disk with an area 113.1 cm^2.

26. Which of the following ratios can be derived from the formula for the circumference of a circle? Select all that apply.

A. $\dfrac{C}{d}$

B. $\dfrac{C}{2r}$

C. $\dfrac{C}{\pi}$

D. $\dfrac{C}{2\pi}$

E. $\dfrac{C}{2c}$

27. A meteorologist measured the eyes of hurricanes to be 15 to 20 miles in diameter during one season. What is the range of areas of the land underneath the eyes of the hurricanes?

28. A circle with a 6 in. diameter is stamped out of a rectangular piece of metal as shown. Find the area of the remaining piece of metal. Use 3.14 for π.

14 in.

8 in.

29. Critique Reasoning A standard bicycle wheel has a diameter of 26 inches. A student claims that during a one-mile bike ride the wheel makes more than 1000 complete revolutions. Do you agree or disagree? Explain. (*Hint:* 1 mile = 5280 feet)

30. Algebra A graphic artist created a company logo from two tangent circles whose diameters are in the ratio 3:2. What percent of the total logo is the area of the region outside of the smaller circle?

31. Communicate Mathematical Ideas In the figure, $\overline{AB}$ is a diameter of circle C, D is the midpoint of $\overline{AC}$, and E is the midpoint of $\overline{AD}$. How does the circumference of circle E compare to the circumference of circle C? Explain.

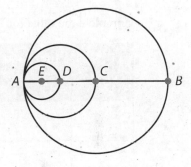

32. Critical Thinking Evelyn divides the circle and rearranges the pieces to make a shape that resembles a parallelogram.

She then divides the circle into more pieces and rearranges them into a shape that resembles a parallelogram. She thinks that the area of the new parallelogram will be closer to the area of a circle. Is she correct? Explain.

Lesson Performance Task

In the lesson, you saw that the more wedges into which you divide a circle, the more closely each wedge resembles a triangle, and the closer to the area of a circle the area of the reassembled wedges becomes. In the branch of mathematics called calculus, this process is called finding a *limit*. Even though you can't cut a circle into millions of tiny wedges to calculate the actual area of the circle, you can see what the area is going to be long before that, by spotting a pattern. You can apply this method in many ways, some of them unexpected.

Mac is a race walker. He is training for a race. He has decided that in the weeks leading up to the race, he'll work up to a level where he is walking 20 kilometers a day. His plan is to walk 10 kilometers the first day of training and increase the distance he walks each day until he reaches his goal.

1. Complete the table for Mac's first 6 days of training.

Day	Increase in distance walked from the day before (in kilometers)	Total distance walked that day (in kilometers)
1	10	10
2	5	$10 + 5 = \boxed{}$
3	2.5	$\boxed{} + 2.5 = \boxed{}$
4		
5		
6		

2. Describe your results in relation to Mac's plan to reach a level where he walks 20 kilometers a day.

3. Suppose Mac continues his training plan. Will Mac ever reach his goal?

16.2 Arc Length and Radian Measure

Essential Question: How do you find the length of an arc?

⊘ Explore   Deriving the Formula for Arc Length

An **arc** is an unbroken part of a circle consisting of two points called the endpoints and all the points on the circle between them. **Arc length** is understood to be the distance along a circular arc measured in linear units (such as feet or centimeters). You can use proportional reasoning to find arc length.

Find the arc length of $\overset{\frown}{AB}$. Express your answer in terms of π and rounded to the nearest tenth.

(A) First find the circumference of the circle.

$C = 2\pi r$ Substitute the radius, 9, for r.

$C = \boxed{}$

(B) The entire circle has 360°. Therefore, the arc's length is $\dfrac{60}{360}$ or $\dfrac{1}{6}$ of the circumference.

Fill in the blanks to find the arc length.

Arc length of $\overset{\frown}{AB} = \dfrac{1}{6} \cdot$ _____   Arc length is $\dfrac{1}{6}$ of the circumference.

$= $ _____   Multiply.

$\approx$ _____   Use a calculator to evaluate. Then round.

So, the arc length of $\overset{\frown}{AB}$ is _____ or _____.

Reflect

1. How could you use the reasoning process you used above to find the length of an arc of the circle that measures $m°$?

_____

_____

You were able to find an arc length using concepts of circumference. Using the same reasoning results in the formula for finding arc length.

Arc Length

The arc length, s, of an arc with measure $m°$ and radius r is given by the formula $s = \dfrac{m}{360} \cdot 2\pi r$.

Example 1 Find the arc length.

(A) On a clock face, the minute hand of a clock is 10 inches long. To the nearest tenth of an inch, how far does the tip of the minute hand travel as the time progresses from 12:00 to 12:15?

The minute hand moves 15 minutes.

$\dfrac{15 \text{ minutes}}{60 \text{ minutes}} = \dfrac{1}{4}$ so the central angle formed is $\dfrac{1}{4} \cdot 360° = 90°$.

$s = \dfrac{m}{360} \cdot 2\pi r$ Use the formula for arc length.

$= \dfrac{90}{360} \cdot 2\pi(10)$ Substitute 10 for r and 90 for m.

$= 5\pi$ Simplify.

≈ 15.7 in.   Simplify.

(B) The minute hand of a clock is 6 inches long. To the nearest tenth of an inch, how far does the tip of the minute hand travel as the time progresses from 12:00 to 12:30?

The minute hand moves 30 minutes.

$\dfrac{30 \text{ minutes}}{60 \text{ minutes}} = \boxed{}$, so the central angle formed is $\dfrac{1}{2} \cdot \boxed{} = \boxed{}$.

$s = \dfrac{m}{360} \cdot \underline{}$ Use the formula for arc length.

                              Substitute _____ for r and _____ for m.

$= \dfrac{\boxed{}}{360} \cdot 2\pi\left(\boxed{}\right)$

$= \boxed{}$ Simplify.

$\approx \boxed{}$ in.   Simplify.

The length of the arc is $\boxed{}$ inches.

Reflect

2. Discussion Why does the formula represent the length of an arc of a circle?

_____

_____

_____

3. The minute hand of a clock is 8 inches long. To the nearest tenth of an inch, how far does the tip of the minute hand travel as the time progresses from 12:00 to 12:45?

🔧 Explain 2 Investigating Arc Lengths in Concentric Circles

Consider a set of concentric circles with center O and radius 1, 2, and 3, and so on. The central angle shown in the figure is a right angle and it cuts off arcs that measure 90°.

Example 2 Find and graph arc lengths for different radii.

(A) For each value of the radius r listed in the table below, find the corresponding arc length. Write the length in terms of π and rounded to the nearest hundredth.

For example, when $r = 1$, the arc length is $\frac{90}{360} \cdot 2\pi(1) = \frac{1}{2}\pi \approx 1.57$.

Radius r	1	2	3	4	5
Arc length s in terms of π	$\frac{1}{2}\pi$				
Arc length s to the nearest hundredth	1.57				

(B) Plot the ordered pairs from your table on the coordinate plane.

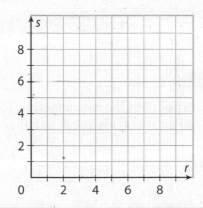

What do you notice about the points?

_____

What type of relationship is the relationship between arc length and radius?

_____

What is the constant of proportionality for this relationship?

_____

4. What happens to the arc length when you double the radius? How is this connected to the idea that all circles are similar?

_____

_____

⚙ Explain 3 Converting Radian Measure

As you discovered in Explain 2, when the central angle is fixed at $m°$, the length of the arc cut off by a central angle is proportional to (or varies directly with) the radius. In fact, you can see that the formula for arc length is a proportional relationship when m is fixed.

$$s = \underbrace{\frac{m}{360}} \cdot 2\pi r$$

constant of proportionality

The constant of proportionality for the proportional relationship is $\frac{m}{360} \cdot 2\pi$. This constant of proportionality is defined to be the **radian measure** of the angle.

Example 3 **Convert each angle measure to radian measure.**

Ⓐ 180°

To convert to a radian measure, let $m = 180$ in the expression $\frac{m}{360} \cdot 2\pi$.

$180° = \dfrac{180}{360} \cdot 2\pi$ Substitute 180 for m.

     $= \pi$ radians   Simplify.

Ⓑ 60°

To convert to a radian measure, let $m = 60$ in the expression $\frac{m}{360} \cdot 2\pi$.

$60° = \dfrac{\boxed{}}{360} \cdot 2\pi$ Substitute _____ for m.

    $= \boxed{}$ radians   Simplify.

Reflect

5. Explain why the radian measure for an angle $m°$ is sometimes defined as the length of the arc cut off on a circle of radius 1 by a central angle of $m°$.

_____

_____

6. Explain how to find the degree measure of an angle whose radian measure is $\dfrac{\pi}{4}$.

_____

_____

Convert each angle measure to radian measure.

7. 90°   **8.** 45°

Elaborate

9. You know that 360° is the degree measure that corresponds to a full circle. What is the radian measure that corresponds to a full circle?

_____

10. Suppose you are given that the measure in radians of an arc of a circle with radius r is θ. How can you find the length of the arc in radians?

_____

11. Essential Question Check-In What two pieces of information do you need to calculate arc length?

_____

⭐ Evaluate: Homework and Practice

- Online Homework
- Hints and Help
- Extra Practice

Use the formula, $s = \dfrac{m}{360} \cdot 2\pi r$, to answer the questions.

1. What part of the circle does the expression $2\pi r$ represent?

2. What part of the circle does $\dfrac{m}{360}$ represent?

3. What part of the circle does the expression $2r$ represent?

4. Critical Thinking Suppose an arc were intercepted by a central angle measuring 15°. The diameter of the circle is 9 cm. Can both of these values be substituted into the arc length formula? Explain.

Find the arc length of $\overset{\frown}{AB}$ to the nearest tenth.

5.

6.

7.

8. The minute hand of a clock is 5 inches long. To the nearest tenth of an inch, how far does the tip of the minute hand travel as the time progresses from 12:00 to 12:25?

9. The circles are concentric. Find the length of the intercepted arc in the larger circle.

10. The circles are concentric. Find the length of $\overset{\frown}{PQ}$

11. Two arcs of concentric circles are intercepted by the same central angle. The resulting arc length of the arc of the larger circle is 16 m and the radius of the larger circle is 12 m. The radius of the smaller circle is 7.5 m. Find the length of the corresponding arc of the smaller circle.

12. Two arcs of concentric circles are intercepted by the same central angle. The resulting arc length of the arc of the smaller circle is 36 ft and its radius is 30 ft. The radius of the larger circle is 45 ft. Find the length of the corresponding arc of the larger circle.

Convert each angle measure to radian measure.

13. 40°

14. 80°

15. 100°

16. 12°

17. It is convenient to know the radian measure for benchmark angles such as 0°, 30°, 45°, and so on. Complete the table by finding the radian measure for each of the given benchmark angles.

Benchmark Angles								
Degree Measure	0°	30°	45°	60°	90°	120°	135°	150°	180°
Radian Measure									

Convert each radian measure to degree measure.

18. $\dfrac{5\pi}{8}$

19. $\dfrac{8\pi}{9}$

20. In the diagram, $\overline{WY}$, and $\overline{XZ}$ are diameters of $\odot T$, and $WY = XZ = 6$.
If $m\widehat{XY} = 140°$, what is the length of $\widehat{YZ}$? Select all that apply.

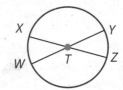

A. $\dfrac{4\pi}{6}$

B. $\dfrac{4\pi}{3}$

C. $\dfrac{2}{3}\pi$

D. 4π

E. 6π

21. Algebra The length of $\widehat{TS}$ is 12 in. Find the length of $\widehat{RS}$.

22. Multi-Step The diagram shows the plan for a putting a decorative trim around a corner desk. The trim will be 4-inch high around the perimeter of the desk. The curve is one quarter of the circumference of a circle. Find the length of trim needed to the nearest half foot.

23. **Explain the Error** A student was asked to find the arc length of $\overset{\frown}{PQ}$. The student's work is shown. Explain the student's error and give the correct arc length.

The entire circumference is $2\pi \cdot 16 = 32\pi$ and $45°$ is $\frac{1}{8}$ of the circle, so the arc length is $\frac{1}{8} \cdot 32\pi = 4\pi$ m.

H.O.T. Focus on Higher Order Thinking

24. **Critique Reasoning** A friend tells you two arcs from different circles have the same arc length if their central angles are equal. Is your friend correct? Explain your reasoning.

25. **Multi-Step** A carpenter is making a tray to fit between two circular pillars in the shape of the shaded area as shown. She is using a jigsaw to cut along the edge of the tray. What is the length of the cut encompassing the tray? Round to the nearest half foot.

26. **Critical Thinking** The pedals of a penny-farthing Bicycle are directly connected to the front wheel.

   a. Suppose a penny-farthing bicycle has a front wheel with a diameter of 5 ft. To the nearest tenth of a foot, how far does the bike move when you turn the pedals through an angle of 90°?

   b. Through what angle should you turn the pedals in order to move forward by a distance of 4.5 ft? Round to the nearest degree.

Lesson Performance Task

The latitude of a point is a measure of its position north or south on the Earth's surface. Latitudes North (N) are measured from 0° N at the equator to 90° N at the North Pole. Latitudes South (S) are measured from 0° S at the equator to 90° S at the South Pole.

The figure shows the latitudes of Washington, D.C. and Lima, Peru. The radius of the Earth is approximately 6,370 kilometers.

1. Find the angle at the Earth's center between radii drawn to Washington and Lima.

2. Find the distance between Washington and Lima. Show your work.

3. A point's longitude is a measure of its position east or west on the Earth's surface. In order for your calculation of the distance between Washington and Lima to be accurate, what must be true about the longitudes of the two cities?

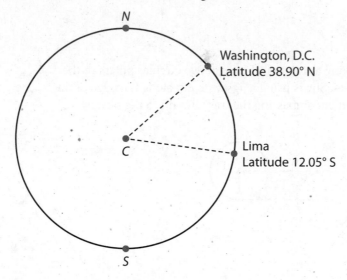

16.3 Sector Area

Essential Question: How do you find the area of a sector of a circle?

Resource
Locker

⊚ Explore   Derive the Formula for the Area of a Sector

A **sector** of a circle is a region bounded by two radii and their intercepted arc. A sector is named by the endpoints of the arc and the center of the circle. For example, the figure shows sector *POQ*.

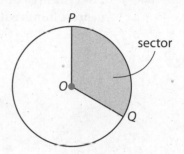

sector

In the same way that you used proportional reasoning to find the length of an arc, you can use proportional reasoning to find the area of a sector.

Find the area of sector *AOB*. Express your answer in terms of π and rounded to the nearest tenth.

Ⓐ First find the area of the circle.

$A = \pi r^2 = \pi(\underline{\quad})^2$

$= \underline{\quad}$

15 mm

O   120°

B

Ⓑ The entire circle is 360°, but $\angle AOB$ measures 120°. Therefore, the sector's area is $\frac{120}{360}$ or $\frac{1}{3}$ of the circle's area.

Area of sector $AOB = \frac{1}{3} \cdot$ _____   The area is $\frac{1}{3}$ of the circle's area.

$= \underline{\quad}$ Simplify.

$= \underline{\quad}$ Use a calculator to evaluate. Then round.

So, the area of sector *AOB* is _____ or _____.

Reflect

1. How could you use the above process to find the area of a sector of the circle whose central angle measures $m°$?

_____

2. **Make a Conjecture** What do you think is the formula for the area of a sector with a central angle of $m°$ and radius *r*?

_____

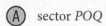

Explain 1   Using the Formula for the Area of a Sector

The proportional reasoning process you used in the Explore can be generalized. Given a sector with a central angle of $m°$ and radius r, the area of the entire circle is πr^2 and the area of the sector is $\frac{m}{360}$ times the circle's area. This gives the following formula.

Area of a Sector
The area A of a sector with a central angle of $m°$ of a circle with radius r is given by $A = \frac{m}{360} \cdot \pi r^2$

Example 1   Find the area of each sector, as a multiple of π and to the nearest hundredth.

Ⓐ   sector POQ

$$A = \frac{m}{360} \cdot \pi r^2$$

$$= \frac{210}{360} \cdot \pi (3)^2$$

$$= \frac{7}{12} \cdot 9\pi$$

$$= \frac{21}{4}\pi$$

$$\approx 16.49 \text{ in}^2$$

Ⓑ   sector HGJ

$$A = \frac{m}{360} \cdot \pi r^2$$

$$= \frac{\boxed{}}{360} \cdot \pi \left(\boxed{}\right)^2$$

$$= \boxed{} \cdot \boxed{}\ \pi$$

$$= \boxed{}\ \pi$$

$$\approx \boxed{}\ \text{m}^2$$

Reflect

3.   **Discussion** Your friend said that the value of $m°$ in the formula for the area of a sector can never be larger than 360°. Do you agree or disagree? Explain your reasoning.

_____

_____

Find the area of each sector, as a multiple of π and to the nearest hundredth.

4. sector AOB

A — 1.6 cm — O — B

5. sector POQ

24 mm
O
22.5°
P
Q

⚙ **Explain 2** | **Applying the Formula for the Area of a Sector**

You can apply the formula for the area of a sector to real-world problems.

Example 2 | **Find the area described.**

Ⓐ A beam from a lighthouse is visible for a distance of 3 mi. To the nearest square mile, what is the area covered by the beam as it sweeps in an arc of 150°?

$A = \dfrac{m}{360} \cdot \pi r^2$

$= \dfrac{150}{360} \cdot \pi(3)^2$

$= \dfrac{5}{12} \cdot 9\pi$

$= 3.75\pi \approx 12 \text{ mi}^2$

Ⓑ A circular plot with a 180 foot diameter is watered by a spray irrigation system. To the nearest square foot, what is the area that is watered as the sprinkler rotates through an angle of 50°?

$d = 180$ ft, so $r =$ _____ ft

$A = \dfrac{m}{360} \cdot \pi r^2$

$= \dfrac{\boxed{}}{360} \cdot \pi\left(\boxed{}\right)^2$

$= \boxed{} \cdot \boxed{} \; \pi$

$= \boxed{} \; \pi \approx \boxed{} \; \text{ft}^2$

6. To the nearest square foot, what is the area watered in Example 2B as the sprinkler rotates through a semicircle?

💬 Elaborate

7. **Discussion** When can you use proportional reasoning to find the area of a sector without knowing or finding its central angle? Explain your reasoning by giving an example.

_____

_____

_____

_____

_____

8. **Essential Question Check-In** What information do you need to find the area of a sector?

_____

☆ Evaluate: Homework and Practice

- Online Homework
- Hints and Help
- Extra Practice

1. The region within a circle that is bounded by two radii and an arc is called a _____.

2. Suppose you know the area and the measure of the central angle of a sector. Describe the process of finding the area of the sector.

3. What is the formula for the area of a circle? Define all variables in the formula.

4. If the angle of a sector measures 45°, what fraction of the circle is the sector?

Find the area of sector *AOB*. Express your answer in terms of π and rounded to the nearest tenth.

5.

6.

7.

8.

9.

10.

11. A round pizza is cut into congruent sectors. If the angle measure of the pizza slice is 20°, how many pieces are in the whole pizza?

12. The area of a piece of pie in the shape of a sector is 7.1 in². The angle of the sector is 40°.

a. What is the area of the entire pie?

b. What is the diameter of the pie?

13. A *lunette* is a semicircular window that is sometimes placed above a doorway or above a rectangular window. The diameter of the lunette is 40 inches. To the nearest square inch, what is the area of the lunette?

Find the area of each sector. Give your answer in terms of π and rounded to the nearest hundredth.

14. sector *PQR*

15. sector *JKL*

16. sector *ABC*

17. sector *RST*

18. The beam from a lighthouse is visible for a distance of 15 mi. To the nearest square mile, what is the area covered by the beam as it sweeps in an arc of 270°?

19. The radius of circle *O* is 6 mm. The area of sector *AOB* is $\frac{9}{2}\pi$ mm². Explain how to find m∠*AOB*.

The Artisan Pizza Co sells take-out pizza in two shapes: an "individual" 6-in. square slice and a circular "party" wheel with an 18 in. diameter. The party wheel is cut into 8 slices/sectors for the customer. An individual slice of the party wheel costs $2.95 and the entire party wheel costs $15.95.

20. Which is larger, the square slice or one sector of the wheel?

21. Which option is the better value, buying by the slice or buying the entire wheel?

22. Greek mathematicians studied the *salinon*, a figure bounded by four semicircles. What is the area of this salinon to the nearest tenth of a square inch?

23. Which of the following express the measure of the angle of a sector, m, as a ratio between the area of the sector and the radius of the circle? Select all that apply.

A. $\dfrac{360\pi}{Ar^2}$

B. $\dfrac{360\,A}{\pi r^2}$

C. $360r^2 \cdot \dfrac{A}{\pi}$

D. $\dfrac{A\pi r^2}{360}$

E. $\dfrac{Ar^2}{360\pi}$

F. $360A \cdot \dfrac{1}{\pi r^2}$

24. Algebra The table shows how students get to school.

Methods	% of Students
Bus	65%
Walk	25%
Other	10%

a. Explain why a circle graph is appropriate for the data.

b. Use a proportion to find the measure of the central angle for each sector. Then use a protractor and a compass to draw the circle graph.

c. Find the area of each sector. Use a radius of 2 inches.

Multi-Step A *segment of a circle* is a region bounded by an arc and its chord. **Find the area of each segment to the nearest hundredth.**

area of segment = area of sector − area of triangle

25.

26.

27. **Critique Reasoning** A student claims that when you double the radius of a sector while keeping the measure of the central angle constant, you double the area of the sector. Do you agree or disagree? Explain

28. **Multi-Step** The exclamation point (!) on a billboard consists of a circle sector and circle. The radius of the sector is 9 ft, and the radius of the circle is 1.5 ft. The angle of the sector is 24°. What is the total area of the exclamation point on the billboard? Round to the nearest tenth.

9 ft

24°

1.5 ft

29. **Analyze Relationships** Compare finding arc length to finding the area of a sector. Name any common and different processes.

30. **Critique Reasoning** Melody says that she needs only to know the length of an arc and radius of a circle to find the area of the corresponding sector. If arc length is L and sector area is A, then $A = \frac{2L}{r}$. Is she correct? Justify your answer.

Lesson Performance Task

The planets orbit the Sun not in circles but in ellipses, which are "flattened" circles. The Earth's orbit, however, isn't flattened much. Its greatest distance from the Sun, 94.5 million miles, differs from its least distance, 91.4 million miles, by only about 3%.

To answer the following questions, make the following assumptions:

a. Summer includes all of the days from June 21 through September 21. During that time Earth travels in a circular orbit with a radius of 94.5 million miles. A year lasts 365 days.

b. Winter includes all of the days from December 21 through March 20. During that time Earth travels in a circular orbit with a radius of 91.4 million miles. The year you will consider lasts 365 days and is not a leap year.

Solve. Show your work. Use 3.14 for π.

1. Find the distances that the Earth travels in summer and in winter. Give your answers in millions of miles rounded to the nearest tenth.

2. Find the Earth's average rate of speed in summer and in winter. Give your answers in millions of miles per day rounded to the nearest hundredth.

3. Find the areas of the sectors that the Earth traverses in summer and in winter. Give your answers in millions of miles squared rounded to the nearest tenth.

Arc Length and Sector Area

Essential Question: How can the arc length and sector area of a circle be used to solve a real-world problem? How are they related?

(Lesson 16.1)

The circumference of a tire is 90 inches. What is its radius? Round to the nearest inch.

$C = 2\pi r$	Write the circumference formula.
$90 = 2\pi r$	Substitute the circumference.
$\dfrac{90}{2\pi} = r$	Simplify.
$14 \text{ in} \approx r$	Substitute 3.14 for π to approximate the solution.

(Lesson 16.2)

Find the arc length of an arc that measures 150° in a circle with a radius of 8 meters. Give your answer in terms of π.

$A = \dfrac{m}{360} \cdot 2\pi r$	Write the arc length formula.
$A = \dfrac{150}{360} \cdot 2\pi 8$	Substitute the angle measure and radius.
$A = \dfrac{20}{3}\pi$	Simplify.

(Lesson 16.3)

A sandwich shop sells sandwiches on two types of bread: a 9-inch square flatbread and a round roll with a 4-inch radius. Which type of bread is larger?

$A = s^2$	Write the area of a square.
$A = (9\,\text{in})^2$	Substitute the side length of the flatbread.
$A = 81\,\text{in}^2$	Simplify.
$A = \pi r^2$	Write the area of a circle.
$A = \pi(4)^2 \text{in}^2$	Substitute the radius of the roll.
$A = 16\pi\,\text{in}^2$	Simplify.
$A \approx 50.24\,\text{in}^2$	Substitute 3.14 for π to approximate the solution.

The flatbread is larger than the roll.

EXERCISES

Find the radius of the circle with the given circumference. *(Lesson 16.1)*

1. $C = 15$ in

2. $C = \pi$ cm

Find the arc length given the angle measure and radius of the circle. Give your answer in terms of π. *(Lesson 16.2)*

3. $m = 180°, r = 4$ inches

Apply the formula for the area of a sector to solve the real-world problem. *(Lesson 16.3)*

4. A paper airplane can be made out of two different pieces of paper: a circular piece 10 inches wide and a square piece 11 inches wide. Which piece of paper will provide the greater area for flight?

MODULE PERFORMANCE TASK

What's the Better Deal on Pizza?

You are ordering pizza and you have two choices: a slice of pizza from a large pizza with a diameter of 22 inches or an entire personal-size pizza that has a diameter of 6 inches. The slice costs $4.95, and the smaller pizza costs $3.75. Assuming that the large pizza is cut into 8 slices, will you get more pizza for your money by buying one slice of the larger pizza or by buying the personal-size pizza?

Use your own paper to complete the task. Be sure to write down all of your assumptions and data. Then use words, diagrams, numbers, or geometry to explain how you came to your conclusion.

16.1–16.3 Arc Length and Sector Area

• Online Homework
• Hints and Help
• Extra Practice

Apply the appropriate area formula. *(Lesson 16.1)*

1. At a campground, the area of a rectangular fire pit is 5 feet by 4 feet. What is the area of the largest circular fire than can be made in this fire pit? Round to the nearest square inch.

Find the arc length. Give your answer in terms of π and round to the nearest hundredth. *(Lesson 16.2)*

2. $\overset{\frown}{AB}$

Apply the formula for the area of a sector to solve the real-world problem. *(Lesson 16.3)*

3. A Mexican restaurant sells quesadillas in two sizes: a "large" 10–inch round quesadilla and a "small" 6–inch round quesadilla. Which is larger, half of the 10-inch quesadilla or the entire 6-inch quesadilla?

ESSENTIAL QUESTION

4. What is the relationship between the arc length and sector area of a circle?

Assessment Readiness

SELECTED RESPONSE

1. Consider each equation. Does it show a true relationship between degree measure and radian measure? Select Yes or No for A–C.

   A. $\frac{5\pi}{12}$ radians $= 75°$ ◯ Yes   ◯ No

   B. $\frac{\pi}{2}$ radians $= 180°$ ◯ Yes   ◯ No

   C. $\frac{\pi}{3}$ radians $= 60°$ ◯ Yes   ◯ No

2. Consider a circle with a radius of 2 meters that has an arc angle of 90°. Choose True or False for each statement.

   A. The arc measure is 90°.   ◯ True   ◯ False

   B. The circumference and the area of this circle, taking away the units, are equal.   ◯ True   ◯ False

   C. The arc length is π meters.   ◯ True   ◯ False

3. $\triangle ABC$ is an equilateral triangle, $AB = 3x + 27$, and $BC = 5x - 9$. Choose True or False for each statement.

   A. $x = 18$ ◯ True   ◯ False

   B. The length of one side of the triangle is 162 units.   ◯ True   ◯ False

   C. The perimeter of the triangle is 243 units.   ◯ True   ◯ False

4. Write an equation that represents the circumference of a circle with a radius of 6 feet. What is the diameter of the circle?

5. Given the sector area, how can the radius be determined? From the radius, how can the arc length be determined?

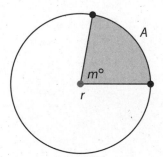

Equations of Circles and Parabolas

Essential Question: How can you use equations of circles and parabolas to solve real-world problems?

REAL WORLD VIDEO
Check out some of the mathematics involved in the flight of rescue helicopters, such as this H-65 helicopter flown by the United States Coast Guard.

MODULE PERFORMANCE TASK PREVIEW

Rescue at Sea

One of the critical functions of the United States Coast Guard is carrying out search and rescue missions at sea. Teams of H-65 helicopters, each carrying two pilots, a flight mechanic, and a rescue swimmer, conduct coordinated sweeps over huge areas of ocean in search of the missing craft. The mathematics involved in executing such missions is complex, but you'll learn some of the basics in this module. Then you'll plan an ocean rescue of your own.

Complete these exercises to review skills you will need for this module.

Circumference

• Online Homework
• Hints and Help
• Extra Practice

Example 1   The center of a circle is $(-4, 1)$, and a point on the circle is $(1, -11)$. Find the circumference of the circle to the nearest tenth.

The circumference formula is $C = 2\pi r$.

$r = \sqrt{(-4-1)^2 + (1-(-11))^2} = 13$ Use the distance formula.

$C = 2\pi(13)$ Substitute.

$C = 26\pi$, or about 81.7.   Simplify.

The center and a point on a circle are given. Find the circumference to the nearest tenth.

1. center: $(5, -5)$
    point on the circle: $(25, 10)$

2. center: $(-12, -20)$
    point on the circle: $(3, -12)$

3. center: $(8, 8)$
    point on the circle: $(-2, 1)$

Characteristics of Quadratic Functions

Example 2   The vertex of a quadratic function is at $(2, 5)$ and one of the x-intercepts is at $(-1, 0)$. Find the other x-intercept.

The missing x-intercept is of the form $(x, 0)$. The midpoint between the two x-intercepts lies on the axis of symmetry, which passes through the vertex of the parabola. The x-value of the vertex is 2, so the axis of symmetry is $x = 2$, and the midpoint between the intercepts is $(2, 0)$. Therefore, 2 is the mean of the x-values of the intercepts: $2 = \dfrac{x + (-1)}{2}$, so $x = 5$. The missing x-intercept is $(5, 0)$.

The vertex and one x-intercept are given. Find the other x-intercept.

4. $(-3, 4), (6, 0)$

5. $(8, 1), (7, 0)$

6. $(-9 -1), (-4, 0)$

17.1 Equation of a Circle

Essential Question: How can you write the equation of a circle if you know its radius and the coordinates of its center?

Resource
Locker

⊘ Explore   Deriving the Equation of a Circle

You have already worked with circles in several earlier lessons. Now you will investigate circles in a coordinate plane and learn how to write an equation of a circle.

We can define a **circle** as the set of all points in the coordinate plane that are a fixed distance r from the center (h, k).

Consider the circle in a coordinate plane that has its center at $C(h, k)$ and that has radius r.

Ⓐ Let P be any point on the circle and let the coordinates of P be (x, y).

Create a right triangle by drawing a horizontal line through C and a vertical line through P, as shown.

What are the coordinates of point A? _____ Explain how you found the coordinates of A.

_____

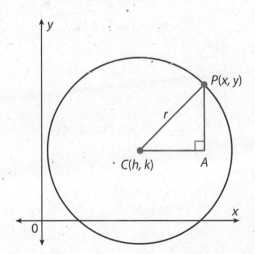

Ⓑ Use absolute value to write expressions for the lengths of the legs of $\triangle CAP$.

$CA =$ _____; $PA =$ _____

Ⓒ Use the Pythagorean Theorem to write a relationship among the side lengths of $\triangle CAP$.

_____ + _____ = _____ .

1. Compare your work with that of other students. Then, write an equation for the circle with center $C(h, k)$ and radius r.

_____

2. Why do you need absolute values when you write expressions for the lengths of the legs in Step B, but not when you write the relationship among the side lengths in Step C?

_____

_____

3. Suppose a circle has its center at the origin. What is the equation of the circle in this case?

_____

⊘ Explain 1 Writing the Equation of a Circle

You can write the equation of a circle given its coordinates and radius.

> **Equation of a Circle**
>
> The equation of a circle with center (h, k) and radius r is $(x - h)^2 + (y - k)^2 = r^2$.

Example 1 Write the equation of the circle with the given center and radius.

(A) Center: $(-2, 5)$; radius: 3

$(x - h)^2 + (y - k)^2 = r^2$ Write the general equation of a circle.

$(x - (-2))^2 + (y - 5)^2 = 3^2$ Substitute -2 for h, 5 for k, and 3 for r.

$(x + 2)^2 + (y - 5)^2 = 9$ Simplify.

(B) Center: $(4, -1)$; radius: $\sqrt{5}$

$(x - h)^2 + (y - k)^2 = r^2$ Write the general equation of a circle.

$\left(x - \boxed{}\right)^2 + \left(y - \boxed{}\right)^2 = \boxed{}$ Substitute $\boxed{}$ for h, $\boxed{}$ for k, and $\boxed{}$ for r.

$\left(x \boxed{}\right)^2 + \left(y \boxed{}\right)^2 = \boxed{}$ Simplify.

4. Suppose the circle with equation $(x - 2)^2 + (y + 4)^2 = 7$ is translated by $(x, y) \rightarrow (x + 3, y - 1)$. What is the equation of the image of the circle? Explain.

_____

_____

_____

Write the equation of the circle with the given center and radius.

5. Center: $(4, 3)$; radius: 4

6. Center: $(-1, -1)$; radius: $\sqrt{3}$

🔧 Explain 2   Finding the Center and Radius of a Circle

Sometimes you may find an equation of a circle in a different form. In that case, you may need to rewrite the equation to determine the circle's center and radius. You can use the process of completing the square to do so.

Example 2   Find the center and radius of the circle with the given equation. Then graph the circle.

(A) $x^2 - 4x + y^2 + 2y = 20$

Step 1 Complete the square twice to write the equation in the form $(x - h)^2 + (y - k)^2 = r^2$.

$x^2 - 4x + (\ )^2 + y^2 + 2y + (\ )^2 = 20 + (\ )^2$ Set up to complete the square.

$x^2 - 4x + \left(\dfrac{-4}{2}\right)^2 + y^2 + 2y + \left(\dfrac{2}{2}\right)^2 = 20 + \left(\dfrac{-4}{2}\right)^2 + \left(\dfrac{2}{2}\right)^2$ Add $\left(\dfrac{-4}{2}\right)^2$ and $\left(\dfrac{2}{2}\right)^2$ to both sides.

$x^2 - 4x + 4 + y^2 + 2y + 1 = 20 + 5$ Simplify.

$(x - 2)^2 + (y + 1)^2 = 25$ Factor

Step 2 Identify h, k, and r to determine the center and radius.

$h = 2 \qquad k = -1 \qquad r = \sqrt{25} = 5$

So, the center is $(2, -1)$ and the radius is 5.

Step 3 Graph the circle.

- Locate the center of the circle.

- Place the point of your compass at the center

- Open the compass to the radius.

- Use the compass to draw the circle.

$x^2 + 6x + y^2 - 4y + 4 = 0$

Step 1 Complete the square twice to write the equation in the form $(x - h)^2 + (y - k)^2 = r^2$.

$$x^2 + 6x + \boxed{}^2 + y^2 - 4y + \boxed{}^2 = -4 + \boxed{}^2 + \boxed{}^2 \quad \text{Add } \boxed{}^2 \text{ and } \boxed{}^2$$

to both sides.

Subtract 4 from both sides.

$$x^2 + 6x + \boxed{} + y^2 - 4y + \boxed{} = -4 + \boxed{} \quad \text{Simplify.}$$

$$\left(x \; \boxed{}\right)^2 + \left(y \; \boxed{}\right)^2 = \boxed{} \quad \text{Factor.}$$

Step 2 Identify h, k, and r to determine the center and radius.

$$h = \boxed{} \qquad k = \boxed{} \qquad r = \sqrt{\boxed{}} = \boxed{}$$

So, the center is $\left(\boxed{}, \boxed{}\right)$ and the radius is $\boxed{}$.

Step 3 Graph the circle.

- Locate the center of the circle.

- Place the point of your compass at the center

- Open the compass to the radius.

- Use the compass to draw the circle.

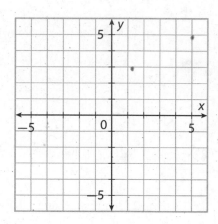

Reflect

7. How can you check your graph by testing specific points from the graph in the original equation? Give an example.

_____

_____

Your Turn

8. Find the center and radius of the circle with the equation.
$x^2 + 2x + y^2 - 8y + 13 = 0$. Then graph the circle.

9. Find the center and radius of the circle with the equation $x^2 + y^2 + 4y = 5$. Then graph the circle.

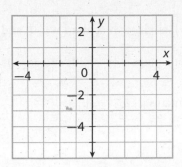

🞥 Explain 3 Writing a Coordinate Proof

You can use a coordinate proof to determine whether or not a given point lies on a given circle in the coordinate plane.

Example 3 **Prove or disprove that the given point lies on the given circle.**

(A) Point $(3, \sqrt{7})$ circle centered at the origin and containing the point $(-4, 0)$

Step 1 Plot a point at the origin and at $(-4, 0)$. Use these to help you draw the circle centered at the origin that contains $(-4, 0)$.

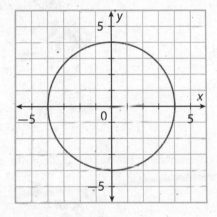

Step 2 Determine the radius: $r = 4$

Step 3 Use the radius and the coordinates of the center to write the equation of the circle.

$(x - h)^2 + (y - k)^2 = r^2$ Write the equation of the circle.

$(x - 0)^2 + (y - 0)^2 = (4)^2$ Substitute 0 for h, 0 for k, and 4 for r.

$x^2 + y^2 = 16$ Simplify.

Step 4 Substitute the x- and y-coordinates of the point $(3, \sqrt{7})$ in the equation of the circle to check whether they satisfy the equation of the circle.

$(3)^2 + (\sqrt{7})^2 \overset{?}{=} 16$ Substitute 3 for x and $\sqrt{7}$ for y.

$9 + 7 = 16$ Simplify.

So, the point $(3, \sqrt{7})$ lies on the circle because the point's x- and y-coordinates satisfy the equation of the circle.

Ⓑ Point $(1, \sqrt{6})$, circle with center $(-1, 0)$ and containing the point $(-1, 3)$

Step 1 Plot a point at $\left(\boxed{}, 0 \right)$ and at $\left(-1, \boxed{} \right)$. Draw the circle centered at $\left(\boxed{}, 0 \right)$ that

contains $\left(-1, \boxed{} \right)$.

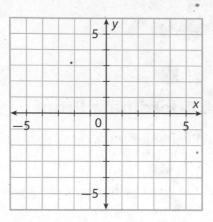

Step 2 Determine the radius: $r = \boxed{}$

Step 3 Use the radius and the coordinates of the center to write the equation of the circle.

$$(x - h)^2 + (y - k)^2 = r^2$$ Write the equation of the circle.

$$\left(x - \boxed{} \right)^2 + \left(y - \boxed{} \right)^2 = \boxed{}^2$$ Substitute $\boxed{}$ for h, $\boxed{}$ for k, and $\boxed{}$ for r.

$$\left(x \boxed{} \right)^2 + y^2 = \boxed{}$$ Simplify.

Step 4 Substitute the x- and y-coordinates of the point $(1, \sqrt{6})$ in the equation of the circle to check whether they satisfy the equation of the circle.

$$\left(\boxed{} \right)^2 + \left(\boxed{} \right)^2 \overset{?}{=} \boxed{}$$ Substitute $\boxed{}$ for x and $\boxed{}$ for y.

$$\boxed{} + \boxed{} \neq \boxed{}$$ Simplify.

So the point $(1, \sqrt{6})$ $\boxed{}$ on the circle because the x- and y-coordinates of the

point $\boxed{}$ the equation of the circle.

Reflect

10. How do you know that the radius of the circle in Example 3A is 4?

_____

_____

11. Name another point with noninteger coordinates that lies on the circle in Example 3A. Explain.

_____

Prove or disprove that the given point lies on the given circle.

12. Point $\left(\sqrt{18}, -4\right)$, circle centered at the origin and containing the point $(6, 0)$

13. Point $(4, -4)$, circle with center $(1, 0)$ and containing the point $(1, 5)$

Elaborate

14. **Discussion** How is the distance formula related to the equation of a circle?

_____

_____

_____

_____

15. **Essential Question Check-In** What information do you need to know to write the equation of a circle?

_____

_____

_____

⭐ Evaluate: Homework and Practice

1. Given the equation, $(x - h)^2 = (y - k)^2 = r^2$, what are the coordinates of the center?

Write the equation of the circle with the given center and radius.

2. center: $(0, 2)$; radius: 5

3. center: $(-1, 3)$; radius 8

4. center: $(-4, -5)$; radius $\sqrt{2}$

5. center: $(9, 0)$; radius $\sqrt{3}$

Find the center and radius of the circle with the given equation. Then graph the circle.

6. $x^2 + y^2 = 16$

7. $x^2 - 6x + y^2 + 8y + 16 = 0$

8. $x^2 - 2x + y^2 + 4y - 4 = 0$

9. $x^2 - 6x + y^2 - 6y + 14 = 0$

10. Prove or disprove that the point $(1, \sqrt{3})$ lies on the circle that is centered at the origin and contains the point $(0, 2)$.

11. Prove or disprove that the point $\left(2, \sqrt{3}\right)$ lies on the circle that is centered at the origin and contains the point $(-3, 0)$.

12. Prove or disprove that the circle with equation $x^2 - 4x + y^2 = -3$ intersects the y-axis.

13. Prove or disprove that the circle with equation $x^2 + y^2 - 10y = -16$ intersects the x-axis.

14. The center of a circle is $(0, -8)$. The radius is 9. What is the equation of the circle? Select all that apply.

   A. $x^2 + (y + 8)^2 = 3$

   B. $x^2 + (y + 8)^2 = 9$

   C. $x^2 + (y + 8)^2 = 81$

   D. $x^2 + y^2 + 16y = 17$

   E. $x^2 + y^2 + 16y = -55$

Algebra Write the equation of each circle.

15.

16.

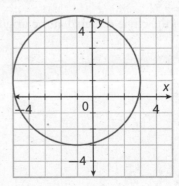

17. Prove or disprove that the circle with equation $x^2 + 4x + y^2 - 4y = 0$ contains the point $(0, 4)$.

18. The point $(2, n)$ lies on the circle whose equation is $(x - 3)^2 + (y + 2)^2 = 26$. Find the value of n.

Determine whether each statement is true or false. If false, explain why.

19. The circle $x^2 + y^2 = 7$ has radius 7.

20. The circle $(x - 2)^2 + (y + 3)^2 = 9$ passes through the point $(-1, -3)$.

21. The center of the circle $(x - 6)^2 + (y + 4)^2 = 1$ lies in the second quadrant.

22. The circle $(x + 1)^2 + (y - 4)^2 = 4$ intersects the y-axis.

23. The equation of the circle centered at the origin with diameter 6 is $x^2 + y^2 = 36$.

24. Multi-Step Carousels can be found in many different settings, from amusement parks to city plazas. Suppose that the center of a carousel is at the origin and that one of the animals on the circumference of the carousel has coordinates $(24, 32)$.

a. If one unit of the coordinate plane equals 1 foot, what is the diameter of the carousel?

b. As the carousel turns, the animals follow a circular path. Write the equation of this circle.

25. Critical Thinking The diameter of a circle has endpoints $(-6, 4)$ and $(0, 2)$.

a. Write an equation for the circle in standard form.

b. Prove or disprove that the point $(0, 4)$ lies on the circle.

26. Communicate Mathematical Ideas Can a unique circle be constructed from three nonlinear points? Explain.

Lesson Performance Task

Cell phone towers are expensive to build, so phone companies try to build as few towers as possible, while still ensuring that all of their customers are within range of a tower. The top figure represents the ranges of three towers that each serve customers within the shaded areas but leave customers outside the shaded areas. The bottom figure shows towers that are too close together. Customers between the towers are not left out, but many customers are served by two towers, a waste of the phone company's money.

On a coordinate grid of three cell phone towers, each unit represents 1 mile. The graph of the range of Tower A has the equation $x^2 + y^2 = 36$. Tower B is 10 miles west of Tower A. Tower C is 10 miles east of Tower A.

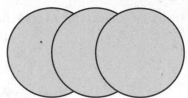

1. Graph the ranges of the three towers. (All three have the same range.)

2. Write the equations of the ranges of Tower B and Tower C.

3. Estimate the area of the overlap between Tower A and Tower B.

4. A new tower with a range of 8 miles is being built 5 miles west and 11 miles north of Tower A. Write the equation of the range of the new tower.

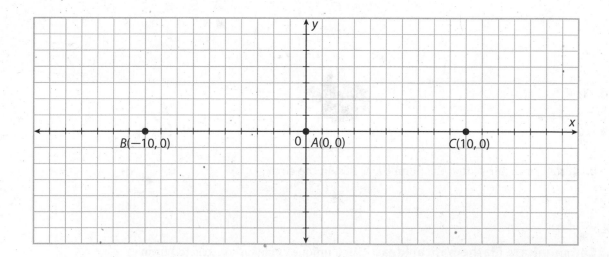

17.2 Equation of a Parabola

Essential Question: How do you write the equation of a parabola that opens up or down given its focus and directrix?

⊙ Explore 1   Identify Points That Are Equidistant From a Point and a Line

Remember that the distance from a point to a line is the length of the perpendicular segment from the point to the line. In the figure, the distance from point A to line ℓ is AB.

You will use the idea of the distance from a point to a line below.

You are given the point R and line ℓ as shown on the graph. Follow these instructions to plot a point.

(A)   Choose a point on line ℓ. Plot point Q at this location.

(B)   Using a straightedge, draw a perpendicular to ℓ that passes through point Q. Label this line m.

(C)   Use the straightedge to draw $\overline{RQ}$. Then use a compass and straightedge to construct the perpendicular bisector of $\overline{RQ}$.

(D)   Plot a point X where the perpendicular bisector intersects the line m.

(E)   Write the approximate coordinates of point X.

(F)   Repeat Steps A–D to plot multiple points. You may want to work together with other students, plotting all of your points on each of your graphs.

The figure shows the construction of point Q, along with several other points constructed using the same method.

1. Explain why point X is equidistant from point R and line ℓ.

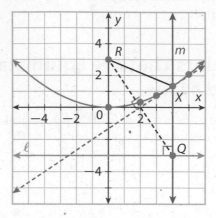

_____

_____

2. What do you notice about the points you plotted?

_____

⊘ Explore 2 Deriving the Equation of a Parabola

A **parabola** is the set of all points P in a plane that are equidistant from a given point, called the **focus**, and a given line, called the **directrix**. The **vertex** of a parabola is the midpoint of the segment, perpendicular to the directrix, that connects the focus and the directrix.

For the parabola shown, the vertex is at the origin.

To derive the general equation of a parabola, you can use the definition of a parabola, the distance formula, and the idea that the distance from a point to a line is the length of the perpendicular segment from the point to the line.

(A) Let the focus of the parabola be $F(0, p)$ and let the directrix be the line $y = -p$. Let P be a point on the parabola with coordinates (x, y).

(B) Let Q be the point of intersection of the perpendicular from P and

the directrix. Then the coordinates of Q are _____.

(C) By the definition of a parabola, $FP = QP$.

By the distance formula, $FP = \sqrt{(x - 0)^2 + (y - p)^2} = \sqrt{x^2 + (y - p)^2}$ and

$QP = \sqrt{(x - x)^2 + (y - (-p))^2} = \sqrt{0 + (y + p)^2} = |y + p|$.

Set FP equal to QP. $\underline{\hspace{3cm}} = |y + p|$

Square both sides. $x^2 + \underline{\hspace{2cm}} = |y + p|^2$

Expand the squared terms. $x^2 + y^2 - \underline{\hspace{1.2cm}} + p^2 = y^2 + \underline{\hspace{1cm}} + p^2$

Subtract y^2 and p^2 from both sides. $\underline{\hspace{1.5cm}} = \underline{\hspace{1cm}}$

Add $2py$ to both sides. $x^2 = \underline{\hspace{1.5cm}}$

Solve for y. $\dfrac{1}{\underline{\hspace{0.8cm}}} x^2 = y$

Reflect

3. Explain how the value of p determines whether the parabola opens up or down.

_____

_____

_____

4. Explain why the origin $(0, 0)$ is always a point on a parabola with focus $F(0, p)$ and directrix $y = -p$.

_____

_____

  Explain 1 # Writing an Equation of a Parabola with Vertex at the Origin

You can use the focus and directrix of a parabola to write an equation of the parabola with vertex at the origin.

Example 1 **Write the equation of the parabola with the given focus and directrix. Then graph the parabola.**

(A) focus: $(0, 5)$; directrix : $y = -5$

- The focus of the parabola is $(0, p)$, so $p = 5$.

    The general equation of a parabola is $y = \frac{1}{4p} x^2$.

    So, the equation of this parabola is $y = \frac{1}{4(5)} x^2$ or $y = \frac{1}{20} x^2$.

- To graph the parabola, complete the table of values. Then plot points and draw the curve.

x	y
−10	5
−5	1.25
0	0
5	1.25
10	5

(B) Write the equation of the parabola with focus $(0, -4)$ and directrix $y = 4$.

- The focus of the parabola is $(0, p)$, so $p = $ _____.

  The general equation of a parabola is $y = \frac{1}{4p} x^2$.

  So, the equation of this parabola is _____.

- To graph the parabola, complete the table of values. Then plot points and draw the curve.

x	y
−4	
−2	
0	
2	
4	

Reflect

5. Describe any symmetry in your graph from Example 1B. Why does this make sense based on the parabola's equation?

_____

_____

_____

Your Turn

Write the equation of the parabola with the given focus and directrix. Then graph the parabola.

6. Parabola with focus $(0, -1)$ and directrix $y = 1$.

Explain 2 **Writing the Equation of a Parabola with Vertex Not at the Origin**

The vertex of a parabola may not be at the origin. But given the focus and directrix of a parabola, you can find the coordinates of the vertex and write an equation of the parabola.

A parabola with vertex (h, k) that opens up or down has equation $(x - h)^2 = 4p(y - k)$ where $|p|$ is the distance from the vertex to the focus.

Example 2 Write the equation of the parabola with the given focus and directrix. Then graph the parabola.

(A) focus: $(3, 5)$, directrix: $y = -3$

- Draw the focus and the directrix on the graph.

- Draw a segment perpendicular to the directrix from the focus.

- Find the midpoint of the segment. The segment is 8 units long, so the vertex is 4 units below the focus. Then $p = 4$, and the coordinates of the vertex are $(3, 1)$.

- Since the formula for a parabola is $(x - h)^2 = 4p(y - k)$, the equation of the parabola is $(x - 3)^2 = 16(y - 1)$.

- To graph the parabola, complete the table of values. Round to the nearest tenth if necessary. Then plot the points and draw the curve.

x	y
−1	2
1	1.3
2	1.1
3	1
4	1.1
6	1.6
7	2

Ⓑ focus: $(-1, 4)$; directrix: $y = 6$

- Draw the focus and the directrix on the graph.

- Draw a segment perpendicular to the directrix through the focus.

- Find the midpoint of the segment. The segment is _____ units long, so the vertex is _____ units above/below the focus. The coordinates of the vertex are _____. The parabola opens down so $p =$ _____.

- Since the formula for a parabola is $(x - h)^2 = 4p(y - k)$, the equation of the parabola is

$$(x - \text{\underline{\hspace{1cm}}})^2 = \text{\underline{\hspace{1cm}}} (y - \text{\underline{\hspace{1cm}}}).$$

- To graph the parabola, complete the table of values. Round to the nearest tenth if necessary. Then plot the points and draw the curve.

x	y
−4	
−3	
−2	
−1	
0	
1	
2	

Reflect

7. **Discussion** Without calculating, how can you determine by considering the focus and directrix of a parabola whether the parabola opens up or down?

_____

_____

_____

_____

_____

Write the equation of the parabola with the given focus and directrix. Then graph the parabola.

8. focus: $(3, 2)$, directrix: $y = -4$

9. focus: $(2, 1)$, directrix: $y = 9$

💬 Elaborate

10. What does the sign of p in the equation of a parabola tell you about the parabola?

_____

11. Explain how to choose appropriate x-values when completing a table of values given the equation of a parabola.

_____

_____

12. **Essential Question Check-In** How is an equation for the general parabola related to the equation for a parabola with a vertex of $(0, 0)$?

_____

_____

• Online Homework
• Hints and Help
• Extra Practice

Write the equation of the parabola with the given focus and directrix. Then graph the parabola.

1. focus: $(0, 2)$; directrix: $y = -2$

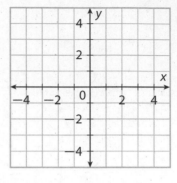

2. focus: $(0, -3)$; directrix: $y = 3$

3. focus: $(0, -5)$; directrix: $y = 5$

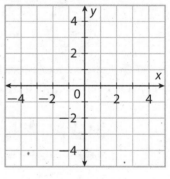

4. focus: $(0, 4)$; directrix: $y = -4$

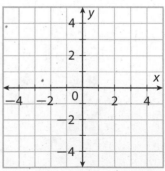

Find the directrix and focus of a parabola with the given equation.

5. $y = -\dfrac{1}{24} x^2$

6. $y = 2x^2$

7. $y = -\frac{1}{2} x^2$

8. $y = \frac{1}{40} x^2$

Write the equation of the parabola with the given focus and directrix. Then graph the parabola.

9. focus: $(2, 3)$; directrix: $y = 7$

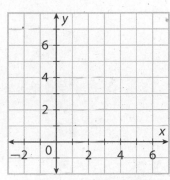

10. focus: $(-3, 2)$; directrix: $y = -4$

11. focus: $(4, 2)$; directrix: $y = -8$

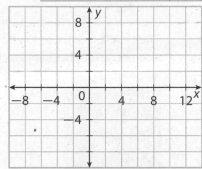

12. focus: $(-3, 8)$; directrix: $y = 9$

Find the focus and directrix of a parabola with the given equation.

13. $(x + 2)^2 = 16(y + 1)$

14. $(x - 4)^2 = 40(y - 4)$

15. $-(x + 5)^2 = y + 3.25$

16. $(x - 3)^2 = -24(y + 4)$

17. Make a Conjecture Complete the table by writing the equation of each parabola. Then use a calculator to graph the equations in the same window to help you make a conjecture: What happens to the graph of a parabola as the focus and directrix move apart?

Focus	$(0, 1)$	$(0, 2)$	$(0, 3)$	$(0, 4)$
Directrix	$y = -1$	$y = -2$	$y = -3$	$y = -4$
Equation				

18. Find the length of the line segment that is parallel to the directrix of a parabola, that passes through the focus, and that has endpoints on the parabola. Explain your reasoning.

19. Represent Real-World Problems The light from the lamp shown has parabolic cross sections. Write an equation for a cross section of the lamp if the bulb is 6 inches from the vertex and the vertex is placed at the origin. (Hint: The bulb of the lamp is the focus of the parabola.)

20. At a bungee-jumping contest, Gavin makes a jump that can be modeled by the equation $(x - 6)^2 = 12(y - 4)$ with dimensions in feet.

   a. Which point on the path identifies the lowest point that Gavin reached? What are the coordinates of this point? How close to the ground was he?

   b. Analyze Relationships Nicole makes a similar jump that can be modeled by the equation $(x - 2)^2 = 8(y - 8.5)$. How close to the ground did Nicole get? Did Nicole get closer to the ground than Gavin? If so, by how much?

21. Critical Thinking Some parabolas open to the left or right rather than up or down. For such parabolas, if $p > 0$, the parabola opens to the right. If $p < 0$, the parabola opens to the left. What is the value of p for the parabola shown? Explain your reasoning.

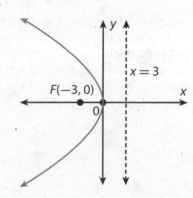

22. Critical Thinking Which equation represents the parabola shown?

A. $(x - 2)^2 = -16(y - 2)$

B. $(y - 2)^2 = -16(x - 2)$

C. $(x - 2)^2 = 16(y - 2)$

D. $(y - 2)^2 = 16(x - 2)$

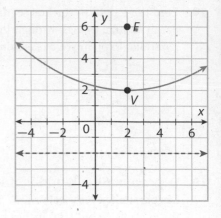

23. Amber and James are lying on the ground, each tossing a ball into the air, and catching it. The paths of the balls can be represented by the following equations, with the x-values representing the horizontal distances traveled thrown and the y-values representing the heights of the balls, both measured in feet.

Amber: $-20(x - 15)^2 = y - 11.25$ James: $-24(x - 12)^2 = y - 6$

a. What are the bounds of the equations for the physical situation? Explain.

b. Whose ball went higher? Which traveled the farthest horizontal distance? Justify your answers.

Lesson Performance Task

Suppose a park wants to build a new half-pipe structure for the skateboarders. To make sure all parts of the ramp are supported, the inside of the ramp needs to be equidistant from a focus point, which is at a height of 3 feet. Find the equation of the half-pipe and sketch it, along with the focus point and the directrix. Would the ramp get steeper or flatten out if the focus point height were at a height of 4 feet? Explain.

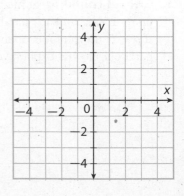

Equations of Circles and Parabolas

Essential Question: How can you use equations of circles and parabolas to solve real-world problems?

Key Vocabulary

circle *(círculo)*

parabola *(parábola)*

focus *(foco)*

directrix *(directriz)*

KEY EXAMPLE   (Lesson 17.1)

Find the center and radius of the circle with the equation $x^2 + 2x + y^2 - 6y = 6$.

$x^2 + 2x + (\ \ )^2 + y^2 - 6y + (\ \ )^2 = 6 + (\ \ )^2$ Set up to complete the square.

$x^2 + 2x + \left(\frac{2}{2}\right)^2 + y^2 - 6y + \left(\frac{-6}{2}\right)^2 = 6 + \left(\frac{2}{2}\right)^2 + \left(\frac{-6}{2}\right)^2$ Add $\left(\frac{2}{2}\right)^2$ and $\left(\frac{-6}{2}\right)^2$ to both sides.

$x^2 + 2x + 1 + y^2 - 6y + 9 = 6 + 10$ Simplify.

$(x + 1)^2 + (y - 3)^2 = 16$ Factor.

$h = -1, k = 3, r = \sqrt{16} = 4$ Identify h, k, and r to determine the center and radius.

The center is $(-1, 3)$ and the radius is 4.

KEY EXAMPLE   (Lesson 17.2)

Find the focus and directrix of the parabola with the equation $y = -\frac{1}{12}x^2$.

$h = 0, k = 0, p = -3$ Use the general equation $y - k = \frac{1}{4p}(x - h)^2$ to identify h, k, and p.

focus: $(0, -3)$ The vertex is at $(0, 0)$, so the focus is at $(0, p)$.

directrix: $y = 3$ The vertex is at $(0, 0)$, so the directrix is $y = -p$.

KEY EXAMPLE   (Lesson 17.2)

Find the equation of the parabola with focus $(1, 6)$ and directrix $y = 2$.

vertex: $(1, 4)$ The vertex is the midpoint of the line through the focus and perpendicular to the directrix.

$h = 1, k = 4, p = 2$ Identify h, k, and p.

$y - 4 = \frac{1}{8}(x - 1)^2$ Substitute h, k, and p in the general equation $y - k = \frac{1}{4p}(x - h)^2$

The equation of the parabola is $y - 4 = \frac{1}{8}(x - 1)^2$.

EXERCISES

Find the center and radius of the circle with the given equation. *(Lesson 17.1)*

1. $(x - 3)^2 + (y + 5)^2 = 49$

2. $(x + 8.5)^2 + y^2 = 75$

3. $x^2 + 6x + y^2 - 2y = 15$

4. $x^2 - 18x + y^2 - 18y + 53 = 0$

Find the focus, vertex, and directrix of the parabola with the given equation. *(Lesson 17.2)*

5. $y = \frac{1}{32}x^2$

6. $y + 3 = -\frac{1}{2}(x + 5)^2$

Find the equation of the parabola with the given focus and directrix. *(Lesson 17.2)*

7. focus $(-2, 3)$; directrix $y = -5$

8. focus $(5, -4)$; directrix $y = 8$

MODULE PERFORMANCE TASK

Rescue at Sea

Radio contact with a sailboat off the coast of California has been lost. The craft's last known position was 35.5° North, 123.7° West. The Coast Guard is mounting a search-and-rescue operation from either Los Angeles International Airport (LAX), located at 33.9° N, 118.4° W; San Francisco International Airport (SFO), located at 37.8° N, 122.4° W; or both. The Coast Guard will use H-65 helicopters with ranges of approximately 290 nautical miles.

Should helicopters be flown from LAX, SFO, or both?

Start by listing in the space below the information you will need to solve the problem. Then use your own paper to work on the task. Use numbers, words, or algebra to explain how you reached your conclusion.

17.1–17.2 Equation of Circles and Parabolas

Solve. Round answers to the nearest tenth. *(Lessons 17.1, 17.2)*

- Online Homework
- Hints and Help
- Extra Practice

1. Find the center and radius of the circle $x^2 + 4x + y^2 - 2y - 4 = 0$.

2. Find the focus, vertex, and directrix of the parabola with the equation $y = (x - 8)^2 - 6$

3. A circle has its center at $(-2, 4)$ and a radius of $5\sqrt{2}$. Does the point $(3, -1)$ lie on the circle? Explain.

4. Does the graph of the parabola $y = -\frac{1}{100}x^2$ open upward or downward? Explain.

5. A new cellular phone tower services all phones within a 17 mile radius. Doreen lives 15 miles east and 8 miles south of the tower. Is she within the area serviced by the tower? Explain. *(Lesson 17.2)*

ESSENTIAL QUESTION

6. What information about a circle and a parabola do you need in order to draw their graphs on the coordinate plane?

Assessment Readiness

1. The graph of the equation $x^2 + 6x + y^2 - 16y = -9$ is a circle. Choose True or False for each statement.

   A. The center of the circle is $(3, -8)$.   ○ True   ○ False

   B. The circle is tangent to the x-axis.   ○ True   ○ False

   C. The circle has a radius of 64.   ○ True   ○ False

2. Consider the graph of the parabola $y = x^2 + 4$. Select Yes or No for A–C.

   A. The vertex is $(0, 4)$ ○ Yes   ○ No

   B. The parabola opens upward.   ○ Yes   ○ No

   C. The directrix is $y = -4.25$.   ○ Yes   ○ No

3. An engineer drew the graph of a new tire on a coordinate plane. The equation of the tire was $x^2 + y^2 - 26y = 0$. How many feet will the tire roll in 100 complete revolutions? Explain.

4. Find the points of intersection of the circle $x^2 + y^2 = 25$ and the parabola $y = x^2 - 5$. Explain how you found the points.

Assessment Readiness

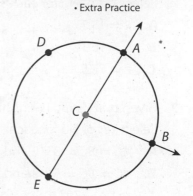

- Online Homework
- Hints and Help
- Extra Practice

1. Determine whether each arc is a minor arc, a major arc, or a semicircle.

   Select the correct answer for each arc.

   A. $\overset{\frown}{AB}$ Minor Arc   Major Arc   Semicircle

   B. $\overset{\frown}{ABE}$ Minor Arc   Major Arc   Semicircle

   C. $\overset{\frown}{ADB}$ Minor Arc   Major Arc   Semicircle

2. Quadrilateral $ABCD$ is inscribed in a circle with angle measures $m\angle A = (11x - 8)°$, $m\angle B = (3x^2 + 1)°$, $m\angle C = (15x + 32)°$, and $m\angle D = (2x^2 - 1)°$. Are each of the following measures of the quadrilateral's angles?

   Select Yes or No for each statement.

   A. $m\angle A = 135°$ ◯ Yes ◯ No

   B. $m\angle B = 109°$ ◯ Yes ◯ No

   C. $m\angle C = 227°$ ◯ Yes ◯ No

   D. $m\angle D = 71°$ ◯ Yes ◯ No

3. $\triangle ABC$ and $\triangle DEF$ are congruent.

   Select True or False for each statement.

   A. $m\angle F = 91°$ ◯ True ◯ False

   B. $m\angle A = 55°$ ◯ True ◯ False

   C. $EF = 11$ ◯ True ◯ False

4. Determine whether the vertex of $\angle 1$ is on the circle, inside the circle, or outside the circle given its measure and the measure of its intercepted arc(s).

   Select the correct answer for each set of angle measures.

   A. $m\angle 1 = 58°$, $m\overset{\frown}{2} = 85°$, $m\overset{\frown}{3} = 31°$ On circle   Inside circle   Outside circle

   B. $m\angle 1 = 52°$, $m\overset{\frown}{2} = 104°$ On circle   Inside circle   Outside circle

   C. $m\angle 1 = 27°$, $m\overset{\frown}{2} = 85°$, $m\overset{\frown}{3} = 31°$ On circle   Inside circle   Outside circle

5. Are each of the following lengths of chords in the circle?

   Select Yes or No for each statement.

   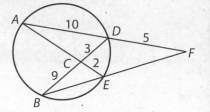

   A. $AC = 13.5$ ◯ Yes   ◯ No

   B. $EF = 7.1$ ◯ Yes   ◯ No

   C. $BF = 2.9$ ◯ Yes   ◯ No

6. Are each of the following lengths of the segments in the triangle?

   Select Yes or No for each statement.

   A. $x = 13.3$ ◯ Yes   ◯ No

   B. $y = 16.1$ ◯ Yes   ◯ No

   C. $z = 13.5$ ◯ Yes   ◯ No

7. Given that $\triangle ABC$ is a right triangle, determine if it is a special right triangle.

   Select Yes or No for each statement.

   A. $AC = BC = 3\sqrt{2}$ and $AB = 6$ ◯ Yes   ◯ No

   B. $AC = BC = 5\sqrt{2}$ and $AB = 10$ ◯ Yes   ◯ No

   C. $m\angle A = 30°$ ◯ Yes   ◯ No

8. Renee is designing a logo for an airline. She starts by making a figure with angle measures as shown. She measures $\overline{AB}$ and finds that the length of the segment is 5 inches. Can she determine the length of $\overline{DB}$ without measuring? If so, explain how. If not, explain why not.

9. A car tire has a diameter of 21.3 inches. What is the circumference and the area of the tire?

Performance Tasks

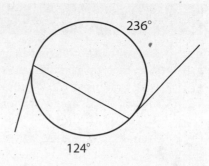

★**10.** A city planner is designing a bridge to cross a circular lake in the park. There will be two footpaths, both tangent to the lake, that connect to each side of the bridge. At what angles do the footpaths connect with the bridge?

★★**11.** Nestor cuts a cake with a 12-inch diameter. One of the pieces he cuts has a central angle of 24°. What is the area of the slice of cake? What fraction of the entire cake is this? Explain.

★★**12.** Jeanine's swimming pool has a diameter of 27 feet. Surrounding the pool is a deck that extends 5 feet from the edges of the pool. Jeanine wants to paint the deck and then put a fence around it. Paint costs $0.85 per square foot and fencing costs $8.25 per foot. How much will it cost Jeanine to paint the deck and add fencing? Explain how you found your answer.

Astronomer During a partial solar eclipse, the moon aligns with the sun and Earth such that it partially covers the sun from view on a circular area on Earth's surface with a radius of 130 kilometers (km). The lines tangent to both the moon and this area meet at a 144° angle. What is the measure and length of the arc on the area in which a person on Earth will be able to witness a partial eclipse?

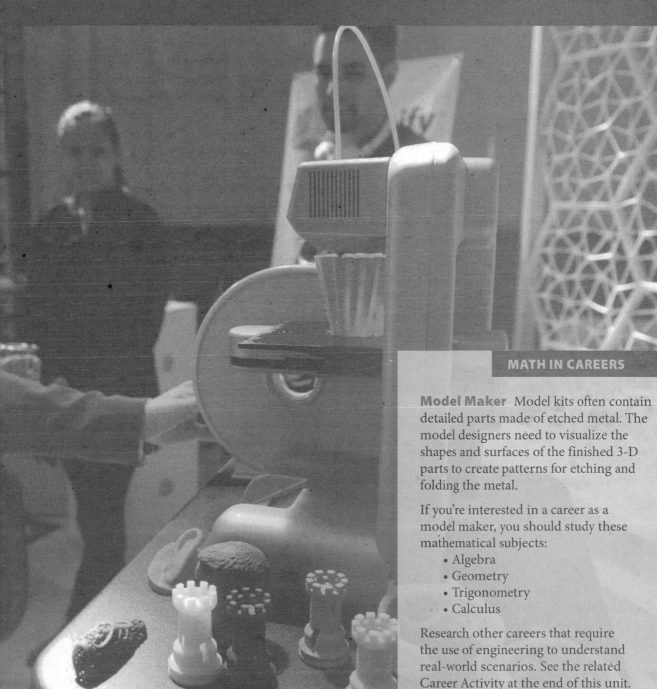

Measurement and Modeling in Two and Three Dimensions

MATH IN CAREERS

Model Maker Model kits often contain detailed parts made of etched metal. The model designers need to visualize the shapes and surfaces of the finished 3-D parts to create patterns for etching and folding the metal.

If you're interested in a career as a model maker, you should study these mathematical subjects:
- Algebra
- Geometry
- Trigonometry
- Calculus

Research other careers that require the use of engineering to understand real-world scenarios. See the related Career Activity at the end of this unit.

Reading Start-Up

Vocabulary

Review Words

✔ area (*área*)

✔ composite figure (*figura compuesta*)

✔ cone (*cono*)

✔ cylinder (*cilindro*)

✔ pyramid (*pirámide*)

✔ sphere (*esfera*)

✔ volume (*volume*)

Preview Words

apothem (*apotema*)

cross section (*sección transversal*)

great circle (*gran círculo*)

net (*neto*)

oblique cylinder (*cilindro oblicuo*)

oblique prism (*prisma oblicuo*)

regular pyramid (*pirámide regular*)

right cone (*cono recto*)

right cylinder (*cilindro recto*)

right prism (*prisma recto*)

surface area (*área de la superficie*)

Visualize Vocabulary

Use the ✔ words and draw examples to complete the chart.

Object	Example

Understand Vocabulary

Complete the sentences using the preview words.

1. A(n) _____ is the region of a plane that intersects a solid figure.

2. A cross section of a sphere with the same radius as the sphere is called a _____.

3. The _____ of a right prism is a two-dimensional image containing six rectangles.

Active Reading

Pyramid Create a Pyramid and organize the adjectives used to describe different objects—right, regular, oblique—on each of its faces. When listening to descriptions of objects, look for these words and associate them with the object that follows.

Volume Formulas

★

Essential Question: How can you use volume formulas to solve real-world problems?

REAL WORLD VIDEO
Check out how volume formulas can be used to find the volumes of real-world objects, including sinkholes.

MODULE PERFORMANCE TASK PREVIEW

How Big Is That Sinkhole?

In 2010, a giant sinkhole opened up in a neighborhood in Guatemala and swallowed up the three-story building that stood above it. In this module, you will choose and apply an appropriate formula to determine the volume of this giant sinkhole.

Are YOU Ready?

Complete these exercises to review skills you will need for this module.

• Online Homework
• Hints and Help
• Extra Practice

Area of a Circle

Example 1 Find the area of a circle with radius equal to 5.

$A = \pi r^2$ Write the equation for the area of a circle of radius r.

$A = \pi(5)^2$ Substitute the radius.

$A = 25\pi$ Simplify.

Find each area.

1. A circle with radius 4 _____

2. A circle with radius 6 _____

3. A circle with radius 3π _____

4. A circle with radius $\frac{2}{\pi}$ _____

Volume Properties

Example 2 Find the number of cubes that are 1 cm^3 in size that fit into a cube of size 1 m^3.

Notice that the base has a length and width of 1 m or 100 cm, so its area is 1 m^2 or 10,000 cm^2.

The 1 m^3 cube is 1 m or 100 cm high, so multiply the area of the base by the height to find the volume of 1,000,000 cm^3.

Find the volume.

5. The volume of a 1 km^3 body of water in m^3

_____

6. The volume of a 1 ft^3 box in in.^{3}

_____

Volume of Rectangular Prisms

Example 3 Find the volume of a rectangular prism with height 4 cm, length 3 cm, and width 5 cm.

$V = Bh$ Write the equation for the volume of a rectangular prism.

$V = (3)(5)(4)$ The volume of a rectangular prism is the area of the base times the height.

$V = 60$ cm^3 Simplify.

Find each volume.

7. A rectangular prism with length 3 m, width 4 m, and height 7 m

_____

8. A rectangular prism with length 2 cm, width 5 cm, and height 12 cm

_____

18.1 Volume of Prisms and Cylinders

Essential Question: How do the formulas for the volume of a prism and cylinder relate to area formulas that you already know?

⊘ Explore   Developing a Basic Volume Formula

The volume of a three-dimensional figure is the number of nonoverlapping cubic units contained in the interior of the figure. This prism is made up of 8 cubes, each with a volume of 1 cubic centimeter, so it has a volume of 8 cubic centimeters. You can use this idea to develop volume formulas.

Volume = 1 cubic unit

In this activity you'll explore how to develop a volume formula for a right prism and a right cylinder.

A **right prism** has lateral edges that are perpendicular to the bases, with faces that are all rectangles.	A **right cylinder** has bases that are perpendicular to its center axis.
right prism	axis right cylinder

(A) On a sheet of paper draw a quadrilateral shape. Make sure the sides aren't parallel. Assume the figure has an area of *B* square units.

area is *B* square units

(B) Use it as the base for a prism. Take a block of Styrofoam and cut to the shape of the base. Assume the prism has a height of 1 unit.

How would changing the area of the base change the volume of the prism?

height is 1 unit

_____

_____

_____

Ⓒ   If the base has an area of B square units, how many cubic units does the prism contain?

_____

Ⓓ   Now use the base to build a prism with a height of h units.

height is h units

How much greater is the volume of this prism compared to the one with a height of 1?

_____

Reflect

1.   Suppose the base of the prism was a rectangle of sides l and w. Write a formula for the volume of the prism using l, w, and h.

_____

2.   A cylinder has a circular base. Use the results of the Explore to write a formula for the volume of a cylinder. Explain what you did.

_____

⊘ Explain 1   Finding the Volume of a Prism

The general formula for the volume of a prism is $V = B \cdot h$. With certain prisms the volume formula can include the formula for the area of the base.

Volume of a Prism	
The formula for the volume of a right rectangular prism with length ℓ, width w, and height h is $V = \ell wh$.	The formula for the volume of a cube with edge length s is $V = s^3$.

Example 1 **Use volume formulas to solve real world problems.**

 A A shark and ray tank at the aquarium has the dimensions shown. Estimate the volume of water in gallons. Use the conversion 1 gallon = 0.134 ft³.

Step 1 Find the volume of the aquarium in cubic feet.

$$V = \ell wh = (120)(60)(8) = 57,600 \text{ ft}^3$$

Step 2 Use the conversion factor $\dfrac{1 \text{ gallon}}{0.134 \text{ ft}^3}$ to estimate the volume of the aquarium in gallons.

$$57,600 \text{ ft}^3 \cdot \frac{1 \text{ gallon}}{0.134 \text{ ft}^3} \approx 429,851 \text{ gallons} \qquad \frac{1 \text{ gallon}}{0.134 \text{ ft}^3} = 1$$

Step 3 Use the conversion factor $\dfrac{1 \text{ gallon}}{8.33 \text{ pounds}}$ to estimate the weight of the water.

$$429,851 \text{ gallons} \cdot \frac{8.33 \text{ pounds}}{1 \text{ gallon}} \approx 3,580,659 \text{ pounds} \qquad \frac{8.33 \text{ pounds}}{1 \text{ gallon}} = 1$$

The aquarium holds about 429,851 gallons. The water in the aquarium weighs about 3,580,659 pounds.

B **Chemistry** Ice takes up more volume than water. This cubic container is filled to the brim with ice. Estimate the volume of water once the ice melts.

Density of ice: 0.9167 g/cm³   Density of water: 1 g/cm³

Step 1 Find the volume of the cube of ice.

$$V = s^3 = \boxed{} = \boxed{} \text{ cm}^3$$

Step 2 Convert the volume to mass using the conversion factor

$$\boxed{} \frac{\text{g}}{\text{cm}^3}.$$

$$\boxed{} \text{ cm}^3 \cdot \boxed{} \frac{\text{g}}{\text{cm}^3} \approx \boxed{} \text{ g}$$

Step 3 Use the mass of ice to find the volume of water. Use the conversion factor $\boxed{}$.

$$24.8 \text{ g} \cdot \boxed{} \approx \boxed{} \text{ cm}^3$$

3. The general formula for the volume of a prism is $V = B \cdot h$. Suppose the base of a prism is a parallelogram of length l and altitude h. Use H as the variable to represent the height of the prism. Write a volume formula for this prism.

_____

4. Find the volume of the figure.

5. Find the volume of the figure.

Volume = 8 cubic units

Each cube has a side of 2*k*.

🔧 Explain 2   Finding the Volume of a Cylinder

You can also find the volume of prisms and cylinders whose edges are not perpendicular to the base.

Oblique Prism	Oblique Cylinder
An **oblique prism** is a prism that has at least one non-rectangular lateral face.	An **oblique cylinder** is a cylinder whose axis is not perpendicular to the bases.

Cavalieri's Principle

If two solids have the same height and the same cross-sectional area at every level, then the two solids have the same volume.

Example 2 To find the volume of an oblique cylinder or oblique prism, use Cavalieri's Principle to find the volume of a comparable right cylinder or prism.

Ⓐ The height of this oblique cylinder is three times that of its radius. What is the volume of this cylinder? Round to the nearest tenth.

Use Cavalieri's Principle to find the volume of a comparable right cylinder.

Represent the height of the oblique cylinder: $h = 3r$

Use the area of the base to find r: $\pi r^2 = 81\pi$ cm^2, so $r = 9$.

Calculate the height: $h = 3r = 27$ cm

Calculate the volume: $V = Bh = (81\pi)27 \approx 6870.7$

The volume is about 6870.7 cubic centimeters.

$B = 81\pi$ cm^2

Ⓑ The height of this oblique square-based prism is four times that of side length of the base. What is the volume of this prism? Round to the nearest tenth.

Calculate the height of the oblique prism:

$h = $ ___ s, where s is the length of the square base.

Use the area of the base to find s.

$s^2 = \boxed{}$ cm^2

$s = \sqrt{\boxed{}}$ cm

Calculate the height.

$h = 4s = 4\boxed{}$ cm

Calculate the volume.

$V = Bh$

$= (75$ cm$^2)\left(\boxed{}$ cm$\right)$

$= \boxed{}$ cm^3

$B = 75$ cm^2

Your Turn

Find the volume.

6.

$r = 12$ in.
$h = 45$ in.

7.

$h = (x + 2)$ cm

$5x$ cm

$4x$ cm

Recall that a composite figure is made up of simple shapes that combine to create a more complex shape. A composite three-dimensional figure is formed from prisms and cylinders. You can find the volume of each separate figure and then add the volumes together to find the volume of the composite figure.

Example 3 Find the volume of each composite figure.

(A) Find the volume of the composite figure, which is an oblique cylinder on a cubic base. Round to the nearest tenth.

The base area of the cylinder is $B = \pi r^2 = \pi(5)^2 = 25\pi$ ft².

The cube has side lengths equal to the diameter of the cylinder's circular base: $s = 10$.

The height of the cylinder is $h = 22 - 10 = 12$ ft.

The volume of the cube is $V = s^3 = 10^3 = 1000$ ft³.

The volume of the cylinder is $V = Bh = (25\pi \text{ ft}^2)(12 \text{ ft}) \approx 942.5$ ft³.

The total volume of the composite figure is the sum of the individual volumes.

$V = 1000 \text{ ft}^3 + 942.5 \text{ ft}^3 = 1942.5 \text{ ft}^3$

(B) This periscope is made up of two congruent cylinders and two congruent triangular prisms, each of which is a cube cut in half along one of its diagonals. The height of each cylinder is 6 times the length of the radius. Use the measurements provided to estimate the volume of this composite figure. Round to the nearest tenth.

Use the area of the base to find the radius. $B = \pi r^2$

$\pi r^2 = \boxed{} \pi$, so $r = \boxed{}$ in.

Calculate the height of each cylinder:

$h = 6r = 6 \cdot \boxed{} = \boxed{}$ in.

The faces of the triangular prism that intersect the cylinders are congruent squares. The side length s of each square is the same as the diameter of the circle.

$s = d = 2 \cdot \boxed{} = \boxed{}$ in.

The two triangular prisms form a cube. What is the volume of this cube?

$V = s^3 = \boxed{}^3 = \boxed{}$ in³

Find the volume of the two cylinders: $V = 2 \cdot 36\pi \cdot \boxed{} = \boxed{}$ in³

The total volume of the composite figure is the sum of the individual volumes.

$V = \boxed{}$ in³ $+ \boxed{}$ in³ $\approx \boxed{}$ in³

8. A pipe consists of two concentric cylinders, with the inner cylinder hollowed out. Describe how you could calculate the volume of the solid pipe. Write a formula for the volume.

_____

_____

_____

_____

_____

Your Turn

9. This robotic arm is made up of two cylinders with equal volume and two triangular prisms for a hand. The volume of each prism is $\frac{1}{2}r \times \frac{1}{3}r \times 2r$, where r is the radius of the cylinder's base. What fraction of the total volume does the hand take up?

💬 Elaborate

10. If an oblique cylinder and a right cylinder have the same height but not the same volume, what can you conclude about the cylinders?

_____

11. A right square prism and a right cylinder have the same height and volume. What can you conclude about the radius of the cylinder and side lengths of the square base?

12. **Essential Question Check-In** How does the formula for the area of a circle relate to the formula for the volume of a cylinder?

_____

_____

☆ Evaluate: Homework and Practice

• Online Homework
• Hints and Help
• Extra Practice

1. The volume of prisms and cylinders can be represented with *Bh*, where *B* represents the area of the base. Identify the type of figure shown and match the prism or cylinder with the appropriate volume formula.

A. $V = (\pi r^2)h$ **B.** $V = \left(\frac{1}{2}bh\right)h$ **C.** $V = \ell wh$

_____ _____ _____

_____ _____ _____

Find the volume of each prism or cylinder. Round to the nearest hundredth.

2.

5.6 mm
3.5 mm
8.4 mm

3.
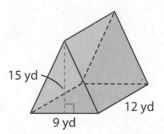

15 yd
12 yd
9 yd

4. The area of the hexagonal base is $\left(\frac{54}{\tan 30°}\right)$ m². Its height is 8 m.

5. The area of the pentagonal base is $\left(\frac{125}{\tan 36°}\right)$ m². Its height is 15 m.

6.

6 cm
9 cm
4 cm

7.

10 ft
12 ft

8. Multi-Step A vase in the shape of an oblique cylinder has the dimensions shown. What is the volume of the vase in liters? Round to the nearest thundredth. (*Hint:* Use the right triangle in the cylinder to find its height.)

17 cm

14 cm

Find the volume of each composite figure. Round to the nearest tenth.

9.

6 ft

4 ft

4 ft

14 ft

12 ft

10.

10 in.   5 in.

15 in.

11.

4 cm

4 cm   4 cm

6 cm

6 cm

6 cm

8 cm

8 cm

8 cm

12. The two figures on each end combine to form a right cylinder.

2 ft

4 ft

4 ft

2 ft

12 ft

13. Colin is buying dirt to fill a garden bed that is a 9 ft by 16 ft rectangle. If he wants to fill it to a depth of 4 in., how many cubic yards of dirt does he need? Round to the nearest cubic yard. If dirt costs $25 per yd³, how much will the project cost?

14. Persevere in Problem Solving A cylindrical juice container with a 3 in. diameter has a hole for a straw that is 1 in. from the side. Up to 5 in. of a straw can be inserted.

a. Find the height h of the container to the nearest tenth.

b. Find the volume of the container to the nearest tenth.

c. How many ounces of juice does the container hold? (*Hint*: 1 in³ ≈ 0.55 oz)

15. Abigail has a cylindrical candle mold with the dimensions shown. If Abigail has a rectangular block of wax measuring 15 cm by 12 cm by 18 cm, about how many candles can she make after melting the block of wax? Round to the nearest tenth.

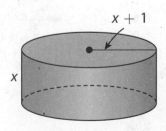

16. Algebra Find the volume of the three-dimensional figure in terms of x.

17. One cup is equal to 14.4375 in³. If a 1-cup measuring cylinder has a radius of 2 in., what is its height? If the radius is 1.5 in., what is its height? Round to the nearest tenth.

18. Make a Prediction A cake is a cylinder with a diameter of 10 in. and a height of 3 in. For a party, a coin has been mixed into the batter and baked inside the cake. The person who gets the piece with the coin wins a prize.

   a. Find the volume of the cake. Round to the nearest tenth.

   b. Keka gets a piece of cake that is a right rectangular prism with a 3 in. by 1 in. base. What is the probability that the coin is in her piece? Round to the nearest hundredth.

H.O.T. Focus on Higher Order Thinking

19. Multi-Step What is the volume of the three-dimensional object with the dimensions shown in the three views?

20. Draw Conclusions You can use *displacement* to find the volume of an irregular object, such as a stone. Suppose a 2 foot by 1 foot tank is filled with water to a depth of 8 in. A stone is placed in the tank so that it is completely covered, causing the water level to rise by 2 in. Find the volume of the stone.

21. Analyze Relationships One juice container is a rectangular prism with a height of 9 in. and a 3 in. by 3 in. square base. Another juice container is a cylinder with a radius of 1.75 in. and a height of 9 in. Describe the relationship between the two containers.

Lesson Performance Task

A full roll of paper towels is a cylinder with a diameter of 6 inches and a hollow inner cylinder with a diameter of 2 inches.

1. Find the volume of the paper on the roll. Explain your method.

2. Each sheet of paper on the roll measures 11 inches by 11 inches by $\frac{1}{32}$ inch. Find the volume of one sheet. Explain how you found the volume.

3. How many sheets of paper are on the roll? Explain.

18.2 Volume of Pyramids

Essential Question: How do you find the volume of a pyramid?

Resource
Locker

◉ Explore Developing a Volume Formula

As shown at the left below, $\overline{AB}$ has length b, and C is any point on line ℓ parallel to $\overline{AB}$. The distance between the line containing $\overline{AB}$ and line ℓ is h. No matter where C is located on line ℓ, the area of the resulting $\triangle ABC$ is always a constant equal to $\frac{1}{2}bh$. Similarly, given a polygon and a plane R that is parallel to the plane containing the polygon, suppose you choose a point on R and create a pyramid with the chosen point as the vertex and the polygon as the base. Both the base area and the height of the pyramid remain constant as you vary the location of the vertex on R, so it is reasonable to assume that the volume of the pyramid remains constant.

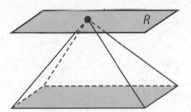

Postulate

Pyramids that have equal base areas and equal heights have equal volumes.

Consider a triangular pyramid with vertex A directly over vertex D of the base BCD. This triangular pyramid A-BCD can be thought of as part of a triangular prism with $\triangle EFA \cong \triangle BCD$. Let the area of the base be B and let $AD = h$.

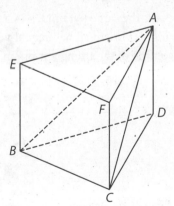

Ⓐ What is the volume of the triangular prism?

_____

Ⓑ Draw $\overline{EC}$ on one face of the triangular prism. Consider the three pyramids: *A-BCD*, *A-EBC*, and *A-CFE*. Explain why the sum of the volumes of these three pyramids is equal to the volume of the prism.

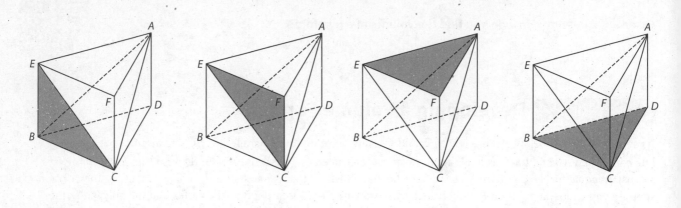

_____

_____

_____

Ⓒ $\overline{EC}$ is the diagonal of a rectangle, so $\triangle EBC \cong \triangle CFE$.
Explain why pyramids *A-EBC* and *A-CFE* have the same volume. Explain why pyramids *C-EFA* and *A-BCD* have the same volume.

_____

_____

_____

_____

Ⓓ *A-CFE* and *C-EFA* are two names for the same pyramid, so you now have shown that the three pyramids that form the triangular prism all have equal volume. Compare the volume of the pyramid *A-BCD* and the volume of the triangular prism. Write the volume of pyramid *A-BCD* in terms of *B* and *h*.

_____

_____

1. Explain how you know that the three pyramids that form the triangular prism all have the same volume.

_____

_____

_____

⏴ Explain 1 Finding the Volume of a Pyramid

In the Explore, you showed that the volume of a "wedge pyramid" having its vertex directly over one of the vertices of the base is one-third the product of the base area and the height. Now consider a general pyramid. As shown in the figure, a pyramid can be partitioned into nonoverlapping wedge pyramids by drawing a perpendicular from the vertex to the base. The volume V of the given pyramid is the sum of the volumes of the wedge pyramids.

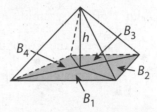

That is, $V = \frac{1}{3}B_1h + \frac{1}{3}B_2h + \frac{1}{3}B_3h + \frac{1}{3}B_4h$.

Using the distributive property, this may be rewritten as $V = \frac{1}{3}h(B_1 + B_2 + B_3 + B_4)$.

Notice that $B_1 + B_2 + B_3 + B_4 = B$, where B is the base area of the given pyramid.

So, $V = \frac{1}{3}Bh$.

The above argument provides an informal justification for the following result.

Volume of a Pyramid
The volume V of a pyramid with base area B and height h is given by $V = \frac{1}{3}Bh$.

Example 1 Solve a volume problem.

(A) Ashton built a model square-pyramid with the dimensions shown. What is the volume of the pyramid?

The pyramid is composed of wooden blocks that are in the shape of cubes. A block has the dimensions 4 cm by 4 by 4 cm. How many wooden blocks did Ashton use to build the pyramid?

- Find the volume of the pyramid.

  The area of the base B is the area of the square with sides of length 24 cm. So, $B = 576$ cm^2.

  The volume V of the pyramid is $\frac{1}{3}Bh = \frac{1}{3} \cdot 576 \cdot 16$.

  So $V = 3072$ cm^3.

- Find the volume of an average block.

  The volume of a cube is given by the formula $V = s^3$. So the volume W of a wooden block is 64 cm^3.

- Find the approximate number of wooden blocks in the pyramid, divide V by W. So the number of blocks that Ashton used is 48.

B The Great Pyramid in Giza, Egypt, is approximately a square pyramid with the dimensions shown. The pyramid is composed of stone blocks that are rectangular prisms. An average block has dimensions 1.3 m by 1.3 m by 0.7 m. Approximately how many stone blocks were used to build the pyramid? Round to the nearest hundred thousand.

- Find the volume of the pyramid.

  The area of the base B is the area of the square with sides of length 230 m. So, _____.

  The volume V of the pyramid is $\frac{1}{3}Bh = \frac{1}{3} \cdot$ _____ $\cdot$ _____.

  So $V \approx$ _____.

- Find the volume of an average block.

  The volume of a rectangular prism is given by the formula _____. So the volume W of an average block is _____.

- Find the approximate number of stone blocks in the pyramid, divide _____ by _____. So the approximate number of blocks is _____.

Reflect

2. What aspects of the model in Part B may lead to inaccuracies in your estimate?

   _____

   _____

3. Suppose you are told that the average height of a stone block 0.69 m rather than 0.7 m. Would the increase or decrease your estimate of the total number of blocks in the pyramid? Explain.

   _____

   _____

Your Turn

4. A piece of pure silver in the shape of a rectangular pyramid with the dimensions shown has a mass of 19.7 grams. What is the density of silver? Round to the nearest tenth.
   $\left(\text{Hint: } density = \frac{mass}{volume}.\right)$

You can add or subtract to find the volume of composite figures.

Example 2   **Find the volume of the composite figure formed by a pyramid removed from a prism. Round to the nearest tenth.**

Ⓐ

15 ft

12 ft

25 ft

- Find the volume of the prism.
  $V = lwh = (25)(12)(15) = 4500 \text{ ft}^3$

- Find the volume of pyramid.
  Area of base: $B = (25)(12) = 300 \text{ ft}^2$

  Volume of pyramid: $V = \frac{1}{3}(300)(15) = 1500 \text{ ft}^3$

- Subtract the volume of the pyramid from volume of the prism to find the volume of the composite figure.
  $4500 - 1500 = 3000$

So the volume of the composite figure is 3000 ft^3.

Ⓑ

15 cm

12 cm

30 cm

- Find the volume of the prism.
  $V = lwh = (30)(\underline{\quad})(\underline{\quad}) = (\underline{\quad\quad}) \text{ cm}^3$

- Find the volume of the pyramid.

  Area of base: $B = $ _____ cm^2

  Volume of pyramid: $V = \frac{1}{3}(\underline{\quad})(\underline{\quad}) = (\underline{\quad}) \text{ cm}^3$

- Subtract volume of pyramid from volume of prism to find volume of composite figure.

  _____ − _____ = _____

So the volume of the composite figure is _____ cm^3.

Find the volume of the composite figure. Round to the nearest tenth.

5. The composite figure is formed from two pyramids. The base of each pyramid is a square with a side length of 6 inches and each pyramid has a height of 8 inches.

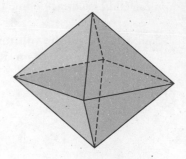

6. The composite figure is formed by a rectangular prism with two square pyramids on top of it.

💬 Elaborate

7. Explain how the volume of a pyramid is related to the volume of a prism with the same base and height.

_____

_____

_____

_____

8. If the length and width of a rectangular pyramid are doubled and the height stays the same, how does the volume of the pyramid change? Explain.

_____

_____

_____

_____

_____

9. **Essential Question Check-In** How do you calculate the volume of a pyramid?

_____

_____

_____

1. Compare the volume of a square pyramid to the volume of a square prism with the same base and height as the pyramid.

2. Which of the following equations could describe a square pyramid? Select all that apply.

   A. $3Vh = B$

   B. $V = \frac{1}{3}\ell wB$

   C. $w = \frac{3V}{\ell h}$

   D. $\frac{V}{B} = \frac{h}{3}$

   E. $V = \frac{w^2 h}{3}$

   F. $\frac{1}{3} = VBh$

3. **Justify Reasoning** As shown in the figure, polyhedron $ABCDEFGH$ is a cube and P is any point on face $EFGH$. Compare the volume of the pyramid $PABCD$ and the volume of the cube. Demonstrate how you came to your answer.

Find the volume of the pyramid. Round your answer to the nearest tenth.

4.

8.1 mm

15.2 mm

12.5 mm

5.

17 in.

6 in.

4 in.

6. Find the volume of a hexagonal pyramid with a base area of 25 ft² and a height of 9 ft.

7. The area of the base of a hexagonal pyramid is $\frac{24}{\tan 30°}$ cm². Find its volume.

4√3 cm

4 cm

Find the volume of the composite figure. Round to the nearest tenth.

8.

18 cm

12 cm

12 cm

12 cm

9.

7.5cm

5 cm

25 cm

12.5 cm

10. Given a square pyramid with a height of 21 ft and a volume of 3969 cubic feet, find the length of one side of the square base. Round to the nearest tenth.

11. Consider a pyramid with height 10 feet and a square base with side length of 7 feet. How does the volume of the pyramid change if the base stays the same and the height is doubled?

12. Algebra Find the value of x if the volume of the pyramid shown is 200 cubic centimeters.

10 cm

10 cm

13. Find the height of a rectangular pyramid with length 3 meters, width 8 meters, and volume 112 cubic meters.

14. A storage container for grain is in the shape of a square pyramid with the dimensions shown.

1 m

1.5 m

   a. What is the volume of the container in cubic centimeters?

   b. Grain leaks from the container at a rate of 4 cubic centimeters per second. Assuming the container starts completely full, about how many hours does it take until the container is empty?

15. A piece of pure copper in the shape of a rectangular pyramid with the dimensions shown has a mass of 16.76 grams. What is the density of copper? Round to the nearest hundredth. $\left(\text{Hint: } density = \dfrac{mass}{volume}.\right)$

1.5 cm

1.5 cm

2.5 cm

16. Represent Real World Problems An art gallery is a 6 story square pyramid with base area $\frac{1}{2}$ acre (1 acre = 4840 yd², 1 story ≈ 10 ft). Estimate the volume in cubic yards and cubic feet.

17. Analyze Relationships How would the volume of the pyramid shown change if each dimension were multiplied by 6? Explain how you found your answer.

4 ft

7 ft   7 ft

18. Geology A crystal is cut into a shape formed by two square pyramids joined at the base. Each pyramid has a base edge length of 5.7 mm and a height of 3 mm. What is the volume of the crystal to the nearest cubic millimeter?

3 mm

5.7 mm

19. A roof that encloses an attic is a square pyramid with a base edge length of 45 feet and a height of 5 yards. What is the volume of the attic in cubic feet? In cubic yards?

5 yd

45 ft

20. Explain the Error Describe and correct the error in finding the volume of the pyramid.

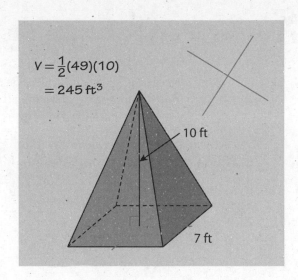

$V = \frac{1}{2}(49)(10)$

$= 245 \text{ ft}^3$

10 ft

7 ft

21. Communicate Mathematical Ideas A pyramid has a square base and a height of 5 ft. The volume of the pyramid is 60 ft³. Explain how to find the length of a side of the pyramid's base.

22. Critical Thinking A rectangular pyramid has a base length of 2, a base width of x, and a height of $3x$. Its volume is 512 cm³. What is the area of the base?

Lesson Performance Task

Genna is making a puzzle using a wooden cube. She's going to cut the cube into three pieces. The figure below shows the lines along which she plans to cut away the first piece. The result will be a piece with four triangular sides and a square side (shaded).

1. Each cut Genna makes will begin at the upper left corner of the cube. Write a rule describing where she drew the lines for the first piece.

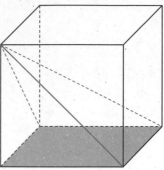

2. The figure below shows two of the lines along which Genna will cut the second piece. Draw a cube and on it, draw the two lines Genna drew. Then, using the same rule you used above, draw the third line and shade the square base of the second piece.

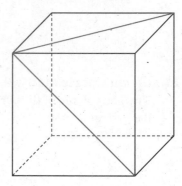

3. When Genna cut away the second piece of the puzzle, the third piece remained. Draw a new cube and then draw the lines that mark the edges of the third piece. Shade the square bottom of the third piece.

4. Compare the volumes of the three pieces. Explain your reasoning.

5. Explain how the model confirms the formula for the volume of a pyramid.

18.3 Volume of Cones

Essential Question: How do you calculate the volumes of composite figures that include cones?

Resource
Locker

⊘ Explore   Developing a Volume Formula

You can approximate the volume of a cone by finding the volumes of inscribed pyramids.

Base of inscribed
pyramid has 3 sides

Base of inscribed
pyramid has 4 sides

Base of inscribed
pyramid has 5 sides

(A) The base of a pyramid is inscribed in the circular base of the cone and is a regular n-gon. Let O be the center of the cone's base, let r be the radius of the cone, and let h be the height of the cone. Draw radii from O to the vertices of the n-gon.

Construct segment $\overline{OM}$ from O to the midpoint M of $\overline{AB}$. How can you prove that $\triangle AOM \cong \triangle BOM$?

_____

_____

_____

(B) How is $\angle 1 \cong \angle 2$?

_____

_____

_____

(C) How many triangles congruent to $\triangle AOB$ surround point O to make up the n-gon that is the base of the pyramid? How can this be used to find the angle measures of $\triangle AOM$ and $\triangle BOM$?

_____

_____

_____

_____

(D) In $\triangle AOM$, $\sin \angle 1 = \frac{x}{r}$, so $x = r\sin \angle 1$. In $\triangle AOM$, $\cos \angle 1 = \frac{y}{r}$, so $y = r\cos \angle 1$. Since $\angle 1$ has a known value, rewrite x and y using substitution.

_____

(E) To write an expression for the area of the base of the pyramid, first write an expression for the area of $\triangle AOB$.

Area of $\triangle AOB = \frac{1}{2} \cdot base \cdot height$

$= \frac{1}{2} \cdot 2x \cdot y$

$= xy$

What is the area of $\triangle AOB$, substituting the new values for x and y? What is the area of the n triangles that make up the base of the pyramid?

(F) Use the area of the base of the pyramid to find an equation for the volume of the pyramid.

Your expression for the pyramid's volume includes the expression $n \sin\left(\dfrac{180°}{n}\right) \cos\left(\dfrac{180°}{n}\right)$. Use a calculator, as follows, to discover what happens to this expression as n gets larger and larger.

- Enter the expression $n \sin\left(\dfrac{180°}{n}\right) \cos\left(\dfrac{180°}{n}\right)$ as Y_1, using x for n.
- Go to the Table Setup menu and enter the values shown.
- View a table for the function and scroll down.

What happens to the expression as n gets very large?

_____

 If $n \sin\left(\dfrac{180°}{n}\right) \cos\left(\dfrac{180°}{n}\right)$ gets closer to π as n becomes greater, what happens to the entire expression for the volume of the inscribed pyramid? How is the area of the circle related to the expression for the base?

_____

_____

Reflect

1. How is the formula for the volume of a cone related to the formula for the volume of a pyramid?

_____

_____

🔑 Explain 1 Finding the Volume of a Cone

The volume relationship for cones that you found in the Explore can be stated as the following formula.

Volume of a Cone

The volume of a cone with base radius r and base area $B = \pi r^2$ and height h is given by $V = \frac{1}{3}Bh$ or by $V = \frac{1}{3}\pi r^2 h$.

You can use a formula for the volume of a cone to solve problems involving volume and capacity.

Example 1   The figure represents a conical paper cup. How many fluid ounces of liquid can the cup hold? Round to the nearest tenth. (*Hint*: $1 \text{ in}^3 \approx 0.554 \text{ fl oz.}$)

2.2 in.

1.8 in.

(A) Find the radius and height of the cone to the nearest hundredth.

The radius is half of the diameter, so $r = \frac{1}{2}(2.2 \text{ in.}) = 1.1 \text{ in.}$

To find the height of the cone, use the Pythagorean Theorem:

$$r^2 + h^2 = (1.8)^2$$

$$(1.1)^2 + h^2 = (1.8)^2$$

$$1.21 + h^2 = 3.24$$

$$h^2 = 2.03, \text{ so } h \approx 1.42 \text{ in.}$$

(B) Find the volume of the cone in cubic inches.

$$V = \frac{1}{3}\pi r^2 h \approx \frac{1}{3}\pi \left(\boxed{}\right)^2 \left(\boxed{}\right) \approx \boxed{} \text{ in}^3$$

(C) Find the capacity of the cone to the nearest tenth of a fluid ounce.

$$\boxed{} \text{ in}^3 \approx \boxed{} \text{ in}^3 \times \frac{0.554 \text{ fl oz}}{1 \text{ in}^3} \approx \boxed{} \text{ fl oz}$$

Your Turn

Right after Cindy buys a frozen yogurt cone, her friend Maria calls her, and they talk for so long that the frozen yogurt melts before Cindy can eat it. The cone has a slant height of 3.9 in. and a diameter of 2.4 in. If the frozen yogurt has the same volume before and after melting, and when melted just fills the cone, how much frozen yogurt did Cindy have before she talked to Maria, to the nearest tenth of a fluid ounce?

2.   Find the radius. Then use the Pythagorean Theorem to find the height of the cone.

2.4 in.

3.9 in.

3.   Find the volume of the cone in cubic inches.

4.   Find the capacity of the cone to the nearest fluid ounce.

Explain 2 Finding the Volume of a Composite Figure

You can find the volume of a composite figure using appropriate volume formulas for the different parts of the figure.

Example 2 Find the volume of the composite figure. Round to the nearest cubic millimeter.

19 mm

32 mm

16 mm

(A) Find the volume of the cylinder.

First, find the radius: $r = \frac{1}{2}(16 \text{ mm}) = 8 \text{ mm}$

$V = \pi r^2 h = \pi (8)^2 (19) = 3{,}820.176 \ldots \text{ mm}^3$

(B) Find the volume of the cone.

The height of the cone is $h =$ ▢ mm − ▢ mm = ▢ mm.

It has the same radius as the cylinder, $r =$ ▢ mm.

$V = \frac{1}{3} \pi r^2 h = \frac{1}{3} \pi \left(\boxed{}\right)^2 \left(\boxed{}\right) \approx \boxed{} \text{ mm}^3$

(C) Find the total volume.

Total volume = volume of cylinder + volume of cone

= $\boxed{}$ mm^3 + $\boxed{}$ mm^3

≈ $\boxed{}$ mm^3

Reflect

5. **Discussion** A composite figure is formed from a cone and a cylinder with the same base radius, and its volume can be calculated by multiplying the volume of the cylinder by a rational number, $\frac{a}{b}$. What arrangements of the cylinder and cone could explain this?

_____

_____

_____

_____

Making a cone-shaped hole in the top of a cylinder forms a composite figure, so that the apex of the cone is at the base of the cylinder. Find the volume of the figure, to the nearest tenth.

4.3 cm

3.6 cm

6. Find the volume of the cylinder.

7. Find the volume of the figure.

⊙ Elaborate

8. Could you use a circumscribed regular *n*-gon as the base of a pyramid to derive the formula for the volume of a cone? Explain.

_____

_____

_____

_____

_____

9. **Essential Question Check-In** How do you calculate the volumes of composite figures that include cones?

_____

_____

_____

1. **Interpret the Answer** Katherine is using a cone to fill a cylinder with sand. If the radii and height are equal on both objects, and Katherine fills the cone to the very top, how many cones will it take to fill the cylinder with sand? Explain your answer.

Find the volume of the cone. Round the answer to the nearest tenth.

2.

1.9 mm

4.2 mm

3.

6.3 ft

5.9 ft

4.

22 cm

20 cm

Find the volume of the cone. Leave the answer in terms of π.

5.

30 in

24 in.

6.

41 m

9 m

Find the volume of the composite figures. Round the answer to the nearest tenth.

7.

4 in. 8 in.

12 in.

6 in.

8.

6 ft

10 ft

9.

2 m

13 m

1 m

10.

5 ft

10 ft

3 ft

12 ft

11. Match the dimensions of a cone on the left with its volume on the right.

   A. radius 3 units, height 7 units   _____ $\frac{25\pi}{6}$ units^3

   B. diameter 5 units, height 2 units   _____ 240π units^3

   C. radius 28 units, slant height 53 units   _____ $11,760\pi$ units^3

   D. diameter 24 units, slant height 13 units.   _____ 21π units^3

12. The roof of a grain silo is in the shape of a cone. The inside radius is 20 feet, and the roof is 10 feet tall. Below the cone is a cylinder 30 feet tall, with the same radius.

   a. What is the volume of the silo?

   b. If one cubic foot of wheat is approximately 48 pounds, and the farmer's crop consists of approximately 2 million pounds of wheat, will all of the wheat fit in the silo?

13. A cone has a volume of 18π in^3. Which are possible dimensions of the cone? Select all that apply.

   A. diameter 1 in., height 18 in.

   B. diameter 6 in., height 6 in.

   C. diameter 3 in., height 6 in.

   D. diameter 6 in., height 3 in.

   E. diameter 4 in., height 13.5 in.

   F. diameter 13.5 in., height 4 in.

14. The figure shows a water tank that consists of a cylinder and a cone. How many gallons of water does the tank hold? Round to the nearest gallon. (Hint: 1 ft³ = 7.48 gal)

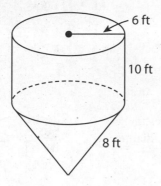

6 ft

10 ft

8 ft

15. Roland is using a special machine to cut cones out of cylindrical pieces of wood. The machine is set to cut out two congruent cones from each piece of wood, leaving no gap in between the vertices of the cones. What is the volume of material left over after two cones are cut out?

12 in.

12 in.

16. Algebra Develop an expression that could be used to solve for the volume of this solid for any value of x.

17. Persevere in Problem Solving A juice stand sells smoothies in cone-shaped cups that are 8 in. tall. The regular size has a 4 in. diameter. The jumbo size has an 8 in. diameter.

8 in.

a. Find the volume of the regular size to the nearest tenth.

b. Find the volume of the jumbo size to the nearest tenth.

c. The regular size costs $1.25. What would be a reasonable price for the jumbo size? Explain your reasoning.

18. Find the volume of a cone with base area 36π ft^2 and a height equal to twice the radius.

19. Find the base circumference of a cone with height 5 cm and volume 125π cm^3.

20. Analyze Relationships Popcorn is available in two cups: a square pyramid or a cone, as shown. The price of each cup of popcorn is the same. Which cup is the better deal? Explain.

21. Make a Conjecture A cylinder has a radius of 5 in. and a height of 3 in. Without calculating the volumes, find the height of a cone with the same base and the same volume as the cylinder. Explain your reasoning.

22. Analyze Relationships A sculptor removes a cone from a cylindrical block of wood so that the vertex of the cone is the center of the cylinder's base, as shown. Explain how the volume of the remaining solid compares with the volume of the original cylindrical block of wood.

23. Explain the Error Which volume is incorrect? Explain the error.

(A)
$$V = \frac{1}{3}(8^2\pi)(17)$$
$$= \frac{1088\pi}{3} \text{ cm}^3$$

(B)
$$V = \frac{1}{3}(8^2\pi)(15)$$
$$= 320\pi \text{ cm}^3$$

Lesson Performance Task

You've just set up your tent on the first night of a camping trip that you've been looking forward to for a long time. Unfortunately, mosquitoes have been looking forward to your arrival even more than you have. When you turn on your flashlight you see swarms of them—an average of 800 mosquitoes per square meter, in fact.

Since you're always looking for a way to use geometry, you decide to solve a problem: How many mosquitoes are in the first three meters of the cone of your flashlight (Zone 1 in the diagram), and how many are in the second three meters (Zone 2)?

1. Explain how you can find the volume of the Zone 1 cone.

2. Find the volume of the Zone 1 cone. Write your answer in terms of π.

3. Explain how you can find the volume of the Zone 2 cone.

4. Find the volume of the Zone 2 cone. Write your answer in terms of π.

5. How many more mosquitoes are there in Zone 2 than there are in Zone 1? Use 3.14 for π.

18.4 Volume of Spheres

Essential Question: How can you use the formula for the volume of a sphere to calculate the volumes of composite figures?

◎ Explore   Developing a Volume Formula

To find the volume of a sphere, compare one of its hemispheres to a cylinder of the same height and radius from which a cone has been removed.

Ⓐ The region of a plane that intersects a solid figure is called a **cross section**. To show that cross sections have the same area at every level, use the Pythagorean Theorem to find a relationship between *r*, *x*, and *R*.

_____

_____

_____

Ⓑ A cross section of the cylinder with the cone removed is a ring.

To find the area of the ring, find the area of the outer circle and of the inner circle. Then subtract the area of the inner circle from the outer circle.

(C) Find an expression for the volume of the cylinder with the cone removed.

(D) Use Cavalieri's principle to deduce the volume of a sphere with radius r.

_____

_____

_____

_____

Reflect

1. How do you know that the height h of the cylinder with the cone removed is equal to the radius r?

_____

_____

2. What happens to the cross-sectional areas when $x = 0$? when $x = r$?

_____

_____

_____

_____

⊘ Explain 1 Finding the Volume of a Sphere

The relationship you discovered in the Explore can be stated as a volume formula.

Volume of a Sphere
The volume of a sphere with radius r is given by $V = \frac{4}{3}\pi r^3$.

You can use a formula for the volume of a sphere to solve problems involving volume and capacity.

Example 1 The figure represents a spherical helium-filled balloon. This tourist attraction allows up to 28 passengers at a time to ride in a gondola suspended underneath the balloon, as it cruises at an altitude of 500 ft. How much helium, to the nearest hundred gallons, does the balloon hold? Round to the nearest tenth. (*Hint:* 1 gal ≈ 0.1337 ft³)

72 ft

Step 1 Find the radius of the balloon.

The radius is half of the diameter, so $r = \frac{1}{2}(72 \text{ ft}) = 36 \text{ ft}$.

Step 2 Find the volume of the balloon in cubic feet.

$$V = \frac{4}{3}\pi r^3$$

$$= \frac{4}{3}\pi \left(\boxed{} \right)^3$$

$$\approx \boxed{} \text{ ft}^3$$

Step 3 Find the capacity of the balloon to the nearest gallon.

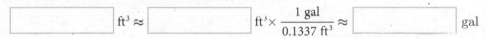

$\boxed{} \text{ ft}^3 \approx \boxed{} \text{ ft}^3 \times \dfrac{1 \text{ gal}}{0.1337 \text{ ft}^3} \approx \boxed{}$ gal

---

Your Turn

A spherical water tank has a diameter of 27 m. How much water can the tank hold, to the nearest liter? (*Hint:* 1,000 L = 1 m³)

3. Find the volume of the tank in cubic meters.

4. Find the capacity of the tank to the nearest liter.

⚙ Explain 2 Finding the Volume of a Composite Figure

You can find the volume of a composite figure using appropriate volume formulas for the different parts of the figure.

Example 2 Find the volume of the composite figure. Round to the nearest cubic centimeter.

5 cm
13 cm

Step 1 Find the volume of the hemisphere.

Step 2 Find the height of the cone.

$$h^2 + \left(\boxed{}\right)^2 = \left(\boxed{}\right)^2$$

$$h^2 + \boxed{} = \boxed{}$$

$$h^2 = \boxed{}$$

$$h = \boxed{}$$

Step 3 Find the volume of the cone.

The cone has the same radius as the hemisphere, $r = \boxed{}$ cm.

$$V = \frac{1}{3}\pi r^2 h$$

$$= \frac{1}{3}\pi \left(\boxed{}\right)^2 \left(\boxed{}\right)$$

$$= \boxed{} \text{ cm}^3$$

Step 4 Find the total volume.

Total volume = volume of hemisphere + volume of cone

$$= \boxed{} \text{ cm}^3 + \boxed{} \text{ cm}^3$$

$$\approx \boxed{} \text{ cm}^3$$

Reflect

5. Is it possible to create a figure by taking a cone and removing from it a hemisphere with the same radius?

_____

_____

_____

Your Turn

6. A composite figure is a cylinder with a hemispherical hole in the top. The bottom of the hemisphere is tangent to the base of the cylinder. Find the volume of the figure, to the nearest tenth.

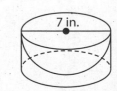
7 in.

7. Discussion Could you use an inscribed prism to derive the volume of a hemisphere? Why or why not? Are there any other ways you could approximate a hemisphere, and what problems would you encounter in finding its volume?

_____

_____

_____

8. Essential Question Check-In A gumball is in the shape of a sphere, with a spherical hole in the center. How might you calculate the volume of the gumball? What measurements are needed?

_____

_____

_____

⭐ Evaluate: Homework and Practice

- Online Homework
- Hints and Help
- Extra Practice

1. Analyze Relationships Use the diagram of a sphere inscribed in a cylinder to describe the relationship between the volume of a sphere and the volume of a cylinder.

Find the volume of the sphere. Round the answer to the nearest tenth.

2.

3.7 in.

3.

11 ft

4.

Circumference
of great circle
is 14π cm

Find the volume of the sphere. Leave the answer in terms of π.

5.

20 cm

6.

1 m

7.

Area of great
circle is 81π in²

Find the volume of the composite figure. Leave the answer in terms of π.

8.

├── 5 ft ──┤ 2 ft

9.

2 in. 8 in.

3 in.

Find the volume of the composite figure. Round the answer to the nearest tenth.

10.

3 cm

4 cm

8 cm

10 cm

11.

10 mm 24 mm

8 mm

12. Analyze Relationships Approximately how many times as great is the volume of a grapefruit with diameter 10 cm as the volume of a lime with diameter 5 cm?

13. A bead is formed by drilling a cylindrical hole with a 2 mm diameter through a sphere with an 8 mm diameter. Estimate the volume of the bead to the nearest whole.

14. Algebra Write an expression representing the volume of the composite figure formed by a hemisphere with radius r and a cube with side length $2r$.

15. One gallon of propane yields approximately 91,500 BTU. About how many BTUs does the spherical storage tank shown provide? Round to the nearest million BTUs. (*Hint:* 1 ft^3 ≈ 7.48 gal)

16. The aquarium shown is a rectangular prism that is filled with water. You drop a spherical ball with a diameter of 6 inches into the aquarium. The ball sinks, causing the water to spill from the tank. How much water is left in the tank? Express your answer to the nearest tenth. (*Hint:* 1 in.^{3} ≈ 0.00433 gal)

17. A sphere with diameter 8 cm is inscribed in a cube. Find the ratio of the volume of the cube to the volume of the sphere.

   A. $\dfrac{6}{\pi}$

   B. $\dfrac{2}{3\pi}$

   C. $\dfrac{3\pi}{4}$

   D. $\dfrac{3\pi}{2}$

For Exercises 18–20, use the table. Round each volume to the nearest billion π.

Planet	Diameter (mi)
Mercury	3,032
Venus	7,521
Earth	7,926
Mars	4,222
Jupiter	88,846
Saturn	74,898
Uranus	31,763
Neptune	30,775

18. **Explain the Error** Margaret used the mathematics shown to find the volume of Saturn.

$$V = \frac{4}{3}\pi r^2 = \frac{4}{3}\pi(74{,}898)^2 \approx \frac{4}{3}\pi(6{,}000{,}000{,}000) \approx 8{,}000{,}000{,}000\pi$$

Explain the two errors Margaret made, then give the correct answer.

19. The sum of the volumes of Venus and Mars is about equal to the volume of which planet?

20. How many times as great as the volume of the smallest planet is the volume of the largest planet? Round to the nearest thousand.

21. Make a Conjecture The *bathysphere* was an early version of a submarine, invented in the 1930s. The inside diameter of the bathysphere was 54 inches, and the steel used to make the sphere was 1.5 inches thick. It had three 8-inch diameter windows. Estimate the volume of steel used to make the bathysphere.

22. Explain the Error A student solved the problem shown. Explain the student's error and give the correct answer to the problem.

A spherical gasoline tank has a radius of 0.5 ft. When filled, the tank provides 446,483 BTU. How many BTUs does one gallon of gasoline yield? Round to the nearest thousand BTUs and use the fact that 1 ft$^3 \approx 7.48$ gal.

> The volume of the tank is $\frac{4}{3}\pi r^3 = \frac{4}{3}\pi(0.5)^3$ ft^3. Multiplying by 7.48 shows that this is approximately 3.92 gal. So the number of BTUs in one gallon of gasoline is approximately 446,483 × 3.92 ≈ 1,750,000 BTU.

23. Persevere in Problem Solving The top of a gumball machine is an 18 in. sphere. The machine holds a maximum of 3300 gumballs, which leaves about 43% of the space in the machine empty. Estimate the diameter of each gumball.

Lesson Performance Task

For his science project, Bizbo has decided to build a scale model of the solar system. He starts with a grapefruit with a radius of 2 inches to represent Earth. His "Earth" weighs 0.5 pounds.

Find each of the following for Bizbo's model. Use the rounded figures in the table. Round your answers to two significant figures. Use 3.14 for π.

	Radius (mi)	Distance from Sun (mi)
Earth	4×10^3	9.3×10^7
Neptune	1.5×10^4	2.8×10^9
Sun	4.3×10^5	

1. the scale of Bizbo's model: 1 inch = _____ miles

2. Earth's distance from the Sun, in inches and in miles

3. Neptune's distance from the Sun, in inches and in miles

4. the Sun's volume, in cubic inches and cubic feet

5. the Sun's weight, in pounds and in tons (Note: the Sun's density is 0.26 times the Earth's density.)

Volume Formulas

Essential Question: How can you use volume formulas to solve real-world problems?

KEY EXAMPLE   *(Lesson 18.1)*

Find the volume of a cylinder with a base radius of 3 centimeters and a height of 5 centimeters. Write an exact answer.

$V = \pi r^2 h$ Write the formula for the volume of a cylinder.

$\quad = \pi(3)^2(5)$ Substitute.

$\quad = 45\pi \text{ cm}^3$ Simplify.

KEY EXAMPLE   *(Lesson 18.2)*

Find the volume of a square pyramid with a base side length of 12 inches and a height of 7 inches.

$V = \frac{1}{3}Bh$ Write the formula for the volume of a pyramid.

$\quad = \frac{1}{3}(12)^2(7)$ Substitute.

$\quad = 336 \text{ in}^3$ Simplify.

KEY EXAMPLE   *(Lesson 18.3)*

Find the volume of a conc with a base diameter of 16 feet and a height of 18 feet. Write an exact answer.

$r = \frac{1}{2}(16 \text{ ft})$ Find the radius.

$\quad = 8 \text{ ft}$ Simplify.

$V = \frac{1}{3}\pi r^2 h$ Write the formula for the volume of a cone.

$\quad = \frac{1}{3}\pi(8)^2(18)$ Substitute.

$\quad = 384\pi \text{ ft}^3$ Simplify.

KEY EXAMPLE   *(Lesson 18.4)*

Find the volume of a sphere with a radius of 30 miles. Write an exact answer.

$V = \frac{4}{3}\pi r^3$ Write the formula for the volume of a sphere.

$\quad = \frac{4}{3}\pi(30)^3$ Substitute.

$\quad = 36{,}000\pi \text{ mi}^3$ Simplify.

Find the volume of each figure. Write an exact answer. *(Lessons 18.1–18.4)*

1.

9
10 5

_____

2.

6.3
4.7
21

_____

3.

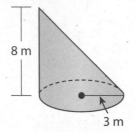

16 cm

33 cm

_____

4.

3.6 ft
4 ft
5 ft

_____

5.

8 m

3 m

_____

6.

12

_____

7.

25 yd   9 yd

_____

MODULE PERFORMANCE TASK

How Big Is That Sinkhole?

In 2010 an enormous sinkhole suddenly appeared in the middle of a Guatemalan neighborhood and swallowed a three-story building above it. The sinkhole has an estimated depth of about 100 feet.

How much material is needed to fill the sinkhole? Determine what information is needed to answer the question. Do you think your estimate is more likely to be too high or too low?

What are some material options for filling the sinkhole, and how much would they cost? Which material do you think would be the best choice?

(Ready) to Go On?

18.1–18.4 Volume Formulas

- Online Homework
- Hints and Help
- Extra Practice

Find the volume of the figure. *(Lessons 18.1–18.4)*

1. An oblique cylinder next to a cube.

2. A prism of volume 3 with a pyramid of the same height cut out.

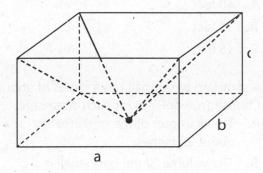

3. A cone with a square pyramid of the same height cut out. The pyramid has height l, and its square base has area l^2.

Top View

4. A cube with sides of length s with the biggest sphere that fits in it cut out.

ESSENTIAL QUESTION

5. How would you find the volume of an ice-cream cone with ice cream in it? What measurements would you need?

Assessment Readiness

1. A simplified model of a particular monument is a rectangular pyramid placed on top of a rectangular prism, as shown. The volume of the monument is 66 cubic feet. Determine whether the given measurement could be the height of the monument.
   Select Yes or No for A–C.

   A. 10 feet   ⚪ Yes   ⚪ No
   B. 13 feet   ⚪ Yes   ⚪ No
   C. 15 feet   ⚪ Yes   ⚪ No

2. A standard basketball has a radius of about 4.7 inches. Choose True or False for each statement.

   A. The diameter of the basketball is about 25 inches.   ⚪ True   ⚪ False

   B. The volume of the basketball is approximately 277.6 in^3.   ⚪ True   ⚪ False

   C. The volume of the basketball is approximately 434.9 in^3.   ⚪ True   ⚪ False

3. A triangle has a side of length 8, a second side of length 17, and a third side of length x. Find the range of possible values for x.

4. Find the approximate volume of the figure at right, composed of a cone, a cylinder, and a hemisphere. Explain how you found the values needed to compute the volume.

Visualizing Solids

Essential Question: How can visualizing solids help you to solve real-world problems?

REAL WORLD VIDEO
Check out how visualization of solids and surface area can be used to determine critical dimensions of the Space Shuttle and other spacecraft.

MODULE PERFORMANCE TASK PREVIEW

How Much Does the Paint on the Space Shuttle Weigh?

At some point, NASA stopped painting the fuel tanks for the Space Shuttle because of the extra weight it added. In this module, you will be challenged to use surface area to come up with an estimate for the weight of that paint. Let's start the countdown!

Complete these exercises to review skills you will need for this module.

Cross Sections

Example 1   What is the cross section of a plane that passes through (but not tangent to) a sphere?

• Online Homework
• Hints and Help
• Extra Practice

No matter how or where the plane passes, the cross section will always be a circle with radius less than or equal to the radius of the sphere.

Find the cross section of the following.

1.   A plane passing through a cylinder parallel to the bases.

_____

Volume

Example 2   Find the exact volume of a right cylinder with a radius 9 and height 5.

$V = Bh$ Volume of a cylinder

$B = \pi r^2$ Area of base equals the area of a circle.

$B = \pi(9)^2 = 81\pi$ Substitute and solve.

$V = (81\pi)(5) = 405\pi$ Substitute and solve to find the volume.

Find the volume of the following. Give exact values.

2.   A sphere with radius 6   _____

3.   A pyramid whose base is a square with a base   _____
having sides of length 17 and whose height is 9

Surface Area

Example 3   Given a cube with a side of length 5, find the surface area.

Since the surface area of a cube is 6 squares of equal area, find the area of one face of the cube and then multiply by 6.

$A = s^2$ Area of a square

$A = (5)^2 = 25$ Substitute and solve.

$SA = 25 \cdot 6 = 150$ Multiply by 6, the number of faces of a cube.

Find the surface area of a cube with the following side lengths.

4.   7   _____

5.   10   _____

19.1 Cross Sections and Solids of Rotation

Essential Question: What tools can you use to visualize solid figures accurately?

Resource Locker

⊘ Explore   Exploring Nets

A **net** is a diagram of the surfaces of a three-dimensional figure that can be folded to form the three-dimensional figure. To identify a three-dimensional figure from a net, look at the number of faces and the shape of each face.

Ⓐ   Complete each row of the table. Express the circumference of the cylinder as a multiple of π.

Type of Solid	Example	Faces	Net
	1.5 m, 2 m, 4 m		4 m, 1.5 m, 2 m, 1.5 m, 2 m
triangular prism		a pair of congruent triangles and 3 rectangles	

Type of Solid	Example	Faces	Net
		a rectangle and 2 pairs of congruent isosceles triangles	11 cm 6 cm
cylinder	7 ft 12 ft		

Reflect

1. **Discussion** Is there more than one way to draw a net for a solid? Are there rules for how the faces of a solid are joined to create a net for it?

_____

_____

_____

🔑 Explain 1   Identifying Cross Sections

Recall that a *cross section* is a region of a plane that intersects a solid figure. Cross sections of three-dimensional figures sometimes turn out to be simple figures such as triangles, rectangles, or circles.

Example 1   Describe the cross section of each figure. Compare the dimensions of the cross section to those of the figure.

Ⓐ The bases of the cylinder are congruent circles.

The cross section is formed by a plane that is parallel to the bases of the cylinder. Any cross section of a cylinder made by a plane parallel to the bases will have the same shape as the bases.

Therefore, the cross section is a circle with the same radius or diameter as the bases.

B. The lateral surface of the cone curves in the horizontal direction, but not the vertical direction. Therefore the two sides of the cross section along this surface are straight line segments with equal lengths.

The third side is a diameter of the base of the cone. Therefore, the cross section is a(n) [   ] triangle. Its base is the [   ] of the cone and its leg length is the [   ] height of the cone.

Reflect

2. A plane intersects a sphere. Make a conjecture about the resulting cross section.

_____

Your Turn

Describe each cross section of each figure. Compare the dimensions of the cross section to those of the figure.

3.

⊘ Explain 2 Generating Three-Dimensional Figures

You can generate a three-dimensional figure by rotating a two-dimensional figure around an appropriate axis.

Example 2 Describe and then sketch the figure that is generated by each rotation in three-dimensional space.

(A) A right triangle rotated around a line containing one of its legs

Leg $\overline{BC}$ is perpendicular to ℓ, so vertex C traces out a circle as it rotates about ℓ, and therefore $\overline{BC}$ traces out a circular base. The hypotenuse, $\overline{AC}$, traces out the curving surface of the cone whose base is formed by $\overline{BC}$. The figure formed by the rotation is a cone.

(B) A rectangle rotated around a line containing one of its sides

Sides $\overline{BC}$ and ☐ are both _____ to ℓ, so they each trace out

congruent _____ with common _____ $BC =$ ☐. Side ☐ is

parallel to ℓ, so it traces out a surface formed by moving a _____ at a constant

distance from ℓ. The figure formed by the rotation is a _____.

4. **Discussion** What principles can you identify for generating a solid by rotation of a two-dimensional figure?

_____

_____

_____

_____

Describe and then sketch the figure that is generated by each rotation in three-dimensional space.

5. A trapezoid with two adjacent acute angles rotated around a line containing the side adjacent to these angles

6. A semicircle rotated around a line containing its diameter

7. Discussion If a solid has been generated by rotating a plane figure around an axis, will the solid always have cross-sections that are circles? Will it always have cross sections that are not circles? Explain.

_____

_____

_____

_____

_____

8. Essential Question Check-In What tools can you use to visualize solid figures? Explain how each tool is helpful.

_____

_____

_____

_____

⭐ Evaluate: Homework and Practice

- Online Homework
- Hints and Help
- Extra Practice

1. Which of the figures is not a net for a cube? Explain.

a.

c.

b.

d.

Describe the three-dimensional figure that can be made from the given net.

2.

3.

Describe the cross-section.

4.

5.

6.

7.

8.

9.

10. Describe the cross section formed by the intersection of a cone and a plane parallel to the base of the cone.

11. Describe the cross section formed by the intersection of a sphere and a plane that passes through the center of the sphere.

Sketch and describe the figure that is generated by each rotation in three-dimensional space.

12. Rotate a semicircle around a line through the endpoints of the semicircle.

13. Rotate an isosceles triangle around the triangle's line of symmetry.

14. Rotate an isosceles right triangle around a line that contains the triangle's hypotenuse

15. Rotate a line segment around a line that is perpendicular to the segment that passes through an endpoint to the segment.

16. Multiple Response Which of the following shapes could be formed by the intersection of a plane and a cube? Select all that apply.

  A. Equilateral Triangle

  B. Scalene Triangle

  C. Square

  D. Rectangle

  E. Circle

17. A student claims that if you dilate the net for a cube using a scale factor of 2, the surface area of the resulting cube is multiplied by 4 and the volume is multiplied by 8. Does this claim make sense?

18. Find the Error A regular hexagonal prism is intersected by a plane as shown. Which cross section is incorrect? Explain.

H.O.T. Focus on Higher Order Thinking

19. Architecture An architect is drawing plans for a building that is a hexagonal prism. Describe how the architect could draw a cutaway of the building that shows a cross section in the shape of a hexagon, and a cross section in the shape of a rectangle.

20. Draw Conclusions Is it possible for a cross section of a cube to be an octagon? Explain.

21. Communicate Mathematical Ideas A cube with sides of length s is intersected by a plane that passes through three of the cube's vertices, forming the cross section shown. What type of triangle is in the cross section? Explain.

22. The three triangles all have the same area because each base and each height are congruent. Make and test a conjecture about the volume of the solids generated by rotating these triangles around the base.

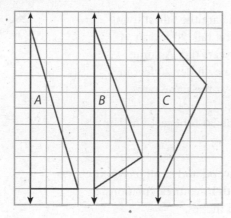

Lesson Performance Task

Each year of its life, a tree grows a new ring just under the outside bark. The new ring consists of two parts, light-colored *springwood*, when the tree grows the fastest, and a darker-colored *summerwood*, when growth slows. When conditions are good and there is lots of sun and rain, the new ring is thicker than the rings formed when there is drought or excessive cold. At the center of the tree is a dark circle called *pith* that is not connected to the age of the tree.

1. Describe the history of the tree in the diagram.

2. The redwood trees of coastal California are the tallest living things on earth. One redwood is 350 feet tall, 20 feet in diameter at its base, and around 2000 years old. Assume that the lower 50 feet of the tree form a cylinder 20 feet in diameter and that all of the rings grew at the same rate.

a. What is the total volume of wood in the 50-foot section? Use 3.14 for π.

b. How wide is each annual ring (springwood and summerwood combined)? Disregard the bark and pith in your calculations. Show your work. Write your answer in inches.

19.2 Surface Area of Prisms and Cylinders

Essential Question: How can you find the surface area of a prism or cylinder?

⊘ Explore   Developing a Surface Area Formula

Surface area is the total area of all the faces and curved surfaces of a three-dimensional figure. The *lateral area* of a prism is the sum of the areas of the lateral faces.

(A) Consider the right prism shown here and the net for the right prism. Complete the figure by labeling the dimensions of the net.

(B) In the net, what type of figure is formed by the lateral faces of the prism?

_____

(C) Write an expression for the length of the base of the rectangle.

_____

(D) How is the base of the rectangle related to the perimeter of the base of the prism?

_____

(E) The lateral area L of the prism is the area of the rectangle. Write a formula for L in terms of h, a, b, and c.

_____

(F) Write the formula for L in terms of P, where P is the perimeter of the base of the prism.

_____

(G) Let B be the area of the base of the prism. Write a formula for the surface area S of the prism in terms of B and L. Then write the formula in terms of B, P, and h.

_____

1. Explain why the net of the lateral surface of any right prism will always be a rectangle.

_____

_____

_____

_____

2. Suppose a rectangular prism has length ℓ, width w, and height h, as shown. Explain how you can write a formula for the surface area of the prism in terms of ℓ, w, and h.

_____

_____

⚙ Explain 1   Finding the Surface Area of a Prism

Lateral Area and Surface Area of Right Prisms

The lateral area of a right prism with height h and base perimeter P is $L = Ph$.

The surface area of a right prism with lateral area L and base area B is $S = L + 2B$, or $S = Ph + 2B$.

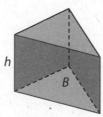

Example 1 Each gift box is a right prism. Find the total amount of paper needed to wrap each box, not counting overlap.

(A) **Step 1** Find the lateral area.

Lateral area formula	$L = Ph$
$P = 2(8) + 2(6) = 28$ cm	$= 28(12)$
Multiply.	$= 336$ cm^2

Step 2 Find the surface area.

Surface area formula	$S = L + 2B$
Substitute the lateral area.	$= 336 + 2(6)(8)$
Simplify.	$= 432$ cm^2

12 cm

6 cm

8 cm

(B) **Step 1** Find the length c of the hypotenuse of the base.

Pythagorean Theorem	$c^2 = a^2 + b^2$
Substitute.	$= \boxed{}^2 + \boxed{}^2$
Simplify.	$= \boxed{}$
Take the square root of each side.	$c = \boxed{}$

10 in   24 in

20 in

Step 2 Find the lateral area.

Lateral area formula	$L = Ph$
Substitute.	$= \boxed{}\left(\boxed{}\right)$
Multiply.	$= \boxed{}$ in^2

Step 3 Find the surface area.

Surface area formula	$S = L + 2B$
Substitute.	$= \boxed{} + 2 \cdot \frac{1}{2}\boxed{} \cdot \boxed{}$
Simplify.	$= \boxed{}$ in^2

Reflect

3. A gift box is a rectangular prism with length 9.8 cm, width 10.2 cm, and height 9.7 cm. Explain how to estimate the amount of paper needed to wrap the box, not counting overlap.

_____

_____

Each gift box is a right prism. Find the total amount of paper needed to wrap each box, not counting overlap.

4.

5 in
5 in
18 in

5.

6 in
3.6 in
8.5 in

⚷ Explain 2 Finding the Surface Area of a Cylinder

Lateral Area and Surface Area of Right Cylinders

The *lateral area* of a cylinder is the area of the curved surface that connects the two bases.

The lateral area of a right cylinder with radius r and height h is $L = 2\pi rh$.

The surface area of a right cylinder with lateral area L and base area B is $S = L + 2B$, or $S = 2\pi rh + 2\pi r^2$.

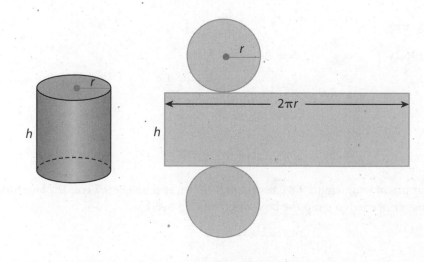

Example 2 Each aluminum can is a right cylinder. Find the amount of paper needed for the can's label and the total amount of aluminum needed to make the can. Round to the nearest tenth.

Ⓐ **Step 1** Find the lateral area.

3 cm

9 cm

Lateral area formula	$L = 2\pi rh$
Substitute.	$L = 2\pi(3)(9)$
Multiply.	$= 54\pi$ cm^2

Step 2 Find the surface area.

Surface area formula	$S = L + 2\pi r^2$
Substitute the lateral area and radius.	$= 54\pi + 2\pi(3)^2$
Simplify.	$= 72\pi$ cm^2

Step 3 Use a calculator and round to the nearest tenth.

The amount of paper needed for the label is the lateral area, $54\pi \approx 169.6$ cm^2.

The amount of aluminum needed for the can is the surface area, $72\pi \approx 226.2$ cm^2.

Ⓑ **Step 1** Find the lateral area.

5 in

2 in

Lateral area formula	$L = 2\pi rh$
Substitute; the radius is half the diameter.	$= 2\pi \left(\boxed{}\right)\left(\boxed{}\right)$
Multiply.	$= \boxed{} \pi$ in^2

Step 2 Find the surface area.

Surface area formula	$S = L + 2\pi r^2$
Substitute the lateral area and radius.	$= \boxed{} \pi + 2\pi \left(\boxed{}\right)^2$
Simplify.	$= \boxed{} \pi$ in^2

Step 3 Use a calculator and round to the nearest tenth.

The amount of paper needed for the label is the lateral area, $\boxed{} \pi \approx \boxed{}$ in^2.

The amount of aluminum needed for the can is the surface area, $\boxed{} \pi \approx \boxed{}$ in^2.

Reflect

6. In these problems, why is it best to round only in the final step of the solution?

_____

_____

Your Turn

Each aluminum can is a right cylinder. Find the amount of paper needed for the can's label and the total amount of aluminum needed to make the can. Round to the nearest tenth.

7.

15 cm

6 cm

8.

80 mm

72 mm

🔑 Explain 3   Finding the Surface Area of a Composite Figure

Example 3   Find the surface area of each composite figure. Round to the nearest tenth.

(A)   **Step 1**   Find the surface area of the right rectangular prism.

Surface area formula	$S = Ph + 2B$
Substitute.	$= 80(20) + 2(24)(16)$
Simplify.	$= 2368 \text{ ft}^2$

4 ft

20 ft

16 ft

24 ft

Step 2   A cylinder is removed from the prism. Find the lateral area of the cylinder and the area of its bases.

Lateral area formula	$L = 2\pi rh$
Substitute.	$= 2\pi(4)(20)$
Simplify.	$= 160\pi \text{ ft}^2$
Base area formula	$B = \pi r^2$
Substitute.	$= \pi(4)^2$
Simplify.	$= 16\pi \text{ ft}^2$

Step 3   Find the surface area of the composite figure. The surface area is the sum of the areas of all surfaces on the exterior of the figure.

$S = (\text{prism surface area}) + (\text{cylinder lateral area}) - (\text{cylinder base areas})$

$= 2368 + 160\pi - 2(16\pi)$

$= 2368 + 128\pi \approx 2770.1 \text{ ft}^2$

Ⓑ Step 1 Find the surface area of the right rectangular prism.

Surface area formula $\quad S = Ph + 2B$

Substitute. $\quad = \boxed{}\left(\boxed{}\right) + 2\boxed{}\left(\boxed{}\right)$

Simplify. $\quad = \boxed{} \text{ cm}^2$

Step 2 Find the surface area of the cylinder.

Lateral area formula $\quad L = 2\pi rh$

Substitute. $\quad = 2\pi\left(\boxed{}\right)\left(\boxed{}\right)$

Simplify. $\quad = \boxed{}\,\pi \text{ cm}^2$

Surface area formula $\quad S = L + 2\pi r^2$

Substitute. $\quad = \boxed{}\,\pi + 2\pi\left(\boxed{}\right)^2$

Simplify. $\quad = \boxed{}\,\pi \text{ cm}^2$

Step 3 Find the surface area of the composite figure. The surface area is the sum of the areas of all surfaces on the exterior of the figure.

$S = $ (prism surface area) $+$ (cylinder surface area) $- 2$(area of one cylinder base)

$= \boxed{} + \boxed{}\,\pi - 2\pi\left(\boxed{}\right)^2$

$= \boxed{} + \boxed{}\,\pi \approx \boxed{} \text{ cm}^2$

Reflect

9. **Discussion** A student said the answer in Part A must be incorrect since a part of the rectangular prism is removed, yet the surface area of the composite figure is greater than the surface area of the rectangular prism. Do you agree with the student? Explain.

_____

_____

_____

_____

Find the surface area of each composite figure. Round to the nearest tenth.

10.

5 in
3 in
3 in 5 in
7 in
9 in

11.

7 mm
6 mm
3 mm

💬 Elaborate

12. Can the surface area of a cylinder ever be less than the lateral area of the cylinder? Explain.

_____

_____

13. Is it possible to find the surface area of a cylinder if you know the height and the circumference of the base? Explain.

_____

_____

14. Essential Question Check-In How is finding the surface area of a right prism similar to finding the surface area of a right cylinder?

_____

_____

• Online Homework
• Hints and Help
• Extra Practice

Find the lateral area and surface area of each prism.

1.

2.

3.

4.

Find the lateral area and surface area of the cylinder. Leave your answer in terms of π.

5.

3 ft

4 ft

6.

11 in.

7 in.

Find the total surface area of the composite figure. Round to the nearest tenth.

7.

4 ft

8 ft

12 ft

8 ft

14 ft

8.

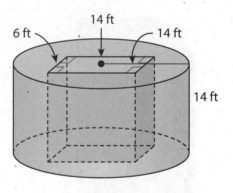

6 ft

14 ft

14 ft

14 ft

Find the total surface area of the composite figure. Round to the nearest tenth.

9.

8 cm

2 cm

6 cm

9 cm

10 cm

10.

2 ft

2 ft

0.5 ft

2 ft

1 ft

11. The greater the lateral area of a florescent light bulb, the more light the bulb produces. One cylindrical light bulb is 16 inches long with a 1-inch radius. Another cylindrical bulb is 23 inches long with a $\frac{3}{4}$-inch radius. Which bulb will produce more light?

12. Find the lateral and surface area of a cube with edge length 9 inches.

13. Find the lateral and surface area of a cylinder with base area 64π m^2 and a height 3 meters less than the radius.

14. Biology Plant cells are shaped approximately like a right rectangular prism. Each cell absorbs oxygen and nutrients through its surface. Which cell can be expected to absorb at a greater rate? (*Hint:* 1 μm = 1 micrometer = 0.000001 meter)

15. Find the height of a right cylinder with surface area 160π ft^2 and radius 5 ft.

16. Find the height of a right rectangular prism with surface area 286 m^2, length 10 m, and width 8 m.

17. Represent Real-World Problems If one gallon of paint covers 250 square feet, how many gallons of paint will be needed to cover the shed, not including the roof? If a gallon of paint costs $25, about how much will it cost to paint the walls of the shed?

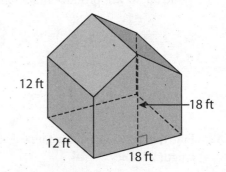

12 ft

18 ft

12 ft

18 ft

18. Match the Surface Area with the appropriate coin in the table.

Coin	Diameter (mm)	Thickness (mm)	Surface Area (mm²)
Penny	19.05	1.55	
Nickel	21.21	1.95	
Dime	17.91	1.35	
Quarter	24.26	1.75	

A. 836.58

B. 579.82

C. 662.81

D. 1057.86

19. Algebra The lateral area of a right rectangular prism is 144 cm². Its length is three times its width, and its height is twice its width. Find its surface area.

20. A cylinder has a radius of 8 cm and a height of 3 cm. Find the height of another cylinder that has a radius of 4 cm and the same surface area as the first cylinder.

21. Analyze Relationships Ingrid is building a shelter to protect her plants from freezing. She is planning to stretch plastic sheeting over the top and the ends of the frame. Assume that the triangles in the frame on the left are equilateral. Which of the frames shown will require more plastic? Explain how finding the surface area of these figures is different from finding the lateral surface area of a figure.

22. Draw Conclusions Explain how the edge lengths of a rectangular prism can be changed so that the surface area is multiplied by 9.

Lesson Performance Task

A manufacturer of number cubes has the bright idea of packaging them individually in cylindrical boxes. Each number cube measures 2 inches on a side.

1. What is the surface area of each cube?

2. What is the surface area of the cylindrical box? Assume the cube fits snugly in the box and that the box includes a top. Use 3.14 for π.

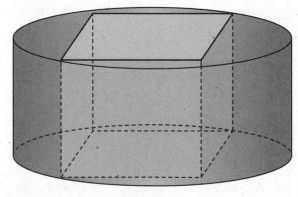

19.3 Surface Area of Pyramids and Cones

Essential Question: How is the formula for the lateral area of a regular pyramid similar to the formula for the lateral area of a right cone?

⊘ Explore   Developing a Surface Area Formula

The base of a **regular pyramid** is a regular polygon, and the lateral faces are congruent isosceles triangles.

(A) The lateral faces of a regular pyramid can be arranged to cover half of a rectangle whose height is equal to the slant height of the pyramid. Complete the figure by labeling the missing dimensions.

(B) Write an expression for the length of the rectangle in terms of s.

_____

(C) How does the length of the rectangle compare to P, the perimeter of the base of the pyramid?

_____

(D) Write an expression for the area of the rectangle in terms of P and ℓ.

_____

(E) Write a formula for the lateral area L of the pyramid. (*Hint*: Use the fact that the lateral faces of the pyramid cover half of the rectangle.)

_____

(F) Let B be the base area of the pyramid. Write a formula for the surface area S of the pyramid in terms of B and L. Then write the formula in terms of B, P, and ℓ.

_____

Reflect

1. **Discussion** The pyramid in the above figure has a square base. Do your formulas only hold for square pyramids or do they hold for other pyramids as well? Explain.

_____

_____

Explain 1 Finding the Surface Area of a Pyramid

Lateral Area and Surface Area of a Regular Pyramid

The lateral area of a regular pyramid with perimeter P and slant height ℓ is $L = \frac{1}{2}P\ell$.

The surface area of a regular pyramid with lateral area L and base area B is $S = L + B$, or $S = \frac{1}{2}P\ell + B$.

Example 1 Find the lateral area and surface area of each regular pyramid.

Ⓐ **Step 1** Find the lateral area.

Lateral area formula $L = \frac{1}{2}P\ell$

$P = 4(5) = 20$ in. $= \frac{1}{2}(20)(9)$

Multiply. $= 90$ in^2

Step 2 Find the surface area.

Surface area formula $S = L + B$

Substitute the lateral area;
$B = 5^2 = 25$ in. $= 90 + 25$

Add. $= 115$ in^2

9 in.

5 in.

Ⓑ **Step 1** Find the slant height ℓ. Use the right triangle shown in the figure.

The legs of the right triangle have lengths ▢ m and ▢ m.

Pythagorean Theorem $\ell^2 = a^2 + b^2$

Substitute. $= \boxed{}^2 + \boxed{}^2$

Simplify. $= \boxed{}$

Take the square root of each side. $\ell = \boxed{}$

12 m

ℓ

10 m

Step 2 Find the lateral area.

Lateral area formula $L = \frac{1}{2}P\ell$

Substitute. $= \frac{1}{2}\left(\boxed{}\right)\left(\boxed{}\right)$

Multiply. $= \boxed{}$ m^2

Step 3 Find the surface area.

Surface area formula $S = L + B$

Substitute. $= \boxed{} + \boxed{}^2$

Simplify. $= \boxed{}$ m^2

Reflect

2. Can you use the formula $L = \frac{1}{2}P\ell$ to find the lateral area of a pyramid whose base is a scalene triangle? If so, describe the dimensions that you need to know. If not, explain why not.

_____

_____

Find the lateral area and surface area of each regular pyramid. Round to the nearest tenth, if necessary.

3.

8 ft

ℓ

6 ft

4.

6 cm

4 cm

⚙ Explain 2 Developing Another Surface Area Formula

The axis of a cone is a segment with endpoints at the vertex and the center of the base. A **right cone** is a cone whose axis is perpendicular to the base.

axis

Right Cone

Example 2 Justify a formula for the surface area of a cone.

(A) A net for a right cone consists of a circle and a sector of a circle, as shown. Complete the figure by labeling the missing dimensions.

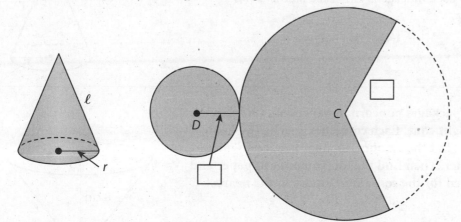

ℓ

r

D

C

(B) Consider the shaded sector in the net. Complete the proportion.

$$\frac{\text{Area of sector}}{\text{Area of} \odot C} = \frac{\text{Arc length of sector}}{\boxed{}}$$

(C) Multiply both sides of the proportion by the area of ⊙ C. Complete the equation.

$$\text{Area of sector} = \frac{\text{Arc length of sector}}{\boxed{}} \cdot \text{Area of} \odot C$$

(D) The arc length of the sector is equal to the circumference of ⊙ D. Therefore, the arc length of the sector equals $2\pi r$. Complete the equation by substituting this expression for the arc length of the sector and by writing the circumference and area of ⊙ C in terms of ℓ.

Area of sector = $\dfrac{\boxed{}}{\boxed{}} \cdot \boxed{}$

(E) Simplify the right side of the equation as much as possible.

Area of sector = $\boxed{}$

(F) The area of the sector in Step E is the lateral area L of the cone. Complete the formula.

$L = \boxed{}$.

(G) Let B be the base area of the cone. Write a formula for the surface area S of the cone in terms of B and L. Then write the formula in terms of r and ℓ.

_____

Reflect

5. In Step D, why is the arc length of the sector equal to the circumference of ⊙ D?

_____

_____

⚙ Explain 3   Finding the Surface Area of a Cone

Lateral Area and Surface Area of a Right Cone

The lateral area of a right cone with radius r and slant height ℓ is $L = \pi r \ell$.

The surface area of a right cone with lateral area L and base area B is $S = L + B$, or $S = \pi r \ell + \pi r^2$.

Example 3 A company packages popcorn in paper containers in the shape of a right cone. Each container also has a plastic circular lid. Find the amount of paper needed to make each container. Then find the total amount of paper and plastic needed for the container. Round to the nearest tenth.

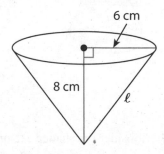

(A) **Step 1** Find the slant height.

Pythagorean Theorem	$\ell^2 = 6^2 + 8^2$
Simplify.	$= 100$
Take the square root of each side.	$\ell = 10$

Step 2 Find the lateral area.

Lateral area formula	$L = \pi r \ell$
Substitute.	$= \pi(6)(10)$
Multiply.	$= 60\pi$ cm^2

Step 3 Find the surface area.

Surface area formula	$S = L + \pi r^2$
Substitute.	$= 60\pi + \pi(6)^2$
Simplify.	$= 96\pi$ cm^2

Step 4 Use a calculator and round to the nearest tenth.

The amount of paper needed for the container is the lateral area, $60\pi \approx 188.5$ cm². The amount of paper and plastic needed for the container is the surface area, $96\pi \approx 301.6$ cm².

Ⓑ **Step 1** Find the radius.

Pythagorean Theorem $\boxed{}^2 = r^2 + \boxed{}^2$

Simplify. $\boxed{} = r^2 + \boxed{}$

Subtract $\boxed{}$ from each side. $\boxed{} = r^2$

Take the square root of each side. $\boxed{} = r$

Step 2 Find the lateral area. $L = \pi r \ell$

Substitute and simplify. $= \pi \left(\boxed{}\right)\left(\boxed{}\right) = \boxed{} \pi$ cm²

Step 3 Find the surface area. $S = L + \pi r^2$

Substitute and simplify. $= \boxed{} \pi + \pi \left(\boxed{}\right)^2 = \boxed{} \pi$ cm²

Step 4 Use a calculator and round to the nearest tenth.

The amount of paper needed for the container is the lateral area, $\boxed{} \pi \approx \boxed{}$ cm².

The amount of paper and plastic needed for the container is $\boxed{} \pi \approx \boxed{}$ cm².

Reflect

6. Two right cones have the same radius. A student said that the cone with the greater slant height must have the greater lateral area. Do you agree? Explain.

_____

_____

Your Turn

A company makes candles in the shape of a right cone. The lateral surface of each candle is covered with paper for shipping and each candle also has a plastic circular base. Find the amount of paper needed to cover the lateral surface of each candle. Then find the total amount of paper and plastic needed. Round to the nearest tenth.

7.

8.

Example 4 Find the surface area of each composite figure. Round to the nearest tenth.

A **Step 1** Find the lateral area of the cone.

The height of the cone is $90 - 45 = 45$ cm.

By the Pythagorean Theorem, $\ell = \sqrt{28^2 + 45^2} = 53$ cm.

Lateral area formula	$L = \pi r \ell$
Substitute.	$= \pi(28)(53)$
Simplify.	$= 1484\pi$ cm^2

Step 2 Find the lateral area of the cylinder.

Lateral area	$L = 2\pi rh$
Substitute.	$= 2\pi(28)(45)$
Simplify.	$= 2520\pi$ cm^2

Step 3 Find the area of the base of the cylinder.

Area of circle	$B = \pi r^2$
Substitute.	$= \pi(28)^2$
Simplify.	$= 784\pi$ cm^2

Step 4 Find the surface area of the composite figure.

$S = $ (cone lateral area) + (cylinder lateral area) + (base area)

$= 1484\pi + 2520\pi + 784\pi$

$= 4788\pi \approx 15,041.9$ cm^2

B **Step 1** Find the slant height of the pyramid.

By the Pythagorean Theorem, $\ell = \sqrt{\boxed{}^2 + \boxed{}^2} = \boxed{}$ yd.

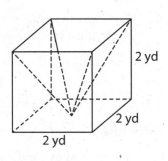

Step 2 Find the lateral area of the pyramid.

Lateral area formula	$L = \frac{1}{2}P\ell$
Substitute.	$= \frac{1}{2}\left(\boxed{}\right)\left(\boxed{}\right)$
Simplify.	$= \boxed{}$ yd^2

Step 3 Find the lateral area of the rectangular prism.

Lateral area formula	$L = Ph$
Substitute.	$= \left(\boxed{}\right)\left(\boxed{}\right)$
Simplify.	$= \boxed{}$ yd^2

Step 4 Find the surface area of the composite figure.

$S = $ (pyramid lateral area) + (prism lateral area) + (base area)

$= \boxed{} + \boxed{} + \boxed{}$

$= \boxed{} \approx \boxed{}$ yd^2

9. How can you check that your answer in Part B is reasonable?

_____

_____

_____

Your Turn

Find the surface area of each composite figure. Round to the nearest tenth.

10.

11.

Elaborate

12. A regular pyramid has a base that is an equilateral triangle with sides 16 inches long. Is it possible to determine the surface area of the pyramid? If not, what additional information do you need?

_____

13. Explain how to estimate the lateral area of a right cone with radius 5 cm and slant height 6 cm. Is your estimate an underestimate or overestimate? Explain.

_____

_____

14. Essential Question Check-In How is the formula for the lateral area of a regular pyramid similar to the formula for the lateral area of a right cone?

_____

_____

_____

_____

1. Multiple Response Which expression represents the surface area of the regular square pyramid shown? Select all that apply.

A. $\dfrac{t^2}{16} + \dfrac{ts}{2}$ **B.** $\dfrac{t^2}{16}$ **C.** $\dfrac{t^2}{4} + t\ell + \dfrac{t\ell}{2}$ **D.** $\dfrac{t}{2}\left(\dfrac{t}{8} + \ell\right)$ **E.** $\dfrac{t}{2}\left(\dfrac{t}{8} + s\right)$

2. Justify Reasoning A frustum of a pyramid is a part of the pyramid with two parallel bases. The lateral faces of the frustum are trapezoids. Use the area formula for a trapezoid to derive a formula for the lateral area of a frustum of a regular square pyramid with base edge lengths b_1 and b_2 and slant height ℓ. Show all of your steps.

3. Draw Conclusions Explain why slant height is not defined for an oblique cone.

Find the lateral and surface area for each pyramid with a regular base. Where necessary, round to the nearest tenth.

4.

12 cm

8 cm   6.93 cm

5.

15 ft

16 ft

16 ft

6.

4 ft

6 ft

6 ft

7.

25 cm

40 cm

Find the lateral and total surface area for each cone. Leave the answer in terms of π.

8.

22 m

14 m

9.

23 cm

23 cm

10.

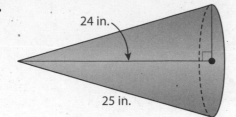

24 in.

25 in.

11.

35 in.

24 in.

Find the surface area for the composite shape. Where appropriate, leave in terms of π. When necessary, round to nearest tenth.

12.

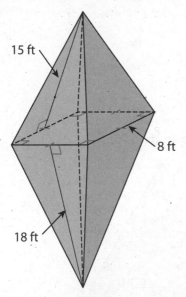

15 ft

8 ft

18 ft

13.

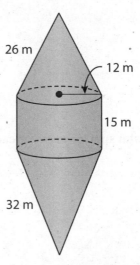

26 m

12 m

15 m

32 m

14.

17 in.

24 in.

7 in.

15.

15 cm   9 cm

19 cm

16.

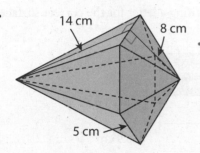

14 cm

8 cm

5 cm

17.

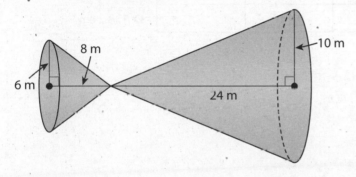

8 m

6 m

10 m

24 m

18. Anna is making a birthday hat from a pattern that is $\frac{3}{4}$ of a circle of colored paper. If Anna's head is 7 inches in diameter, will the hat fit her? Explain.

6 in.

19. It is a tradition in England to celebrate May 1st by hanging cone-shaped baskets of flowers on neighbors' door handles. Addy is making a basket from a piece of paper that is a semicircle with diameter 12 in. What is the diameter of the basket?

├─────── 12 in. ───────┤

20. Match the figure with the correct surface area. Indicate a match by writing a letter for the correct surface area in the final column for each shape.

Shape	Base Area	Slant Height	Surface Area	
Regular square pyramid	36 cm²	5 cm		**A.** 9.4 cm²
Regular triangular pyramid	√3 cm²	√3 cm		**B.** 6.9 cm²
Right cone	16π cm²	7 cm		**C.** 96 cm²
Right cone	π cm²	2 cm		**D.** 138.2 cm²

21. The Pyramid Arena in Memphis, Tennessee, is a square pyramid with base edge lengths of 200 yd and a height of 32 stories. Estimate the area of the glass on the sides of the pyramid. (*Hint:* 1 story ≈ 10 ft)

22. A juice container is a regular square pyramid with the dimensions shown.

    a. Find the surface area of the container to the nearest tenth.

    10 cm

    8 cm

    b. The manufacturer decides to make a container in the shape of a right cone that requires the same amount of material. The base diameter must be 9 cm. Find the slant height of the container to the nearest tenth.

23. **Persevere in Problem Solving** A *frustum* of a cone is a part of the cone with two parallel bases. The height of the frustum of the cone that is shown is half the height of the original cone.

    a. Find the surface area of the original cone.

    5 cm

    20 cm

    10 cm

    b. Find the lateral area of the top of the cone.

    c. Find the area of the top base of the frustum.   **d.** Use your results from parts a, b, and c to find the surface area of the frustum of the cone.

> **H.O.T. Focus on Higher Order Thinking**

24. **Communicate Mathematical Ideas** Explain how you would find the volume of a cone, given the radius and the surface area.

_____

_____

_____

_____

25. **Draw Conclusions** Explain why the slant height of a regular square pyramid must be greater than half the base edge length.

_____

_____

_____

_____

Lesson Performance Task

The pyramid in the figure is built in two levels.

$AC = 200$ feet

You have a summer job as an intern archaeologist. The archaeologists you are working
with need to apply a liquid microbial biofilm inhibitor to the pyramid to prevent bacterial
degradation of the stones and have asked you to calculate the volume of inhibitor needed for
the job. You find that you need 36,000 gallons of inhibitor for the top level. How many gallons
will you need for the bottom level? (Keep in mind that you won't be treating the square bases of
the levels.) Explain how you found the answer.

19.4 Surface Area of Spheres

Essential Question: How can you use the formula for the surface area of a sphere to calculate the surface areas of composite figures?

Resource Locker

🧭 Explore   Developing a Surface Area Formula

You can derive the formula for the surface area of a sphere with radius r by imagining that it is filled with a large number of pyramids, whose apexes all meet at the center of the sphere and whose bases rest against the sphere's surface. It does not matter exactly what shape each base is, as long as all the bases have the same area, B, and they are not too far from regular polygons in shape. The figure shows a sphere with the first three pyramids inscribed.

(A) What is the approximate volume of each pyramid?

_____

_____

(B) Express the approximate volume of the sphere in terms of the n pyramids.

_____

(C) Use the formula for the volume of a sphere to write an approximate equation that can be solved for B, and solve it.

_____

_____

(D) Write an approximate expression for the sphere's surface area S in terms of the pyramid bases.

_____

_____

(E) Substitute your expression for the base area B of each pyramid from step C into your expression from step D. This gives you an approximate expression for the surface area S that does not involve the pyramids.

_____

_____

1. As n gets larger and larger, what do you think will happen to the closeness of the approximations in steps A, B, C, and E? Explain.

_____

_____

2. As a conjecture, write the formula for the surface area S of a sphere with radius r.

_____

⚙ Explain 1 Finding the Surface Area of a Sphere

Surface Area of a Sphere

The surface area of a sphere with radius r is given by $S = 4\pi r^2$.

You can use a formula for the surface area of a sphere to solve real-world problems.

Example 1 **A spherical water tank is 21.5 ft in diameter. The corrosion-resistant alloy skin of the tank is $\frac{1}{8}$ in thick. How much alloy is used to make the tank, to the nearest cubic inch?**

(A) Find the radius of the tank in inches.

The radius of the tank is $\frac{1}{2}(21.5 \text{ ft}) = 10.75 \text{ ft} \times \dfrac{12 \text{ in.}}{1 \text{ ft}} = 129 \text{ in.}$

(B) Find the surface area of the tank.

$S = 4\pi r^2 = 4\pi \left(\boxed{} \right)^2 = \boxed{} ... \text{in}^2$

(C) Find the amount of alloy, to the nearest cubic inch.

Amount of alloy = surface area × thickness

$= \left(\boxed{} ... \text{in}^2 \right) \times \left(\boxed{} \text{in.} \right) \approx \boxed{} \text{in}^3$

Your Turn

A basketball is a sphere 29.5 in. in circumference. A baseball is a sphere of circumference 9.0 in. How much material is needed to make each ball, and how does the ratio of these amounts compare to the ratio of the circumferences?

3. How much material is needed to make a basketball, to the nearest tenth of a square inch?

4. How much material is needed to make a baseball, to the nearest tenth?

5. Compare the ratio of the amounts of material to the ratio of the circumferences. What do you notice?

_____

_____

⚙ **Explain 2** **Finding the Surface Area of a Composite Figure**

You can find the surface area of a composite figure using appropriate formulas for the areas of the different surfaces of the figure.

Example 2 Find the surface area of the composite figure, in terms of π and to the nearest tenth.

5 cm

14 cm

Ⓐ Find the area of the base of the cylinder.

$A_1 = \pi r^2 = \pi(5)^2 = 25\pi$ cm^2

Ⓑ Find the area of the curved surface of the cylinder.

$A_2 = 2\pi rh = 2\pi\left(\boxed{}\right)\left(\boxed{}\right) = \boxed{}\,\pi$ cm^2

Ⓒ Find the surface area of the hemisphere.

$A_3 = \frac{1}{2}(4\pi r^2) = 2\pi\left(\boxed{}\right)^2 = \boxed{}\,\pi$ cm^2

Ⓓ Find the surface area of the composite figure.

$S = A_1 + A_2 + A_3$

$= \boxed{}\,\pi$ cm$^2 + \boxed{}\,\pi$ cm$^2 + \boxed{}\,\pi$ cm^2

$= \boxed{}\,\pi$ cm$^2 \approx \boxed{}$ cm^2

Reflect

6. **Discussion** Could you have used the formula for the surface area of a cylinder? Explain.

_____

_____

Find the surface area of the composite figure, in terms of π and to the nearest tenth.

8 in.

5 in.

7. Find the lateral area of the cylinder.

8. Find the surface area of each hemisphere.

9. Find the surface area of the composite figure.

💬 Elaborate

10. How does deriving the formula for the surface area of a sphere depend on knowing the formula for its volume?

_____

_____

_____

_____

11. Essential Question Check-In How can you use the formula for the surface area of a sphere to calculate the surface areas of composite figures?

_____

_____

_____

_____

1. Using your knowledge of surface area and area, create a formula that will work to find the total surface area of the closed hemisphere for any value of r.

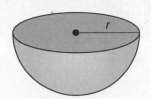

Find the surface area of the sphere. Leave the answer in terms of π.

2.

16 yd

3.

21 in.

4.

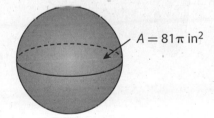

$A = 81\pi$ in^2

5.

$A = 49\pi$ cm^2

Find the surface area of the composite figure. Leave the answer in terms of π.

6.

5 ft

2 ft

7.

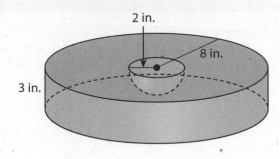

2 in.

8 in.

3 in.

8.

3 cm

4 cm

7 cm

10 cm

9.

24 mm

10 mm

8 mm

10. Find the surface area of the closed hemisphere.

8 yd

11. Find the circumference of the sphere with a surface area of 60π in². Leave the answer in terms of π.

12. Geography Earth's radius is approximately 4000 mi. About two-thirds of Earth's surface is covered by water. Estimate the land area on Earth.

13. A baseball has a radius of approximately 1.5 inches. Estimate the amount of leather used to cover the baseball. Leave the answer in terms of π.

14. Which of the following expressions represents the ratio of the surface area of a cylinder to the surface area of a sphere with the same radius, r?

  A. $\dfrac{1}{2} + \dfrac{h}{r}$

  B. $\dfrac{\pi + h}{r^2}$

  C. $\dfrac{h}{4\pi}$

  D. $\dfrac{r + h}{4r}$

  E. $\dfrac{r + h}{2r}$

15. Explain the Error Susana solved for the surface area of the sphere using the following method:

$S = \dfrac{4}{3}\pi r^2$

$ = \dfrac{4}{3}\pi (10)^2$

$ = \dfrac{4}{3}\pi 100$

$ = \dfrac{400}{3}\pi \text{ m}^2$

20 m

Find her error, and explain how to fix it.

16. Use the table to answer the question.

    a. Which is greater, the sum of the surface areas of Uranus and Neptune or the surface area of Saturn?

Planet	Diameter (mi)
Mercury	3,032
Venus	7,521
Earth	7,926
Mars	4,222
Jupiter	88,846
Saturn	74,898
Uranus	31,763
Neptune	30,775

    b. About how many times as great is the surface area of Earth as the surface area of Mars?

17. A globe has a volume of 288π in^3. What is the surface area of the globe? Give your answer in terms of π.

18. A bead is formed by drilling a cylindrical hole, with a 2 mm diameter, through a sphere with an 8 mm diameter. Estimate the surface area of the bead.

19. The size of a cultured pearl is typically indicated by its diameter in mm. About how many times as great is the surface area of the 9 mm pearl as the surface area of the 6 mm pearl?

20. The diameter of an orange is 10 cm and the diameter of a lime is 5 cm. About how many times as great is the surface area of a half of the orange as the surface area of a half of the lime?

21. A hemisphere has a surface area of 972π cm^2. If the radius is multiplied by $\frac{1}{3}$, what will be the surface area of the new hemisphere?

22. Communicate Mathematical Ideas Describe the effect on the surface area if the dimension on the sphere is doubled.

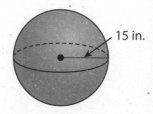

15 in.

23. Analyze Relationships What is the relationship between the surface area of the sphere and the lateral area of the cylinder?

24. Persevere in Problem Solving A company sells orange juice in spherical containers that look like oranges. Each container has a surface area of approximately 50.3 in^2.

a. What is the volume of the container? Round to the nearest tenth.†

b. The company decides to increase the radius of the container by 10%. What is the surface area of the new container?

25. Draw Conclusions Suppose a sphere and a cube have equal surface areas. Using r for the radius of the sphere and s for the side of a cube, write an equation to show the relationship between r and s.

Lesson Performance Task

Locations on Earth are measured in relation to longitude and latitude lines. Longitude lines run north and south through the North and South poles. The 0° longitude line is called the Prime Meridian and runs through Greenwich, England. Latitude lines circle the Earth parallel to the Equator, which is designated 0° latitude. Longitude and latitude lines intersect one another at right angles.

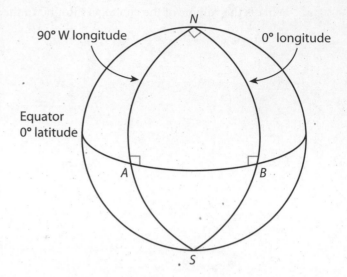

1. Triangle *ABN* is formed by the Equator and two lines of longitude. It is called a spherical triangle. Describe the ways that it is similar to a plane triangle and the ways that it differs.

2. Find the area of spherical triangle *ABN*. Explain how you found the area. Use 7912 miles as the diameter of the Earth. Use 3.14 for π.

Visualizing Solids

Essential Question: How can you use visualizing solids to solve real-world problems?

Key Vocabulary

net *(red)*

surface area *(área de la superficie)*

regular pyramid *(pirámide regular)*

right cone *(cono recto)*

KEY EXAMPLE   *(Lesson 19.1)*

Describe the cross section formed when a plane cuts through the center of a sphere. Compare the dimensions of the cross section to those of the figure.

Since the sphere and the plane are both rotationally symmetric about the perpendicular axis, the cross section is also rotationally symmetric and is therefore a circle. Since it passes through the sphere's widest part, the circle's radius is equal to the radius of the sphere.

KEY EXAMPLE   *(Lesson 19.2)*

Find the surface area of a right prism with length of 10, width of 5, and height of 4.

$L = Ph$	Apply the lateral area formula.
$L = (2 \cdot 10 + 2 \cdot 5)4 = 120$	Substitute and solve.
$S = L + 2B$	Apply the surface area formula.
$S = 120 + 2 \cdot 10 \cdot 5 = 220$	Substitute and solve.

KEY EXAMPLE   *(Lesson 19.3)*

Find the surface area of a right cone with radius 12 and height 16.

$l^2 = 12^2 + 16^2$	Use the Pythagorean Theorem to find the slant height.
$l = 20$	Solve.
$L = \pi r l$	Find the lateral area.
$L = \pi(12)(20) = 240\pi$	Substitute and multiply.
$S = L + \pi r^2$	Find the surface area.
$S = 240\pi + \pi(12)^2 = 384\pi$	Substitute and solve.

KEY EXAMPLE   *(Lesson 19.4)*

Find the surface area of a sphere with radius 14.

$S = 4\pi r^2$	Use the formula for surface area of a sphere.
$S = 4\pi(14)^2 = 784\pi$	Substitute and solve.

EXERCISES

Determine if it is possible to form the following shapes by rotating a two-dimensional shape around the *y*-axis. If so, state the shape needed to do so. *(Lesson 19.1)*

1. sphere _____

2. right prism _____

3. cylinder _____

Find the exact surface area of the following shapes. *(Lessons 19.2 , 19.3, 19.4)*

4. right prism with length 3, width 4, and height 5 _____

5. cylinder with radius 8 and height 3 _____

6. regular pyramid with side length 12 and height 8 _____

7. right cone with diameter 8 and height 3 _____

8. sphere with radius 8 _____

9. hemisphere with radius 9 _____

MODULE PERFORMANCE TASK

How Much Does the Paint on a Space Shuttle Weigh?

NASA used to paint the fuel tanks for the Space Shuttle with white latex paint, but they decided to stop painting them because of the extra weight that the paint added. Just how much could that paint weigh?

The photo gives you a good sense of the shape of the fuel tank. According to NASA, the tank has a height of 153.8 feet and a diameter of 27.6 feet. Use one or more of the formulas you have learned to find the surface area of the tank. Then use your calculation to come up with your best estimate of the weight of the paint required to cover the fuel tank.

Start by listing in the space below any additional information you will need to solve the problem. Then use your own paper to complete the task. Be sure to write down all of your assumptions and data. Use tables, diagrams, words, or numbers to explain how you came to your conclusion.

19.1–19.4 Visualizing Solids

State the figure obtained when rotating the figure about an axis along its largest side, and find the exact surface area of the resulting figure.

1. A rectangle with length 18 and width 14. *(Lesson 19.1)*

Find the exact surface area of the following. *(Lessons 19.2, 19.3, 19.4)*

2.

ESSENTIAL QUESTION

3. When finding the surface area of a composite figure, why is it often necessary to subtract sides common to each individual shape?

Assessment Readiness

1. A rectangular prism has a surface area of 922 square units. Consider each set of dimensions. Could these be the dimensions of the right prism?
Select Yes or No for A–C.

   A. length = 23, width = 7, height = 10   ◯ Yes   ◯ No

   B. length = 17, width = 8, height = 13   ◯ Yes   ◯ No

   C. length = 10, width = 9, height = 12   ◯ Yes   ◯ No

2. A sphere has a radius of 27. Choose True or False for each statement.

   A. The surface area of the sphere is
   729π square units.   ◯ True   ◯ False

   B. The volume of the sphere is
   $26{,}244\pi$ cubic units.   ◯ True   ◯ False

   C. The surface area of the sphere is
   2916π square units.   ◯ True   ◯ False

3. $\triangle ABC$ maps to $\triangle DEF$ with the transformation $(x, y) \rightarrow \left(\frac{1}{4}x, \frac{1}{4}y\right)$. Choose True or False for each statement.

   A. If $BC = 8$, $EF = 2$.   ◯ True   ◯ False

   B. If $BC = 4$, $EF = 16$.   ◯ True   ◯ False

   C. If $BC = 20$, $EF = 5$.   ◯ True   ◯ False

4. What solid is formed when rotating a square about a horizontal or vertical axis through the center of the square? Does this solid have a square for a base? Does this solid have a square for a cross-section?

5. Draw the net of a right cylinder with a radius of 2 and a height of 6, and then explain if this answer is the only possible net for this cylinder.

Modeling and Problem Solving

Essential Question: How can you use modeling to solve real-world problems?

REAL WORLD VIDEO
Check out how GPS coordinates can be used to calculate the area of a region of the Earth's surface.

MODULE PERFORMANCE TASK PREVIEW

Population Density

It's easy to find the population density of a region once you know the population and the area. What's not always so easy is counting the population (New York City, 8,336,697 in 2012) and calculating the area (New York City, 302.64 square miles). Of course, there are some regions whose populations are much smaller than that of New York City and whose areas are easier to calculate. You'll find the population density of one of them after you complete this module.

Complete these exercises to review skills you will need for this module.

Scale Factor and Scale Drawings

Example 1

The width on an architectural plan for a rectangular room is 8 cm. The actual room will be 12 ft wide and 18 ft long. How long is the length of the room on the plan?

• Online Homework
• Hints and Help
• Extra Practice

$$\frac{\text{plan width}}{\text{actual width}} = \frac{\text{plan length}}{\text{actual length}} \rightarrow \frac{8}{12} = \frac{x}{18}$$

$$x = \frac{18 \cdot 8}{12} = 12 \qquad \text{Multiply and simplify.}$$

The plan length is 12 cm.

Find the missing length for a rectangular room.

1. plan length: 4 in.
    actual width: 28 ft
    actual length: 32 ft
    Find the plan width.

2. plan width: 6 in.
    plan length: 8 in.
    actual length: 24 yd
    Find the actual width.

3. plan width: 2.4 cm
    plan length: 9 cm
    actual width: 3.6 m
    Find the actual length.

Volume

Example 2

The volume of a cylinder is 42 cm³. Its height is 3.5 cm. Find the diameter of the cylinder.

$$V = \pi r^2 h \qquad\qquad \text{Write the formula.}$$

$$42 = \pi r^2 (3.5) \qquad \text{Substitute.}$$

$$r^2 = \frac{42}{3.5\pi} = \frac{12}{\pi} \qquad \text{Solve for } r^2.$$

$$r \approx 1.954 \qquad\qquad \text{Solve for } r \text{ to the nearest thousandth.}$$

$$2r \approx 3.91 \qquad\qquad \text{Find the diameter.}$$

The diameter of the cylinder is about 3.91 cm.

Find the missing measure of the cylinder to the nearest hundredth.

4. diameter: 7 ft
    height: 2 ft
    Find the volume.

5. radius: 10 in.
    volume: 490 in³
    Find the height.

6. diameter: 1.2 m
    volume: 4.8 m³
    Find the height.

20.1 Scale Factor

Essential Question: How does multiplying one or more of the dimensions of a figure affect its attributes?

Resource Locker

⊘ Explore   Exploring Effects of Changing Dimensions on Perimeter and Area

Changes made to the dimensions of a figure can affect the perimeter and the area.

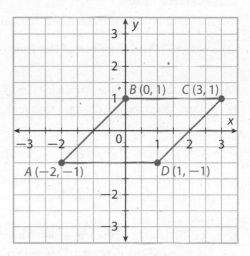

Use the figure to investigate how changing one or more dimensions of the figure affect its perimeter and area.

Ⓐ Apply the transformation $(x, y) \to (3x, y)$. Find the perimeter and the area.

Original Dimensions	Dimensions after $(x, y) \to (3x, y)$
$P = 6 + 4\sqrt{2}$	$P = \boxed{}$
$A = 6$	$A = \boxed{}$

Ⓑ Apply the transformation $(x, y) \to (x, 3y)$. Find the perimeter and the area.

Original Dimensions	Dimensions after $(x, y) \to (x, 3y)$
$P = 6 + 4\sqrt{2}$	$P = \boxed{}$
$A = 6$	$A = \boxed{}$

Ⓒ Apply the transformation $(x, y) \to (3x, 3y)$. Find the perimeter and the area.

Original Dimensions	Dimensions after $(x, y) \to (3x, 3y)$
$P = 6 + 4\sqrt{2}$	$P = \boxed{}$
$A = 6$	$A = \boxed{}$

1. Describe the changes that occurred in Steps A and B. Did the perimeter or area change by a constant factor?

_____

_____

2. Describe the changes that occurred in Step C. Did the perimeter or area change by a constant factor?

_____

_____

🔧 Explain 1   Describe a Non-Proportional Dimension Change

In a non-proportional dimension change, you do not use the same factor to change each dimension of a figure.

Example 1   Find the area of the figure.

(A) Find the area of the parallelogram. Then multiply the length by 2 and determine the new area. Describe the changes that took place.

Original Figure   Transformed Figure

$A = bh = 6 \cdot 5 = 30 \text{ ft}^2$ $A = bh = 12 \cdot 5 = 60 \text{ ft}^2$

When the length of the parallelogram changes by a factor of 2, the area changes by a factor of 2.

(B) Find the area of the trapezoid. Then multiply the height by 0.5 and determine the new area. Describe the changes that took place.

Original Figure $A = \frac{1}{2}(b_1 + b_2)h = $ ⬚

Transformed Figure $A = \frac{1}{2}(b_1 + b_2)h = $ ⬚

When the height of the trapezoid changes by a factor of _____, the

area of the trapezoid changes by a factor of _____.

Reflect

3. **Discussion** When a non-proportional change is applied to the dimensions of a figure, does the perimeter change in a predictable way?

_____

_____

Your Turn

4. Find the area of a triangle with vertices $(-5, -2)$, $(-5, 7)$, and $(3, 1)$. Then apply the transformation $(x, y) \rightarrow (x, 4y)$ and determine the new area. Describe the changes that took place.

5. Find the area of the figure. Then multiply the width by 5 and determine the new area. Describe the changes that took place.

⚙ Explain 2   Describe a Proportional Dimension Change

In a proportional dimension change, you use the same factor to change each dimension of a figure.

Example 2   Find the area and perimeter of a circle.

Ⓐ Find the circumference and area of the circle. Then multiply the radius by 3 and find the new circumference and area. Describe the changes that took place.

Original Figure $C = 2\pi(4) = 8\pi$

$A = \pi(4)^2 = 16\pi$

Transformed Figure $C = 2\pi(12) = 24\pi$

$A = \pi(12)^2 = 144\pi$

The circumference changes by a factor of 3, and the area changes by a factor of 9 or 3^2.

Ⓑ Find the perimeter and area of the figure. Then multiply the length and height by $\frac{1}{3}$ and find the new perimeter and area. Describe the changes that took place.

Original Figure	Transformed Figure
$P = \underline{\hspace{3cm}}$	$P = \underline{\hspace{3cm}}$
$A = \underline{\hspace{3cm}}$	$A = \underline{\hspace{3cm}}$

The perimeter changes by a factor of _____, and the area changes by a factor of _____.

Reflect

6. Fill in the table to describe the effect on perimeter (or circumference) and area when the dimensions of a figure are changed proportionally.

Effects of Changing Dimensions Proportionally		
Change in Dimensions	**Perimeter or Circumference**	**Area**
All dimensions multiplied by a		

7. Find the circumference and area of the circle. Then multiply the radius by 0.25 and find the new circumference and area. Describe the changes that took place.

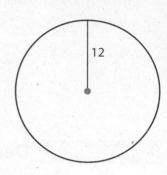

⚙ Explain 3 Describe a Proportional Dimension Change for a Solid

In a proportional dimension change to a solid, you use the same factor to change each dimension of a figure.

Example 3 **Find the volume of the composite solid.**

(A) A company is planning to create a similar version of this storage tank, a cylinder with hemispherical caps at each end. Find the volume and surface area of the original tank. Then multiply all the dimensions by 2 and find the new volume and surface area. Describe the changes that took place.

The volume of the solid is $V = \pi r^2 h + \frac{4}{3}\pi r^3$, and the surface area is $S = 2\pi rh + 4\pi r^2$.

Original Solid

$V = \pi(3)^2(12) + \frac{4}{3}\pi(3)^3 = 144\pi$ cu. ft.

$S = 2\pi(3 \cdot 12) + 4\pi(3)^2 = 108\pi$ sq. ft.

Transformed Solid

$V = \pi(6)^2(24) + \frac{4}{3}\pi(6)^3 = 1152\pi$ cu. ft.

$S = 2\pi(6 \cdot 24) + 4\pi(6)^2 = 432\pi$ sq. ft.

The volume changes by a factor of 8, and the surface area changes by a factor of 4.

(B) A children's toy is shaped like a hemisphere with a conical top. A company decides to create a smaller version of the toy. Find the volume and surface area of the original toy. Then multiply all dimensions by $\frac{2}{3}$ and find the new volume and surface area. Describe the changes that took place.

The volume of the solid is $V = \frac{1}{3}\pi r^2 h + \frac{2}{3}\pi r^3$,

and the surface area is $S = \pi r\sqrt{r^2 + h^2} + 2\pi r^2$.

Original Solid

$V = $ [   ] cu. in.

$S = $ [   ] sq. in.

Transformed Solid

$V = $ [   ] cu. in.

$S = $ [   ] sq. in.

The volume changes by a factor of _____, and the surface area changes by a factor of _____.

8. Fill in the table to describe the effect on surface area and volume when the dimensions of a figure are changed proportionally.

Effects of Changing Dimensions Proportionally		
Change in Dimensions	**Surface Area**	**Volume**
All dimensions multiplied by a		

Your Turn

9. A farmer has made a scale model of a new grain silo. Find the volume and surface area of the model. Use the scale ratio 1 : 36 to find the volume and surface area of the silo. Compare the volumes and surface areas relative to the scale ratio. Be consistent with units of measurement.

3 in.

3 in.

8 in.

🗩 Elaborate

10. Two square pyramids are similar. If the ratio of a pair of corresponding edges is $a : b$, what is the ratio of their volumes? What is the ratio of their surface areas?

_____

_____

11. **Essential Question Check-In** How is a non-proportional dimension change different from a proportional dimension change?

_____

_____

A trapezoid has the vertices $(0, 0)$, $(4, 0)$, $(4, 4)$, and $(-3, 4)$.

1. Describe the effect on the area if only the x-coordinates of the vertices are multiplied by $\frac{1}{2}$.

2. Describe the effect on the area if only the y-coordinates of the vertices are multiplied by $\frac{1}{2}$.

3. Describe the effect on the area if both the x- and y-coordinates of the vertices are multiplied by $\frac{1}{2}$.

4. Describe the effect on the area if the x-coordinates are multiplied by 2 and y-coordinates are multiplied by $\frac{1}{2}$.

Describe the effect of the change on the area of the given figure.

5. The height of the triangle is doubled.

12 m

21 m

6. The height of a trapezoid with base lengths 12 cm and 8 cm and height 5 cm is multiplied by $\frac{1}{3}$.

7. The base of the parallelogram is multiplied by $\frac{2}{3}$.

9 in.

24 in.

8. **Communicate Mathematical Ideas**

A triangle has vertices $(1, 5)$, $(2, 3)$, and $(-1, -6)$. Find the effect that multiplying the height of the triangle by 4 has on the area of the triangle, without doing any calculations. Explain.

Describe the effect of each change on the perimeter or circumference and the area of the given figure.

9. The base and height of an isosceles triangle with base 12 in. and height 6 in. are both tripled.

10. The base and height of the rectangle are both multiplied by $\frac{1}{2}$.

18 ft

6 ft

11. The dimensions are multiplied by 5.

2 yd

3 yd

12. The dimensions are multiplied by $\frac{3}{5}$.

10 m

5 m

13. For each change, check whether the change is non-proportional or proportional.

    A. The height of a triangle is doubled.   ◯ proportional   ◯ non-proportional

    B. All sides of a square are quadrupled.   ◯ proportional   ◯ non-proportional

    C. The length of a rectangle is multiplied by $\frac{3}{4}$.   ◯ proportional   ◯ non-proportional

    D. The height of a triangular prism is tripled.   ◯ proportional   ◯ non-proportional

    E. The radius of a sphere is multiplied by $\sqrt{5}$.   ◯ proportional   ◯ non-proportional

14. Tina and Kleu built rectangular play areas for their dogs. The play area for Tina's dog is 1.5 times as long and 1.5 times as wide as the play area for Kleu's dog. If the play area for Kleu's dog is 60 square feet, how big is the play area for Tina's dog?

15. A map has the scale 1 inch = 10 miles. On the map, the area of Big Bend National Park in Texas is about 12.5 square inches. Estimate the actual area of the park in acres. (*Hint*: 1 square mile = 640 acres)

16. A restaurant has a weekly ad in a local newspaper that is 2 inches wide and 4 inches high and costs $36.75 per week. The cost of each ad is based on its area. If the owner of the restaurant decided to double the width and height of the ad, how much will the new ad cost?

17. Suppose the dimensions of a triangle with a perimeter of 18 inches are doubled. Find the perimeter of the new triangle in inches.

A rectangular prism has vertices (0, 0, 0), (0, 3, 0), (7, 0, 0), (7, 3, 0), (0, 0, 6), (0, 3, 6), (7, 0, 6) and (7, 3, 6).

18. Suppose all the dimensions are tripled. Find the new vertices.

19. Find the effect of the change on the volume of the prism.

20. How would the effect of the change be different if only the height had been tripled?

21. Analyze Relationships How could you change the dimensions of a parallelogram to increase the area by a factor of 5 if the parallelogram does not have to be similar to the original parallelogram? if the parallelogram does have to be similar to the original parallelogram?

22. Algebra A square has a side length of $(2x + 5)$ cm.

   a. If the side length is mulitplied by 5, what is the area of the new square?

   b. Use your answer to part (a) to find the area of the original square without using the area formula. Justify your answer.

23. Algebra A circle has a diameter of 6 in. If the circumference is multiplied by $(x + 3)$, what is the area of the new circle? Justify your answer.

24. Communicate Mathematical Ideas The dimensions of a prism with volume V and surface area S are multiplied by a scale factor of k to form a similar prism. Make a conjecture about the ratio of the surface area of the new prism to its volume. Test your conjecture using a cube with an edge length of 1 and a scale factor of 2.

Lesson Performance Task

On a computer screen, lengths and widths are measured not in inches or millimeters but in pixels. A pixel is the smallest visual element that a computer is capable of processing. A common size for a large computer screen is 1024 × 768 pixels. (Widths rather than heights are conventionally listed first.) For the following, assume you're working on a 1024 × 768 screen.

1. You have a photo measuring 640 × 300 pixels and you want to enlarge it proportionally so that it is as wide as the computer screen. Find the measurements of the photo after it has been scaled up. Explain how you found the answer.

2. **a.** Explain why you can't enlarge the photo proportionally so that it is as tall as the computer screen.

   b. Why can't you correct the difficulty in (a) by scaling the width of the photo by a factor of 1024 ÷ 640 and the height by a factor of 768 ÷ 300?

3. You have some square photos and you would like to fill the screen with them, so there is no overlap and there are no gaps between photos. Find the dimensions of the largest such photos you can use (all of them the same size), and find the number of photos. Explain your reasoning.

1024 pixels

768 pixels

20.2 Modeling and Density

Essential Question: How can you model real-world situations involving density?

Resource Locker

(◎) Explore   Comparing Density

Density is the amount of matter that an object has in a given unit of volume. The density of an object is calculated by dividing its mass by its volume.

$$\text{density} = \frac{\text{mass}}{\text{volume}}$$

Density can be used to help distinguish between similar materials, like identifying different types of wood.

Data about two approximately cylindrical wood logs is shown in the table. Determine which wood is denser.

Type of wood	Diameter (cm)	Height (cm)	Mass (kg)
Douglas fir	6	17	254
American redwood	8	12	271

(A) Make a prediction, based on the data but without calculating, about which wood is denser. Describe your reasoning

_____

_____

(B) Determine the volume of each log.

(C) Determine the density of each log. Identify the denser wood.

Reflect

1. What do your results tell you about the two types of wood?

_____

_____

Calculating a Population Density

You can define density in other situations that involve area or volume besides mass per unit volume. For example, the population density of a region, or the population per unit area, can be found by using the density formula.

Example 1 **Find the approximate population density.**

Ⓐ Burlington, Vermont has an area of about 160 km² and a population of 109,000 people. What is the approximate population density of Burlington?

$$\text{Population density} = \frac{\text{population}}{\text{area}} = \frac{109{,}000}{160} \approx 681 \text{ persons/km}^2$$

Ⓑ The state of Vermont has a population of 626,000. Vermont's territory can be modeled as a trapezoid, as shown in the figure. Each unit on the coordinate grid represents one mile. Find the approximate population density of Vermont.

$$\text{Area} = \frac{1}{2}\,(b_1+b_2)h = \frac{1}{2}\!\left(40 + \boxed{}\right)\!\left(\boxed{}\right) = \boxed{} \text{ mi}^2$$

$$\text{Population density} = \frac{\text{population}}{\text{area}} = \frac{\boxed{}}{\boxed{}} \approx \boxed{} \text{ persons/mi}^2$$

Reflect

2. **Discussion** The actual area of Vermont is 9,620 mi². Is your approximation an overestimate or underestimate? Explain.

_____

_____

_____

3. How would the population density of Vermont change if its given population doubled by 2100? Why?

_____

_____

4. Critique Reasoning Marya claims that Burlington is about 10 times more densely populated than the state average. Is she correct? Explain your reasoning.

_____

_____

_____

_____

Your Turn

5. Chicago has a population of about 2,715,000. Its territory can be modeled as a parallelogram, as shown in the figure. Each unit on the coordinate grid represents one mile. Find the approximate population density of Chicago.

⚙ Explain 2 Calculating Measures of Energy

A British thermal unit (BTU), a unit of energy, is approximately the amount of energy needed to increase the temperature of one pound of water by one degree Fahrenheit. The energy content of a fuel may be measured in BTUs per unit of volume.

Example 2 A spherical tank is filled with a gas and it has the dimensions shown. Find the number of BTUs produced by one cubic foot of the gas. Round to the nearest BTU.

(A) When the tank is filled with natural gas, it provides 116,151 BTUs.

Find the volume of the spherical tank.

$$r = \frac{1}{2}(6 \text{ ft}) = 3 \text{ ft}$$

$$V = \frac{4}{3}\pi r^3 = \frac{4}{3}\pi(3)^3 = 36\pi \text{ ft}^3$$

Divide to find the number of BTUs in one cubic foot of natural gas.

$$\frac{\text{BTUs}}{1 \text{ ft}^3} = \frac{\text{BTUs in tank}}{\text{volume of tank}}$$

$$= \frac{116,151 \text{ BTUs}}{36\pi \text{ ft}^3}$$

$$\approx 1,027 \text{ BTUs}$$

(B) When the tank is filled with kerosene, it provides about 114,206,000 BTUs.

The volume of the tank is _____.

$$\frac{\text{BTUs}}{1\ \text{ft}^3} = \frac{\text{BTUs in tank}}{\text{volume of tank}}$$

$$= \frac{\boxed{} \cdot\ \text{BTUs}}{\boxed{}\ \text{ft}^3}$$

$$\approx \boxed{}\ \text{BTUs}$$

Reflect

6. Which fuel has a higher energy density?

_____

7. One pint of water weighs approximately one pound. How many pints of water can be heated from 74°F to 75°F by one cubic foot of natural gas? How many pints of water can be heated from 75°F to 85°F by one cubic foot of natural gas?

_____

_____

_____

Your Turn

8. A cylindrical tank has the dimensions shown. How many BTUs will the tank provide when filled with natural gas?

5 ft

14 ft

💬 Elaborate

9. Pressure is defined in terms of force per unit area. Is pressure an example of a density?

_____

_____

_____

10. **Essential Question Check-In** Describe the general concept of *density* and give two real-world examples.

_____

_____

_____

_____

☆ Evaluate: Homework and Practice

Determine which is denser.

1. Cylindrical logs of wood

Type of wood	Diameter (ft)	Height (ft)	Mass (lb)
Aspen	3.6	4.5	1,195
Juniper	3.0	6.0	1,487

2. Cylindrical bars of alloy

Alloy	Radius (cm)	Height (cm)	Mass (g)
Nichrome	3.9	27.2	10,800
Mild steel	4.6	18.8	9,840

3. Spherical tanks of liquefied gases

Liquefied Gas	Radius (m)	Mass (kg)
Oxygen (O_2), at $-186°C$	0.8	2477
Hydrogen (H_2), at $-256°C$	1.2	514

4. Colorado has a population of 5,268,367. Its territory can be modeled by a rectangle approximately 280 mi by 380 mi. Find the approximate population density of Colorado.

5. Tennessee has a population of 6,495,978. Its territory can be modeled by a trapezoid, as shown in the figure. Each unit on the coordinate grid represents one mile. Find the approximate population density of Tennessee.

6. New Hampshire has a population of 1,323,459. Its territory can be modeled by a triangle, as shown in the figure. Each unit on the coordinate grid represents one mile. Find the approximate population density of New Hampshire.

7. A spherical gas tank has a 10 foot diameter. When filled with propane, it provides 358,000,000 BTUs. How many BTUs does 1 cubic foot of propane yield? Round to the nearest thousand.

8. Ethan has collected information about the energy content of various fuels. Order the fuels by their energy density from greatest to least. $\left(1 \text{ barrel} = 42 \text{ gallons}; 1 \text{ gallon} = 8 \text{ pints}\right)$

Fuel	Heat Content
Jet fuel	5,670,000 BTUs/barrel
Gasoline	160,937 BTUs/gallon
Home fuel	138,690 BTUs/gallon
Propane	11,417 BTUs/pint

9. A fuel tank has a volume of 32 gallons. When filled with biodiesel, it provides 4,000,000 BTUs. How many BTUs does 1 gallon of biodiesel yield?

10. A piece of marble has been machine-carved into the shape of a cone with the dimensions shown. It has a mass of 169 kg. What is the density of the marble, to the nearest kilogram per cubic meter?

0.7 m

0.3 m

11. Metallurgy The purity of gold is measured in carats. 24-carat gold is pure gold, and has a density of 19.3 g/cm^3. 18-carat gold is often used for jewelry because it holds its shape better than pure gold. An 18-carat gold ring, which is 75% pure gold, has a mass of 18 g. What volume of pure gold was used to make the ring, to the nearest hundredth?

12. Agriculture The maximum grain yield for corn is achieved by planting at a density of 38,000 plants per acre. A farmer wants to maximize the yield for the field represented on the coordinate grid. Each unit on the coordinate grid represents one foot. How many corn plants, to the nearest thousand, does the farmer need? (*Hint:* 1 acre = 43,560 ft^2)

13. The density of water at 4°C is 1000 kg/m^3. A cubic meter of water, when frozen to −20°C, has a volume of 1.0065 m^3. What is the density of ice at this temperature, to the nearest tenth?

14. Space A launch vehicle is designed to carry up to 35 tons of payload into orbit. When fully fueled, it will contain 1,216,000 kg of liquid oxygen (LO$_2$) at a density of 1155 kg/m^3 and 102,000 kg of liquid hydrogen (LH$_2$) at a density of 71 kg/m^3. What is the total volume of liquefied gases carried by the launch vehicle, to the nearest tenth?

15. Manila, Philippines, has one of the highest population densities in the world with 111,002 people/mi². Manila's total population is 1,652,171. How large is Manilla, to the nearest tenth of a square mile?

16. Multistep A building has apartments on 67 floors and each floor measures 110 feet by 85 feet. Currently, 2340 people live in the building. Find the population density of the building to the nearest person per square mile, in terms of the area occupied by the building at street level. Also find the population density of the building in terms of its total floor area. (*Hint:* 1 mi² = 27,878,400 ft²)

17. The caloric density of foods is a useful tool when comparing calorie counts. The table shows typical serving sizes for several foods and the number of calories per serving. Complete the fourth column. Then use the final column to number the foods from the lowest caloric density to the highest. Round to the nearest calorie per gram.

Food	Grams (g)	Calories (Cal)	Cal per 100 g	
1 cubic inch cheddar cheese	17	69		
1 large hard boiled egg	50	78		
1 medium apple	138	72		
1.5 ounces raisins	43	129		

H.O.T. Focus on Higher Order Thinking

18. Analyze Relationships The graph shows the relationship between mass and volume for pure silver. Use the graph to determine the density of pure silver to the nearest tenth and explain your method.

19. Communicate Mathematical Ideas According to Archimedes' Principle, an object placed in water will experience an upward force equal to the weight of water the object displaces. It is this upward force that causes objects less dense than water to float. For example, a cork floats when it is displacing a weight of water exactly equal to its own weight. When placed in water, what percent of a cork's volume will remain above the surface? Explain your answer.

	Density
Cork	0.24 g/cm³
Water	1.00 g/cm³

Lesson Performance Task

A regular pyramid made of pure gold with the dimensions shown has a mass of 160.5 grams. Find the density of gold. Round to the nearest tenth. If the dimensions of the pyramid doubled, what would change about the mass and density?

2.5 cm

2.5 cm

4 cm

20.3 Problem Solving with Constraints

Essential Question: How can you model situations to meet real-world constraints?

Resource
Locker

⊘ Explore Maximizing Volume

Real-world problems often involve constraints. For example, for a given surface area, a sphere maximizes volume, but this is not usually the best shape for a package design.

Suppose you want to build a storage box from a rectangular piece of plywood that measures 4 ft by 8 ft. You must use six pieces, for the top, bottom, and sides of the box, and you can only make cuts perpendicular to the edges of the plywood. Given these constraints, what design appears to give the maximum possible volume for the box?

Ⓐ Consider the top, bottom, front, and back of the box. Which dimensions must these rectangular pieces have in common?

_____

_____

Ⓑ Sketch two possible sets of cuts of the plywood. You do not have to use all the plywood in your design. Label your sketch with all the dimension information you have, using variable expressions if necessary.

Ⓒ Calculate the volume of the resulting box for each of your designs.

Ⓓ Which design is better? Do you think one of your designs provides the greatest possible volume given the constraints of the problem?

_____

_____

1. How effective is this design in maximizing the volume? Explain.

_____

_____

_____

_____

2. **Discussion** Compare results with others in your class. What seems to be a good strategy?

_____

_____

🔘 Explain 1 **Determining Dimensions Given a Volume**

Volume formulas are useful for solving problems where the constraint is to use a given volume of material for a given shape. For instance, suppose you want to make a cylindrical candle using a given amount of wax. You can use the formula for the volume of a cylinder to determine the candle's dimensions.

Example 1 **Determine the necessary dimensions.**

(A) You have 150 cm³ of wax and want to make a cylindrical candle. If you want the candle's height and diameter to be equal, what radius and height should it have, to the nearest tenth?

The diameter of the candle is $2r$. The height is equal to the diameter, so $h = 2r$.

The candle's volume is: $\qquad\qquad V = \pi r^2 h$

Substitute $2r$ for h: $\qquad\qquad V = \pi r^2 (2r)$

Simplify: $\qquad\qquad\qquad V = 2\pi r^3$

Substitute the given volume of wax: $\qquad 150 = 2\pi r^3$

Solve for r^3. $\qquad\qquad\qquad r^3 = \dfrac{150}{2\pi} \approx 23.9$

Use a graphing calculator to graph each side of the equation as a separate function.

Graph $y = r^3$ and $y = 23.9$. The coordinates of the intersection are $(2.879..., 23.9)$.

The radius of the candle should be 2.9 cm. The height of the candle should be twice the radius or 5.8 cm.

Ⓑ You have 300 cm³ of wax and want to make a candle in the shape of a square prism. If you want the candle to be twice as tall as it is wide, what side lengths should it have, to the nearest tenth?

Let the length of the base be b. The height h is twice the base or _____.

The candle's volume is: _____

Substitute $2b$ for h: _____

Simplify: _____

Substitute the given volume of wax: _____

Solve for b^3. _____

Graph $y = b^3$ and $y =$ _____. The coordinates of the intersection are _____.

The side lengths of the square base of the candle should be _____. The height of the

candle should be twice the base or _____.

Reflect

3. How can you check that your answer to Example 1B is reasonable?

_____

_____

Your Turn

4. You want to make a conical candle using 15 in³ of wax. If the candle's height is twice its diameter, what radius and height should it have, to the nearest tenth?

5. You have an octagonal candle mold that has a base that is three inches across and has side length 1.2 inches. If you use this mold to make a candle using 50 in³ of wax, how tall will the candle be?

3 in.

1.2 in.

🔧 Explain 2   Modeling to Meet Constraints

A full-grown tree needs to have a minimum size canopy to photosynthesize enough sugar to feed the tree's bulk. This constraint can be modeled by relating the tree's canopy surface area to the volume of its trunk. By making some simplifying assumptions, you can explore this relationship.

Example 2   What is the minimum radius for the described tree, to the nearest foot?

(A)   Suppose a full-grown oak tree with trunk diameter 6 ft requires at least 8 ft²
of exterior canopy area per cubic foot of trunk volume. Model the canopy
with a hemisphere, and model the trunk with a cylinder whose height is
three times its diameter.

Find the volume of the trunk.

Radius of trunk $= \frac{1}{2}(6 \text{ ft}) = 3$ ft   Height of trunk $= 3(6 \text{ ft}) = 18$ ft

Volume of trunk $= \pi r^2 h = \pi(3)^2(18) = 162\pi$ ft³

Find the minimum exterior canopy area for this size of trunk.

Minimum exterior canopy area $= \frac{8 \text{ ft}^2}{1 \text{ ft}^3} \times (162\pi \text{ ft}^3) = 1{,}296\pi$ ft²

Write an expression for the curved surface area of a hemisphere with radius r.

Surface area $= \frac{1}{2}(4\pi r^2) = 2\pi r^2$

Write an equation that shows the relation between the surface area and the canopy area.

Surface area $=$ Minimum canopy area

$2\pi r^2 = 1{,}296\pi$

$r^2 = \frac{1{,}296\pi}{2\pi} = 648$ $r = \sqrt{648} \approx 25$ft

The minimum radius of canopy required for this oak tree is 25 feet.

(B)   Suppose a growing oak tree with trunk diameter 12 inches requires at least 12 ft² of exterior
canopy area per cubic foot of trunk volume. Model the canopy with a hemisphere, and
model the trunk with a cylinder whose height is 24 times its diameter.

radius of trunk $= \boxed{}$ ft   height of trunk $= \boxed{}$

Volume of trunk $= \pi r^2 h = \pi \left(\boxed{}\right)^2 \left(\boxed{}\right) = \boxed{}\pi$ ft³

Curved surface area $=$ Minimum canopy area

$\frac{1}{2}(4\pi r^2) = \frac{\boxed{} \text{ ft}^2}{1 \text{ ft}^3} \times \left(\boxed{}\pi \text{ ft}^3\right)$

$2\pi r^2 = \boxed{}\pi$ ft²

$r^2 = \frac{\boxed{}}{\boxed{}} = \boxed{}$ $r = \boxed{} = \boxed{}$

The minimum radius of canopy required for this oak tree is 6 feet.

6. **Discussion** How could you use this model to make decisions about planting trees?

_____

_____

_____

_____

Your Turn

7. Assume a mature sequoia tree requires at least 0.6 m² of exterior canopy area per cubic meter of trunk volume. Also assume that the canopy can be modeled by a cone whose slant height is 4 times its radius, and that the trunk of the tree can be modeled by a cone whose height is 12 times its diameter. The formula for the lateral surface area of a cone is $A = \pi(\text{radius})(\text{slant height})$. What is the minimum base radius of canopy required for a sequoia with trunk diameter 5 m? Round your answer to the nearest tenth.

5 m

Elaborate

8. What is the role of a constraint in solving a real-world problem?

_____

_____

_____

9. Essential Question Check-In How can you model situations to meet real-world constraints?

_____

_____

_____

_____

⭐ Evaluate: Homework and Practice

- Online Homework
- Hints and Help
- Extra Practice

Find the volume of each design for a box built from a piece of plywood measuring 60 cm by 180 cm.

1.

2.

3.

4.

5. A cylindrical candle is to be made from 18 in³ of wax. If the candle's height is twice its diameter, what radius and height should it have, to the nearest tenth?

6. A conical candle is to be made from 240 cm³ of wax. If the candle's height is three times its diameter, what radius and height should it have, to the nearest tenth?

7. The design specifications for a coffee mug state that it should be cylindrical, with height 1.5 times its diameter, and with a capacity of 450 mL when filled to the brim. What interior radius and height should the coffee mug have, to the nearest tenth of a centimeter? (*Hint:* 1 mL $\doteq$ 1 cm³)

8. A bob for a pendulum clock will be a cone of equal height and diameter, made from 3 in³ of metal. What radius and height should the bob have, to the nearest tenth?

9. Assume a full-grown oak tree requires at least 8 ft² of exterior canopy area per cubic foot of trunk volume. Model the canopy with a hemisphere, and model the trunk using a cylinder whose height is three times its diameter. What is the minimum radius of canopy required for an oak with trunk diameter 9 ft? Round your answer to the nearest foot.

10. A mature beech tree requires at least 20 m² of exterior canopy area per cubic meter of trunk volume. Model the canopy with a hemisphere, and model the trunk using a cylinder whose height is three times its diameter. What is the minimum radius of canopy required for a beech with trunk diameter 2 m? Round your answer to the nearest foot.

11. Assume a mature sequoia tree requires at least 0.6 m² of exterior canopy area per cubic meter of trunk volume. Model the canopy with a cone whose slant height is 4 times its radius. Model the trunk with a cone whose height is 12 times its diameter. What is the minimum base radius of canopy required for a sequoia with trunk diameter 8 m? Round your answer to the nearest tenth.

12. Assume a mature Douglas fir requires at least 2 ft² of exterior canopy area per cubic foot of trunk volume. Model the canopy with a cone whose slant height is 4 times its diameter, and model the trunk with a cone whose height is 12 times its diameter. What is the minimum base radius of canopy required for a Douglas fir with trunk diameter 4 ft? Round your answer to the nearest tenth.

13. None of the designs in Questions 1–4 actually maximize the volume of a box made from a 60 cm by 180 cm plywood sheet. Find a design that does maximize the volume. (*Hint:* Use two variables, x and y, for the dimensions of the two side pieces.)

180 cm

60 cm

14. Jack is planning to build an aquarium in the shape of a rectangular prism. He wants the base to measure 90 cm by 40 cm. The maximum safe weight this type of aquarium can support is 150 kg. Given that the density of water is 0.001 kg/cm³ and that Jack estimates he will have 5 kg of rocks, sand, and fish to put in the aquarium, what is the aquarium's maximum height, to the nearest centimeter?

15. Rita is making a box from a 2 ft by 5 ft piece of plywood. The box does not need a top, so only five pieces are needed. Suggest two designs to maximize the volume of the box. Check your designs by calculating the volume.

5 ft

2 ft

5 ft

2 ft

16. Multi-step A propane tank is designed in the shape of a cylinder with two hemispherical ends. The cylinder's height is twice its diameter, and the tank's capacity is 1,000 gal. What is the radius of the tank, to the nearest tenth of a foot? (*Hint:* 1 ft^3 = 7.48 gal)

17. A cylindrical space station is 5 m in diameter and 12 m long, and it requires 0.2 m^2 of solar panels per cubic meter of volume to provide power. If it has two sets of rectangular solar panels, each 2 m wide, how long should each set of panels be? Round your answer to the nearest tenth.

18. Create a design to make a cylinder, including both circular ends, from a sheet of metal that measures 150 cm by 60 cm. Calculate the volume of your design, to the nearest thousand cubic centimeters.

150 cm

60 cm

19. A roll of aluminum foil is 15 in. wide. It has an interior diameter of 1.2 in. and an exterior diameter of 1.6 in. If the foil is 0.001 in. thick, what length of foil is rolled up, to the nearest foot? (*Hint:* Start by finding the volume of a 1-ft length of foil 15 in. wide.)

15 in.

1.2 in.   1.6 in.

20. Assume a full-grown oak tree requires at least 8 ft^2 of exterior canopy area per cubic foot of trunk volume. Model the canopy with a hemisphere. Model the trunk with a cylinder whose height is three times its diameter. Develop a formula for the minimum radius R of canopy required for an oak with trunk radius r, in feet.

H.O.T. Focus on Higher Order Thinking

21. **What If?** An animal's weight is proportional to its volume. The strength in its legs to support its weight is proportional to their cross-sectional area. Imagine magnifying a mouse to the size of an elephant. If its length is multiplied by 50, and its density and proportions stay the same, what are the multipliers for its weight and the cross-sectional areas for its legs? Would a mouse this size be able to support itself?

22. **Multi-step** A stopper will be the shape of the frustum of a cone. The height of the complete cone would be 8 times its base diameter, but the stopper's height is to be only twice the larger base diameter. The stopper is to be made from 10 cm³ of silicone. What should the stopper's base radius R, base radius r, and height be, to the nearest tenth?

23. **Look for a Pattern** An aluminum soda can holds 12 fl oz. Investigate the least amount of aluminum needed to make the can: Use the given volume to find a formula for the can's height h in terms of its radius r, substitute into a formula for the can's surface area, and use trial values to determine the values of r and h, to the nearest tenth of an inch, that minimize the can's surface area. (*Hint*: 1 fl oz = 1.73 in³)

24. Persevere in Problem Solving People have a wide variety of body plans, from endomorphic (short and stocky) to ectormorphic (tall and slender). These body plans represent adaptations to cold or hot climates from earlier in human history. A higher surface area to volume ratio allows body heat to be shed more easily in a hot climate, while a lower ratio helps to retain body heat in very cold conditions. Complete the table. Find the ratio of surface area to volume for each body plan. How much greater is the ratio for the ectomorphic body plan than for the endomorphic one? (For each cylindrical form, count only one circular base in addition to the curved surface.)

Endomorphic body plan			
Part of Body	Form and Dimensions	Volume	Exterior Surface Area
Head	sphere, $d = 6$ in.		
Torso	cylinder, $d = 15$ in., $h = 30$ in.		
Arms	cylinder, $d = 3$ in., $h = 24$ in.		
Legs	cylinder, $d = 6$ in., $h = 28$ in.		
Whole body			

Ectomorphic body plan			
Part of Body	Form and Dimensions	Volume	Exterior Surface Area
Head	sphere, $d = 6$ in.		
Torso	cylinder, $d = 10$ in., $h = 32$ in.		
Arms	cylinder, $d = 2$ in., $h = 34$ in.		
Legs	cylinder, $d = 4$ in., $h = 36$ in.		
Whole body			

Lesson Performance Task

In trying to disguise a gift, Henry decides to put a box of blocks into a cylindrical box. The set of blocks is a cube that measures 4 inches on each side. About how much extra wrapping paper will Henry use as a result of this decision?

Modeling and Problem Solving

Essential Question: How can you use modeling to solve real-world problems?

Key Vocabulary

density *(densidad)*

scale factor *(factor de escala)*

KEY EXAMPLE   (Lesson 20.1)

Find the surface area and volume of a rectangular prism-shaped box measuring 6 inches by 8 inches by 12 inches. Then multiply the dimensions by 2 and find the new surface area and volume. Describe the changes that took place.

$2(6 \times 8) + 2(6 \times 12) + 2(8 \times 12) = 96 + 144 + 192$ Find the original surface area.

$= 432 \text{ in}^2$

$6 \times 8 \times 12 = 576 \text{ in}^3$ Find the original volume.

$2(12 \times 16) + 2(12 \times 24) + 2(16 \times 24) = 384 + 576 + 768$ Find the new surface area.

$= 1{,}728 \text{ in}^2$

$12 \times 16 \times 24 = 4608 \text{ in}^3$ Find the new volume

$\dfrac{1728}{432} = 4$ Compare the surface areas. $\dfrac{4608}{576} = 8$ Compare the volumes.

The surface area is multiplied by 4. The volume is multiplied by 8.

KEY EXAMPLE   (Lesson 20.2)

Logan County, Kansas, has a population of 2,784. Its border can be modeled by a rectangle with vertices $A(-18, 15)$, $B(18, 15)$, $C(18, -15)$, and $D(-18, -15)$, where each unit on the coordinate plane represents 1 mile. Find the approximate population density of Logan County. Round to the nearest tenth.

$18 - (-18) = 36 \text{ mi}$ The width of Logan County is the difference of the *x*-coordinates.

$15 - (-15) = 30 \text{ mi}$ The height of Logan County is the difference of the *y*-coordinates.

$36 \times 30 = 1080 \text{ mi}^2$ area = length × width

$\dfrac{2784}{1080} \approx 2.6$ Population density $= \dfrac{\text{population}}{\text{area}}$

The population density is about 2.6 persons per square mile.

KEY EXAMPLE   (Lesson 20.3)

The height of a filing cabinet is 1.5 times the width. The depth is twice the width. The volume of the cabinet is 12,288 in³. What are the cabinet's dimensions?

Volume $= l \times w \times h$ Write the formula for the volume.

$12{,}288 = x \times 1.5x \times 2x$ Substitute for the volume, width, height, and depth.

$x = \sqrt[3]{4096}$ Simplify.

$x = 16$ Evaluate the cube root.

Width: 16 inches. Height: 1.5 × 16 = 24 inches. Depth: 2 × 16 = 32 inches.

EXERCISES

1. One side of a rhombus measures 12 inches. Two angles measure 60°. Find the perimeter and area of the rhombus. Then multiply the side lengths by 3. Find the new perimeter and area. Describe the changes that took place. *(Lesson 20.1)*

2. A box of cereal measures 2.25 inches by 7.5 inches by 10 inches. The box contains 16 ounces of cereal. Find the cereal density, to the nearest thousandth. *(Lesson 20.2)*

3. The height and diameter of a cylindrical water tank are equal. The tank has a volume of 1200 cubic feet. Find the height of the tank to the nearest tenth. *(Lesson 20.3)*

MODULE PERFORMANCE TASK
Population Density

Unlike most geographical regions, the Canadian province of Saskatchewan has a shape that is almost exactly a regular geometric figure. That figure is an isosceles trapezoid. Here are the lengths of the province's four borders:

North: 277 miles South: 390 miles East: 761 miles   West: 761 miles

- Saskatchewan's population in the 2011 census was 1,033,381. What was its population density?

- Saskatchewan is divided into 18 census divisions. Division 18, which makes up the northern half of the province (actually 49.3% of the area), has a population of 36,557. How does the population density of Division 18 compare with that of the southern half of the province?

Start by listing on your own paper the information you will need to solve the problem. Then complete the task. Use numbers, words, or algebra to explain how you reached your conclusion.

20.1–20.3 Modeling and Problem Solving

Solve. Round answers to the nearest tenth. *(Lessons 20.1, 20.2, 20.3)*

- Online Homework
- Hints and Help
- Extra Practice

1. A circle containing the point $(4, -2)$ has its center at $(1, 2)$. Describe the changes in the circumference and area of the circle if the radius is multiplied by 2.

2. Seven hundred people are gathered in a trapezoidal park with bases measuring 60 yards and 80 yards and a height of 50 yards.

   a. Find the population density of the park.

   b. Find the population density if the bases and height are halved.

3. An aquarium in the shape of a rectangular prism has a bottom, no top, two square sides, and two sides the same height as the square sides but twice their length. The total area of the five sides is 1800 in^2. Find the volume of the aquarium. Explain your reasoning.

4. A triangle has base b and height h. The base is doubled. Describe how the height must change so that the area remains the same. Explain your reasoning.

ESSENTIAL QUESTION

5. How can you use mathematics to model real-world situations?

Assessment Readiness

1. The dimensions of a cube are tripled. Choose True or False for each statement.

   A. The perimeter of each face is tripled. ○ True ○ False

   B. The surface area of the cube is multiplied by 6. ○ True ○ False

   C. The volume of the cube is multiplied by 27. ○ True ○ False

2. A solid figure has a volume of 300 cubic centimeters. The radius and the height of the figure are equal. Select Yes or No for A–C.

   A. The figure could be a cylinder with a radius of $\sqrt{\frac{300}{\pi}}$. ○ Yes ○ No

   B. The figure could be a cone with a radius of $\sqrt[3]{\frac{900}{\pi}}$. ○ Yes ○ No

   C. The figure could be a cylinder with a height of $\sqrt[3]{\frac{300}{\pi}}$. ○ Yes ○ No

3. A 4-square-mile community of prairie dogs in South Dakota has a total population of 12,000. Over a 3-year period, the total population increases at an average rate of 2% per year. Describe the change in the population density, assuming the total area of the community remains unchanged.

4. A city park in the shape of a right triangle has an area of $450\sqrt{3}$ square yards. One leg of the triangle measures half the length of the hypotenuse. What are the dimensions of the park? Explain your reasoning.

1. Consider each congruence theorem below.
Can you use the theorem to determine whether $\triangle ABC \cong \triangle ABD$?

Select Yes or No for A–C.

A. ASA Triangle Congruence Theorem   ◯ Yes   ◯ No

B. SAS Triangle Congruence Theorem   ◯ Yes   ◯ No

C. SSS Triangle Congruence Theorem   ◯ Yes   ◯ No

2. For each pyramid, determine whether the statement regarding its volume is true.

Select True or False for each statement.

A. A rectangular pyramid with $\ell = 3$ m, $w = 4$ m, $h = 7$ m has volume 84 m³.   ◯ True   ◯ False

B. A triangular pyramid with base $B = 14$ ft² and $h = 5$ ft has volume 60 ft².   ◯ True   ◯ False

C. A pyramid with the same base and height of a prism has less volume.   ◯ True   ◯ False

3. For each shape, determine whether the statement regarding its volume is true.

Select True or False for each statement.

A. A cone with base radius $r = 5$ in. and $h = 12$ in. has volume 100π in³.   ◯ True   ◯ False

B. A sphere with radius $r = \frac{6}{\pi}$ m has volume $\frac{8}{\pi^2}$ m³.   ◯ True   ◯ False

C. A sphere is composed of multiple cones with the same radius.   ◯ True   ◯ False

4. DeMarcus draws $\triangle ABC$. Then he translates it along the vector $\langle -4, -3 \rangle$ rotates it 180°, and reflects it across the x-axis.

Choose True or False for each statement.

A. The final image of $\triangle ABC$ is in Quadrant IV.   ◯ True   ◯ False

B. The final image of $\triangle ABC$ is a right triangle.   ◯ True   ◯ False

C. DeMarcus will get the same result if he performs the reflection followed by the translation and rotation.   ◯ True   ◯ False

5. Determine whether each statement regarding surface area is true.
   Select True or False for each statement.
   A. The surface area of a cone is the sum of the
      areas of a circle and sector of a circle.   ○ True   ○ False
   B. The surface area of a sphere is greater
      than a cube's with $s = r$.   ○ True   ○ False
   C. A composite figure's surface area is the sum
      of each individual figure's surface area.   ○ True   ○ False

6. Can each of the shapes below be expressed as a composite figure of equilateral
   triangles? Select Yes or No for each shape.
   A. A pyramid   ○ Yes   ○ No
   B. A hexagon   ○ Yes   ○ No
   C. A pentagon   ○ Yes   ○ No

7. The figure shows a composite figure formed by two right
   triangles, a square, and a circle. Determine whether the
   probability of throwing a dart into each shape is correct,
   assuming that the dart will always land in one of the shapes.
   Select True or False for each statement.

   A. The probability of
      landing in the circle is $\frac{\pi}{8}$.   ○ True   ○ False

   B. The probability of landing
      in one of the triangles is $\frac{1}{4}$.   ○ True   ○ False

   C. The probability of
      landing in the square is $\frac{1}{2}$.   ○ True   ○ False

8. A cube is dilated by a factor of 4. By what factor does its volume increase? Explain
   your reasoning.

9. The perimeter of $\triangle PQR$ is 44 cm, and $\triangle PQR \sim \triangle WXY$. If $PQ = 12$ and
   $XY + WY = 24$, what is the perimeter of WXY?

Performance Tasks

★**10.** A scientist wants to compare the densities of two cylinders, but one is twice as high and has a diameter two times as long as the other. How should the scientist compare the two densities of the cylinders if he doesn't know the volume of the larger cylinder? If the volume of the smaller cylinder is 30 cm^3, what is the volume of the larger cylinder?

★★**11.** You are trying to pack in preparation for a trip and need to fit a collection of children's toys in a box. Each individual toy is a composite figure of four cubes, and all of the toys are shown in the figure. Arrange the toys in an orderly fashion so that they will fit in the smallest box possible. Draw the arrangement. What is the volume of the box if each of the cubes have side lengths of 10 cm?

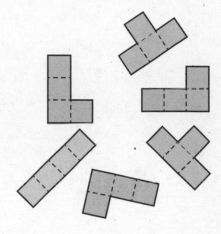

★★**12.** A carpenter has a wooden cone with a slant height of 16 inches and a diameter of 12 inches. The vertex of the cone is directly above the center of its base. He measures halfway down the slant height and makes a cut parallel to the base. He now has a truncated cone and a cone half the height of the original.

   A. He expected the two parts to weigh about the same, but they don't. Which is heavier? Why?

   B. Find the ratio of the weight of the small cone to that of the truncated cone. Show your work.

Model Maker A model maker wants to create a scale model of a sphere with a volume of 1000 m³. The model should have a volume of 1000 cm³. What scale factor should the model maker use? If a triangle drawn on the model has three right angles, what is its area?

Probability

MATH IN CAREERS

Epidemiologist Epidemiologists study infectious agents like viruses and bacteria and use the data they collect to prevent outbreaks from spreading. Using math, an epidemiologist can predict how fast an epidemic might spread.

If you're interested in a career as an epidemiologist, you should study these mathematical subjects:
- Algebra
- Statistics
- Linear Algebra

Research other careers that require the use of statistical modeling to understand real-world scenarios. See the related Career Activity at the end of this unit.

Reading Start-Up

Visualize Vocabulary

Match the review words to their descriptions to complete the chart.

Word	Description
	The measure of how likely an event is to occur
	All possible outcomes of an experiment
	Any set of outcomes
	A single repetition or observation of an experiment
	A result of an experiment

Understand Vocabulary

Complete the sentences using the preview words.

1. The _____ contains no elements.

2. If the occurrence of one event does not affect the occurrence of another event, then the events are called _____.

3. A(n) _____ is a group of objects in a particular order.

4. To find the _____ of a positive integer, find the product of the number and all of the positive integers less than the number.

Active Reading

Key-Term Fold Create a Key-Term Fold with vocabulary words on the flaps and descriptions of the words behind them. Focus on how the vocabulary words for the unit relate. When speaking, describe the words when needed to make sure your ideas clear.

Vocabulary

Review Words

✔ event (*evento*)

✔ outcome (*resultado*)

✔ probability (*probabilidad*)

✔ sample space (*muestra de espacio*)

✔ trial (*prueba*)

Preview Words

combination (*combinación*)
complement (*complementar*)
conditional probability (*probabilidad condicional*)
dependent events (*eventos dependientes*)
element (*elemento*)
empty set (*conjunto vacío*)
factorial (*factorial*)
independent events (*eventos independientes*)
intersection (*intersección*)
permutation (*permutación*)
set (*conjunto*)
subset (*subconjunto*)
union (*unión*)

Introduction to Probability

Essential Question: How can you use probability to solve real-world problems?

REAL WORLD VIDEO
Check out how principles of statistics and probability are used to derive and interpret baseball players' statistics.

MODULE PERFORMANCE TASK PREVIEW

Baseball Probability

In this module, you will use concepts of probability to determine the chances of various outcomes for a baseball player at bat. To successfully complete this task, you'll need to calculate a theoretical probability for a real-world situation. Batter up!

Are YOU Ready?

Complete these exercises to review skills you will need for this module.

Probability of Simple Events

• Online Homework
• Hints and Help
• Extra Practice

Example 1 Find the probability of rolling a 4 when using a normal six-sided die with each side having equal probability.

Each of the six faces has equal probability, so the probability of any face being rolled is $\frac{1}{6}$.

There is only one face with a four on it, so the probability of rolling a four is also $\frac{1}{6}$.

Find each probability.

1. The probability of flipping a coin and getting a heads, given that the probability of getting a tails is the same, and there is no chance that the coin lands on its side

   _____

2. The probability of drawing a Jack of Hearts from a 52-card deck given the deck is properly shuffled

   _____

3. The probability of any particular day being Sunday

   _____

Probability of Compound Events

Example 2 Find the probability of drawing a red card or a black card when the probability of either is $\frac{1}{4}$ and you only draw one card.

Only one card is drawn and either card has a $\frac{1}{4}$ probability, so the probability of drawing one or the other is the sum of their probabilities.

Probability of drawing a red card or black card $\frac{1}{4} + \frac{1}{4} = \frac{1}{2}$.

Find each probability.

4. The probability of rolling a twelve-sided die and getting a 4 or a 6 given the probability of getting a 4 is $\frac{1}{12}$ and is equal to the probability of getting a 6

   _____

5. The probability of pulling a red or a blue marble from a jar given the probability of drawing a red marble is $\frac{1}{4}$ and the probability of pulling a blue marble is $\frac{1}{2}$ and you only pull one marble

   _____

21.1 Probability and Set Theory

Essential Question: How are sets and their relationships used to calculate probabilities?

Resource Locker

⊘ Explore   Working with Sets

A **set** is a collection of distinct objects. Each object in a set is called an **element** of the set. A set is often denoted by writing the elements in braces.

The set with no elements is the **empty set**, denoted by ⊘ or { }.

The set of all elements under consideration is the **universal set**, denoted by U.

Identifying the number of elements in a set is important for calculating probabilities.

(A)   Use set notation to identify each set described in the table and identify the number of elements in each set.

Set	Set Notation	Number of Elements in the Set
Set A is the set of prime numbers less than 10.	$A = \left\{ 2, 3, \boxed{}, 7 \right\}$	$n(A) = 4$
Set B is the set of even natural numbers less than 10.	$B = \left\{ \boxed{}, \boxed{}, \boxed{}, \boxed{} \right\}$	$n(B) = \boxed{}$
Set C is the set of natural numbers less than 10 that are multiples of 4.	$\boxed{} = \left\{ 4, \boxed{} \right\}$	$n(C) = \boxed{}$
The universal set is all natural numbers less than 10.	$U =$	$\boxed{}\left(\boxed{} \right) = 9$

The following table identifies terms used to describe relationships among sets. Use sets A, B, C, and U from the previous table. You will supply the missing Venn diagrams in the Example column, including the referenced elements of the sets, as you complete steps B–I following.

Term	Notation	Venn Diagram	Example
Set C is a **subset** of set B if every element of C is also an element of B.	$C \subset B$		
The **intersection** of sets A and B is the set of all elements that are in both A *and* B.	$A \cap B$	 $A \cap B$ is the double-shaded region.	
The **union** of sets A and B is the set of all elements that are in A or B.	$A \cup B$	 $A \cup B$ is the entire shaded region.	
The **complement** of set A is the set of all elements in the universal set U that are *not* in A.	A^c or $\sim A$	 A^c is the shaded region.	

(B) Since C is a subset of B, every element of set C, which consists of the numbers _____ and _____, is located not only in oval C, but also within oval B. Set B includes the elements of C as well as the additional elements _____ and _____, which are located in oval B outside of oval C. The universal set includes the elements of sets B and C as well as the additional elements _____, _____, _____, _____, and _____, which are located in region U outside of ovals B and C.

(C) In the first row of the table, draw the corresponding Venn diagram that includes the elements of B, C, and U.

(D) To determine the intersection of A and B, first define the elements of set A and set B separately, then identify all the elements found in both sets A *and* B.

$A = \{\Box, \Box, \Box, \Box\}$

$B = \{\Box, \Box, \Box, \Box\}$

$A \cap B = \{\Box\}$

(E) In the second row of the table, draw the Venn diagram for $A \cap B$ that includes the elements of A, B, and U and the double-shaded intersection region.

(F) To determine the union of sets A and B, identify all the elements found in either set A or set B by combining all the elements of the two sets into the union set.

$A \cup B = \left\{ \boxed{}, \boxed{}, \boxed{}, \boxed{}, \boxed{}, \boxed{}, \boxed{} \right\}$

(G) In the third row of the table, draw the Venn diagram for $A \cup B$ that includes the elements of A, B, and U and the shaded union region.

(H) To determine the complement of set A, first identify the elements of set A and universal set U separately, then identify all the elements in the universal set that are *not* in set A.

$A = \left\{ \boxed{}, \boxed{}, \boxed{}, \boxed{} \right\}$

$U = \left\{ \boxed{}, \boxed{}, \boxed{}, \boxed{}, \boxed{}, \boxed{}, \boxed{}, \boxed{} \right\}$

$A^C = \left\{ \boxed{}, \boxed{}, \boxed{}, \boxed{}, \boxed{} \right\}$

(I) In the fourth row of the table, draw the Venn diagram for A^c that includes the elements of A and U and the shaded region that represents the complement of A.

Reflect

1. **Draw Conclusions** Do sets always have an intersection that is not the empty set? Provide an example to support your conclusion.

_____

_____

⚷ **Explain 1** ## Calculating Theoretical Probabilities

A *probability experiment* is an activity involving chance. Each repetition of the experiment is called a *trial* and each possible result of the experiment is termed an *outcome*. A set of outcomes is known as an *event,* and the set of all possible outcomes is called the *sample space.*

Probability measures how likely an event is to occur. An event that is impossible has a probability of 0, while an event that is certain has a probability of 1. All other events have a probability between 0 and 1. When all the outcomes of a probability experiment are equally likely, the **theoretical probability** of an event A in the sample space S is given by

$$P(A) = \frac{\text{number of outcomes in the event}}{\text{number of outcomes in the sample space}} = \frac{n(A)}{n(S)}.$$

Example 1 Calculate $P(A)$, $P(A \cup B)$, $P(A \cap B)$, and $P(A^c)$ for each situation.

Ⓐ You roll a number cube. Event A is rolling a prime number. Event B is rolling an even number.

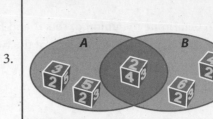

$S = \{1, 2, 3, 4, 5, 6\}$, so $n(S) = 6$. $A = \{2, 3, 5\}$, so $n(A) = 3$.

So, $P(A) = \dfrac{n(A)}{n(S)} = \dfrac{3}{6} = \dfrac{1}{2}$.

$A \cup B = \{2, 3, 4, 5, 6\}$, so $n(A \cup B) = 5$. So, $P(A \cup B) = \dfrac{n(A \cup B)}{n(S)} = \dfrac{5}{6}$.

$A \cap B = \{2\}$, so $n(A \cap B) = 1$. So, $P(A \cap B) = \dfrac{n(A \cap B)}{n(S)} = \dfrac{1}{6}$.

$A^C = \{1, 4, 6\}$, so $n(A^C) = 3$. So, $P(A^C) = \dfrac{n(A^C)}{n(S)} = \dfrac{3}{6} = \dfrac{1}{2}$.

Ⓑ Your grocery basket contains one bag of each of the following items: oranges, green apples, green grapes, green broccoli, white cauliflower, orange carrots, and green spinach. You are getting ready to transfer your items from your cart to the conveyer belt for check-out. Event A is picking a bag containing a vegetable first. Event B is picking a bag containing a green food first. All bags have an equal chance of being picked first.

$S = \{\text{orange, apple, grape, broccoli, cauliflower, carrot, spinach}\}$, so $n(S) = \boxed{}$.

$A = \{\text{broccoli, cauliflower, } \underline{\hspace{1.5cm}}, \underline{\hspace{1.5cm}}\}$, so $n(A) = \boxed{}$. So $P(A) = \dfrac{n\left(\boxed{}\right)}{n\left(\boxed{}\right)} = \dfrac{\boxed{}}{\boxed{}}$.

$A \cup B = \{\text{broccoli, } \underline{\hspace{1.5cm}}, \underline{\hspace{1.5cm}}, \underline{\hspace{1.5cm}}, \underline{\hspace{1.5cm}}, \text{grape}\}$, so $n(A \cup B) = \boxed{}$.

$P(A \cup B) = \dfrac{\boxed{}\left(\boxed{}\right)}{\boxed{}\left(\boxed{}\right)} = \dfrac{\boxed{}}{\boxed{}}$

$A \cap B = \{\underline{\hspace{1.5cm}}, \underline{\hspace{1.5cm}}\}$, so $n(A \cap B) = \boxed{}$

$P(A \cap B) = \dfrac{\boxed{}\left(\boxed{}\right)}{\boxed{}\left(\boxed{}\right)} = \dfrac{\boxed{}}{\boxed{}}$

$P\left(\boxed{}\right) = \dfrac{\boxed{}\left(\boxed{}\right)}{\boxed{}\left(\boxed{}\right)} = \dfrac{\boxed{}}{\boxed{}}$

2. **Discussion** In Example 1B, which is greater, $P(A \cup B)$ or $P(A \cap B)$? Do you think this result is true in general? Explain.

_____

_____

_____

_____

Your Turn

The numbers 1 through 30 are written on slips of paper that are then placed in a hat. Students draw a slip to determine the order in which they will give an oral report. Event A is being one of the first 10 students to give their report. Event B is picking a multiple of 6. If you pick first, calculate each of the indicated probabilities.

3. $P(A)$

4. $P(A \cup B)$

5. $P(A \cap B)$

6. $P(A^c)$

Explain 2 Using the Complement of an Event

You may have noticed in the previous examples that the probability of an event occurring and the probability of the event not occurring (i.e., the probability of the complement of the event) have a sum of 1. This relationship can be useful when it is more convenient to calculate the probability of the complement of an event than it is to calculate the probability of the event.

Probabilities of an Event and Its Complement	
$P(A) + P(A^c) = 1$	The sum of the probability of an event and the probability of its complement is 1.
$P(A) = 1 - P(A^c)$	The probability of an event is 1 minus the probability of its complement.
$P(A^c) = 1 - P(A)$	The probability of the complement of an event is 1 minus the probability of the event.

Example 2 Use the complement to calculate the indicated probabilities.

(A) You roll a blue number cube and a white number cube at the same time. What is the probability that you do not roll doubles?

Step 1 Define the events. Let A be that you do not roll doubles and A^c that you do roll doubles.

Step 2 Make a diagram. A two-way table is one helpful way to identify all the possible outcomes in the sample space.

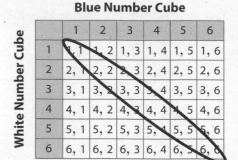

Blue Number Cube

White Number Cube

	1	2	3	4	5	6
1	1, 1	1, 2	1, 3	1, 4	1, 5	1, 6
2	2, 1	2, 2	2, 3	2, 4	2, 5	2, 6
3	3, 1	3, 2	3, 3	3, 4	3, 5	3, 6
4	4, 1	4, 2	4, 3	4, 4	4, 5	4, 6
5	5, 1	5, 2	5, 3	5, 4	5, 5	5, 6
6	6, 1	6, 2	6, 3	6, 4	6, 5	6, 6

Step 3 Determine $P(A^c)$. Since there are fewer outcomes for rolling doubles, it is more convenient to determine the probability of rolling doubles, which is $P(A^c)$. To determine $n(A^c)$, draw a loop around the outcomes in the table that correspond to A^c and then calculate $P(A^c)$.

$$P(A^c) = \frac{n(A^c)}{n(S)} = \frac{6}{36} = \frac{1}{6}$$

Step 4 Determine $P(A)$. Use the relationship between the probability of an event and its complement to determine $P(A)$.

$$P(A) = 1 - P(A^c) = 1 - \frac{1}{6} = \frac{5}{6}$$

So, the probability of not rolling doubles is $\frac{5}{6}$.

(B) One pile of cards contains the numbers 2 through 6 in red hearts. A second pile of cards contains the numbers 4 through 8 in black spades. Each pile of cards has been randomly shuffled. If one card from each pile is chosen at the same time, what is the probability that the sum will be less than 12?

Step 1 Define the events. Let A be the event that the sum is less than 12 and A^c be the event that _____.

Step 2 Make a diagram. Complete the table to show all the outcomes in the sample space.

Step 3 Determine $P(A^c)$. Circle the outcomes in the table that correspond to A^c, then determine $P(A^c)$.

$$P(A^c) = \frac{\boxed{}\left(\boxed{}\right)}{\boxed{}\left(\boxed{}\right)} = \frac{\boxed{}}{\boxed{}}$$

Red Hearts ♥

Black Spades ♠

	2	3	4	5	6
4	4+2	4+3			
5	5+2				
6					
7					
8					

Step 4 Determine P(A). Use the relationship between the probability of an event and its complement to determine $P(A^c)$.

$$P(A) = \boxed{} - \boxed{} \left(\boxed{} \right) = \boxed{} - \frac{\boxed{}}{\boxed{}} = \frac{\boxed{}}{\boxed{}}$$

So, the probability that the sum of the two cards is _____ is $\dfrac{\boxed{}}{\boxed{}}$.

Reflect

7. Describe a different way to calculate the probability that the sum of the two cards will be less than 12.

_____

_____

Your Turn

One bag of marbles contains two red, one yellow, one green, and one blue marble. Another bag contains one marble of each of the same four colors. One marble from each bag is chosen at the same time. Use the complement to calculate the indicated probabilities.

8. Probability of selecting two different colors

9. Probability of not selecting a yellow marble

💬 Elaborate

10. Can a subset of A contain elements of A^c? Why or why not?

_____

_____

_____

11. For any set A, what does $A \cap \varnothing$ equal? What does $A \cup \varnothing$ equal? Explain.

_____

_____

_____

12. **Essential Question Check-In** How do the terms *set*, *element*, and *universal set* correlate to the terms used to calculate theoretical probability?

_____

_____

_____

_____

Set A is the set of factors of 12, set B is the set of even natural numbers less than 13, set C is the set of odd natural numbers less than 13, and set D is the set of even natural numbers less than 7. The universal set for these questions is the set of natural numbers less than 13.

So, $A = \left\{1, 2, 3, 4, 6, 12\right\}$, $B = \left\{2, 4, 6, 8, 10, 12\right\}$,

$C = \left\{1, 3, 5, 7, 9, 11\right\}$, $D = \left\{2, 4, 6\right\}$, and

$U = \left\{1, 2, 3, 4, 5, 6, 7, 8, 9, 10, 11, 12\right\}$. Answer each question.

1. Is $D \subset A$? Explain why or why not.

2. Is $B \subset A$? Explain why or why not.

3. What is $A \cap B$?

4. What is $A \cap C$?

5. What is $A \cup B$?

6. What is $A \cup C$?

7. What is A^C?

8. What is B^C?

You have a set of 10 cards numbered 1 to 10. You choose a card at random. Event A is choosing a number less than 7. Event B is choosing an odd number. Calculate the probability.

9. $P(A)$

10. $P(B)$

11. $P(A \cup B)$

12. $P(A \cap B)$

13. $P(A^C)$

14. $P(B^C)$

Use the complement of the event to find the probability.

15. You roll a 6-sided number cube. What is the probability that you do not roll a 2?

16. You choose a card at random from a standard deck of cards. What is the probability that you do not choose a red king?

17. You spin the spinner shown. The spinner is divided into 12 equal sectors. What is the probability of not spinning a 2?

18. A bag contains 2 red, 5 blue, and 3 green balls. A ball is chosen at random. What is the probability of not choosing a red ball?

19. Cards numbered 1–12 are placed in a bag. A card is chosen at random. What is the probability of not choosing a number less than 5?

20. Slips of paper numbered 1–20 are folded and placed into a hat, and then a slip of paper is drawn at random. What is the probability the slip drawn has a number which is not a multiple of 4 or 5?

21. You are going to roll two number cubes, a white number cube and a red number cube, and find the sum of the two numbers that come up.

    a. What is the probability that the sum will be 6?

    b. What is the probability that the sum will not be 6?

22. You have cards with the letters A, B, C, D, E, F, G, H, I, J, K, L, M, N, O, P. Event U is choosing the cards A, B, C or D. Event V is choosing a vowel. Event W is choosing a letter in the word "APPLE". Find $P(U \cap V \cap W)$.

A standard deck of cards has 13 cards (2, 3, 4, 5, 6, 7, 8, 9, 10, jack, queen, king, ace) in each of 4 suits (hearts, clubs, diamonds, spades). The hearts and diamonds cards are red. The clubs and spades cards are black. Answer each question.

23. You choose a card from a standard deck of cards at random. What is the probability that you do not choose an ace? Explain.

24. You choose a card from a standard deck of cards at random. What is the probability that you do not choose a club? Explain.

25. You choose a card from a standard deck of cards at random. Event A is choosing a red card. Event B is choosing an even number. Event C is choosing a black card. Find $P(A \cap B \cap C)$. Explain.

26. You are selecting a card at random from a standard deck of cards. Match each event with the correct probability. Indicate a match by writing the letter of the event on the line in front of the corresponding probability.

A. Picking a card that is both red and a heart.   _____ $\dfrac{1}{52}$

B. Picking a card that is both a heart and an ace.   _____ $\dfrac{1}{4}$

C. Picking a card that is not both a heart and an ace.   _____ $\dfrac{51}{52}$

H.O.T.   Focus on Higher Order Thinking

27. Critique Reasoning A bag contains white tiles, black tiles, and gray tiles. Someone is going to choose a tile at random. $P(W)$, the probability of choosing a white tile, is $\frac{1}{4}$. A student claims that the probability of choosing a black tile, $P(B)$, is $\frac{3}{4}$ since $P(B) = 1 - P(W) = 1 - \frac{1}{4} = \frac{3}{4}$. Do you agree? Explain.

28. Communicate Mathematical Ideas A bag contains 5 red marbles and 10 blue marbles. You are going to choose a marble at random. Event A is choosing a red marble. Event B is choosing a blue marble. What is $P(A \cap B)$? Explain.

29. Critical Thinking Jeffery states that for a sample space S where all outcomes are equally likely, $0 \le P(A) \le 1$ for any subset A of S. Create an argument that will justify his statement or state a counterexample.

Lesson Performance Task

For the sets you've worked with in this lesson, membership in a set is binary: Either something belongs to the set or it doesn't. For instance, 5 is an element of the set of odd numbers, but 6 isn't.

In 1965, Lofti Zadeh developed the idea of "fuzzy" sets to deal with sets for which membership is not binary. He defined a *degree* of membership that can vary from 0 to 1. For instance, a membership function $m_L(w)$ for the set L of large dogs where the degree of membership m is determined by the weight w of a dog might be defined as follows:

- A dog is a full member of the set L if it weighs 80 pounds or more. This can be written as $m_L(w) = 1$ for $w \geq 80$.

- A dog is not a member of the set L if it weighs 60 pounds or less. This can be written as $m_L(w) = 0$ for $w \leq 60$.

- A dog is a partial member of the set L if it weighs between 60 and 80 pounds. This can be written as $0 < m_L(w) < 1$ for $60 < w < 80$.

The "large dogs" portion of the graph shown displays the membership criteria listed above. Note that the graph shows only values of $m(w)$ that are positive.

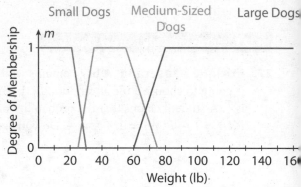

1. Using the graph, give the approximate weights for which a dog is considered a full member, a partial member, and not a member of the set S of small dogs.

2. The union of two "fuzzy" sets A and B is given by the membership rule $m_{A \cup B}(x) = \text{maximum}\big(m_A(x), m_B(x)\big)$. So, for a dog of a given size, the degree of its membership in the set of small or medium-sized dogs $(S \cup M)$ is the greater of its degree of membership in the set of small dogs and its degree of membership in the set of medium-sized dogs.

   The intersection of A and B is given by the membership rule $m_{A \cap B}(x) = \text{minimum}\big(m_A(x), m_B(x)\big)$. So, for a dog of a given size, the degree of its membership in the set of dogs that are both small and medium-sized $(S \cap M)$ is the lesser of its degree of membership in the set of small dogs and its degree of membership in the set of medium-sized dogs.

   Using the graph above and letting S be the set of small dogs, M be the set of medium-sized dogs, and L be the set of large dogs, draw the graph of each set.

   a. $S \cup M$

   b. $M \cap L$

21.2 Permutations and Probability

Essential Question: When are permutations useful in calculating probability?

⊘ Explore   Finding the Number of Permutations

A **permutation** is a selection of objects from a group in which order is important. For example, there are 6 permutations of the letters A, B, and C.

| ABC | ACB | BAC | BCA | CAB | CBA |

You can find the number of permutations with the **Fundamental Counting Principle**.

Fundamental Counting Principle

If there are n items and a_1 ways to choose the first item, a_2 ways to select the second item after the first item has been chosen, and so on, there are $a_1 \times a_2 \times \ldots \times a_n$ ways to choose n items.

There are 7 members in a club. Each year the club elects a president, a vice president, and a treasurer.

Ⓐ What is the number of permutations of all 7 members of the club?

There are _____ different ways to make the first selection.

Once the first person has been chosen, there are _____ different ways to make the second selection.

Once the first two people have been chosen, there are _____ different ways to make the third selection.

Continuing this pattern, there are _____ permutations of all the members of the club.

Ⓑ The club is holding elections for a president, a vice president, and a treasurer. How many different ways can these positions be filled?

There are _____ different ways the position of president can be filled.

Once the president has been chosen, there are _____ different ways the position of vice president can be filled. Once the president and vice president have been chosen, there are _____ different ways the position of treasurer can be filled.

So, there are _____ different ways that the positions can be filled.

(C) What is the number of permutations of the members of the club who were not elected as officers?

After the officers have been elected, there are _____ members remaining. So there are _____ different ways to make the first selection.

Once the first person has been chosen, there are _____ different ways to make the second selection.

Continuing this pattern, there are _____ permutations of the unelected members of the club.

(D) Divide the number of permutations of all the members by the number of permutations of the unelected members.

There are _____ permutations of all the members of the club.

There are _____ permutations of the unelected members of the club.

The quotient of these two values is _____.

Reflect

1. How does the answer to Step D compare to the answer to Step B?

_____

2. **Discussion** Explain the effect of dividing the total number of permutations by the number of permutations of items not selected.

_____

_____

🔑 Explain 1   Finding a Probability Using Permutations

The results of the Explore can be generalized to give a formula for permutations. To do so, it is helpful to use *factorials*. For a positive integer n, **n factorial**, written $n!$, is defined as follows.

$$n! = n \times (n - 1) \times (n - 2) \times \ldots \times 3 \times 2 \times 1$$

That is, $n!$ is the product of n and all the positive integers less than n. Note that $0!$ is defined to be 1.

In the Explore, the number of permutations of the 7 objects taken 3 at a time is

$$7 \times 6 \times 5 = \frac{7 \times 6 \times 5 \times 4 \times 3 \times 2 \times 1}{4 \times 3 \times 2 \times 1} = \frac{7!}{4!} = \frac{7!}{(7 - 3)!}$$

This can be generalized as follows.

Permutations
The number of permutations of n objects taken r at a time is given by $_nP_r = \dfrac{n!}{(n - r)!}$.

Example 1 Use permutations to find the probabilities.

(A) A research laboratory requires a four-digit security code to gain access to the facility. A security code can contain any of the digits 0, 1, 2, 3, 4, 5, 6, 7, 8, and 9, but no digit is repeated. What is the probability that a scientist is randomly assigned a code with the digits 1, 2, 3, and 4 in any order?

The sample space S consists of permutations of 4 digits selected from 10 digits.

$$n(S) = {}_{10}P_4 = \frac{10!}{(10-4)!} = \frac{10!}{6!} = 5040$$

Event A consists of permutations of a security code with the digits 1, 2, 3, and 4.

$$n(A) = {}_4P_4 = \frac{4!}{(4-4)!} = \frac{4!}{0!} = 24$$

The probability of getting a security code with the digits 1, 2, 3, and 4 is

$$P(A) = \frac{n(A)}{n(S)} = \frac{24}{5040} = \frac{1}{210}.$$

(B) A certain motorcycle license plate consists of 5 digits that are randomly selected. No digit is repeated. What is the probability of getting a license plate consisting of all even digits?

The sample space S consists of permutations of _____ selected from _____.

$$n(S) = {}_\square P_\square = \frac{\square}{\square} = \boxed{}$$

Event A consists of permutations of a license plate with _____.

$$n(A) = {}_\square P_\square = \frac{\square}{\square} = \square$$

The probability of getting a license plate with _____ is

$$P(A) = \frac{n(A)}{n(S)} = \frac{\square}{\square} = \frac{\square}{\square}.$$

Your Turn

There are 8 finalists in the 100-meter dash at the Olympic Games. Suppose 3 of the finalists are from the United States, and that all finalists are equally likely to win.

3. What is the probability that the United States will win all 3 medals in this event?

4. What is the probability that the United States will win no medals in this event?

Explain 2 Finding the Number of Permutations with Repetition

Up to this point, the problems have focused on finding the permutations of distinct objects. If some of the objects are repeated, this will reduce the number of permutations that are distinguishable.

For example, here are the permutations of the letters A, B, and C.

ABC	ACB	BAC	BCA	CAB	CBA

Next, here are the permutations of the letters M, O, and M. Bold type is used to show the different positions of the repeated letter.

MO**M**	**M**O**M**	**MM**O	**MM**O	O**MM**	O**MM**

Shown without the bold type, here are the permutations of the letters M, O, and M.

MOM	MOM	MMO	MMO	OMM	OMM

Notice that since the letter M is repeated, there are only 3 distinguishable permutations of the letters. This can be generalized with a formula for permutations with repetition.

Permutations with Repetition

The number of different permutations of n objects where one object repeats a times, a second object repeats b times, and so on is

$$\frac{n!}{a! \times b! \times \ldots}$$

Example 2 Find the number of permutations.

(A) How many different permutations are there of the letters in the word ARKANSAS?

There are 8 letters in the word, and there are 3 A's and 2 S's, so the number of permutations

of the letters in ARKANSAS is $\frac{8!}{3!2!} = 3360$.

(B) One of the zip codes for Anchorage, Alaska, is 99522. How many permutations are there of the numbers in this zip code?

There are ___ digits in the zip code, and there are _____, and _____ in the zip code, so the number of permutations of the zip code is

---

Your Turn

5. How many different permutations can be formed using all the letters in MISSISSIPPI?

6. One of the standard telephone numbers for directory assistance is 555–1212. How many different permutations of this telephone number are possible?

Finding a Probability Using Permutations with Repetition

Permutations with repetition can be used to find probablilities.

Example 3 The school jazz band has 4 boys and 4 girls, and they are randomly lined up for a yearbook photo.

Ⓐ Find the probability of getting an alternating boy-girl arrangement.

The sample space S consists of permutations of 8 objects, with 4 boys and 4 girls.

$n(S) \dfrac{8!}{4!4!} = 70$

Event A consists of permutations that alternate boy-girl or girl-boy. The possible permutations are BGBGBGBG and GBGBGBGB.

$n(A) = 2$

The probability of getting an alternating boy-girl arrangement is $P(A) = \dfrac{n(A)}{n(S)} = \dfrac{2}{70} = \dfrac{1}{35}$.

Ⓑ Find the probability of getting all of the boys grouped together.

The sample space S consists of permutations of _____, with _____.

$n(S) = \dfrac{\square}{\square} = \square$

Event A consists of permutations with _____. The possible permutations are BBBBGGGG, GBBBBGGG, _____.

$n(A) = \square$

The probability of getting all the boys grouped together is $P(A) = \dfrac{n(A)}{n(S)} = \dfrac{\square}{\square} = \dfrac{\square}{\square}$.

Your Turn

7. There are 2 mystery books, 2 romance books, and 2 poetry books to be randomly placed on a shelf. What is the probability that the mystery books are next to each other, the romance books are next to each other, and the poetry books are next to each other?

8. What is the probability that a random arrangement of the letters in the word APPLE will have the two P's next to each other?

Elaborate

9. If $_nP_a = _nP_b$, what is the relationship between a and b? Explain your answer.

_____

10. It was observed that there are 6 permutations of the letters A, B, and C. They are ABC, ACB, BAC, BCA, CAB, and CBA. If the conditions are changed so that the order of selection does not matter, what happens to these 6 different groups?

_____

_____

11. **Essential Question Check-In** How do you determine whether choosing a group of objects involves permutations?

_____

⭐ Evaluate: Homework and Practice

- Online Homework
- Hints and Help
- Extra Practice

1. An MP3 player has a playlist with 12 songs. You select the shuffle option, which plays each song in a random order without repetition, for the playlist. In how many different orders can the songs be played?

2. There are 10 runners in a race. Medals are awarded for 1st, 2nd, and 3rd place. In how many different ways can the medals be awarded?

3. There are 9 players on a baseball team. In how many different ways can the coach choose players for first base, second base, third base, and shortstop?

4. A bag contains 9 tiles, each with a different number from 1 to 9. You choose a tile without looking, put it aside, choose a second tile without looking, put it aside, then choose a third tile without looking. What is the probability that you choose tiles with the numbers 1, 2, and 3 in that order?

5. There are 11 students on a committee. To decide which 3 of these students will attend a conference, 3 names are chosen at random by pulling names one at a time from a hat. What is the probability that Sarah, Jamal, and Mai are chosen in any order?

6. A clerk has 4 different letters that need to go in 4 different envelopes. The clerk places one letter in each envelope at random. What is the probability that all 4 letters are placed in the correct envelopes?

7. A swim coach randomly selects 3 swimmers from a team of 8 to swim in a heat. What is the probability that she will choose the three strongest swimmers?

8. How many different sequences of letters can be formed using all the letters in ENVELOPE?

9. Yolanda has 3 each of red, blue, and green marbles. How many possible ways can the 9 marbles be arranged in a row?

10. Jane has 16 cards. Ten of the cards look exactly the same and have the number 1 on them. The other 6 cards look exactly the same and have the number 2 on them. Jane is going to make a row containing all 16 cards. How many different ways can she order the row?

11. Ramon has 10 cards, each with one number on it. The numbers are 1, 2, 3, 4, 4, 6, 6, 6, 6, 6. Ramon is going to make a row containing all 10 cards. How many different ways can he order the row?

12. A grocer has 5 apples and 5 oranges for a window display. The grocer makes a row of the 10 pieces of fruit by choosing one piece of fruit at random, making it the first piece in the row, choosing a second piece of fruit at random, making it the second piece in the row, and so on. What is the probability that the grocer arranges the fruits in alternating order? (Assume that the apples are not distinguishable and that the oranges are not distinguishable.)

13. The letters G, E, O, M, E, T, R, Y are on 8 tiles in a bag, one letter on each tile. If you select tiles randomly from the bag and place them in a row from left to right, what is the probability the tiles will spell out GEOMETRY?

14. There are 11 boys and 10 girls in a classroom. A teacher chooses a student at random and puts that student at the head of a line, chooses a second student at random and makes that student second in the line, and so on, until all 21 students are in the line. What is the probability that the teacher puts them in a line alternating boys and girls, where no two of the same gender stand together?

15. There are 4 female and 4 male kittens are sleeping together in a row. Assuming that the arrangement is a random arrangement, what is the probability that all the female kittens are together, and all the male kittens are together?

16. If a ski club with 12 members votes to choose 3 group leaders, what is the probability that Marsha, Kevin, and Nicola will be chosen in any order for President, Treasurer, and Secretary?

17. There are 7 books numbered 1–7 on the summer reading list. Peter randomly chooses 2 books. What is the probability that Peter chooses books numbered 1 and 2, in either order?

18. On an exam, students are asked to list 5 historical events in the order in which they occurred. A student randomly orders the events. What is the probability that the student chooses the correct order?

19. A fan makes 6 posters to hold up at a basketball game. Each poster has a letter of the word TIGERS. Six friends sit next to each other in a row. The posters are distributed at random. What is the probability that TIGERS is spelled correctly when the friends hold up the posters?

20. The 10 letter tiles S, A, C, D, E, E, M, I, I, and O are in a bag. What is the probability that the letters S-A-M-E will be drawn from the bag at random, in that order?

21. If three cards are drawn at random from a standard deck of 52 cards, what is the probability that they will all be 7s? (There are four 7s in a standard deck of 52 cards.)

22. A shop classroom has ten desks in a row. If there are 6 students in shop class and they choose their desks at random, what is the probability they will sit in the first six desks?

23. Match each event with its probability. All orders are chosen randomly.

A. There are 15 floats that will be in a town parade. Event A: The mascot float is chosen to be first and the football team float is chosen to be second.

B. Beth is one of 10 students performing in a school talent show. Event B: Beth is chosen to be the fifth performer and her best friend is chosen to be fourth.

C. Sylvester is in a music competition with 14 other musicians. Event C: Sylvester is chosen to be last, and his two best friends are chosen to be first and second.

_____ $\dfrac{1}{1365}$

_____ $\dfrac{1}{210}$

_____ $\dfrac{1}{90}$

H.O.T. Focus on Higher Order Thinking

24. Explain the Error Describe and correct the error in evaluating the expression.

$$_5P_3 = \frac{5!}{3!} = \frac{5 \times 4 \times \cancel{3!}}{\cancel{3!}} = 20$$

25. Make a Conjecture If you are going to draw four cards from a deck of cards, does drawing four aces from the deck have the same probability as drawing four 3s? Explain.

26. Communicate Mathematical Ideas Nolan has Algebra, Biology, and World History homework. Assume that he chooses the order that he does his homework at random. Explain how to find the probability of his doing his Algebra homework first.

27. Explain the Error A student solved the problem shown. The student's work is also shown. Explain the error and provide the correct answer.

A bag contains 6 tiles with the letters A, B, C, D, E, and F, one letter on each tile. You choose 4 tiles one at a time without looking and line them up from left to right as you choose them. What is the probability that your tiles spell BEAD?

Let S be the sample space and let A be the event that the tiles spell BEAD.

$$n(S) = {}_6P_4 = \frac{6!}{(6-4)!} = \frac{6!}{2!} = 360$$

$$n(A) = {}_4P_4 = \frac{4!}{(4-4)!} = \frac{4!}{0!} = 24$$

$$P(A) = \frac{n(A)}{n(S)} = \frac{24}{360} = \frac{1}{5}$$

Lesson Performance Task

How many different ways can a blue card, a red card, and a green card be arranged? The diagram shows that the answer is six.

1. Now solve this problem: What is the least number of colors needed to color the pattern shown here, so that no two squares with a common boundary have the same color? Draw a sketch to show your answer.

2. Now try this one. Again, find the least number of colors needed to color the pattern so that no two regions with a common boundary have the same color. Draw a sketch to show your answer.

3. In 1974, Kenneth Appel and Wolfgang Haken solved a problem that had confounded mathematicians for more than a century. They proved that no matter how complex a map is, it can be colored in a maximum of four colors, so that no two regions with a common boundary have the same color. Sketch the figure shown here. Can you color it in four colors? Can you color it in three colors?

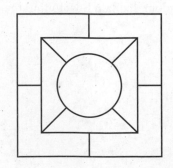

21.3 Combinations and Probability

Essential Question: What is the difference between a permutation and a combination?

⊘ Explore Finding the Number of Combinations

A **combination** is a selection of objects from a group in which order is unimportant. For example, if 3 letters are chosen from the group of letters A, B, C, and D, there are 4 different combinations.

ABC	ABD	ACD	BCD

A restaurant has 8 different appetizers on the menu, as shown in the table. They also offer an appetizer sampler, which contains any 3 of the appetizers served on a single plate. How many different appetizer samplers can be created? The order in which the appetizers are selected does not matter.

Appetizers	
Nachos	Chicken Wings
Chicken Quesadilla	Vegetarian Egg Rolls
Potato Skins	Soft Pretzels
Beef Chili	Guacamole Dip

(A) Find the number appetizer samplers that are possible if the order of selection does matter. This is the number of permutations of 8 objects taken 3 at a time.

$$_8P_3 = \frac{\boxed{}}{\left(\boxed{} - \boxed{}\right)!} = \frac{\boxed{}}{\boxed{}} = \boxed{}$$

(B) Find the number of different ways to select a particular group of appetizers. This is the number of permutations of 3 objects.

$$_3P_3 = \frac{\boxed{}}{\left(\boxed{} - \boxed{}\right)!} = \frac{\boxed{}}{\boxed{}} = \boxed{}$$

C To find the number of possible appetizer samplers if the order of selection does not matter, divide the answer to part A by the answer to part B.

So the number of appetizer samplers that can be created is $\dfrac{\boxed{}}{\boxed{}} = \boxed{}$.

Reflect

1. Explain why the answer to Part A was divided by the answer to Part B.

_____

_____

_____

2. On Mondays and Tuesdays, the restaurant offers an appetizer sampler that contains any 4 of the appetizers listed. How many different appetizer samplers can be created?

_____

3. In general, are there more ways or fewer ways to select objects when the order does not matter? Why?

_____

_____

⊘ Explain 1 Finding a Probability Using Combinations

The results of the Explore can be generalized to give a formula for combinations. In the Explore, the number of combinations of the 8 objects taken 3 at a time is

$$_8P_3 \div _3P_3 = \frac{8!}{(8-3)!} \div \frac{3!}{(3-3)!} = \frac{8!}{(8-3)!} \cdot \frac{0!}{3!} = \frac{8!}{(8-3)!} \cdot \frac{1}{3!} = \frac{8!}{3!(8-3)!}$$

This can be generalized as follows.

Combinations

The number of combinations of n objects taken r at a time is given by

$$_nC_r = \frac{n!}{r!(n-r)!}$$

Example 1 Find each probability.

A There are 4 boys and 8 girls on the debate team. The coach randomly chooses 3 of the students to participate in a competition. What is the probability that the coach chooses all girls?

The sample space S consists of combinations of 3 students taken from the group of 12 students.

$$n(S) = {}_{12}C_3 = \frac{12!}{3!9!} = 220$$

Event A consists of combinations of 3 girls taken from the set of 8 girls.

$$n(A) = {}_8C_3 = \frac{8!}{3!5!} = 56$$

The probability that the coach chooses all girls is $P(A) = \dfrac{n(A)}{n(S)} = \dfrac{56}{220} = \dfrac{14}{55}$.

Ⓑ There are 52 cards in a standard deck, 13 in each of 4 suits: clubs, diamonds, hearts, and spades. Five cards are randomly drawn from the deck. What is the probability that all five cards are diamonds?

The sample space S consists of combinations of _____ cards drawn from 52 cards.

$$n(S) = {}_{\square}C_{\square} = \frac{\boxed{}}{\boxed{}} = \boxed{}$$

Event A consists of combinations of 5 cards drawn from the _____ diamonds.

$$n(A) = {}_{\square}C_{\square} = \frac{\boxed{}}{\boxed{}} = \boxed{}$$

The probability of randomly selecting _____ cards that are diamonds is

$$P(A) = \frac{n(A)}{n(S)} = \frac{\boxed{}}{\boxed{}} = \frac{\boxed{}}{\boxed{}}.$$

Your Turn

4. A coin is tossed 4 times. What is the probability of getting exactly 3 heads?

5. A standard deck of cards is divided in half, with the red cards (diamonds and hearts) separated from the black cards (spades and clubs). Four cards are randomly drawn from the red half. What is the probability they are all diamonds?

Sometimes, counting problems involve the phrases "at least" or "at most." For these problems, combinations must be added.

For example, suppose a coin is flipped 3 times. The coin could show heads 0, 1, 2, or 3 times. To find the number of combinations with at least 2 heads, add the number of combinations with 2 heads and the number of combinations with 3 heads $\left({}_3C_2 + {}_3C_3\right)$.

Example 2 **Find each probability.**

(A) A coin is flipped 5 times. What is the probability that the result is heads at least 4 of the 5 times?

The number of outcomes in the sample space S can be found by using the Fundamental Counting Principle since each flip can result in heads or tails.

$$n(S) = 2 \cdot 2 \cdot 2 \cdot 2 \cdot 2 = 2^5 = 32$$

Let A be the event that the coin shows heads at least 4 times. This is the sum of 2 events, the coin showing heads 4 times and the coin showing heads 5 times. Find the sum of the combinations with 4 heads from 5 coins and with 5 heads from 5 coins.

$$n(A) = {}_5C_4 + {}_5C_5 = \frac{5!}{4!1!} + \frac{5!}{5!0!} = 5 + 1 = 6$$

The probability that the coin shows at least 4 heads is $P(A) = \dfrac{n(A)}{n(S)} = \dfrac{6}{32} = \dfrac{3}{16}$.

(B) Three number cubes number cubes are rolled and the result is recorded. What is the probability that at least 2 of the number cubes show 6?

The number of outcomes in the sample space S can be found by using the Fundamental Counting Principle since each roll can result in 1, 2, 3, 4, 5, or 6.

$$n(S) = \boxed{} = \boxed{}$$

Let A be the event that at least 2 number cubes show 6. This is the sum of 2 events,

_____ or _____. The event of getting

6 on 2 number cubes occurs _____ since there are ____ possibilities for the other

number cube.

$$n(A) = \boxed{} + \boxed{} = \boxed{} + \boxed{} = \boxed{} + \boxed{} = \boxed{}$$

The probability of getting a 6 at least twice in 3 rolls is $P(A) = \dfrac{n(A)}{n(S)} = \dfrac{\boxed{}}{\boxed{}} = \dfrac{\boxed{}}{\boxed{}}$.

6. A math department has a large database of true-false questions, half of which are true and half of which are false, that are used to create future exams. A new test is created by randomly selecting 6 questions from the database. What is the probability the new test contains at most 2 questions where the correct answer is "true"?

7. There are equally many boys and girls in the senior class. If 5 seniors are randomly selected to form the student council, what is the probability the council will contain at least 3 girls?

Elaborate

8. Discussion A coin is flipped 5 times, and the result of heads or tails is recorded. To find the probability of getting tails at least once, the events of 1, 2, 3, 4, or 5 tails can be added together. Is there a faster way to calculate this probability?

_____

_____

9. If $_nC_a = {_nC_b}$, what is the relationship between a and b? Explain your answer.

_____

10. Essential Question Check-In How do you determine whether choosing a group of objects involves combinations?

_____

1. A cat has a litter of 6 kittens. You plan to adopt 2 of the kittens. In how many ways can you choose 2 of the kittens from the litter?

2. An amusement park has 11 roller coasters. In how many ways can you choose 4 of the roller coasters to ride during your visit to the park?

3. Four students from 30-member math club will be selected to organize a fundraiser. How many groups of 4 students are possible?

4. A school has 5 Spanish teachers and 4 French teachers. The school's principal randomly chooses 2 of the teachers to attend a conference. What is the probability that the principal chooses 2 Spanish teachers?

5. There are 6 fiction books and 8 nonfiction books on a reading list. Your teacher randomly assigns you 4 books to read over the summer. What is the probability that you are assigned all nonfiction books?

6. A bag contains 26 tiles, each with a different letter of the alphabet written on it. You choose 3 tiles from the bag without looking. What is the probability that you choose the tiles with the letters A, B, and C?

7. You are randomly assigned a password consisting of 6 different characters chosen from the digits 0 to 9 and the letters A to Z. As a percent, what is the probability that you are assigned a password consisting of only letters? Round your answer to the nearest tenth of a percent.

8. A bouquet of 6 flowers is made up by randomly choosing between roses and carnations. What is the probability the bouquet will have at most 2 roses?

9. A bag of fruit contains 10 pieces of fruit, chosen randomly from bins of apples and oranges. What is the probability the bag contains at least 6 oranges?

10. You flip a coin 10 times. What is the probability that you get at most 3 heads?

11. You flip a coin 8 times. What is the probability you will get at least 5 heads?

12. You flip a coin 5 times. What is the probability that every result will be tails?

13. There are 12 balloons in a bag: 3 each of blue, green, red, and yellow. Three balloons are chosen at random. Find the probability that all 3 balloons are green.

14. There are 6 female and 3 male kittens at an adoption center. Four kittens are chosen at random. What is the probability that all 4 kittens are female?

There are 21 students in your class. The teacher wants to send 4 students to the library each day. The teacher will choose the students to go to the library at random each day for the first four days from the list of students who have not already gone. Answer each question.

15. What is the probability you will be chosen to go on the first day?

16. If you have not yet been chosen to go on days 1–3, what is the probability you will be chosen to go on the fourth day?

17. Your teacher chooses 2 students at random to represent your homeroom. The homeroom has a total of 30 students, including your best friend. What is the probability that you and your best friend are chosen?

There are 12 peaches and 8 bananas in a fruit basket. You get a snack for yourself and three of your friends by choosing four of the pieces of fruit at random. Answer each question.

18. What is the probability that all 4 are peaches?

19. What is the probability that all 4 are bananas?

20. There are 30 students in your class. Your science teacher will choose 5 students at random to create a group to do a project. Find the probability that you and your 2 best friends in the science class will be chosen to be in the group.

21. On a television game show, 9 members of the studio audience are randomly selected to be eligible contestants.

   a. Six of the 9 eligible contestants are randomly chosen to play a game on the stage. How many combinations of 6 players from the group of eligible contestants are possible?

   b. You and your two friends are part of the group of 9 eligible contestants. What is the probability that all three of you are chosen to play the game on stage? Explain how you found your answer.

22. Determine whether you should use permutations or combinations to find the number of possibilities in each of the following situations. Select the correct answer for each lettered part.

a. Selecting a group of 5 people from a group of 8 people ⃝ permutation ⃝ combination

b. Finding the number of combinations for a combination lock ⃝ permutation ⃝ combination

c. Awarding first and second place ribbons in a contest ⃝ permutation ⃝ combination

d. Choosing 3 books to read in any order from a list of 7 books ⃝ permutation ⃝ combination

H.O.T. Focus on Higher Order Thinking

23. Communicate Mathematical Ideas Using the letters A, B, and C, explain the difference between a permutation and a combination.

24. Draw Conclusions Calculate $_{10}C_6$ and $_{10}C_4$.

a. What do you notice about these values? Explain why this makes sense.

b. Use your observations to help you state a generalization about combinations.

25. Justify Reasoning Use the formula for combinations to make a generalization about $_nC_n$. Explain why this makes sense.

26. Explain the Error Describe and correct the error in evaluating $_9C_4$.

$$_9C_4 = \frac{9!}{(9-4)!} = \frac{9!}{5!} = 3024$$

Lesson Performance Task

1. In the 2012 elections, there were six candidates for the United States Senate in Vermont. In how many different orders, from first through sixth, could the candidates have finished?

2. The winner of the Vermont Senatorial election received 208,253 votes, 71.1% of the total votes cast. The candidate coming in second received 24.8% of the vote. How many votes did the second-place candidate receive? Round to the nearest ten.

3. Following the 2012 election there were 53 Democratic, 45 Republican, and 2 Independent senators in Congress.

   a. How many committees of 5 Democratic senators could be formed?

   b. How many committees of 48 Democratic senators could be formed?

   c. Explain how a clever person who knew nothing about combinations could guess the answer to (b) if the person knew the answer to (a).

4. Following the election, a newspaper printed a circle graph showing the make-up of the Senate. How many degrees were allotted to the sector representing Democrats, how many to Republicans, and how many to Independents?

21.4 Mutually Exclusive and Overlapping Events

Essential Question: How are probabilities affected when events are mutually exclusive or overlapping?

Resource Locker

⊙ Explore 1 Finding the Probability of Mutually Exclusive Events

Two events are **mutually exclusive events** if they cannot both occur in the same trial of an experiment. For example, if you flip a coin it cannot land heads up and tails up in the same trial. Therefore, the events are mutually exclusive.

A number dodecahedron has 12 sides numbered 1 through 12. What is the probability that you roll the cube and the result is an even number or a 7?

Ⓐ Let A be the event that you roll an even number. Let B be the event that you roll a 7. Let S be the sample space.

Complete the Venn diagram by writing all outcomes in the sample space in the appropriate region.

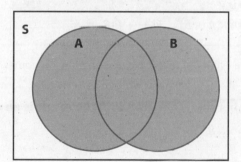

Ⓑ Calculate $P(A)$.

$$P(A) = \dfrac{\boxed{}}{\boxed{}} = \dfrac{\boxed{}}{\boxed{}}$$

Ⓒ Calculate $P(B)$.

$$P(B) = \dfrac{\boxed{}}{\boxed{}}$$

Ⓓ Calculate $P(A \text{ or } B)$.

$$n(S) = \boxed{}.$$

$$n(A \text{ or } B) = n(A) + n(B)$$

$$= \boxed{} + \boxed{} = \boxed{}$$

So, $P(A \text{ or } B) = \dfrac{n(A \text{ or } B)}{n(S)} = \dfrac{\boxed{}}{\boxed{}}.$

Ⓔ Calculate $P(A) + P(B)$. Compare the answer to Step D.

$$P(A) + P(B) = \dfrac{\boxed{}}{\boxed{}} + \dfrac{\boxed{}}{\boxed{}} = \dfrac{\boxed{}}{\boxed{}}$$

$$P(A) + P(B) \,\rule{2cm}{0.4pt}\, P(A \text{ or } B).$$

1. **Discussion** How would you describe mutually exclusive events to another student in your own words? How could you use a Venn diagram to assist in your explanation?

_____

_____

_____

_____

2. Look back over the steps. What can you conjecture about the probability of the union of events that are mutually exclusive?

_____

_____

_____

_____

⊘ Explore 2 Finding the Probability of Overlapping Events

The process used in the previous Explore can be generalized to give the formula for the probability of mutually exclusive events.

Mutually Exclusive Events

If A and B are mutually exclusive events, then $P(A \text{ or } B) = P(A) + P(B)$.

Two events are **overlapping events** (or inclusive events) if they have one or more outcomes in common.

What is the probability that you roll number dodecahedron and the result is an even number or a number greater than 7?

(A) Let A be the event that you roll an even number. Let B be the event that you roll a number greater than 7. Let S be the sample space.

Complete the Venn diagram by writing all outcomes in the sample space in the appropriate region.

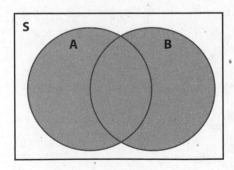

Ⓑ Calculate $P(A)$.

$$P(A) = \frac{\boxed{}}{\boxed{}} = \frac{\boxed{}}{\boxed{}}$$

Ⓒ Calculate $P(B)$.

$$P(B) = \frac{\boxed{}}{\boxed{}}$$

Ⓓ Calculate $P(A \text{ and } B)$.

$$P(A \text{ and } B) = \frac{\boxed{}}{\boxed{}} = \frac{\boxed{}}{\boxed{}}$$

Ⓔ Use the Venn diagram to find $P(A \text{ or } B)$.

$$P(A \text{ or } B) = \frac{\boxed{}}{\boxed{}} = \frac{\boxed{}}{\boxed{}}$$

Ⓕ Now, use $P(A)$, $P(B)$, and $P(A \text{ and } B)$ to calculate $P(A \text{ or } B)$.

$$P(A) = \boxed{} \qquad P(B) = \boxed{} \qquad P(A \text{ and } B) = \boxed{}$$

$$P(A) + P(B) - P(A \text{ and } B) = \boxed{} + \boxed{} - \boxed{} = \boxed{}$$

Reflect

3. Why must you subtract $P(A \text{ and } B)$ from $P(A) + P(B)$ to determine $P(A \text{ or } B)$?

_____

_____

_____

4. Look back over the steps. What can you conjecture about the probability of the union of two events that are overlapping?

_____

_____

_____

🔑 **Explain 1** **Finding a Probability From a Two-Way Table of Data**

The previous Explore leads to the following rule.

The Addition Rule

$P(A \text{ or } B) = P(A) + P(B) - P(A \text{ and } B)$

Example 1 Use the given two-way tables to determine the probabilities.

Ⓐ $P(\text{senior or girl})$

	Freshman	Sophomore	Junior	Senior	TOTAL
Boy	98	104	100	94	396
Girl	102	106	96	108	412
Total	200	210	196	202	808

To determine $P(\text{senior or girl})$, first calculate $P(\text{senior})$, $P(\text{girl})$, and $P(\text{senior and girl})$.

1121

$P(\text{senior}) = \frac{202}{808} = \frac{1}{4}; P(\text{girl}) = \frac{412}{808} = \frac{103}{202}$ $P(\text{senior and girl}) = \frac{108}{808} = \frac{27}{202}$

Use the addition rule to determine $P(\text{senior or girl})$.

$P(\text{senior or girl}) = P(\text{senior}) + P(\text{girl}) - P(\text{senior and girl})$

$\qquad = \frac{1}{4} + \frac{103}{202} - \frac{27}{202}$

$\qquad = \frac{253}{404}$

Therefore, the probability that a student is a senior or a girl is $\frac{253}{404}$.

(B) $P\left((\text{domestic or late})^c\right)$

	Late	On Time	Total
Domestic Flights	12	108	120
International Flights	6	54	60
Total	18	162	180

To determine $P\left((\text{domestic or late})^c\right)$, first calculate $P(\text{domestic or late})$.

$P(\text{domestic}) = \dfrac{\boxed{}}{\boxed{}} = \dfrac{\boxed{}}{\boxed{}}; P(\text{late}) = \dfrac{\boxed{}}{\boxed{}} = \dfrac{\boxed{}}{\boxed{}}; P(\text{domestic and late}) = \dfrac{\boxed{}}{\boxed{}} = \dfrac{\boxed{}}{\boxed{}}$

Use the addition rule to determine $P(\text{domestic or late})$.

$P(\text{domestic or late}) = P(\text{domestic}) + P(\text{late}) - P(\text{domestic and late})$

$\qquad = \dfrac{\boxed{}}{\boxed{}} + \dfrac{\boxed{}}{\boxed{}} - \dfrac{\boxed{}}{\boxed{}} = \dfrac{\boxed{}}{\boxed{}}$

Therefore, $P\left((\text{domestic or late})^c\right) = 1 - P(\text{domestic or late})$

$\qquad = 1 - \dfrac{\boxed{}}{\boxed{}}$

$\qquad = \dfrac{\boxed{}}{\boxed{}}$

5. Use the table to determine P(headache or no medicine).

	Took Medicine	No Medicine	TOTAL
Headache	12	15	27
No Headache	48	25	73
TOTAL	60	40	100

💬 Elaborate

6. Give an example of mutually exclusive events and an example of overlapping events.

_____

_____

_____

_____

_____

7. **Essential Question Check-In** How do you determine the probability of mutually exclusive events and overlapping events?

_____

_____

_____

☆ Evaluate: Homework and Practice

- Online Homework
- Hints and Help
- Extra Practice

1. A bag contains 3 blue marbles, 5 red marbles, and 4 green marbles. You choose one without looking. What is the probability that it is red or green?

2. A number icosahedron has 20 sides numbered 1 through 20. What is the probability that the result of a roll is a number less than 4 or greater than 11?

3. A bag contains 26 tiles, each with a different letter of the alphabet written on it. You choose a tile without looking. What is the probability that you choose a vowel (a, e, i, o, or u) or a letter in the word GEOMETRY?

4. **Persevere in Problem Solving** You roll two number cubes at the same time. Each cube has sides numbered 1 through 6. What is the probability that the sum of the numbers rolled is even or greater than 9? (*Hint*: Create and fill out a probability chart.)

The table shows the data for car insurance quotes for 125 drivers made by an insurance company in one week.

	Teen	Adult (20 or over)	Total
0 accidents	15	53	68
1 accident	4	32	36
2+ accidents	9	12	21
Total	28	97	125

You randomly choose one of the drivers. Find the probability of each event.

5. The driver is an adult.

6. The driver is a teen with 0 or 1 accident.

7. The driver is a teen.

8. The driver has 2+ accidents.

9. The driver is a teen and has 2+ accidents.

10. The driver is a teen or a driver with 2+ accidents.

Use the following information for Exercises 11–16. The table shown shows the results of a customer satisfaction survey for a cellular service provider, by location of the customer. In the survey, customers were asked whether they would recommend a plan with the provider to a friend.

	Arlington	Towson	Parkville	Total
Yes	40	35	41	116
No	18	10	6	34
Total	58	45	47	150

One of the customers that was surveyed was chosen at random. Find the probability of each event.

11. The customer was from Towson and said No.　　**12.** The customer was from Parkville.

13. The customer said Yes.　　**14.** The customer was from Parkville and said Yes.

15. The customer was from Parkville or said Yes.

16. Explain why you cannot use the rule $P(A \text{ or } B) = P(A) + P(B)$ in Exercise 15.

Use the following information for Exercises 17–21. Roberto is the owner of a car dealership. He is assessing the success rate of his top three salespeople in order to offer one of them a promotion. Over two months, for each attempted sale, he records whether the salesperson made a successful sale or not. The results are shown in the chart.

	Successful	Unsuccessful	Total
Becky	6	6	12
Raul	4	5	9
Darrell	6	9	15
Total	16	20	36

Roberto randomly chooses one of the attempted sales.

17. Find the probability that the sale was one of Becky's or Raul's successful sales.

18. Find the probability that the sale was one of the unsuccessful sales or one of Raul's successful sales.

19. Find the probability that the sale was one of Darrell's unsuccessful sales or one of Raul's unsuccessful sales.

20. Find the probability that the sale was an unsuccessful sale or one of Becky's attempted sales.

21. Find the probability that the sale was a successful sale or one of Raul's attempted sales.

22. You are going to draw one card at random from a standard deck of cards. A standard deck of cards has 13 cards (2, 3, 4, 5, 6, 7, 8, 9, 10, jack, queen, king, ace) in each of 4 suits (hearts, clubs, diamonds, spades). The hearts and diamonds cards are red. The clubs and spades cards are black. Which of the following have a probability of less than $\frac{1}{4}$? Choose all that apply.

    a. Drawing a card that is a spade and an ace

    b. Drawing a card that is a club or an ace

    c. Drawing a card that is a face card or a club

    d. Drawing a card that is black and a heart

    e. Drawing a red card and a number card from 2–9

23. **Draw Conclusions** A survey of 1108 employees at a software company finds that 621 employees take a bus to work and 445 employees take a train to work. Some employees take both a bus and a train, and 321 employees take only a train. To the nearest percent, find the probability that a randomly chosen employee takes a bus or a train to work. Explain.

24. Communicate Mathematical Ideas Explain how to use a Venn diagram to find the probability of randomly choosing a multiple of 3 or a multiple of 4 from the set of numbers from 1 to 25. Then find the probability.

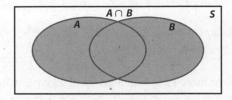

25. Explain the Error Sanderson attempted to find the probability of randomly choosing a 10 or a diamond from a standard deck of playing cards. He used the following logic:

Let S be the sample space, A be the event that the card is a 10, and B be the event that the card is a diamond.

There are 52 cards in the deck, so $n(S) = 52$.

There are four 10s in the deck, so $n(A) = 4$.

There are 13 diamonds in the deck, so $n(B) = 13$.

One 10 is a diamond, so $n(A \cap B) = 1$.

$$P(A \cup B) = \frac{n(A \cup B)}{n(S)} = \frac{n(A) \cdot n(B) - n(A \cap B)}{n(S)} = \frac{4 \cdot 13 - 1}{52} = \frac{51}{52}$$

Describe and correct Sanderson's mistake.

Lesson Performance Task

What is the smallest number of randomly chosen people that are needed in order for there to be a better than 50% probability that at least two of them will have the same birthday? The astonishing answer is 23. Follow these steps to find why.

1. Can a person have a birthday on two different days? Use the vocabulary of this lesson to explain your answer.

Looking for the probability that two or more people in a group of 23 have matching birthdays is a challenge. Maybe there is one match but maybe there are five matches or seven or fourteen. A much easier way is to look for the probability that there are *no* matches in a group of 23. In other words, all 23 have different birthdays. Then use that number to find the answer.

2. There are 365 days in a non-leap year.

   a. Write an expression for the number of ways you can assign different birthdays to 23 people. (Hint: Think of the people as standing in a line, and you are going to assign a different number from 1 to 365 to each person.)

   b. Write an expression for the number of ways you can assign any birthday to 23 people. (Hint: Now think about assigning any number from 1 to 365 to each of 23 people.)

   c. How can you use your answers to (a) and (b) to find the probability that no people in a group of 23 have the same birthday? Use a calculator to find the probability to the nearest ten-thousandth.

   d. What is the probability that at least two people in a group of 23 have the same birthday? Explain your reasoning.

Introduction to Probability

Essential Question: How can you use probability to solve real-world problems?

Key Vocabulary

set *(conjunto, juego)*
element *(elemento)*
empty set *(conjunto vacío)*
universal set *(conjunto universal)*
subset *(subconjunto)*
intersection *(intersección)*
union *(unión)*
complement *(complemento)*
theoretical probability *(probabilidad teórica)*
permutation *(permutación)*
Fundamental Counting Principle *(principio fundamental de conteo)*
factorial *(factorial)*
combination *(combinación)*

KEY EXAMPLE   *(Lesson 21.1)*

When rolling two fair number cubes, what is the probability that the sum of the two cubes will not be even or prime?

The sum of two number cubes can be any integer from 2 through 12. Of these, the only possible sum that is not even or prime is 9. There are 36 possible outcomes for rolling two number cubes. Of these, the only ones that sum to 9 are (3, 6), (6, 3), (4, 5), and (5, 4). So, P(sum is not even or prime) $= \frac{4}{36} = \frac{1}{9}$.

KEY EXAMPLE   *(Lesson 21.2)*

Ten marbles are placed in a jar. Of the 10 marbles, 3 are blue, 2 are red, 3 are green, 1 is orange, and 1 is yellow. The 10 marbles are randomly placed in a line. What is the probability that all marbles of the same color are next to each other?

Marbles of the same color are indistinguishable objects. The sample space S consists of permutations of 10 objects, with 3 of one type, 3 of another type, and 2 of a third type.

$$n(S) = \frac{10!}{3!3!2!} = 50,400$$

Event A consists of permutations that have all marbles of the same color next to each other, so it is the number of ways of ordering the 5 colors.

$$n(A) = 5! = 120$$

The probability that all marbles of the same color are next to each other is

$$P(A) = \frac{n(A)}{n(S)} = \frac{120}{50,400} = \frac{1}{420}.$$

KEY EXAMPLE   *(Lesson 21.3)*

A class of 15 boys and 15 girls is putting together a random group of 3 students to do classroom chores. What is the probability that at least 2 of the students are boys?

The sample space S consists of combinations of three student groups.

$$n(S) = \frac{30!}{3!27!} = 4060$$

Event A consists of combinations that have 2 boys or 3 boys in the group. The event of getting 2 boys in the group occurs 15 times, once for each individual girl in the class.

$$n(A) = 15 \cdot {}_{15}C_2 + {}_{15}C_3 = 15 \cdot \frac{15!}{2!13!} + \frac{15!}{3!12!} = 2030$$

The probability that there will be at least 2 boys in the group is $P(A) = \frac{n(A)}{n(S)} = \frac{2030}{4060} = \frac{1}{2}$.

EXERCISES

Use the sets below to find the indicated set for problems 1–4. *(Lesson 21.1)*

$U = \{1, 2, 3, 4, 5, 6, 7, 8, 9\}$

$A = \{1, 3, 5, 7, 9\}$

$B = \{2, 4, 6, 8\}$

$C = \{1, 2, 4, 5, 7, 9\}$

1. $A \cup C$ _____

2. $B \cap C$ _____

3. A^C _____

4. $A \cap B$ _____

5. A computer password can use all digits (0–9) and all letters (*a–z*) that are case sensitive (upper and lower). How many different permutations of 5-figure passwords are there if there is no repeated input? *(Lesson 21.2)*

6. Brandon is rolling a 10-sided number cube 5 times. What is the probability that he will roll at least two 7s? *(Lesson 21.3)*

Determine if the given events are mutually exclusive. If not, explain why. *(Lesson 21.4)*

7. Rolling a 3 or a 4 on a regular number cube

8. Drawing a queen or a red card from a standard deck of 52 cards

9. Flipping a coin and having it land on heads or tails

10. Rolling an even number or a prime number on a number cube

MODULE PERFORMANCE TASK

Baseball Probability

A baseball player will be batting three times during today's game. So far this season, the player has gotten an average of 1 hit in every 3 times at bat. Based on this data, what is the probability that the player will get exactly one hit in today's game? Is that outcome more or less likely than getting no hits?

Start by making notes in the space below about your plan for solving the problem. Then use your own paper to complete the task, using words, numbers, or diagrams to explain how your reached your conclusions.

21.1–21.4 Introduction to Probability

- Online Homework
- Hints and Help
- Extra Practice

Find the probabilities. *(Lessons 21.3, 21.4)*

1. Twenty-six tiles with the letters A through Z are placed face down on a table and mixed. (For the purpose of this exercise assume that the letter Y is a vowel.) Five tiles are drawn in order. Compute the probability that only consonants are selected.

2. The two-way table shows the results of a poll in a certain country that asked voters, sorted by political party, whether they supported or opposed a proposed government initiative. Find the given probabilities.

	Party A	Party B	Other Party	No Party	Total
Support	97	68	8	19	192
Oppose	32	81	16	11	140
Undecided	9	23	10	26	68
Total	138	172	34	56	400

a. $P\left(\text{no party or undecided}\right)$

b. $P\left(\left(\text{party A or support}\right)^c\right)$

ESSENTIAL QUESTION

3. A teacher is assigning 32 presentation topics to 9 students at random. Each student will get 3 topics, and no topic will be repeated. Somil is very interested in 5 topics. What is the probability that Somil will be assigned at least one of his preferred topics? Explain how you arrived at your answer.

Assessment Readiness

1. Jonah is arranging books on a shelf. The order of the books matters to him. There are 336 ways he can arrange the books. Choose Yes or No for each statement.

   A. He might be arranging 3 books from a selection of 8 different books. ◯ Yes ◯ No

   B. He might be arranging 4 books from a selection of 8 different books. ◯ Yes ◯ No

   C. He might be arranging 5 books from a selection of 8 different books. ◯ Yes ◯ No

2. Decide whether the probability of tossing the given sum with two dice is $\frac{5}{36}$. Select Yes or No for A–C.

   A. A sum of 6 ◯ Yes ◯ No

   B. A sum of 7 ◯ Yes ◯ No

   C. A sum of 8 ◯ Yes ◯ No

3. Let H be the event that a coin flip lands with heads showing, and let T be the event that a flip lands with tails showing. (Note that $P(H) = P(T) = 0.5$.) What is the probability that you will get heads at least once if you flip the coin ten times? Explain your reasoning.

4. There are 8 girls and 6 boys on the student council. How many committees of 3 girls and 2 boys can be formed? Show your work.

Conditional Probability and Independence of Events

Essential Question: How can you use conditional probability and independence of events to solve real-world problems?

REAL WORLD VIDEO
Check out how principles of conditional probability are used to understand the chances of events in playing cards.

MODULE PERFORMANCE TASK PREVIEW
Playing Cards

In this module, you will use concepts of conditional probability to determine the chance of drawing a hand of cards with a certain property. To successfully complete this task, you'll need to master these skills:

- Distinguish between independent and dependent events.
- Apply the conditional probability formula to a real-world situation.
- Use the Multiplication Rule appropriately.

Are (YOU) Ready?

Complete these exercises to review skills you will need for this module.

Probability of Compound Events

- Online Homework
- Hints and Help
- Extra Practice

Example 1 Find the probability of rolling a pair of six-sided dice and the sum of their faces being even or equal to 3.

Three is not even, so the two probabilities are mutually exclusive. The probability is equal to the sums of the probabilities of rolling an even sum or rolling a sum of 3.

Probability of rolling an even sum $= \frac{18}{36}$ **Count the number of outcomes for the first event.**

Probability of rolling a sum of 3 $= \frac{2}{36}$ **Count the number of outcomes for the second event.**

Probability of rolling an even sum or a sum of 3 $= \frac{18}{36} + \frac{2}{36} = \frac{20}{36} = \frac{5}{9}$

Find each probability.

1. The probability of rolling two dice at the same time and getting a 4 with either die or the sum of the dice is 6. _____

2. The probability of rolling two dice at the same time and getting a 4 with either die and the sum of the dice is 6. _____

3. The probability of pulling red or blue marbles (or both) from a jar of only red and blue marbles when you pull out two marbles given that pulling red and pulling blue are equally likely events. _____

4. The probability of pulling a red marble and a blue marble from a jar of only red and blue marbles when you pull out two marbles given that pulling red and pulling blue are equally likely events. _____

5. The probability of flipping a coin three times and getting exactly two heads or at least one tails given the probability of getting a heads is $\frac{1}{2}$ and the probability of getting a tails is $\frac{1}{2}$. _____

6. The probability of flipping a coin three times and getting exactly two heads and at least one tails given the probability of getting a heads is $\frac{1}{2}$ and the probability of getting a tails is $\frac{1}{2}$. _____

7. The probability of flipping a coin three times and getting at least two heads or at least one tails given the probability of getting a heads is $\frac{1}{2}$ and the probability of getting a tails is $\frac{1}{2}$. _____

22.1 Conditional Probability

Essential Question: How do you calculate a conditional probability?

 Explore 1 **Finding Conditional Probabilities from a Two-Way Frequency Table**

The probability that event *A* occurs given that event *B* has already occurred is called the **conditional probability** of *A* given *B* and is written $P(A \mid B)$.

One hundred migraine headache sufferers participated in a study of a new medicine. Some were given the new medicine, and others were not. After one week, participants were asked if they had experienced a headache during the week. The two-way frequency table shows the results.

	Took medicine	No medicine	Total
Headache	11	13	24
No headache	54	22	76
Total	65	35	100

Let event *A* be the event that a participant did not get a headache. Let event *B* be the event that a participant took the medicine.

(A) To the nearest percent, what is the probability that a participant who took the medicine did not get a headache?

_____ participants took the medicine.   So, $P(A \mid B) = \dfrac{\boxed{}}{\boxed{}} \approx \boxed{}$%.

Of these, _____ did not get a headache.

(B) To the nearest percent, what is the probability that a participant who did not get a headache took the medicine?

_____ participants did not get a headache.   So, $P(B \mid A) = \dfrac{\boxed{}}{\boxed{}} \approx \boxed{}$%.

Of these, _____ took the medicine.

 Let $n(A)$ be the number of participants who did not get a headache, $n(B)$ be the number of participants who took the medicine, and $n(A \cap B)$ be the number of participants who took the medicine and did not get a headache.

$n(A) = \boxed{}$ $n(B) = \boxed{}$ $n(A \cap B) = \boxed{}$

Express $P(A \mid B)$ and $P(B \mid A)$ in terms of $n(A)$, $n(B)$, and $n(A \cap B)$.

$P(A \mid B) = \dfrac{\boxed{}}{\boxed{}}$ $P(B \mid A) = \dfrac{\boxed{}}{\boxed{}}$

1. For the question "What is the probability that a participant who did not get a headache took the medicine?", what event is assumed to have already occurred?

_____

2. In general, does it appear that $P(A|B) = P(B|A)$? Why or why not?

_____

_____

⊘ Explore 2 Finding Conditional Probabilities from a Two-Way Relative Frequency Table

You can develop a formula for $P(A|B)$ that uses relative frequencies (which are probabilities) rather than frequencies (which are counts).

	Took medicine	No medicine	Total
Headache	11	13	24
No headache	54	22	76
Total	65	35	100

Ⓐ To obtain relative frequencies, divide every number in the table by 100, the total number of participants in the study.

	Took medicine	No medicine	Total
Headache			
No headache			
Total			1

Ⓑ Recall that event A is the event that a participant did not get a headache and that event B is the event that a participant took the medicine. Use the relative frequency table from Step A to find $P(A)$, $P(B)$, and $P(A \cap B)$.

_____

_____

Ⓒ In the first Explore, you found the conditional probabilities $P(A|B) \approx 83\%$ and $P(B|A) \approx 71\%$ by using the frequencies in the two-way frequency table. Use the relative frequencies from the table in Step A to find the equivalent conditional probabilities.

$$P(A|B) = \frac{P(A \cap B)}{P(B)} = \frac{\boxed{}}{\boxed{}} \approx \boxed{} \%$$

$$P(B|A) = \frac{P(A \cap B)}{P(A)} = \frac{\boxed{}}{\boxed{}} \approx \boxed{} \%$$

(D) Generalize the results by using $n(S)$ as the number of elements in the sample space (in this case, the number of participants in the study). For instance, you can write $P(A) = \frac{n(A)}{n(S)}$. Write each of the following probabilities in a similar way.

$$P(B) = \frac{\boxed{}}{\boxed{}} \qquad P(A \cap B) = \frac{\boxed{}}{\boxed{}} \qquad P(A \mid B) = \frac{\dfrac{n(A \cap B)}{\boxed{}}}{\dfrac{}{n(B)}} = \frac{P(A \cap B)}{\boxed{}}$$

Reflect

3. Why are the two forms of $P(A \cap B)$, $\frac{n(A \cap B)}{n(B)}$ and $\frac{P(A \cap B)}{P(B)}$, equivalent?

_____

4. What is a formula for $P(B \mid A)$ that involves probabilities rather than counts? How do you obtain this formula from the fact that $P(B \mid A) = \frac{n(A \cap B)}{n(A)}$?

_____

🔑 Explain 1 Using the Conditional Probability Formula

In the previous Explore, you discovered the following formula for conditional probability.

> **Conditional Probability**
>
> The conditional probability of A given B (that is, the probability that event A occurs given that event B occurs) is as follows:
>
> $$P(A \mid B) = \frac{P(A \cap B)}{P(B)}$$

Example 1 Find the specified probability.

(A) For a standard deck of playing cards, find the probability that a red card randomly drawn from the deck is a jack.

Step 1 Find $P(R)$, the probability that a red card is drawn from the deck.

There are 26 red cards in the deck of 52 cards, so $P(R) = \frac{26}{52}$.

Step 2 Find $P(J \cap R)$, the probability that a red jack is drawn from the deck.

There are 2 red jacks in the deck, so $P(J \cap R) = \frac{2}{52}$.

Step 3 Substitute the probabilities from Steps 1 and 2 into the formula for conditional probability.

$$P(J|R) = \frac{P(J \cap R)}{P(R)} = \frac{\frac{2}{52}}{\frac{26}{52}}$$

Step 4 Simplify the result.

$$P(J|R) = \frac{\frac{2}{52} \cdot 52}{\frac{26}{52} \cdot 52} = \frac{2}{26} = \frac{1}{13}$$

(B) For a standard deck of playing cards, find the probability that a jack randomly drawn from the deck is a red card.

Step 1 Find $P(J)$, the probability that a jack is drawn from the deck.

There are _____ jacks in the deck of 52 cards, so $P(J) = \dfrac{\square}{52}$.

Step 2 Find $P(J \cap R)$, the probability that a red jack is drawn from the deck.

There are _____ red jacks in the deck, so $P(J \cap R) = \dfrac{\square}{52}$.

Step 3 Substitute the probabilities from Steps 1 and 2 into the formula for conditional probability.

$$P(R|J) = \frac{P(J \cap R)}{P(J)} = \frac{\frac{\square}{52}}{\frac{\square}{52}}$$

Step 4 Simplify the result.

$$P(R|J) = \frac{\frac{\square}{52} \cdot 52}{\frac{\square}{52} \cdot 52} = \frac{\square}{\square} = \frac{1}{\square}$$

Your Turn

5. For a standard deck of playing cards, find the probability that a face card randomly drawn from the deck is a king. (The ace is *not* a face card.)

6. For a standard deck of playing cards, find the probability that a queen randomly drawn from the deck is a diamond.

7. When calculating a conditional probability from a two-way table, explain why it doesn't matter whether the table gives frequencies or relative frequencies.

_____

_____

8. **Discussion** Is it possible to have $P(B|A) = P(A|B)$ for some events A and B? What conditions would need to exist?

_____

_____

9. **Essential Question Check-In** In a two-way frequency table, suppose event A represents a row of the table and event B represents a column of the table. Describe how to find the conditional probability $P(A|B)$ using the frequencies in the table.

_____

_____

☆ Evaluate: Homework and Practice

- Online Homework
- Hints and Help
- Extra Practice

In order to study the relationship between the amount of sleep a student gets and his or her school performance, a researcher collected data from 120 students. The two-way frequency table shows the number of students who passed and failed an exam and the number of students who got more or less than 6 hours of sleep the night before. Use the table to answer the questions in Exercises 1–3.

	Passed exam	Failed exam	Total
Less than 6 hours of sleep	12	10	22
More than 6 hours of sleep	90	8	98
Total	102	18	120

1. To the nearest percent, what is the probability that a student who failed the exam got less than 6 hours of sleep?

2. To the nearest percent, what is the probability that a student who got less than 6 hours of sleep failed the exam?

3. To the nearest percent, what is the probability that a student got less than 6 hours of sleep and failed the exam?

4. You have a standard deck of playing cards from which you randomly select a card. Event D is getting a diamond, and event F is getting a face card (a jack, queen, or king).

Show that $P(D|F) = \dfrac{n(D \cap F)}{n(F)}$ and $P(D|F) = \dfrac{P(D \cap F)}{P(F)}$ are equal.

The table shows data in the previous table as relative frequencies (rounded to the nearest thousandth when necessary). Use the table for Exercises 5–7.

	Passed exam	Failed exam	Total
Less than 6 hours of sleep	0.100	0.083	0.183
More than 6 hours of sleep	0.750	0.067	0.817
Total	0.850	0.150	1.000

5. To the nearest percent, what is the probability that a student who passed the exam got more than 6 hours of sleep?

6. To the nearest percent, what is the probability that a student who got more than 6 hours of sleep passed the exam?

7. Which is greater, the probability that a student who got less than 6 hours of sleep passed the exam or the probability that a student who got more than 6 hours of sleep failed the exam? Explain.

You randomly draw a card from a standard deck of playing cards. Let *A* be the event that the card is an ace, let *B* be the event that the card is black, and let *C* be the event that the card is a club. Find the specified probability as a fraction.

8. $P(A \mid B)$

9. $P(B \mid A)$

10. $P(A \mid C)$

11. $P(C \mid A)$

12. $P(B \mid C)$

13. $P(C \mid B)$

14. A botanist studied the effect of a new fertilizer by choosing 100 orchids and giving 70% of these plants the fertilizer. Of the plants that got the fertilizer, 40% produced flowers within a month. Of the plants that did not get the fertilizer, 10% produced flowers within a month.

a. Use the given information to complete the two-way frequency table.

	Received fertilizer	Did not receive fertilizer	Total
Did not flower in one month			
Flowered in one month			
Total			

b. To the nearest percent, what is the probability that an orchid that produced flowers got fertilizer?

c. To the nearest percent, what is the probability that an orchid that got fertilizer produced flowers?

15. At a school fair, a box contains 24 yellow balls and 76 red balls. One-fourth of the balls of each color are labeled "Win a prize." Match each description of a probability with its value as a percent.

A. The probability that a randomly selected   _____ 76%
ball labeled "Win a prize" is yellow

B. The probability that a randomly selected   _____ 25%
ball labeled "Win a prize" is red

C. The probability that a randomly selected   _____ 24%
ball is labeled "Win a prize" and is red

D. The probability that a randomly selected   _____ 19%
yellow ball is labeled "Win a prize"

16. A teacher gave her students two tests. If 45% of the students passed both tests and 60% passed the first test, what is the probability that a student who passed the first test also passed the second?

17. You randomly select two marbles, one at a time, from a pouch containing blue and green marbles. The probability of selecting a blue marble on the first draw and a green marble on the second draw is 25%, and the probability of selecting a blue marble on the first draw is 56%. To the nearest percent, what is the probability of selecting a green marble on the second draw, given that the first marble was blue?

You roll two number cubes, one red and one blue. The table shows the probabilities for events based on whether or not a 1 is rolled on each number cube. Use the table to find the specified conditional probability, expressed as a fraction. Then show that the conditional probability is correct by listing the possible outcomes as ordered pairs of the form (number on red cube, number on blue cube) and identifying the successful outcomes.

	Rolling a 1 on the red cube	Not rolling a 1 on the red cube	Total
Rolling a 1 on the blue cube	$\frac{1}{36}$	$\frac{5}{36}$	$\frac{1}{6}$
Not rolling a 1 on the blue cube	$\frac{5}{36}$	$\frac{25}{36}$	$\frac{5}{6}$
Total	$\frac{1}{6}$	$\frac{5}{6}$	1

18. P(not rolling a 1 on the blue cube | rolling a 1 on the red cube)

19. P(not rolling a 1 on the blue cube | not rolling a 1 on the red cube)

20. The table shows the results of a quality-control study at a computer factory.

	Shipped	Not shipped	Total
Defective	3	7	10
Not defective	89	1	90
Total	92	8	100

a. To the nearest tenth of a percent, what is the probability that a shipped computer is not defective?

b. To the nearest tenth of a percent, what is the probability that a defective computer is shipped?

H.O.T. Focus on Higher Order Thinking

21. Analyze Relationships In the Venn diagram, the circles representing events *A* and *B* divide the sample space *S* into four regions: the overlap of the circles, the part of *A* not in the overlap, the part of *B* not in the overlap, and the part of *S* not in *A* or *B*. Suppose that the area of each region is proportional to the number of outcomes that fall within the region. Which conditional probability is greater: $P(A|B)$ or $P(B|A)$? Explain.

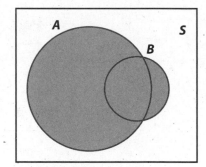

22. Explain the Error A student was asked to use the table shown to find the probability, to nearest percent, that a participant in a study of a new medicine for migraine headaches did not take the medicine, given that the participant reported no headaches.

	Took medicine	No medicine	Total
Headache	11	13	24
No headache	54	22	76
Total	65	35	100

The student made the following calculation.

$P(\text{no medicine} \mid \text{no headache}) = \dfrac{22}{35} \approx 0.63 = 63\%$

Explain the student's error, and find the correct probability.

23. Communicate Mathematical Ideas Explain how a conditional probability based on a two-way frequency table effectively reduces it to a one-way table. In your explanation, refer to the two-way table shown, which lists frequencies for events A, B, and their complements. Highlight the part of the table that supports your explanation.

	A	Not A	Total
B	$n(A \cap B)$	$n(\text{not } A \cap B)$	$n(B)$
Not B	$n(A \cap \text{not } B)$	$n(\text{not } A \cap \text{not } B)$	$n(\text{not } B)$
Total	$n(A)$	$n(\text{not } A)$	$n(S)$

Lesson Performance Task

The two-way frequency table gives the results of a survey that asked students this question: Which of these would you most like to meet: a famous singer, a movie star, or a sports star?

	Famous singer	Movie star	Sports star	Total
Boys	20	15	55	
Girls	40	50	20	
Total				

a. Complete the table by finding the row totals, column totals, and grand total.

b. To the nearest percent, what is the probability that a student who chose "movie star" is a girl?

c. To the nearest percent, what is the probability that a student who chose "famous singer" is a boy?

d. To the nearest percent, what is the probability that a boy chose "sports star"?

e. To the nearest percent, what is the probability that a girl chose "famous singer"?

f. To the nearest percent, what is the probability that a student who chose either "famous singer" or "movie star" is a boy?

g. To the nearest percent, what is the probability that a girl did not choose "sports star"?

22.2 Independent Events

Essential Question: What does it mean for two events to be independent?

Resource Locker

⊘ Explore   Understanding the Independence of Events

Suppose you flip a coin and roll a number cube. You would expect the probability of getting heads on the coin to be $\frac{1}{2}$ regardless of what number you get from rolling the number cube. Likewise, you would expect the probability of rolling a 3 on the number cube to be $\frac{1}{6}$ regardless of whether of the coin flip results in heads or tails.

When the occurrence of one event has no effect on the occurrence of another event, the two events are called **independent events**.

Ⓐ A jar contains 15 red marbles and 17 yellow marbles. You randomly draw a marble from the jar. Let R be the event that you get a red marble, and let Y be the event that you get a yellow marble.

Since the jar has a total of _____ marbles, $P(R) = \dfrac{\boxed{}}{\boxed{}}$ and $P(Y) = \dfrac{\boxed{}}{\boxed{}}$.

Ⓑ Suppose the first marble you draw is a red marble, and you put that marble back in the jar before randomly drawing a second marble. Find $P(Y|R)$, the probability that you get a yellow marble on the second draw after getting a red marble on the first draw. Explain your reasoning.

Since the jar still has a total of _____ marbles and _____ of them are yellow, $P(Y|R) = \dfrac{\boxed{}}{\boxed{}}$.

Ⓒ Suppose you *don't* put the red marble back in the jar before randomly drawing a second marble. Find $P(Y|R)$, the probability that you get a yellow marble on the second draw after getting a red marble on the first draw. Explain your reasoning.

Since the jar now has a total of _____ marbles and _____ of them are yellow, $P(Y|R) = \dfrac{\boxed{}}{\boxed{}}$.

Reflect

1. In one case you replaced the first marble before drawing the second, and in the other case you didn't. For which case was $P(Y|R)$ equal to $P(Y)$? Why?

_____

_____

2. In which of the two cases would you say the events of getting a red marble on the first draw and getting a yellow marble on the second draw are independent? What is true about $P(Y|R)$ and $P(Y)$ in this case?

_____

_____

Explain 1   Determining if Events are Independent

To determine the independence of two events A and B, you can check to see whether $P(A|B) = P(A)$ since the occurrence of event A is unaffected by the occurrence of event B if and only if the events are independent.

Example 1   The two-way frequency table gives data about 180 randomly selected flights that arrive at an airport. Use the table to answer the question.

	Late Arrival	On Time	Total
Domestic Flights	12	108	120
International Flights	6	54	60
Total	18	162	180

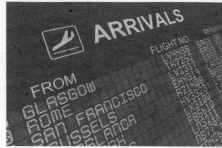

(A)   Is the event that a flight is on time independent of the event that a flight is domestic?

Let O be the event that a flight is on time. Let D be the event that a flight is domestic. Find $P(O)$ and $P(O|D)$. To find $P(O)$, note that the total number of flights is 180, and of those flights, there are 162 on-time flights. So, $P(O) = \frac{162}{180} = 90\%$.

To find $P(O|D)$, note that there are 120 domestic flights, and of those flights, there are 108 on-time flights.

So, $P(O|D), = \frac{108}{120} = 90\%$.

Since $P(O|D) = P(O)$, the event that a flight is on time is independent of the event that a flight is domestic.

(B)   Is the event that a flight is international independent of the event that a flight arrives late?

Let I be the event that a flight is international. Let L be the event that a flight arrives late. Find $P(I)$ and $P(I|L)$. To find $P(I)$, note that the total number of flights is 180, and of those

flights, there are ____ international flights. So, $P(I) = \dfrac{\boxed{}}{180} = \boxed{}\%$.

To find $P(I|L)$, note that there are ____ flights that arrive late, and of those flights, there are ____

international flights. So, $P(I|L) = \dfrac{\boxed{}}{\boxed{}} = \boxed{}\%$.

Since $P(I|L)\ \boxed{}\ P(I)$, the event that a flight is international [is/is not] independent of the

event that a flight arrives late.

The two-way frequency table gives data about 200 randomly selected apartments in a city. Use the table to answer the question.

	1 Bedroom	2+ Bedrooms	Total
Single Occupant	64	12	76
Multiple Occupants	26	98	124
Total	90	110	200

3. Is the event that an apartment has a single occupant independent of the event that an apartment has 1 bedroom?

_____

_____

_____

4. Is the event that an apartment has 2 or more bedrooms independent of the event that an apartment has multiple occupants?

_____

_____

_____

🔑 Explain 2   Finding the Probability of Independent Events

From the definition of conditional probability you know that $P(A|B) = \dfrac{P(A \cap B)}{P(B)}$ for any events A and B. If those events happen to be independent, you can replace $P(A|B)$ with $P(A)$ and get $P(A) = \dfrac{P(A \cap B)}{P(B)}$. Solving the last equation for $P(A \cap B)$ gives the following result.

> **Probability of Independent Events**
>
> Events A and B are independent if and only if $P(A \cap B) = P(A) \cdot P(B)$.

Example 2   Find the specified probability.

(A) Recall the jar with 15 red marbles and 17 yellow marbles from the Explore. Suppose you randomly draw one marble from the jar. After you put that marble back in the jar, you randomly draw a second marble. What is the probability that you draw a yellow marble first and a red marble second?

Let Y be the event of drawing a yellow marble first. Let R be the event of drawing a red marble second. Then $P(Y) = \frac{17}{32}$ and, because the first marble drawn is replaced before the second marble is drawn, $P(R|Y) = P(R) = \frac{15}{32}$. Since the events are independent, you can multiply their probabilities: $P(Y \cap R) = P(Y) \cdot P(R) = \frac{17}{32} \cdot \frac{15}{32} = \frac{255}{1024} \approx 25\%$.

Ⓑ You spin the spinner shown two times. What is the probability that the spinner stops on an even number on the first spin, followed by an odd number on the second spin?

Let E be the event of getting an even number on the first spin. Let O be the event of getting an odd number on the second spin. Then $P(E) = \dfrac{\square}{8}$ and, because the first spin has no effect on the second spin, $P(O|E) = P(O) = \dfrac{\square}{8}$. Since the events are independent, you can multiply their probabilities:

$$P(E \cap O) = P(E) \cdot P(O) = \frac{\square}{8} \cdot \frac{\square}{8} = \frac{\square}{64} \approx \boxed{} \%.$$

Reflect

5. In Part B, what is the probability that the spinner stops on an odd number on the first spin, followed by an even number on the second spin? What do you observe? What does this tell you?

_____

_____

_____

_____

Your Turn

6. You spin a spinner with 4 red sections, 3 blue sections, 2 green sections, and 1 yellow section. If all the sections are of equal size, what is the probability that the spinner stops on green first and blue second?

7. A number cube has the numbers 3, 5, 6, 8, 10, and 12 on its faces. You roll the number cube twice. What is the probability that you roll an odd number on both rolls?

Explain 3 Showing That Events Are Independent

So far, you have used the formula $P(A \cap B) = P(A) \cdot P(B)$ when you knew that events A and B are independent. You can also use the formula to determine whether two events are independent.

Example 3 Determine if the events are independent.

(A) The two-way frequency table shows data for 120 randomly selected patients who have the same doctor. Determine whether a patient who takes vitamins and a patient who exercises regularly are independent events.

	Takes Vitamins	No Vitamins	Total
Regular Exercise	48	28	76
No regular Exercise	12	32	44
Total	60	60	120

Let V be the event that a patient takes vitamins. Let E be the event that a patient exercises regularly.

Step 1 Find $P(V)$, $P(E)$, and $P(V \cap E)$. The total number of patients is 120.

There are 60 patients who take vitamins, so $P(V) = \dfrac{60}{120} = \dfrac{1}{2}$.

There are 76 patients who exercise regularly, so $P(B) = \dfrac{76}{120} = \dfrac{19}{30}$.

There are 48 patients who take vitamins and exercise regularly, so $P(V \cap E) = \dfrac{48}{120} = 40\%$.

Step 2 Compare $P(V \cap E)$ and $P(V) \cdot P(E)$.

$$P(V) \cdot P(E) = \frac{1}{2} \cdot \frac{19}{30} = \frac{19}{60} \approx 32\%$$

Because $P(V \cap E) \neq P(V) \cdot P(E)$, the events are not independent.

(B) The two-way frequency table shows data for 60 randomly selected children at an elementary school. Determine whether a child who knows how to ride a bike and a child who knows how to swim are independent events.

	Knows how to Ride a Bike	Doesn't Know how to Ride a Bike	Total
Knows how to Swim	30	10	40
Doesn't Know how to Swim	15	5	20
Total	45	15	60

Let B be the event a child knows how to ride a bike. Let S be the event that a child knows how to swim.

Step 1 Find $P(B)$, $P(S)$, and $P(B \cap S)$. The total number of children is 60.

There are ____ children who know how to ride a bike, so $P(B) = \dfrac{\boxed{}}{60} = \dfrac{\boxed{}}{4}$.

There are ____ children who know how to swim, so $P(S) = \dfrac{\boxed{}}{60} = \dfrac{\boxed{}}{3}$.

There are ____ children who know how to ride a bike and swim, so $P(B \cap S) = \dfrac{\boxed{}}{60} = \dfrac{\boxed{}}{2}$.

Step 2 Compare $P(B \cap S)$ and $P(B) \cdot P(S)$.

$$P(B) \cdot P(S) = \frac{\boxed{}}{4} \cdot \frac{\boxed{}}{3} = \frac{\boxed{}}{2}$$

Because $P(B \cap S)\ \boxed{}\ P(B) \cdot P(S)$, the events [are/are not] independent.

Your Turn

8. A farmer wants to know if an insecticide is effective in preventing small insects called aphids from damaging tomato plants. The farmer experiments with 80 plants and records the results in the two-way frequency table. Determine whether a plant that was sprayed with insecticide and a plant that has aphids are independent events.

	Has Aphids	No Aphids	Total
Sprayed with Insecticide	12	40	52
Not Sprayed with Insecticide	14	14	28
Total	26	54	80

9. A student wants to know if right-handed people are more or less likely to play a musical instrument than left-handed people. The student collects data from 250 people, as shown in the two-way frequency table. Determine whether being right-handed and playing a musical instrument are independent events.

	Right-Handed	Left-Handed	Total
Plays a Musical Instrument	44	6	50
Does not Play a Musical Instrument	176	24	200
Total	220	30	250

10. What are the ways that you can show that two events A and B are independent?

_____

_____

11. How can you find the probability that two independent events A and B both occur?

_____

12. Essential Question Check-In Give an example of two independent events and explain why they are independent.

_____

_____

_____

_____

⭐ Evaluate: Homework and Practice

• Online Homework
• Hints and Help
• Extra Practice

1. A bag contains 12 red and 8 blue chips. Two chips are separately drawn at random from the bag.

   a. Suppose that a single chip is drawn at random from the bag. Find the probability that the chip is red and the probability that the chip is blue.

   b. Suppose that two chips are separately drawn at random from the bag and that the first chip is returned to the bag before the second chip is drawn. Find the probability that the second chip drawn is blue given the first chip drawn was red.

   c. Suppose that two chips are separately drawn at random from the bag and that the first chip is not returned to the bag before the second chip is drawn. Find the probability that the second chip drawn is blue given the first chip drawn was red.

   d. In which situation—the first chip is returned to the bag or not returned to the bag—are the events that the first chip is red and the second chip is blue independent? Explain.

2. Identify whether the events are independent or not independent.

a. Flip a coin twice and get tails both times. ◯ Independent ◯ Not Independent

b. Roll a number cube and get 1 on the first roll and 6 on the second. ◯ Independent ◯ Not Independent

c. Draw an ace from a shuffled deck, put the card back and reshuffle the deck, and then draw an 8. ◯ Independent ◯ Not Independent

d. Rotate a bingo cage and draw the ball labeled B-4, set it aside, and then rotate the cage again and draw the ball labled N-38. ◯ Independent ◯ Not Independent

Answer the question using the fact that $P(A|B) = P(A)$ only when events A and B are independent.

3. The two-way frequency table shows data for 80 randomly selected people who live in a metropolitan area. Is the event that a person prefers public transportation independent of the event that a person lives in the city?

	Prefers to Drive	Prefers Public Transportation	Total
Lives in the City	12	24	36
Lives in the Suburbs	33	11	44
Total	45	35	80

4. The two-way frequency table shows data for 120 randomly selected people who take vacations. Is the event that a person prefers vacationing out of state independent of the event that a person is a woman?

	Prefers Vacationing Out of State	Prefers Vacationing in State	Total
Men	48	32	80
Women	24	16	40
Total	72	48	120

A jar contains marbles of various colors as listed in the table. Suppose you randomly draw one marble from the jar. After you put that marble back in the jar, you randomly draw a second marble. Use this information to answer the question, giving a probability as a percent and rounding to the nearest tenth of percent when necessary.

Color of Marble	Number of Marbles
Red	20
Yellow	18
Green	12
Blue	10

5. What is the probability that you draw a blue marble first and a red marble second?

6. What is the probability that you draw a yellow marble first and a green marble second?

7. What is the probability that you draw a yellow marble both times?

8. What color marble for the first draw and what color marble for the second draw have the greatest probability of occurring together? What is that probability?

You spin the spinner shown two times. Each section of the spinner is the same size. Use this information to answer the question, giving a probability as a percent and rounding to the nearest tenth of a percent when necessary.

9. What is the probability that the spinner stops on 1 first and 2 second?

10. What is the probability that the spinner stops on 4 first and 3 second?

11. What is the probability that the spinner stops on an odd number first and an even number second?

12. What first number and what second number have the least probability of occurring together? What is that probability?

13. Find the probability of getting heads on every toss of a coin when the coin is tossed 3 times.

14. You are randomly choosing cards, one at a time and with replacement, from a standard deck of cards. Find the probability that you choose an ace, then a red card, and then a face card. (Remember that face cards are jacks, queens, and kings.)

Determine whether the given events are independent using the fact that $P(A \cap B) = P(A) \cdot P(B)$ only when events A and B are independent.

15. The manager of a produce stand wants to find out whether there is a connection between people who buy fresh vegetables and people who buy fresh fruit. The manager collects data on 200 randomly chosen shoppers, as shown in the two-way frequency table. Determine whether buying fresh vegetables and buying fresh fruit are independent events.

	Bought Vegetables	No Vegetables	Total
Bought Fruit	56	20	76
No Fruit	49	75	124
Total	105	95	200

16. The owner of a bookstore collects data about the reading preferences of 60 randomly chosen customers, as shown in the two-way frequency table. Determine whether being a female and preferring fiction are independent events.

	Prefers Fiction	Prefers Nonfiction	Total
Female	15	10	25
Male	21	14	35
Total	36	24	60

17. The psychology department at a college collects data about whether there is a relationship between a student's intended career and the student's like or dislike for solving puzzles. The two-way frequency table shows the collected data for 80 randomly chosen students. Determine whether planning for a career in a field involving math or science and a like for solving puzzles are independent events.

	Plans a Career in a Math/Science Field	Plans a Career in a Non-Math/Science Field	Total
Likes Solving Puzzles	35	15	50
Dislikes Solving Puzzles	9	21	30
Total	44	36	80

18. A local television station surveys some of its viewers to determine the primary reason they watch the station. The two-way frequency table gives the survey data. Determine whether a viewer is a man and a viewer primarily watches the station for entertainment are independent events.

	Primarily Watches for Information (News, Weather, Sports)	Primarily Watches for Entertainment (Comedies, Dramas)	Total
Men	28	12	40
Women	35	15	50
Total	63	27	90

19. Using what you know about independent events, complete the two-way frequency table in such a way that any event from a column will be independent of any event from a row. Give an example using the table to demonstrate the independence of two events.

	Women	Men	Total
Prefers Writing with a Pen			100
Prefers Writing with a Pencil			50
Total	60	90	150

20. Make a Prediction A box contains 100 balloons. The balloons come in two colors: 80 are yellow and 20 are green. The balloons are also either marked or unmarked: 50 are marked "Happy Birthday!" and 50 are not. A balloon is randomly chosen from the box. How many yellow "Happy Birthday!" balloons must be in the box if the event that a balloon is yellow and the event that a balloon is marked "Happy Birthday!" are independent? Explain.

21. Construct Arguments Given that events A and B are independent, prove that the complement of event A, A^c, is also independent of event B.

22. Multi-Step The two-way frequency table shows two events, A and B, and their complements, A^c and B^c. Let $P(A) = a$ and $P(B) = b$. Using a, b, and the grand total T, form the products listed in the table to find the number of elements in $A \cap B$, $A \cap B^c$, $A^c \cap B$, and $A^c \cap B^c$.

	A	A^c	Total
B	abT	$(1-a)bT$	
B^c	$a(1-b)T$	$(1-a)(1-b)T$	
Total			T

a. Find the table's missing row and column totals in simplest form.

b. Show that events A and B are independent using the fact that $P(A \mid B) = P(A)$ only when events A and B are independent.

c. Show that events A and B^c are independent.

d. Show that events A^c and B are independent.

e. Show that events A^c and B^c are independent.

Lesson Performance Task

Before the mid-1800s, little was known about the way that plants pass along characteristics such as color and height to their offspring. From painstaking observations of garden peas, the Austrian monk Gregor Mendel discovered the basic laws of heredity. The table shows the results of three of Mendel's experiments. In each experiment, he looked at a particular characteristic of garden peas by planting seeds exclusively of one type.

Characteristic	Type Planted	Results in Second Generation
Flower color	100% violet	705 violet, 224 white
Seed texture	100% round	5474 round, 1850 wrinkled
Seed color	100% yellow	6022 yellow, 2011 green

1. Suppose you plant garden peas with violet flowers and round, yellow seeds. Estimate the probability of obtaining second-generation plants with violet flowers, the probability of obtaining second-generation plants with round seeds, and the probability of obtaining second-generation plants with yellow seeds. Explain how you made your estimates.

Mendel saw that certain traits, such as violet flowers and round seeds, seemed stronger than others, such white flowers and wrinkled seeds. He called the stronger traits "dominant" and the weaker traits "recessive." Both traits can be carried in the genes of a plant, because a gene consists of two *alleles*, one received from the mother and one from the father. (For plants, the "father" is the plant from which the pollen comes, and the "mother" is the plant whose pistil receives the pollen.) When at least one of the alleles has the dominant trait, the plant exhibits the dominant trait. Only when both alleles have the recessive trait does the plant exhibit the recessive trait.

You can use a 2 × 2 Punnett square, like the one shown, to see the results of crossing the genes of two parent plants. In this Punnett square, V represents the dominant flower color violet and v represents the recessive flower color white. If each parent's genes contain both V and v alleles, the offspring may receive, independently and with equal probability, either a V allele or a v allele from each parent.

	V	v
V	VV	Vv
v	vV	vv

2. After planting a first generation of plants exhibiting only dominant traits, Mendel observed that the second generation consisted of plants with a ratio of about 3:1 dominant-to-recessive traits. Does the Punnett square support or refute Mendel's observation? Explain.

3. Draw a 4 × 4 Punnett square for finding the results of crossing two violet-flower-and-round-seed parent plants. Let *V* and *R* represent the dominant traits violet flowers and round seeds, respectively. Let *v* and *r* represent the recessive traits white flowers and wrinkled seeds, respectively. Each column heading and row heading of your Punnett square should contain a two-letter combination of *V* or *v* and *R* or *r*. Each cell of your Punnett square will then contain four letters. Use the Punnett square to find the probability that a second-generation plant will have white flowers and round seeds. Explain your reasoning.

22.3 Dependent Events

Essential Question: How do you find the probability of dependent events?

Resource
Locker

⊘ Explore   Finding a Way to Calculate the Probability of Dependent Events

You know two tests for the independence of events A and B:

1. If $P(A|B) = P(A)$, then A and B are independent.

2. If $P(A \cap B) = P(A) \cdot P(B)$, then A and B are independent.

Two events that fail either of these tests are **dependent events** because the occurrence of one event affects the occurrence of the other event.

Ⓐ The two-way frequency table shows the results of a survey of 100 people who regularly walk for exercise. Let O be the event that a person prefers walking outdoors. Let M be the event that a person is male. Find $P(O)$, $P(M)$, and $P(O \cap M)$ as fractions. Then determine whether events O and M are independent or dependent.

	Prefers walking outdoors	Prefers walking on a treadmill	Total
Male	40	10	50
Female	20	30	50
Total	60	40	100

_____

_____

Ⓑ Calculate the conditional probabilities $P(O|M)$ and $P(M|O)$.

$$P(O|M) = \frac{n(O \cap M)}{n(M)} = \frac{\boxed{}}{\boxed{}} = \frac{\boxed{}}{5}$$

$$P(M|O) = \frac{n(O \cap M)}{n(O)} = \frac{\boxed{}}{\boxed{}} = \frac{\boxed{}}{3}$$

Ⓒ Complete the multiplication table using the fractions for $P(O)$ and $P(M)$ from Step A and the fractions for $P(O|M)$ and $P(M|O)$ from Step B.

×	P(O)	P(M)
P(O|M)		
P(M|O)		

Ⓓ Do any of the four products in Step C equal $P(O \cap M)$, calculated in Step A? If so, which of the four products?

_____

Reflect

1. In a previous lesson you learned the conditional probability formula $P(B|A) = \frac{P(A \cap B)}{P(A)}$. How does this formula explain the results you obtained in Step D?

_____

_____

_____

2. Let F be the event that a person is female. Let T be the event that a person prefers walking on a treadmill. Write two formulas you can use to calculate $P(F \cap T)$. Use either one to find the value of $P(F \cap T)$, and then confirm the result by finding $P(F \cap T)$ directly from the two-way frequency table.

_____

_____

_____

🔧 Explain 1   Finding the Probability of Two Dependent Events

You can use the Multiplication Rule to find the probability of dependent events.

> **Multiplication Rule**
>
> $P(A \cap B) = P(A) \cdot P(B|A)$ where $P(B|A)$ is the conditional probability of event B, given that event A has occurred.

Example 1   There are 5 tiles with the letters A, B, C, D, and E in a bag. You choose a tile without looking, put it aside, and then choose another tile without looking. Use the Multiplication Rule to find the specified probability, writing it as a fraction.

(A) Find the probability that you choose a vowel followed by a consonant.

Let V be the event that the first tile is a vowel. Let C be the event that the second tile is a consonant. Of the 5 tiles, there are 2 vowels, so $P(V) = \frac{2}{5}$.

Of the 4 remaining tiles, there are 3 consonants, so $P(C|V) = \frac{3}{4}$.

By the Multiplication Rule, $P(V \cap C) = P(V) \cdot P(V|C) = \frac{2}{5} \cdot \frac{3}{4} = \frac{6}{20} = \frac{3}{10}$.

(B) Find the probability that you choose a vowel followed by another vowel.

Let $V1$ be the event that the first tile is a vowel. Let $V2$ be the event that the second tile is also a vowel. Of the 5 tiles, there are ___ vowels, so $P(V1) = \frac{\boxed{}}{5}$.

Of the 4 remaining tiles, there is ___ vowel, so $P(V2|V1) = \frac{\boxed{}}{4}$.

By the Multiplication Rule, $P(V1 \cap V2) = P(V1) \cdot P(V2|V1) = \frac{\boxed{}}{5} \cdot \frac{\boxed{}}{4} = \frac{\boxed{}}{20} = \frac{\boxed{}}{10}$.

Your Turn

A bag holds 4 white marbles and 2 blue marbles. You choose a marble without looking, put it aside, and choose another marble without looking. Use the Multiplication Rule to find the specified probability, writing it as a fraction.

3. Find the probability that you choose a white marble followed by a blue marble.

4. Find the probability that you choose a white marble followed by another white marble.

⚙ Explain 2 Finding the Probability of Three or More Dependent Events

You can extend the Multiplication Rule to three or more events. For instance, for three events A, B, and C, the rule becomes $P(A \cap B \cap C) = P(A) \cdot P(B|A) \cdot P(C|A \cap B)$.

Example 2 You have a key ring with 7 different keys. You're attempting to unlock a door in the dark, so you try keys one at a time and keep track of which ones you try.

Ⓐ Find the probability that the third key you try is the right one.

Let $W1$ be the event that the first key you try is wrong. Let $W2$ be the event that the second key you try is also wrong. Let R be the event that the third key you try is right.

On the first try, there are 6 wrong keys among the 7 keys, so $P(W1) = \frac{6}{7}$.

On the second try, there are 5 wrong keys among the 6 remaining keys, so $P(W2|W1) = \frac{5}{6}$.

On the third try, there is 1 right key among the 5 remaining keys, so $P(R|W2 \cap W1) = \frac{1}{5}$.

By the Multiplication Rule, $P(W1 \cap W2 \cap R) = P(W1) \cdot P(W2|W1) \cdot P(R|W1 \cap W2) = \frac{6}{7} \cdot \frac{5}{6} \cdot \frac{1}{5} = \frac{1}{7}$.

Ⓑ Find the probability that one of the first three keys you try is right.

There are two ways to approach this problem:

1. You can break the problem into three cases: (1) the first key you try is right; (2) the first key is wrong, but the second key is right; and (3) the first two keys are wrong, but the third key is right.

2. You can use the complement: The complement of the event that one of the first three keys is right is the event that *none* of the first three keys is right.

Use the second approach.

Let $W1$, $W2$, and $W3$ be the events that the first, second, and third keys, respectively, are wrong.

From Part A, you already know that $P(W1) = \frac{\boxed{}}{7}$ and $P(W2|W1) = \frac{\boxed{}}{6}$.

On the third try, there are 4 wrong keys among the 5 remaining keys, so $P(W3|W2 \cap W1) = \frac{\boxed{}}{5}$.

By the Multiplication Rule,

$$P(W1 \cap W2 \cap W3) = P(W1) \cdot P(W2|W1) \cdot P(W3|W1 \cap W2) = \frac{\boxed{}}{7} \cdot \frac{\boxed{}}{6} \cdot \frac{\boxed{}}{5} = \frac{\boxed{}}{\boxed{}}$$

The event $W1 \cap W2 \cap W3$ is the complement of the one you want. So, the probability that one of

the first three keys you try is right is $1 - P(W1 \cap W2 \cap W3) = 1 - \frac{\boxed{}}{\boxed{}} = \frac{\boxed{}}{\boxed{}}$.

5. In Part B, show that the first approach to solving the problem gives the same result.

_____

_____

_____

_____

_____

_____

_____

_____

6. In Part A, suppose you don't keep track of the keys as you try them. How does the probability change? Explain.

_____

_____

_____

_____

Your Turn

Three people are standing in line at a car rental agency at an airport. Each person is willing to take whatever rental car is offered. The agency has 4 white cars and 2 silver ones available and offers them to customers on a random basis.

7. Find the probability that all three customers get white cars.

8. Find the probability that two of the customers get the silver cars and one gets a white car.

💬 Elaborate

9. When are two events dependent?

_____

_____

10. Suppose you are given a bag with 3 blue marbles and 2 red marbles, and you are asked to find the probability of drawing 2 blue marbles by drawing one marble at a time and not replacing the first marble drawn. Why does not replacing the first marble make these events dependent? What would make these events independent? Explain.

_____

_____

_____

_____

_____

_____

11. Essential Question Check-In According to the Multiplication Rule, when finding $P(A \cap B)$ for dependent events A and B, you multiply $P(A)$ by what?

_____

1. Town officials are considering a property tax increase to finance the building of a new school. The two-way frequency table shows the results of a survey of 110 town residents.

	Supports a property tax increase	Does not support a property tax increase	Total
Lives in a household with children	50	20	70
Lives in a household without children	10	30	40
Total	60	50	110

a. Let C be the event that a person lives in a household with children. Let S be the event that a person supports a property tax increase. Are the events C and S independent or dependent? Explain.

b. Find $P(C|S)$ and $P(S|C)$. Which of these two conditional probabilities can you multiply with $P(C)$ to get $P(C \cap S)$? Which of the two can you multiply with $P(S)$ to get $P(C \cap S)$?

2. A mall surveyed 120 shoppers to find out whether they typically wait for a sale to get a better price or make purchases on the spur of the moment regardless of price. The two-way frequency table shows the results of the survey.

	Waits for a Sale	Buys on Impulse	Total
Woman	40	10	50
Man	50	20	70
Total	90	30	120

a. Let W be the event that a shopper is a woman. Let S be the event that a shopper typically waits for a sale. Are the events W and S independent or dependent? Explain.

b. Find $P(W|S)$ and $P(S|W)$. Which of these two conditional probabilities can you multiply with $P(W)$ to get $P(W \cap S)$? Which of the two can you multiply with $P(S)$ to get $P(W \cap S)$?

There are 4 green, 10 red, and 6 yellow marbles in a bag. Each time you randomly choose a marble, you put it aside before choosing another marble at random. Use the Multiplication Rule to find the specified probability, writing it as a fraction.

3. Find the probability that you choose a red marble followed by a yellow marble.

4. Find the probabilty that you choose one yellow marble followed by another yellow marble.

5. Find the probability that you choose a red marble, followed by a yellow marble, followed by a green marble.

6. Find the probability that you choose three red marbles.

The table shows the sums that are possible when you roll two number cubes and add the numbers. Use this information to answer the questions.

+	1	2	3	4	5	6
1	2	3	4	5	6	7
2	3	4	5	6	7	8
3	4	5	6	7	8	9
4	5	6	7	8	9	10
5	6	7	8	9	10	11
6	7	8	9	10	11	12

7. Let *A* be the event that you roll a 2 on the number cube represented by the row labeled 2. Let *B* be the event that the sum of the numbers on the cubes is 7.

   a. Are these events independent or dependent? Explain.

   b. What is $P(A \cap B)$?

8. Let *A* be the event that you roll a 3 on the number cube represented by the row labeled 3. Let *B* be the event that the sum of the numbers on the cubes is 5.

   a. Are these events independent or dependent? Explain.

   b. What is $P(A \cap B)$?

9. A cooler contains 6 bottles of apple juice and 8 bottles of grape juice. You choose a bottle without looking, put it aside, and then choose another bottle without looking. Match each situation with its probability. More than one situation can have the same probability.

   a. Choose apple juice and then grape juice.   _____ $\dfrac{4}{13}$

   b. Choose apple juice and then apple juice.   _____ $\dfrac{24}{91}$

   c. Choose grape juice and then apple juice.   _____ $\dfrac{15}{91}$

   d. Choose grape juice and then grape juice.

10. Jorge plays all tracks on a playlist with no repeats. The playlist he's listening to has 12 songs, 4 of which are his favorites.

   a. What is the probability that the first song played is one of his favorites, but the next two songs are not?

   b. What is the probability that the first three songs played are all his favorites?

   c. Jorge can also play the tracks on his playlist in a random order with repeats possible. If he does this, how does your answer to part b change? Explain why.

11. You are playing a game of bingo with friends. In this game, balls are labeled with one of the letters of the word BINGO and a number. Some of these letter-number combinations are written on a bingo card in a 5 × 5 array, and as balls are randomly drawn and announced, players mark their cards if the ball's letter-number combination appears on the cards. The first player to complete a row, column, or diagonal on a card says "Bingo!" and wins the game. In the game you're playing, there are 20 balls left. To complete a row on your card, you need N-32 called. To complete a column, you need G-51 called. To complete a diagonal, you need B-6 called.

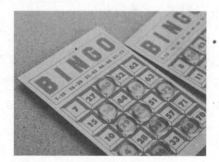

   a. What is the probability that the next two balls drawn do not have a letter-number combination you need, but the third ball does?

   b. What is the probability that none of the letter-number combinations you need is called from the next three balls?

12. You are talking with 3 friends, and the conversation turns to birthdays.

    a. What is the probability that no two people in your group were born in the same month?

    b. Is the probability that at least two people in your group were born in the same month greater or less than $\frac{1}{2}$? Explain.

    c. How many people in a group would it take for the probability that at least two people were born in the same month to be greater than $\frac{1}{2}$? Explain.

13. **Construct Arguments** Show how to extend the Multiplication Rule to three events A, B, and C.

14. **Make a Prediction** A bag contains the same number of red marbles and blue marbles. You choose a marble without looking, put it aside, and then choose another marble. Is there a greater-than-50% chance or a less-than-50% chance that you choose two marbles with different colors? Explain.

Lesson Performance Task

To prepare for an accuracy landing competition, a team of skydivers has laid out targets in a large open field. During practice sessions, team members attempt to land inside a target.

Two rectangular targets are shown on each field. Assuming a skydiver lands at random in the field, find the probabilities that the skydiver lands inside the specified target(s).

1. Calculate the probabilities using the targets shown here.

   a. $P(A)$

   b. $P(B)$

   c. $P(A \cap B)$

   d. $P(A \cup B)$

   e. $P(A|B)$

   f. $P(B|A)$

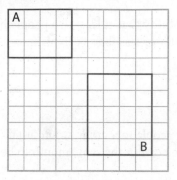

2. Calculate the probabilities using the targets shown here.

   a. $P(A)$

   b. $P(B)$

   c. $P(A \cap B)$

   d. $P(A \cup B)$

   e. $P(A|B)$

   f. $P(B|A)$

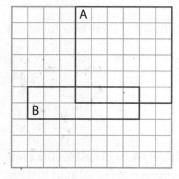

3. Calculate the probabilities using the targets shown here.

   a. $P(A)$

   b. $P(B)$

   c. $P(A \cap B)$

   d. $P(A \cup B)$

   e. $P(A|B)$

   f. $P(B|A)$

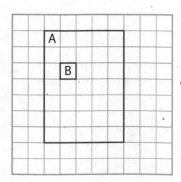

Conditional Probability and Independence of Events

Essential Question: How can you use conditional probability and independence of events to solve real-world problems?

KEY EXAMPLE   *(Lesson 22.1)*

Find the probability that a black card drawn from the deck is a queen. (The deck is a standard one of 52 cards.)

The deck has 52 cards and 26 of them are black, so the probability of

drawing a black card is $P(B) = \dfrac{26}{52}$.

There are 2 black queens in the deck, so the probability of drawing one of them from the deck is

$P(Q \cap B) = \dfrac{2}{52} = \dfrac{1}{26}$.

Using the formula for conditional probability, $P(Q \mid B) = \dfrac{P(Q \cap B)}{P(B)} = \dfrac{\frac{2}{52}}{\frac{26}{52}} = \dfrac{1}{13}$.

KEY EXAMPLE   *(Lesson 22.2)*

Jim rolled a set of two number cubes. If these are standard 6-sided number cubes, what is the probability of obtaining 12? (That means the values of the top faces add up to 12.)

The only way to get 12 is for both of the top sides of the number cubes to be 6. The events of obtaining 6s are independent. Each of these events has the probability of $\frac{1}{6}$ (1 out of 6 options), so the probability of getting 12 is $\frac{1}{6} \cdot \frac{1}{6} = \frac{1}{36}$ by the multiplication rule.

KEY EXAMPLE   *(Lesson 22.3)*

What is the probability of selecting 2 blue marbles out of a jar of 20, half of them blue? How did you obtain it?

Let event A be selecting a blue marble on the first pick. Let event B be selecting a blue marble on the second one. The first marble is not replaced, so these are dependent events. Of the 20 marbles, half of them are blue, so $P(A) = \frac{1}{2}$. Of the remaining 19 marbles, 9 of them are blue, so the probability of selecting one is $P(B) = \frac{9}{19}$. Thus, the probability of selecting 2 blue marbles is $P(A \text{ and } B) = \frac{1}{2} \cdot \frac{9}{19} = \frac{9}{38}$, using the multiplication rule.

Exercises

Determine the conditional probability. *(Lesson 22.1)*

1. What is the probability that a diamond that is drawn from the deck is a queen?

2. What is the probability that a queen drawn is a diamond?

Show that the following situation refers to independent events. *(Lesson 22.2)*

3. Isabelle believes that right- and left-footed soccer players are equally likely to score goals. She collected data from 260 players from a local soccer league. Using the following two-way frequency table, show that being right-footed and scoring goals are independent events.

	Right-Footed	Left-Footed	Total
Has scored a goal	39	13	52
Has not scored a goal	156	52	208
TOTAL	195	65	260

Identify whether a situation involves independent or dependent events. *(Lesson 22.3)*

4. Jim has 2 blue, 2 green, and 2 black socks in his drawer. He picks out 2 socks, one after the other. Determine the probability of him getting a matching pair of blue socks.

MODULE PERFORMANCE TASK

Drawing Aces

You have a standard deck of 52 playing cards. You pick three cards in a row without replacement. What is the probability that all three are aces?

Now you replace the three cards, shuffle, and pick four cards in a row without replacement. What is the probability that none are aces?

Begin by making notes in the space below about your plan for approaching this problem. Then complete the task on your own paper, using words, numbers, or diagrams to explain how you reached your conclusions.

(Ready) to Go On?

22.1–22.3 Conditional Probability and Independence of Events

- Online Homework
- Hints and Help
- Extra Practice

Compute the requested probability and explain how you obtained it.

1. A farmer wants to know if a particular fertilizer can cause blackberry shrubs to produce fruit early. Using the following two-way table, compute the probability of a plant producing fruit early without receiving fertilizer. *(Lesson 22.1)*

	Early Fruit	No Fruit	Total
Received fertilizer	37	3	40
Did not receive fertilizer	19	21	40
TOTAL	56	24	80

2. Lisa flipped the same coin twice. Determine the probability of the coin landing on tails on the second try. *(Lesson 22.2)*

3. Lisa flipped the same coin three times. What is the probability she obtained all tails? *(Lesson 22.2)*

ESSENTIAL QUESTION

4. A jar contains 12 pennies, 5 nickels, and 18 quarters. You select 2 coins at random, one after the other.

   Does selecting a nickel affect the probability of selecting another nickel? Does not selecting a dime affect the probability of selecting a nickel? Describe how you would find the probability of selecting 2 nickels.

Assessment Readiness

1. Are the events independent? Choose Yes or No for each situation.

   A. Picking a penny and a marble out of a jar of pennies and marbles. ○ Yes   ○ No

   B. Drawing cards from a deck to form a 4-card hand. ○ Yes   ○ No

   C. Rolling a 3 on a fair number cbe and flipping tails on a fair coin. ○ Yes   ○ No

2. Of the boys running for School President, 2 are juniors and 3 are seniors. Of the girls who are running, 4 are juniors and 1 is a senior. Decide whether the situation has a probability of $\frac{2}{5}$. Select Yes or No for A–C.

   A. A girl wins. ○ Yes   ○ No

   B. A candidate who is a boy is a junior. ○ Yes   ○ No

   C. A candidate who is a junior is a boy. ○ Yes   ○ No

3. You shuffle a standard deck of playing cards and deal one card. What is the probability that you deal an ace or a club? Explain your reasoning.

4. Claude has 2 jars of marbles. Each jar has 10 blue marbles and 10 green marbles. He selects 2 marbles from each jar. What is the probability they are all blue? Explain your reasoning.

Probability and Decision Making

Essential Question: How can you use probability to solve real-world problems?

REAL WORLD VIDEO
Physicians today use many sophisticated tests and technologies to help diagnose illnesses, but they must still consider probability in their diagnoses and decisions about treatment.

MODULE PERFORMANCE TASK PREVIEW

What's the Diagnosis?

The science of medicine has come a long way since surgeries were performed by the neighborhood barber and leeches were used to treat just about every ailment. Nevertheless, modern medicine isn't perfect, and widely used tests for diagnosing illnesses aren't always 100 percent accurate. In this module, you'll learn how probability can be used to measure the reliability of tests and then use what you learned to evaluate decisions about a diagnosis.

Complete these exercises to review skills you will need for this module.

Probability of Simple Events

- Online Homework
- Hints and Help
- Extra Practice

Example 1

Two 6-sided conventional number cubes are tossed.
What is the probability that their sum is greater than 8?

+	1	2	3	4	5	6
1	2	3	4	5	6	7
2	3	4	5	6	7	8
3	4	5	6	7	8	9
4	5	6	7	8	9	10
5	6	7	8	9	10	11
6	7	8	9	10	11	12

There are 10 values greater than 8 and a total number of 36 values.

$$\frac{\text{number of favorable outcomes}}{\text{total number of outcomes}} = \frac{10}{36} = \frac{5}{18}$$

The probability that the sum of the two number cubes is greater than 8 is $\frac{5}{18}$.

Two number cubes are tossed. Find each probability.

1. The sum is prime.

2. The product is prime.

3. The product is a perfect square.

Making Predictions with Probability

Example 2

A fly lands on the target shown. What is the probability that the fly landed on red?

The area of the entire target is 6^2, or 36 units^2.

Red area is: $A = \pi r^2 = \pi(1)^2 = \pi$.

$$\frac{\text{number of favorable outcomes}}{\text{total number of outcomes}} = \frac{\pi}{36} \approx 8.7\%$$

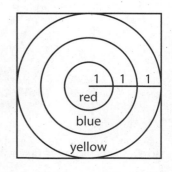

Use the target to find the percent probability, to the nearest tenth.

4. Blue

5. Yellow or red

6. Not within a circle

23.1 Using Probability to Make Fair Decisions

Essential Question: How can you use probability to help you make fair decisions?

Explore **Using Probabilities When Drawing at Random**

You are sharing a veggie supreme pizza with friends. There is one slice left and you and a friend both want it. Both of you have already had two slices. What is a fair way to solve this problem?

Ⓐ Suppose you both decide to have the same amount of pizza. This means that the last slice will be cut into two pieces. Describe a fair way to split this last piece.

_____

_____

Ⓑ Suppose instead you decide that one of you will get the whole slice. Complete the table so that the result of each option gives a fair chance for each of you to get the last slice. Why do each of these possibilities give a fair chance?

Option	Result (you get last slice)	Result (friend gets last slice)
Flip a coin	Heads	
Roll a standard die		1, 3, 5
Play Rock, Paper, Scissors	You win.	You _____.
Draw lots using two straws of different lengths		Short straw

_____

_____

Reflect

1. Suppose, when down to the last piece, you tell your friend, "I will cut the last piece, and I will choose which piece you get." Why is this method unfair?

_____

_____

2. Your friend suggests that you shoot free throws to decide who gets the last piece. Use probability to explain why this might not be a fair way to decide.

_____

_____

⊘ Explain 1   Awarding a Prize to a Random Winner

Suppose you have to decide how to award a prize to a person at an event. You might want every person attending to have the same chance of winning, or you might want people to do something to improve their chance of winning. How can you award the prize fairly?

Example 1   Explain whether each method of awarding a prize is fair.

(A) The sponsor of an event wants to award a door prize to one attendee. Each person in attendance is given a ticket with a unique number on it. All of the numbers are placed in a bowl, and one is drawn at random. The person with the matching number wins the prize.

The method of awarding a door prize is fair. Each number has the same chance of being chosen, so each attendee has an equal probability of winning the prize. If n attendees are at the event, then the probability of winning the prize is $\frac{1}{n}$ for each attendee.

(B) A fundraiser includes a raffle in which half of the money collected goes to a charity, and the other half goes to one winner. Tickets are sold for $5 each. Copies of all the tickets are placed in a box, and one ticket is drawn at random. The person with the matching ticket wins the raffle.

The method of choosing a raffle winner is fair/not fair because

each _____ has an equal probability of being drawn.

Reflect

3. In Example 1B, the probability may not be the same for each person to win the raffle. Explain why the method is still fair.

_____

_____

Your Turn

4. Each month, a company wants to award a special parking space to an employee at random. Describe a fair way to do this. Include a way to ensure that a person doesn't win a second time before each employee has won once.

_____

_____

_____

Explain 2 Solving Real-World Problems Fairly

You can use a random number generator to choose a winner of a prize.

Example 2 Use a problem solving plan.

A class of 24 students sold 65 magazine subscriptions to raise money for a trip. As an incentive to participate, you will award a prize to one student in the class. Describe a method of awarding the prize fairly. Use probabilities to explain why your method is fair for the students listed.

Student	Subscriptions Sold
Miri	5
Liam	2
Madison	0

 Analyze Information

Identify the important information.

- There are _____ students.
- They sold _____ magazine subscriptions.
- There is one prize, so there will be one winner.

 Formulate a Plan

To be fair, students who sold more subscriptions should have a better chance of winning the prize than the students who sold fewer.

Find a method of assigning and choosing chances to win so that the chance of winning is proportional to the number of subscriptions sold.

Solve

The class sold 65 subscriptions, so assign the numbers 1–65 to the students. Each student gets as many numbers as the number of subscriptions he or she sold.

Student	Subscriptions Sold	Numbers Assigned	Probability of Winning
Miri	5	1–5	$\dfrac{\boxed{}}{65} \approx \boxed{}$
Liam	2	6, 7	$\dfrac{\boxed{}}{65} \approx \boxed{}$
Madison	0	none	$\dfrac{\boxed{}}{65} = \boxed{}$

Then use a calculator to find a random integer from 1 to 65. If the result is 7, then Liam wins the prize.

 Justify and Evaluate

This method seems fair/unfair because it gives everyone who sold subscriptions a chance of winning. You could award a prize to the student who sold the most subscriptions, but this might not be possible if multiple students all sold the same number, and it might not seem fair if some students have better access to buyers than others.

5. A student suggests that it would be better to assign the numbers to students randomly rather than in numerical order. Would doing this affect the probability of winning?

_____

_____

6. A charity is giving a movie ticket for every 10 coats donated. Jacob collected 8 coats, Ben collected 6, and Ryan and Zak each collected 3. They decide to donate the coats together so that they will get 2 movie tickets. Describe how to use a random number generator to decide which 2 boys get a ticket.

_____

_____

_____

_____

🖋 Explain 3 **Solving the Problem of Points**

The decision-making situation that you will apply in this example is based on the "Problem of Points" that was studied by the French mathematicians Blaise Pascal and Pierre de Fermat in the 17th century. Their work on the problem launched the branch of mathematics now known as probability.

Example 3 **Two students, Lee and Rory, find a box containing 100 baseball cards. To determine who should get the cards, they decide to play a game with the rules shown.**

Game Rules
• One of the students repeatedly tosses a coin.
• When the coin lands heads up, Lee gets a point.
• When the coin lands tails up, Rory gets a point.
• The first student to reach 20 points wins the game and gets the baseball cards.

As Lee and Rory are playing the game they are interrupted and are unable to continue. How should the 100 baseball cards be divided between the students given that the game was interrupted at the described moment?

Ⓐ When they are interrupted, Lee has 19 points and Rory has 17 points.

At most, 3 coin tosses would have been needed for someone to win the game.

Make a list of all possible results using H for heads and T for tails. Circle the outcomes in which Lee wins the game.

0T, 3H	1T, 2H	2T, 1H	3T, 0H
HHHH	THH	TTH	TTT
	HTH	THT	
	HHT	HTT	

There are 8 possible results. Lee wins in 7 of them and Rory wins in 1 of them.

The probability of Lee winning is $\frac{7}{8}$, so he should get $\frac{7}{8}$ of the cards which is 87.5 cards. The probability of Rory winning is $\frac{1}{8}$, so he should get $\frac{1}{8}$ of the cards which is 12.5 cards. Rather than split a card into two, they might decide to flip a coin for that card or to let Lee have it because he was more likely to win it.

(B) When they are interrupted, Lee has 18 points and Rory has 17 points.

At most, _____ more coin tosses would have been needed.

List all possible results. Circle the outcomes in which Lee wins.

   0T, 4H   1T, 3H   2T, 2H   3T, 1H   4T, 0H

There are _____ possible results. Lee wins in _____ of them and Rory wins

in _____ of them.

The probability of Lee winning is _____ , so he should get _____ cards.

The probability of Rory winning is _____ , so he should get _____ cards.

Reflect

7. **Discussion** A student suggests that a better way to divide the cards in Example 3B would be to split the cards based on the number of points earned so far. Which method do you think is better?

_____

_____

_____

Your Turn

8. Describe a situation where the game is interrupted, resulting in the cards needing to be divided evenly between the two players.

_____

_____

9. Discussion In the situation described in the Explore, suppose you like the crust and your friend does not. Is there a fair way to cut the slice of pizza that might not result in two equal size pieces?

_____

_____

10. How would the solution to Example 2 need to change if there were two prizes to award? Assume that you do not want one student to win both prizes.

_____

_____

_____

_____

_____

_____

11. Essential Question Check-In Describe a way to use probability to make a fair choice of a raffle winner.

_____

_____

_____

 Evaluate: Homework and Practice

• Online Homework
• Hints and Help
• Extra Practice

1. You and a friend split the cost of a package of five passes to a climbing gym. Describe a way that you could fairly decide who gets to use the fifth pass.

2. In addition to prizes for first, second, and third place, the organizers of a race have a prize that they want each participant to have an equal chance of winning. Describe a fair method of choosing a winner for this prize.

Decide whether each method is a fair way to choose a winner if each person should have an equal chance of winning. Explain your answer by evaluating each probability.

3. Roll a standard die. Meri wins if the result is less than 3. Riley wins if the result is greater than 3.

4. Draw a card from a standard deck of cards. Meri wins if the card is red. Riley wins if the card is black.

5. Flip a coin. Meri wins if it lands heads. Riley wins if it lands tails.

6. Meri and Riley both jump as high as they can. Whoever jumps higher wins.

7. Roll a standard die. Meri wins if the result is even. Riley wins if the result is odd.

8. Draw a stone from a box that contains 5 black stones and 4 white stones. Meri wins if the stone is black. Riley wins if the stone is white.

9. A chess club has received a chess set to give to one of its members. The club decides that everyone should have a chance of winning the set based on how many games they have won this season. Describe a fair method to decide who wins the set. Find the probability that each member will win it.

Member	Games Won	Probability of Winning	Member	Games Won	Probability of Winning
Kayla	30		Hailey	12	
Noah	23		Gabe	12	
Ava	18		Concour	5	

10. Owen, Diego, and Cody often play a game during lunch. When they can't finish, they calculate the probability that each will win given the current state of the game and assign partial wins. Today, when they had to stop, it would have taken at most 56 more moves for one of them to win. Owen would have won 23 of the moves, Diego would have won 18 of them, and Cody would have won 15. To 2 decimal places, how should they assign partial wins?

Represent Real-World Problems Twenty students, including Paige, volunteer to work at the school banquet. Each volunteer worked at least 1 hour. Paige worked 4 hours. The students worked a total of 45 hours. The organizers would like to award a prize to 1 of the volunteers.

11. Describe a process for awarding the prize so that each volunteer has an equal chance of winning. Find the probability of Paige winning.

12. Describe a process for awarding the prize so that each volunteer's chance of winning is proportional to how many hours the volunteer worked. Find the probability of Paige winning.

There are 10,000 seats available in a sports stadium. Each seat has a package beneath it, and 20 of the seats have an additional prize winning package with a family pass for the entire season.

13. Is this method of choosing a winner for the family passes fair?

14. What is the probability of winning a family pass if you attend the game?

15. What is the probability of not winning a family pass if you attend the game?

A teacher tells students, "For each puzzle problem you complete, I will assign you a prize entry." In all, 10 students complete 53 puzzle problems. Leon completed 7. To award the prize, the teacher sets a calculator to generate a random integer from 1 to 53. Leon is assigned 18 to 24 as "winners".

16. What is the probability that a specific number is chosen?

17. What is the probability that one of Leon's numbers will be chosen?

18. What is the probability that one of Leon's numbers will not be chosen?

19. Is this fair to Leon according to the original instructions? Explain.

20. Make a Conjecture Two teams are playing a game against one another in class to earn 10 extra points on an assignment. The teacher said that the points will be split fairly between the two teams, depending on the results of the game. If Team A earned 1300 points, and Team B earned 2200 points, describe one way the teacher could split up the 10 extra points. Explain.

21. Persevere in Problem Solving Alexa and Sofia are at a yard sale, and they find a box of 20 collectible toys that they both want. They can't agree about who saw it first, so they flip a coin until Alexa gets 10 heads or Sofia gets 10 tails. When Alexa has 3 heads and Sofia has 6 tails, they decide to divide the toys proportionally based on the probability each has of winning under the original rules. How should they divide the toys?

Lesson Performance Task

Three games are described below. For each game, tell whether it is fair (all players are equally likely to win) or unfair (one player has an advantage). Explain how you reached your decision, being sure to discuss how probability entered into your decision.

1. You and your friend each toss a quarter. If two heads turn up, you win. If a head and a tail turn up, your friend wins. If two tails turn up, you play again.

2. You and your friend each roll a die. If the sum of the numbers is odd, you get 1 point. If the sum is even, your friend gets 1 point.

3. You and your friend each roll a die. If the product of the numbers is odd, you get 1 point. If the product is even, your friend gets 1 point.

23.2 Analyzing Decisions

Essential Question: How can conditional probability help you make real-world decisions?

Resource
Locker

⊘ **Explore**   **Analyzing a Decision Using Probability**

Suppose scientists have developed a test that can be used at birth to determine whether a baby is right-handed or left-handed. The test uses a drop of the baby's saliva and instantly gives the result. The test has been in development, long enough for the scientists to track the babies as they grow into toddlers and to see whether their test is accurate. About 10% of babies turn out to be left-handed.

The scientists have learned that when children are left-handed, the test correctly identifies them as left-handed 92% of the time. Also when children are right-handed, the test correctly identifies them as right-handed 95% of the time.

Ⓐ In the first year on the market, the test is used on 1,000,000 babies. Complete the table starting with the Totals. Then use the given information to determine the expected number in each category.

	Tests Left-handed	Tests Right-handed	Total
Truly Left-handed			
Truly Right-handed			
Total			1,000,000

Ⓑ What is the probability that a baby who tests left-handed actually is left-handed?

Ⓒ What is the probability that a baby who tests right-handed actually is right-handed?

Reflect

1. Is the test a good test of right-handedness?

_____

2. A baby is tested, and the test shows the baby will be left-handed. The parents decide to buy a left-handed baseball glove for the baby. Is this a reasonable decision?

_____

_____

3. **Discussion** Describe two ways in which the test can become a more reliable indicator of left-handedness.

_____

_____

_____

⊘ Explore 2 Deriving Bayes' Theorem

You can generalize your results so that they are applicable to other situations in which you want to analyze decisions. Now, you will derive a formula known as Bayes' Theorem.

(A) Complete the steps to derive Bayes' Theorem.

Write the formula for $P(B|A)$.

Solve for $P(A \text{ and } B)$.

Write the formula for $P(A|B)$.

Substitute the expression for $P(A \text{ and } B)$.

(B) Explain how you can use a table giving the number of results for each case to find $P(B)$.

	B	B^c	Total
A	n	p	$n + p$
A^c	m	q	$m + q$
Total	$n + m$	$p + q$	$n + m + p + q$

(C) Explain how you can use the tree diagram to find $P(B)$.

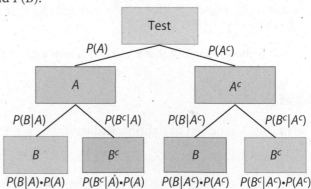

(D) Use your result from Step C to rewrite your final expression from Step A to get another form of Bayes' Theorem.

4. Explain in words what each expression means in the context of Explore 1.

$P(A)$ is the probability of actually being left-handed.

$P(B)$ is the probability of testing left-handed.

$P(A|B)$ is _____ .

$P(B|A)$ is _____ .

5. Use Bayes' Theorem to calculate the probability that a baby actually is left-handed, given that the baby tests left-handed. Explain what this probability means.

_____

_____

_____

⊘ Explain 1   Using Bayes' Theorem

Bayes' Theorem is a useful tool when you need to analyze decisions.

Bayes' Theorem

Given two events A and B with $P(B) \neq 0$, $P(A|B) = \dfrac{P(B|A) \cdot P(A)}{P(B)}$.

Another form is $P(A|B) = \dfrac{P(B|A) \cdot P(A)}{P(B|A) \cdot P(A) + P(B|A^c) \cdot P(A^c)}$.

Example 1 Suppose Walter operates an order-filling machine that has an error rate of 0.5%. He installs a new order-filling machine that has an error rate of only 0.1%. The new machine takes over 80% of the order-filling tasks.

Ⓐ One day, Walter gets a call from a customer complaining that her order wasn't filled properly. Walter blames the problem on the old machine. Was he correct in doing so?

First, find the probability that the order was filled by the old machine given that there was an error in filling the order, $P(\text{old} \mid \text{error})$.

$P(\text{old}|\text{error}) = \dfrac{P(\text{error}|\text{old}) \cdot P(\text{old})}{P(\text{error})}$

$= \dfrac{0.005 \cdot (0.20)}{0.001 + 0.0008} = \dfrac{0.001}{0.0018} = \dfrac{5}{9} \approx 0.56$

Given that there is a mistake, the probability is about 56% that the old machine filled the order. The probability that the new machine filled the order is $1 - 0.56 = 0.44 = 44\%$. The old machine is only slightly more likely than the new machine to have filled the order. Walter shouldn't blame the old machine.

(B) Walter needs to increase capacity for filling orders, so he increases the number of orders being filled by the old machine to 30% of the total orders. What percent of errors in filled orders are made by the old machine? Is Walter unreasonably increasing the risk of shipping incorrectly filled orders?

Find the probability that _____

given that _____ ,

P(____ | ____).

Use Bayes' Theorem.

_____

_____

Describe the result of making this change.

_____

_____

_____

Machine
Old   New
Error   No error   Error   No error

Reflect

6. The old machine fills so few orders. How can it be responsible for more than half of the errors?

_____

Your Turn

In the situation described in the Explore, suppose the scientists have changed the test so that now it correctly identifies left-handed children 100% of the time, and still correctly identifies right-handed children 95% of the time.

7. Complete the tree diagram.

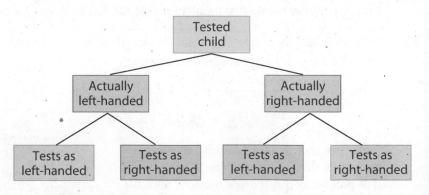

Tested child
Actually left-handed   Actually right-handed
Tests as left-handed   Tests as right-handed   Tests as left-handed   Tests as right-handed

8. With the new test, what is the probability that a child who tests as left-handed will be left-handed? How does this compare to the original test?

9. With the new test, what is the probability that a child who tests as right-handed will be left-handed? How does this compare to the original test?

⊙ Elaborate

10. **Discussion** Compare the probabilities you found in the Explore and Your Turn 8 and 9. Why did the percent of babies who test as right-handed and are actually left-handed increase?

_____

_____

_____

11. **Essential Question Check-In** How can you use probability to help you analyze decisions?

_____

_____

_____

★ Evaluate: Homework and Practice

• Online Homework
• Hints and Help
• Extra Practice

1. A factory manager is assessing the work of two assembly-line workers. Helen has been on the job longer than Kyle. Their production rates for the last month are in the table. Based on comparing the number of defective products, the manager is considering putting Helen on probation. Is this a good decision? Why or why not?

	Helen	Kyle	Total
Defective	50	20	70
Not defective	965	350	1,315
Total	1,015	370	1,385

2. **Multiple Step** A reporter asked 150 voters if they plan to vote in favor of a new library and a new arena. The table shows the results. If you are given that a voter plans to vote *no* to the new arena, what is the probability that the voter also plans to vote no to the new library?

		Library		
		Yes	No	**Total**
Arena	Yes	21	30	51
	No	57	42	99
	Total	78	72	**150**

3. You want to hand out coupons for a local restaurant to students who live off campus at a rural college with a population of 10,000 students. You know that 10% of the students live off campus and that 98% of those students ride a bike. Also, 62% of the students who live on campus do not have a bike. You decide to give a coupon to any student you see who is riding a bike. Complete the table. Then explain whether this a good decision.

	bike	no bike	Total
on campus			
off campus			
Total			

4. A test for a virus correctly identifies someone who has the virus (by returning a positive result) 99% of the time. The test correctly identifies someone who does not have the virus (by returning a negative result) 99% of the time. It is known that 0.5% of the population has the virus. A doctor decides to treat anyone who tests positive for the virus. Complete the two-way table assuming a total population of 1,000,000 people have been tested. Is this a good decision?

	Tests Positive	Tests Negative	Total
Virus			
No virus			
Total			1,000,000

5. It is known that 2% of the population has a certain allergy. A test correctly identifies people who have the allergy 98% of the time. The test correctly identifies people who do not have the allergy 95% of the time. A website recommends that anyone who tests positive for the allergy should begin taking medication. Complete the two-way table. Do you think this is a good recommendation? Why or why not?

	Test Positive	Test Negative	Total
Total			10,000

6. Use the tree diagram shown.

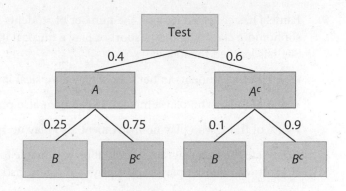

a. Find $P(B|A^c) \cdot P(A^c)$.

b. Find $P(B)$.

c. Use Bayes Theorem to find $P(A^c|B)$.

7. The probabilities of drawing lemons and limes from a bag are shown in the tree diagram. Find the probability of drawing the two pieces of fruit randomly from the bag.

a. two lemons

b. two limes

c. lime, then lemon

d. lemon, then lime

8. **Multiple Step** A school principal plans a school picnic for June 2. A few days before the event, the weather forecast predicts rain for June 2, so the principal decides to cancel the picnic. Consider the following information.

- In the school's town, the probability that it rains on any day in June is 3%.
- When it rains, the forecast correctly predicts rain 90% of the time.
- When it does not rain, the forecast incorrectly predicts rain 5% of the time.

a. Find $P(\text{prediction of rain}|\text{rains})$ and $P(\text{rains})$.

b. Complete the tree diagram, and find $P(\text{Prediction of rain})$.

c. Find $P(\text{rains}|\text{prediction of rain})$.

d. Is the decision to cancel the picnic reasonable?

9. Pamela has collected data on the number of students in the sophomore class who play a sport or play a musical instrument. She has learned the following.

- 42.5% of all students in her school play a musical instrument.

- 20% of those who play a musical instrument also play a sport.

- 40% of those who play no instrument also play no sport.

Complete the tree diagram. Would it be reasonable to conclude that a student who doesn't play a sport plays a musical instrument?

10. Interpret the Answer Company X supplies 35% of the phones to an electronics store and Company Y supplies the remainder. The manager of the store knows that 25% of the phones in the last shipment from Company X were defective, while only 5% of the phones from Company Y were defective. The manager chooses a phone at random and finds that it is defective. The manager decides that the phone must have come from Company X. Do you think this is a reasonable conclusion? Why or why not?

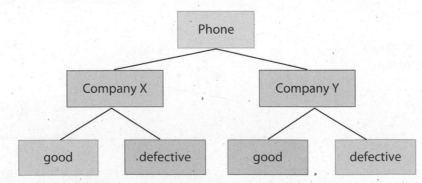

11. Suppose that strep throat affects 2% of the population and a test to detect it produces an accurate result 99% of the time. Create a tree diagram and use Bayes, Theorem to find the probability that someone who tests positive actually has strep throat.

12. A hand-made quilt is first prize in a fund-raiser raffle. The table shows information about all the ticket buyers. Given that the winner of the quilt is a man, what is the probability that he resides in Sharonville?

	Men	Women	Total
Forestview	35	45	80
Sharonville	15	25	40

13. Recall that the Multiplication Rule says the $P(A \cap B) = P(A) \cdot P(B \mid A)$. If you switch the order of events A and B, then the rule becomes $P(B \cap A) = P(B) \cdot P(A \mid B)$. Use the Multiplication Rule and the fact that $P(B \cap A) = P(A \cap B)$ to prove Bayes' Theorem. (*Hint*: Divide each side by $P(B)$.)

14. Sociology A sociologist collected data on the types of pets in 100 randomly selected households. Suppose you want to offer a service to households that own both a cat and a dog. Based on the data in the table, would it be more effective to hand information to people walking dogs or to people buying cat food?

		Owns a Cat		
		Yes	No	
Owns a Dog	Yes	15	24	
	No	18	43	

15. Interpret the Answer It is known that 1% of all mice in a laboratory have a genetic mutation. A test for the mutation correctly identifies mice that have the mutation 98% of the time. The test correctly identifies mice that do not have the mutation 96% of the time. A lab assistant tests a mouse and finds that the mouse tests positive for the mutation. The lab assistant decides that the mouse must have the mutation. Is this a good decision? Complete the tree diagram and explain your answer.

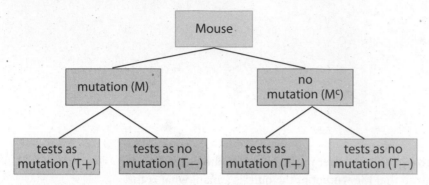

16. Interpret the Answer It is known that 96% of all dogs do not get trained. One professional trainer claims that 54% of trained dogs will sit on one of the first four commands and that no other dogs will sit on command. A condominium community wants to impose a restriction on dogs that are not trained. They want each dog owner to show that his or her dog will sit on one of the first four commands. Assuming that the professional trainer's claim is correct, is this a fair way to identify dogs that have not been trained? Explain.

17. Multiple Steps Tomas has a choice of three possible routes to work. On each day, he randomly selects a route and keeps track of whether he is late. Based on this 40-day trial, which route makes Tomas least likely to be late for work?

	Late	Not Late
Route A	IIII	HHT HHT
Route B	III	HHT II
Route C	IIII	HHT HHT II

18. **Critique Reasoning** When Elisabeth saw this tree diagram, she said that the calculations must be incorrect. Do you agree? Justify your answer.

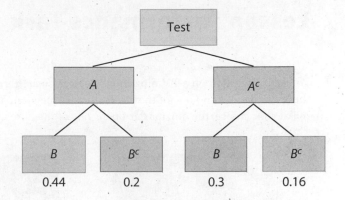

19. **Multiple Representations** The Venn diagram shows how many of the first 100 customers of a new bakery bought either bread or cookies, both, or neither. Taryn claims that the data indicate that a customer who bought cookies is more likely to have bought bread than a customer who bought bread is likely to have bought cookies. Is she correct?

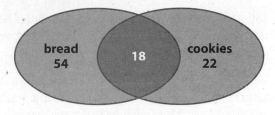

20. **Persevere in Problem Solving** At one high school, the probability that a student is absent today, given that the student was absent yesterday, is 0.12. The probability that a student is absent today, given that the student was present yesterday, is 0.05. The probability that a student was absent yesterday is 0.1. A teacher forgot to take attendance in several classes yesterday, so he assumed that attendance in his class today is the same as yesterday. If there were 40 students in these classes, how many errors would you expect by doing this?

Lesson Performance Task

You're a contestant on a TV quiz show. Before you are three doors. Behind two of the doors, there's a goat. Behind one of the doors, there's a new car. You are asked to pick a door. After you make your choice, the quizmaster opens one of the doors you *didn't* choose, revealing a goat.

Door 1

Door 2

Door 3

Now there are only two doors. You can stick with your original choice or you can switch to the one remaining door. Should you switch?

Intuition tells most people that, with two doors left, there's a 50% probability that they're right and a 50% probability that they're wrong. They conclude that it doesn't matter whether they switch or not.

Does it? Using Bayes' Theorem, it can be shown mathematically that you're much better off switching! You can reach the same conclusion using logical thinking skills. Assume that the car is behind Door #1. (The same reasoning that follows can be applied if the car is behind one of the other doors.) You've decided to switch your choice after the first goat is revealed. There are three possibilities.

Essential Question: How can you use probability to solve real-world problems?

KEY EXAMPLE   (Lesson 23.1)

Determine whether the method of awarding a prize is fair. Explain.

A festival has a baked goods fundraising raffle in which tickets are drawn for winners. The tickets are sold for $2 each, and the purchaser of the ticket places his or her name on the ticket before placing the ticket into a fishbowl on a table. There are 20 cakes for prizes. A ticket is drawn at random from the fishbowl for each cake.

The method of awarding the prize is fair. This is because each ticket has an equal probability of being drawn. For each of n tickets bought, that ticket has a $\frac{1}{n}$ chance of being drawn. The more tickets someone buys, the better chance they have of winning a cake.

KEY EXAMPLE   (Lesson 23.2)

Suppose Rhonda's Block Warehouse operates a block-making machine that has an error rate of 0.7%. Then Rhonda installs a new block-making machine that has an error rate of only 0.3%. The new machine takes over 75% of the block-making tasks. One day, Rhonda gets a call from a customer complaining that his block is not made properly. Rhonda blames the problem on the old machine. Was she correct in doing so?

Find Event A, Event B, $P(A|B)$, $P(B)$, and $P(A)$.

Event A is the error making the block, Event B is that the old machine made the block, $P(A|B)$ is the error rate of the old machine (0.007), $P(B)$ is the probability the old machine made the block (0.25), and $P(A)$ is $0.75 \cdot 0.003 + 0.25 \cdot 0.007 = 0.004$.

$$P(B|A) = \frac{P(A|B)P(B)}{P(A)} \qquad \text{Bayes' Theorem}$$

$$P(\text{old machine|bad block}) = \frac{0.007 \cdot 0.25}{0.004} \qquad \text{Substitute known probabilities}$$

$$P(\text{old machine|bad block}) = 0.4375 = 43.75\%$$

Given that the probability that a bad block is made by the old machine is less than 50%, Rhonda should not blame the old machine for the bad block.

EXERCISES

Determine whether the method of awarding a prize is fair. Explain. If it is not fair, describe a way that would be fair. *(Lesson 23.1)*

1. A teacher gives a ticket to each student who earns a 90 or above on any homework assignment. At the end of each week, the teacher draws from the ticket jar and gives the winning student a free homework pass for the next week.

Suppose that a card dealing machine has a probability of 23% for pulling a face card. An older machine has a 14% chance of pulling a face card. Use Bayes' Theorem to find the probability. *(Lesson 23.2)*

2. If each machine is used 50% of the time, and a face card is the next card drawn, what is the probability the new machine drew the card?

MODULE PERFORMANCE TASK

What's the Diagnosis?

Lenny works in a factory that makes cleaning products. Lately he has been suffering from headaches. He asks his doctor if the chemicals used in the factory might be responsible for his headaches. The doctor performs a blood test that is routinely used to diagnose the kind of illness Lenny is concerned about.

Use the following facts to gauge the probability that Lenny has the illness if he tests positive:

1. The test has a reliability rate of 85 percent.

2. The test has a false positive rate of 8 percent.

3. The illness affects 3 percent of people who are Lenny's age and who work in conditions similar to those he works in.

Start by listing on your own paper the information you will need to solve the problem. Then complete the task. Use numbers, words, or algebra to explain how you reached your conclusion.

23.1–23.2 Probability and Decision Making

• Online Homework
• Hints and Help
• Extra Practice

Determine whether the method of awarding a prize is fair. Explain briefly.
(Lesson 23.1)

1. Prize to every 500th customer

2. Ticket to every customer; drawing

3. Choose number 1–10; draw number

4. Ticket to all cars; two to red cars

Rodney's Repair Service has a lug nut tightening machine that works well 89% of the time. They got a new machine that works well 98% of the time. Each machine is used 50% of the time. Use Bayes' Theorem to find each probability. *(Lesson 23.2)*

5. new machine malfunctioned

6. old machine malfunctioned

7. old machine worked well

8. new machine worked well

ESSENTIAL QUESTION

9. How can probability and decision making help the organizer of a raffle?

Assessment Readiness

1. Consider the situation. Is the method of awarding the prize fair?
   Select Yes or No for A–C.

   A. Ticket for every $10 spent ○ Yes ○ No

   B. Coupon every 10 guests .. ○ Yes ○ No

   C. Entry for every mile driven ○ Yes ○ No

2. Consider the situation of having four tiles in a bag spelling M–A–T–H drawn randomly without replacement. Choose True or False for each statement.

   A. There is one way to draw all 4 tiles from the bag, if order doesn't matter. ○ True ○ False

   B. There are six ways to draw 2 tiles from the bag, if order matters. ○ True ○ False

   C. There are twenty four ways to draw 3 tiles from the bag if order matters. ○ True ○ False

3. The band class has two trumpet players. Of the two, the first trumpet player plays a wrong note 4% of the time, and the second trumpet player plays a wrong note 9% of the time. If one song has the first trumpet player playing 75% of the song, and the second trumpet player playing the rest, use Bayes' Theorem to find the probability that a wrong note was played by the second trumpet. Explain whether your answer makes sense.

4. Given a triangle with a side of length 11 and another side of length 6, find the range of possible values for x, the length of the third side. Explain your reasoning.

1. Figure *ABCDE* is similar to figure *LMNOP*. Select True or False for each mathematical statement.

   A. $\dfrac{BC}{AE} = \dfrac{MN}{OP}$ ○ True   ○ False

   B. $\dfrac{AB}{DE} = \dfrac{LM}{OP}$ ○ True   ○ False

   C. $\dfrac{BD}{AE} = \dfrac{MN}{LP}$ ○ True   ○ False

2. The transformation $(x, y) \rightarrow (x - 2, y + 1)$ is applied to $\triangle XYZ$. Select True or False for each statement.

   A. The area of $\triangle X'Y'Z'$ is the same   ○ True   ○ False
   as the area of $\triangle XYZ$.

   B. The distance from X to X' is equal   ○ True   ○ False
   to the distance from Z to Z'.

   C. The transformation is a rotation.   ○ True   ○ False

3. Does each scenario describe independent events? Select Yes or No for each situation.

   A. Drawing two cards from a standard   ○ Yes   ○ No
   deck of cards that are both aces

   B. Rolling a fair number cube twice and   ○ Yes   ○ No
   getting 6 on both rolls

   C. Rolling a 3 on a fair number cube and   ○ Yes   ○ No
   flipping tails on a fair coin

4. Each student in a class has been assigned at random to draw a parallelogram, a rectangle, a rhombus, or a square. Select True or False for each statement about the likelihood that a student will draw a parallelogram.

   A. It is unlikely because the probability   ○ True   ○ False
   is less than 0.5.

   B. It is likely because the probability is   ○ True   ○ False
   between 0.5 and 0.75.

   C. It is impossible for it not to happen   ○ True   ○ False
   because the probability is 1.

5. The events A and B are independent. Select True or False for each statement.

   A. $P(A \mid B) = P(B \mid A)$ ○ True   ○ False

   B. $P(A \text{ and } B) = P(B)P(A)$ ○ True   ○ False

   C. $P(A) = P(B)$ ○ True   ○ False

6. Vera needs to place 15 student volunteers at a local fire station. Five students will wash fire trucks, 7 will be assigned to paint, and 3 will be assigned to wash windows. What is the number of possible job assignments expressed using factorials and as a simplified number?

7. The table below shows the number of days that a meteorologist predicted it would be sunny and the number of days it was sunny. Based on the data in the table, what is the conditional probability that it will be sunny on a day when the meteorologist predicts it will be sunny? Show your work.

	Sunny	Not Sunny	Total
Predicts Sunny	570	20	590
Does Not Predict Sunny	63	347	410
Total	633	367	1000

8. Complete the two-way table below. Then find the fraction of red cards in a standard 52-card deck that have a number on them and find the fraction of numbered cards that are red.

	Red	Black	Total
Number			
No Number			
Total			

Performance Tasks

★ **9.** Sixteen cards numbered 1 through 16 are placed face down, and Stephanie chooses one at random. What is the probability that the number on Stephanie's card is less than 5 or greater than 10? Show your work.

★★10. Students in 4 different classes are surveyed about their favorite movie type. What is the probability that a randomly selected student in class B prefers comedies? What is the probability that a randomly selected student who prefers comedies is in class B? Explain why the two probabilities are not the same. Show your work.

	A	B	C	D
Action	12	9	8	11
Comedy	13	11	15	4
Drama	6	11	7	18

★★11. A Chinese restaurant has a buffet that includes ice cream for dessert. The table shows the selections made last week.

	Chocolate	Vanilla	Strawberry
Cone	24	18	12
Dish	12	21	15

A. Which flavor is the most popular? Which serving method? Is the combination of the most popular flavor and serving method the most popular dessert choice overall? Explain.

B. Which of the following is more likely? Explain.

• A customer chooses vanilla, given that the customer chose a cone.

• A customer chooses a cone, given that the customer chose vanilla.

C. A class of 24 students gets the buffet for lunch. If all the students get ice cream, about how many will get a cone or vanilla? Explain.

Epidemiologist An epidemiologist is aiding in the treatment of a community plagued by two different infectious agents, X and Z. Each infectious agent must be treated differently with a new treatment if the patient has been infected by both agents. The community has a total population of 15,000 people, where 5% are not affected by either agent and 60% are afflicted by the X infection. 39% of the population is afflicted by X but not by Z. Unfortunately, the treatment for the X infection fails 35% of the time. The same incident happened to 10 other communities with similar results as the first. What is the probability that people will be healthy? have the X affliction? have the Z affliction? have both afflictions?

Glossary/Glosario

A

acute angle An angle that measures greater than 0° and less than 90°.

ángulo agudo Ángulo que mide más de 0° y menos de 90°.

---

acute triangle A triangle with three acute angles.

triángulo acutángulo Triángulo con tres ángulos agudos.

---

adjacent angles Two angles in the same plane with a common vertex and a common side, but no common interior points.

ángulos adyacentes Dos ángulos en el mismo plano que tienen un vértice y un lado común pero no comparten puntos internos.

∠1 and ∠2 are adjacent angles.

---

adjacent arcs Two arcs of the same circle that intersect at exactly one point.

arcos adyacentes Dos arcos del mismo círculo que se cruzan en un punto exacto.

$\overarc{RS}$ and $\overarc{ST}$ are adjacent arcs.

---

alternate exterior angles For two lines intersected by a transversal, a pair of angles that lie on opposite sides of the transversal and outside the other two lines.

ángulos alternos externos Dadas dos líneas cortadas por una transversal, par de ángulos no adyacentes ubicados en los lados opuestos de la transversal y fuera de las otras dos líneas.

∠4 and ∠5 are alternate exterior angles.

---

alternate interior angles For two lines intersected by a transversal, a pair of nonadjacent angles that lie on opposite sides of the transversal and between the other two lines.

ángulos alternos internos Dadas dos líneas cortadas por una transversal, par de ángulos no adyacentes ubicados en los lados opuestos de la transversal y entre las otras dos líneas.

∠3 and ∠6 are alternate interior angles.

---

altitude of a cone A segment from the vertex to the plane of the base that is perpendicular to the plane of the base.

altura de un cono Segmento que se extiende desde el vértice hasta el plano de la base y es perpendicular al plano de la base.

h

ENGLISH	SPANISH	EXAMPLES

altitude of a cylinder A segment with its endpoints on the planes of the bases that is perpendicular to the planes of the bases.

altura de un cilindro Segmento con sus extremos en los planos de las bases que es perpendicular a los planos de las bases.

altitude of a prism A segment with its endpoints on the planes of the bases that is perpendicular to the planes of the bases.

altura de un prisma Segmento con sus extremos en los planos de las bases que es perpendicular a los planos de las bases.

altitude of a pyramid A segment from the vertex to the plane of the base that is perpendicular to the plane of the base.

altura de una pirámide Segmento que se extiende desde el vértice hasta el plano de la base y es perpendicular al plano de la base.

altitude of a triangle A perpendicular segment from a vertex to the line containing the opposite side.

altura de un triángulo Segmento perpendicular que se extiende desde un vértice hasta la línea que forma el lado opuesto.

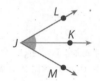

angle bisector A ray that divides an angle into two congruent angles.

bisectriz de un ángulo Rayo que divide un ángulo en dos ángulos congruentes.

$\overrightarrow{JK}$ is an angle bisector of $\angle LJM$.

angle of rotation An angle formed by a rotating ray, called the terminal side, and a stationary reference ray, called the initial side.

ángulo de rotación Ángulo formado por un rayo rotativo, denominado lado terminal, y un rayo de referencia estático, denominado lado inicial.

angle of rotational symmetry The smallest angle through which a figure with rotational symmetry can be rotated to coincide with itself.

ángulo de simetría de rotación El ángulo más pequeño alrededor del cual se puede rotar una figura con simetría de rotación para que coincida consigo misma.

apothem The perpendicular distance from the center of a regular polygon to a side of the polygon.

apotema Distancia perpendicular desde el centro de un polígono regular hasta un lado del polígono.

ENGLISH	SPANISH	EXAMPLES
arc An unbroken part of a circle consisting of two points on the circle, called the endpoints, and all the points on the circle between them.	**arco** Parte continua de una circunferencia formada por dos puntos de la circunferencia denominados extremos y todos los puntos de la circunferencia comprendidos entre éstos.	*R* *S* (circle)
arc length The distance along an arc measured in linear units.	**longitud de arco** Distancia a lo largo de un arco medida en unidades lineales.	10 ft, *D*, 90°, *C*, m$\overset{\frown}{CD}$ = 5π ft
arc marks Marks used on a figure to indicate congruent angles.	**marcas de arco** Marcas utilizadas en una figura para indicar ángulos congruentes.	*C*, *D*, Arc marks, *E*, *F*, *A*, *B*
auxiliary line A line drawn in a figure to aid in a proof.	**línea auxiliar** Línea dibujada en una figura como ayuda en una demostración.	Auxiliary line, *B*, 4, 2, 5, ℓ, *A*, 1, 3, *C*
axiom *See* postulate.	**axioma** *Ver* postulado.	
axis of a cone The segment with endpoints at the vertex and the center of the base.	**eje de un cono** Segmento cuyos extremos se encuentran en el vértice y en el centro de la base.	Axis (cone)
axis of a cylinder The segment with endpoints at the centers of the two bases.	**eje de un cilindro** Segmentos cuyos extremos se encuentran en los centros de las dos bases.	Axis
axis of symmetry A line that divides a plane figure or a graph into two congruent reflected halves.	**eje de simetría** Línea que divide una figura plana o una gráfica en dos mitades reflejadas congruentes.	Axis of symmetry, *y* = |*x*| (graph)

B

base angle of a trapezoid One of a pair of consecutive angles whose common side is a base of the trapezoid.

ángulo base de un trapecio Uno de los dos ángulos consecutivos cuyo lado en común es la base del trapecio.

base angle of an isosceles triangle One of the two angles that have the base of the triangle as a side.

ángulo base de un triángulo isósceles Uno de los dos ángulos que tienen como lado la base del triángulo.

base of a geometric figure A side of a polygon; a face of a three-dimensional figure by which the figure is measured or classified.

base de una figura geométrica Lado de un polígono; cara de una figura tridimensional por la cual se mide o clasifica la figura.

between Given three points A, B, and C, B is between A and C if and only if all three of the points lie on the same line, and $AB + BC = AC$.

entre Dados tres puntos A, B y C, B está entre A y C si y sólo si los tres puntos se encuentran en la misma línea y $AB + BC = AC$.

biconditional statement A statement that can be written in the form "p if and only if q."

enunciado biconditional Enunciado que puede expresarse en la forma "p si y sólo si q".

A figure is a triangle if and only if it is a three-sided polygon.

bisect To divide into two congruent parts.

trazar una bisectriz Dividir en dos partes congruentes.

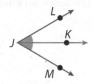

$\overrightarrow{JK}$ bisects $\angle LJM$.

C

center of a circle The point inside a circle that is the same distance from every point on the circle.

centro de un círculo Punto dentro de un círculo que se encuentra a la misma distancia de todos los puntos del círculo.

center of dilation The intersection of the lines that connect each point of the image with the corresponding point of the preimage.

centro de dilatación Intersección de las líneas que conectan cada punto de la imagen con el punto correspondiente de la imagen original.

ENGLISH	SPANISH	EXAMPLES
center of rotation The point around which a figure is rotated.	**centro de rotación** Punto alrededor del cual rota una figura.	
central angle of a circle An angle with measure less than or equal to 180° whose vertex is the center of a circle.	**ángulo central de un círculo** Ángulo con medida inferior o igual a 180° cuyo vértice es el centro de un círculo.	
centroid of a triangle The point of concurrency of the three medians of a triangle. Also known as the *center of gravity*.	**centroide de un triángulo** Punto donde se encuentran las tres medianas de un triángulo. También conocido como *centro de gravedad*.	 The centroid is *P*.
chord A segment whose endpoints lie on a circle.	**cuerda** Segmento cuyos extremos se encuentran en un círculo.	
circle The set of points in a plane that are a fixed distance from a given point called the center of the circle.	**círculo** Conjunto de puntos en un plano que se encuentran a una distancia fija de un punto determinado denominado centro del círculo.	
circumcenter of a triangle The point of concurrency of the three perpendicular bisectors of a triangle.	**circuncentro de un triángulo** Punto donde se cortan las tres mediatrices de un triángulo.	 The circumcenter is *P*.
circumcircle See circumscribed circle.	**circuncírculo** *Véase* círculo circunscrito.	
circumference The distance around the circle.	**circunferencia** Distancia alrededor del círculo.	
circumscribed angle An angle formed by two rays from a common endpoint that are tangent to a circle	**ángulo circunscrito** Ángulo formado por dos semirrectas tangentes a un círculo que parten desde un extremo común.	

Glossary/Glosario

circumscribed circle Every vertex of the polygon lies on the circle.

círculo circunscrito Todos los vértices del polígono se encuentran sobre el círculo.

circumscribed polygon Each side of the polygon is tangent to the circle.

polígono circunscrito Todos los lados del polígono son tangentes al círculo.

coincide To correspond exactly; to be identical.

coincidir Corresponder exactamente, ser idéntico.

collinear Points that lie on the same line.

colineal Puntos que se encuentran sobre la misma línea.

K,L, and M are collinear points.

combination A selection of a group of objects in which order is *not* important. The number of combinations of *r* objects chosen from a group of *n* objects is denoted $_nC_r$.

combinación Selección de un grupo de objetos en la cual el orden *no* es importante. El número de combinaciones de *r* objetos elegidos de un grupo de *n* objetos se expresa así: $_nC_r$.

For 4 objects A, B, C, and D, there are $_4C_2 = 6$ different combinations of 2 objects: AB, AC, AD, BC, BD, CD.

common tangent A line that is tangent to two circles.

tangente común Línea que es tangente a dos círculos.

 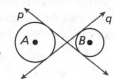

complement of an angle The sum of the measures of an angle and its complement is 90°.

complemento de un ángulo La suma de las medidas de un ángulo y su complemento es 90°.

The complement of a 53° angle is a 37° angle.

complement of an event All outcomes in the sample space that are not in an event *E*, denoted $\bar{E}$.

complemento de un suceso Todos los resultados en el espacio muestral que no están en el suceso *E* y se expresan $\bar{E}$.

In the experiment of rolling a number cube, the complement of rolling a 3 is rolling a 1, 2, 4, 5, or 6.

complementary angles Two angles whose measures have a sum of 90°.

ángulos complementarios Dos ángulos cuyas medidas suman 90°.

ENGLISH	SPANISH	EXAMPLES
component form The form of a vector that lists the vertical and horizontal change from the initial point to the terminal point.	**forma de componente** Forma de un vector que muestra el cambio horizontal y vertical desde el punto inicial hasta el punto terminal.	 The component form of $\overrightarrow{CD}$ is $\langle 2, 3 \rangle$.
composite figure A plane figure made up of triangles, rectangles, trapezoids, circles, and other simple shapes, or a three-dimensional figure made up of prisms, cones, pyramids, cylinders, and other simple three-dimensional figures.	**figura compuesta** Figura plana compuesta por triángulos, rectángulos, trapecios, círculos y otras figuras simples, o figura tridimensional compuesta por prismas, conos, pirámides, cilindros y otras figuras tridimensionales simples.	
composition of transformations One transformation followed by another transformation.	**composición de transformaciones** Una transformación seguida de otra transformación.	
compound event An event made up of two or more simple events.	**suceso compuesto** Suceso formado por dos o más sucesos simples.	In the experiment of tossing a coin and rolling a number cube, the event of the coin landing heads and the number cube landing on 3.
concave polygon A polygon in which a diagonal can be drawn such that part of the diagonal contains points in the exterior of the polygon.	**polígono cóncavo** Polígono en el cual se puede trazar una diagonal tal que parte de la diagonal contiene puntos ubicados fuera del polígono.	 Concave quadrilateral
conclusion The part of a conditional statement following the word *then*.	**conclusión** Parte de un enunciado condicional que sigue a la palabra *entonces*.	If $x + 1 = 5$, then $\underline{x = 4}$. Conclusion
concurrent Three or more lines that intersect at one point.	**concurrente** Tres o más líneas que se cortan en un punto.	
conditional probability The probability of event *B*, given that event *A* has already occurred or is certain to occur, denoted $P(B \mid A)$; used to find probability of dependent events.	**probabilidad condicional** Probabilidad del suceso *B*, dado que el suceso *A* ya ha ocurrido o es seguro que ocurrirá, expresada como $P(B \mid A)$; se utiliza para calcular la probabilidad de sucesos dependientes.	

ENGLISH	SPANISH	EXAMPLES
conditional relative frequency The ratio of a joint relative frequency to a related marginal relative frequency in a two-way table.	**frecuencia relativa condicional** Razón de una frecuencia relativa conjunta a una frecuencia relativa marginal en una tabla de doble entrada.	
conditional statement A statement that can be written in the form "if p, then q," where p is the hypothesis and q is the conclusion.	**enunciado condicional** Enunciado que se puede expresar como "si p, entonces q", donde p es la hipótesis y q es la conclusión.	If $x + 1 = 5$, then $x = 4$. Hypothesis Conclusion
cone A three-dimensional figure with a circular base and a curved lateral surface that connects the base to a point called the vertex.	**cono** Figura tridimensional con una base circular y una superficie lateral curva que conecta la base con un punto denominado vértice.	
congruence statement A statement that indicates that two polygons are congruent by listing the vertices in the order of correspondence.	**enunciado de congruencia** Enunciado que indica que dos polígonos son congruentes enumerando los vértices en orden de correspondencia.	$\triangle HKL \cong \triangle YWX$
congruence transformation *See* isometry.	**transformación de congruencia** *Ver* isometría.	
congruent Having the same size and shape, denoted by $\cong$.	**congruente** Que tiene el mismo tamaño y la misma forma, expresado por $\cong$.	$\overline{PQ} \cong \overline{SR}$
congruent polygons Two polygons whose corresponding sides and angles are congruent.	**polígonos congruentes** Dos polígonos cuyos lados y ángulos correspondientes son congruentes.	
conjecture A statement that is believed to be true.	**conjetura** Enunciado que se supone verdadero.	A sequence begins with the terms 2, 4, 6, 8, 10. A reasonable conjecture is that the next term in the sequence is 12.
consecutive interior angles *See* same-side interior angles.	**ángulos internos consecutivos** *Ver* ángulos internos del mismo lado.	
contrapositive The statement formed by both exchanging and negating the hypothesis and conclusion of a conditional statement.	**contrarrecíproco** Enunciado que se forma al intercambiar y negar la hipótesis y la conclusión de un enunciado condicional.	Statement: If $n + 1 = 3$, then $n = 2$. Contrapositive: If $n \neq 2$, then $n + 1 \neq 3$.

Glossary/Glosario

converse The statement formed by exchanging the hypothesis and conclusion of a conditional statement.

recíproco Enunciado que se forma intercambiando la hipótesis y la conclusión de un enunciado condicional.

Statement: If $n + 1 = 3$, then $n = 2$.
Converse: If $n = 2$, then $n + 1 = 3$.

---

convex polygon A polygon in which no diagonal contains points in the exterior of the polygon.

polígono convexo Polígono en el cual ninguna diagonal contiene puntos fuera del polígono.

Convex quadrilateral

---

coordinate A number used to identify the location of a point. On a number line, one coordinate is used. On a coordinate plane, two coordinates are used, called the x-coordinate and the y-coordinate. In space, three coordinates are used, called the x-coordinate, the y-coordinate, and the z-coordinate.

coordenada Número utilizado para identificar la ubicación de un punto. En una recta numérica se utiliza una coordenada. En un plano cartesiano se utilizan dos coordenadas, denominadas coordenada x y coordenada y. En el espacio se utilizan tres coordenadas, denominadas coordenada x, coordenada y y coordenada z.

The coordinate of point A is 3.

The coordinates of point B are (1, 4).

---

coordinate proof A style of proof that uses coordinate geometry and algebra.

prueba de coordenadas Tipo de demostración que utiliza geometría de coordenadas y álgebra.

---

coplanar Points that lie in the same plane.

coplanar Puntos que se encuentran en el mismo plano.

---

corollary A theorem whose proof follows directly from another theorem.

corolario Teorema cuya demostración proviene directamente de otro teorema.

---

corresponding angles of lines intersected by a transversal For two lines intersected by a transversal, a pair of angles that lie on the same side of the transversal and on the same sides of the other two lines.

ángulos correspondientes de líneas cortadas por una transversal Dadas dos líneas cortadas por una transversal, el par de ángulos ubicados en el mismo lado de la transversal y en los mismos lados de las otras dos líneas.

$\angle 1$ and $\angle 3$ are corresponding.

---

corresponding angles of polygons Angles in the same position in two different polygons that have the same number of angles.

ángulos correspondientes de los polígonos Ángulos que tienen la misma posición en dos polígonos diferentes que tienen el mismo número de ángulos.

$\angle A$ and $\angle D$ are corresponding angles.

Glossary/Glosario

ENGLISH	SPANISH	EXAMPLES
corresponding sides of polygons Sides in the same position in two different polygons that have the same number of sides.	**lados correspondientes de los polígonos** Lados que tienen la misma posición en dos polígonos diferentes que tienen el mismo número de lados.	 $\overrightarrow{AB}$ and $\overline{DE}$ are corresponding sides.
cosecant In a right triangle, the cosecant of angle A is the ratio of the length of the hypotenuse to the length of the side opposite A. It is the reciprocal of the sine function.	**cosecante** En un triángulo rectángulo, la cosecante del ángulo A es la razón entre la longitud de la hipotenusa y la longitud del cateto opuesto a A. Es la inversa de la función seno.	 $\csc A = \dfrac{\text{hypotenuse}}{\text{opposite}} = \dfrac{1}{\sin A}$
cosine In a right triangle, the cosine of angle A is the ratio of the length of the leg adjacent to angle A to the length of the hypotenuse. It is the reciprocal of the secant function.	**coseno** En un triángulo rectángulo, el coseno del ángulo A es la razón entre la longitud del cateto adyacente al ángulo A y la longitud de la hipotenusa. Es la inversa de la función secante.	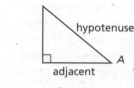 $\cos A = \dfrac{\text{adjacent}}{\text{hypotenuse}} = \dfrac{1}{\sec A}$
cotangent In a right triangle, the cotangent of angle A is the ratio of the length of the side adjacent to A to the length of the side opposite A. It is the reciprocal of the tangent function.	**cotangente** En un triángulo rectángulo, la cotangente del ángulo A es la razón entre la longitud del cateto adyacente a A y la longitud del cateto opuesto a A. Es la inversa de la función tangente.	 $\cot A = \dfrac{\text{adjacent}}{\text{opposite}} = \dfrac{1}{\tan A}$
counterexample An example that proves that a conjecture or statement is false.	**contraejemplo** Ejemplo que demuestra que una conjetura o enunciado es falso.	
CPCTC An abbreviation for "Corresponding Parts of Congruent Triangles are Congruent," which can be used as a justification in a proof after two triangles are proven congruent.	**PCTCC** Abreviatura que significa "Las partes correspondientes de los triángulos congruentes son congruentes", que se puede utilizar para justificar una demostración después de demostrar que dos triángulos son congruentes (CPCTC, por sus siglas en inglés).	
cross section The intersection of a three-dimensional figure and a plane.	**sección transversal** Intersección de una figura tridimensional y un plano.	

Glossary/Glosario

ENGLISH	SPANISH	EXAMPLES
cube A prism with six square faces.	**cubo** Prisma con seis caras cuadradas.	
cylinder A three-dimensional figure with two parallel congruent circular bases and a curved lateral surface that connects the bases.	**cilindro** Figura tridimensional con dos bases circulares congruentes y paralelas y una superficie lateral curva que conecta las bases.	

D

ENGLISH	SPANISH	EXAMPLES
decagon A ten-sided polygon.	**decágono** Polígono de diez lados.	
deductive reasoning The process of using logic to draw conclusions.	**razonamiento deductivo** Proceso en el que se utiliza la lógica para sacar conclusiones.	
definition A statement that describes a mathematical object and can be written as a true biconditional statement.	**definición** Enunciado que describe un objeto matemático y se puede expresar como un enunciado bicondicional verdadero.	
degree A unit of angle measure; one degree is $\frac{1}{360}$ of a circle.	**grado** Unidad de medida de los ángulos; un grado es $\frac{1}{360}$ de un círculo.	
density The amount of matter that an object has in a given unit of volume. The density of an object is calculated by dividing its mass by its volume.	**densidad** La cantidad de materia que tiene un objeto en una unidad de volumen determinada. La densidad de un objeto se calcula dividiendo su masa entre su volumen.	$\text{density} = \frac{\text{mass}}{\text{volume}}$
dependent events Events for which the occurrence or nonoccurrence of one event affects the probability of the other event.	**sucesos dependientes** Dos sucesos son dependientes si el hecho de que uno de ellos se cumpla o no afecta la probabilidad del otro.	From a bag containing 3 red marbles and 2 blue marbles, drawing a red marble, and then drawing a blue marble without replacing the first marble.
diagonal of a polygon A segment connecting two nonconsecutive vertices of a polygon.	**diagonal de un polígono** Segmento que conecta dos vértices no consecutivos de un polígono.	
diameter A segment that has endpoints on the circle and that passes through the center of the circle; also the length of that segment.	**diámetro** Segmento que atraviesa el centro de un círculo y cuyos extremos están sobre la circunferencia; longitud de dicho segmento.	

dilation A transformation in which the lines connecting every point P with its preimage P' all intersect at a point C known as the center of dilation, and $\frac{CP'}{CP}$ is the same for every point P; a transformation that changes the size of a figure but not its shape.

dilatación Transformación en la cual las líneas que conectan cada punto P con su imagen original P' se cruzan en un punto C conocido como centro de dilatación, y $\frac{CP'}{CP}$ es igual para cada punto P; transformación que cambia el tamaño de una figura pero no su forma.

directed line segment A segment between two points A and B with a specified direction, from A to B or from B to A.

segmento de una línea con dirección Un segmento entro dos puntos con una dirección especificada.

direction of a vector The orientation of a vector, which is determined by the angle the vector makes with a horizontal line.

dirección de un vector Orientación de un vector, determinada por el ángulo que forma el vector con una línea horizontal.

directrix A fixed line used to define a *parabola*. Every point on the parabola is equidistant from the directrix and a fixed point called the *focus*.

directriz Línea fija utilizada para definir una *parábola*. Cada punto de la parábola es equidistante de la directriz y de un punto fijo denominado *foco*.

$$P_1D_1 = P_1F \quad P_2D_2 = P_2F$$

distance between two points The absolute value of the difference of the coordinates of the points.

distancia entre dos puntos Valor absoluto de la diferencia entre las coordenadas de los puntos.

$$AB = |a - b| = |b - a|$$

distance from a point to a line The length of the perpendicular segment from the point to the line.

distancia desde un punto hasta una línea Longitud del segmento perpendicular desde el punto hasta la línea.

The distance from P to $\overleftrightarrow{AC}$ is 5 units.

dodecagon A 12-sided polygon.

dodecágono Polígono de 12 lados.

E

element of a set An item in a set.

elemento de un conjunto Componente de un conjunto.

4 is an element of the set of even numbers.

$$4 \in \left\{ \text{even numbers} \right\}$$

Glossary/Glosario

ENGLISH	SPANISH	EXAMPLES
empty set A set with no elements.	**conjunto vacío** Conjunto sin elementos.	The solution set of $|x| < 0$ is the empty set, $\{\ \}$, or $\varnothing$.
endpoint A point at an end of a segment or the starting point of a ray.	**extremo** Punto en el final de un segmento o punto de inicio de un rayo.	
enlargement A dilation with a scale factor greater than 1. In an enlargement, the image is larger than the preimage.	**agrandamiento** Dilatación con un factor de escala mayor que 1. En un agrandamiento, la imagen es más grande que la imagen original.	
equally likely outcomes Outcomes are equally likely if they have the same probability of occurring. If an experiment has n equally likely outcomes, then the probability of each outcome is $\frac{1}{n}$.	**resultados igualmente probables** Los resultados son igualmente probables si tienen la misma probabilidad de ocurrir. Si un experimento tiene n resultados igualmente probables, entonces la probabilidad de cada resultado es $\frac{1}{n}$.	If a coin is tossed, and heads and tails are equally likely, then $P(\text{heads}) = P(\text{tails}) = \frac{1}{2}$.
equiangular polygon A polygon in which all angles are congruent.	**polígono equiangular** Polígono cuyos ángulos son todos congruentes.	
equiangular triangle A triangle with three congruent angles.	**triángulo equiangular** Triángulo con tres ángulos congruentes.	
equidistant The same distance from two or more objects.	**equidistante** Igual distancia de dos o más objetos.	X is equidistant from A and B.
equilateral polygon A polygon in which all sides are congruent.	**polígono equilátero** Polígono cuyos lados son todos congruentes.	
equilateral triangle A triangle with three congruent sides.	**triángulo equilátero** Triángulo con tres lados congruentes.	

Glossary/Glosario

Glossary/Glosario

ENGLISH	SPANISH	EXAMPLES
Euclidean geometry The system of geometry described by Euclid. In particular, the system of Euclidean geometry satisfies the Parallel Postulate, which states that there is exactly one line through a given point parallel to a given line.	**geometría euclidiana** Sistema geométrico desarrollado por Euclides. Específicamente, el sistema de la geometría euclidiana cumple con el postulado de las paralelas, que establece que por un punto dado se puede trazar una única línea paralela a una línea dada.	
event An outcome or set of outcomes in a probability experiment.	**suceso** Resultado o conjunto de resultados en un experimento de probabilidad.	In the experiement of rolling a number cube, the event "an odd number" consists of the outcomes 1, 3, 5.
experiment An operation, process, or activity in which outcomes can be used to estimate probability.	**experimento** Una operación, proceso o actividad en la que se usan los resultados para estimar una probabilidad.	Tossing a coin 10 times and noting the number of heads.
experimental probability The ratio of the number of times an event occurs to the number of trials, or times, that an activity is performed.	**probabilidad experimental** Razón entre la cantidad de veces que ocurre un suceso y la cantidad de pruebas, o veces, que se realiza una actividad.	Kendra made 6 of 10 free throws. The experimental probability that she will make her next free throw is $P\left(\text{free throw}\right) = \frac{\text{number made}}{\text{number attempted}} = \frac{6}{10}$.
exterior of a circle The set of all points outside a circle.	**exterior de un círculo** Conjunto de todos los puntos que se encuentran fuera de un círculo.	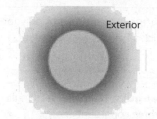
exterior of an angle The set of all points outside an angle.	**exterior de un ángulo** Conjunto de todos los puntos que se encuentran fuera de un ángulo.	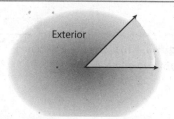
exterior of a polygon The set of all points outside a polygon.	**exterior de un polígono** Conjunto de todos los puntos que se encuentran fuera de un polígono.	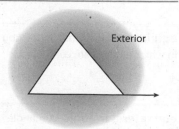
exterior angle of a polygon An angle formed by one side of a polygon and the extension of an adjacent side.	**ángulo externo de un polígono** Ángulo formado por un lado de un polígono y la prolongación del lado adyacente.	∠4 is an exterior angle.

ENGLISH	SPANISH	EXAMPLES

external secant segment A segment of a secant that lies in the exterior of the circle with one endpoint on the circle.

segmento secante externo Segmento de una secante que se encuentra en el exterior del círculo y tiene un extremo sobre el círculo.

$\overline{NM}$ is an external secant segment.

F

factorial If n is a positive integer, then n factorial, written $n!$, is $n \cdot (n-1) \cdot (n-2) \cdot ... \cdot 2 \cdot 1$. The factorial of 0 is defined to be 1.

factorial Si n es un entero positivo, entonces el factorial de n, expresado como $n!$, es $n \cdot (n-1) \cdot (n-2) \cdot ... \cdot 2 \cdot 1$. Por definición, el factorial de 0 será 1.

$7! = 7 \cdot 6 \cdot 5 \cdot 4 \cdot 3 \cdot 2 \cdot 1 = 5040$
$0! = 1$

fair When all outcomes of an experiment are equally likely.

justo Cuando todos los resultados de un experimento son igualmente probables.

When tossing a fair coin, heads and tails are equally likely. Each has a probability of $\frac{1}{2}$.

favorable outcome The occurrence of one of several possible outcomes of a specified event or probability experiment.

resultado favorable Cuando se produce uno de varios resultados posibles de un suceso específico o experimento de probabilidad.

In the experiment of rolling an odd number on a number cube, the favorable outcomes are 1, 3, and 5.

focus (pl. foci) of a parabola A fixed point F used with a *directrix* to define a *parabola*.

foco de una parábola Punto fijo F utilizado con una *directriz* para definir una *parábola*.

Fundamental Counting Principle For n items, if there are m_1 ways to choose a first item, m_2 ways to choose a second item after the first item has been chosen, and so on, then there are $m_1 \cdot m_2 \cdot ... \cdot m_n$ ways to choose n items.

Principio fundamental de conteo Dados n elementos, si existen m_1 formas de elegir un primer elemento, m_2 formas de elegir un segundo elemento después de haber elegido el primero, y así sucesivamente, entonces existen $m_1 \cdot m_2 \cdot ... \cdot m_n$ formas de elegir n elementos.

If there are 4 colors of shirts, 3 colors of pants, and 2 colors of shoes, then there are $4 \cdot 3 \cdot 2 = 24$ possible outfits.

G

geometric mean For positive numbers a and b, the positive number x such that $\frac{a}{x} = \frac{x}{b}$. In a geometric sequence, a term that comes between two given nonconsecutive terms of the sequence.

media geométrica Dados los números positivos a y b, el número positivo x tal que $\frac{a}{x} = \frac{x}{b}$. En una sucesión geométrica, un término que está entre dos términos no consecutivos dados de la sucesión.

$\frac{a}{x} = \frac{x}{b}$
$x^2 = ab$
$x = \sqrt{ab}$

Glossary/Glosario

geometric probability A form of theoretical probability determined by a ratio of geometric measures such as lengths, areas, or volumes.

probabilidad geométrica Una forma de la probabilidad teórica determinada por una razón de medidas geométricas, como longitud, área o volumen.

The probability of the pointer landing on 80° is $\frac{2}{9}$.

glide reflection A composition of a translation and a reflection across a line parallel to the translation vector.

deslizamiento con inversión Composición de una traslación y una reflexión sobre una línea paralela al vector de traslación.

First translate the preimage along $\vec{v}$.

Then reflect the image across line ℓ.

great circle A circle on a sphere that divides the sphere into two hemispheres.

círculo máximo En una esfera, círculo que divide la esfera en dos hemisferios.

Great circle

H

height of a figure The length of an altitude of the figure.

altura de una figura Longitud de la altura de la figura.

hemisphere Half of a sphere.

hemisferio Mitad de una esfera.

heptagon A seven-sided polygon.

heptágono Polígono de siete lados.

hexagon A six-sided polygon.

hexágono Polígono de seis lados.

hypotenuse The side opposite the right angle in a right triangle.

hipotenusa Lado opuesto al ángulo recto de un triángulo rectángulo.

hypotenuse

ENGLISH	SPANISH	EXAMPLES
hypothesis The part of a conditional statement following the word *if*.	**hipótesis** La parte de un enunciado condicional que sigue a la palabra *si*.	If $x + 1 = 5$, then $x = 4$. Hypothesis

I

ENGLISH	SPANISH	EXAMPLES
identity An equation that is true for all values of the variables.	**identidad** Ecuación verdadera para todos los valores de las variables.	$3 = 3$ $2(x - 1) = 2x - 2$
image A shape that results from a transformation of a figure known as the preimage.	**imagen** Forma resultante de la transformación de una figura conocida como imagen original.	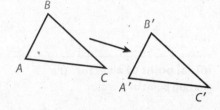
incenter of a triangle The point of concurrency of the three angle bisectors of a triangle.	**incentro de un triángulo** Punto donde se encuentran las tres bisectrices de los ángulos de un triángulo.	
incircle *See* inscribed circle.	**incírculo** *Véase* círculo inscrito.	
included angle The angle formed by two adjacent sides of a polygon.	**ángulo incluido** Ángulo formado por dos lados adyacentes de un polígono.	
included side The common side of two consecutive angles of a polygon.	**lado incluido** Lado común de dos ángulos consecutivos de un polígono.	
independent events Events for which the occurrence or nonoccurrence of one event does not affect the probability of the other event.	**sucesos independientes** Dos sucesos son independientes si el hecho de que se produzca o no uno de ellos no afecta la probabilidad del otro suceso.	From a bag containing 3 red marbles and 2 blue marbles, drawing a red marble, replacing it, and then drawing a blue marble.
indirect measurement A method of measurement that uses formulas, similar figures, and/or proportions.	**medición indirecta** Método para medir objetos mediante fórmulas, figuras semejantes y/o proporciones.	

indirect proof A proof in which the statement to be proved is assumed to be false and a contradiction is shown.

demostración indirecta Prueba en la que se supone que el enunciado a demostrar es falso y se muestra una contradicción.

---

indirect reasoning *See* indirect proof.

razonamiento indirecto *Ver* demostración indirecta.

---

inductive reasoning The process of reasoning that a rule or statement is true because specific cases are true.

razonamiento inductivo Proceso de razonamiento por el que se determina que una regla o enunciado son verdaderos porque ciertos casos específicos son verdaderos.

---

initial point of a vector The starting point of a vector.

punto inicial de un vector Punto donde comienza un vector.

---

initial side The ray that lies on the positive *x*-axis when an angle is drawn in standard position.

lado inicial Rayo que se encuentra sobre el eje *x* positivo cuando se traza un ángulo en posición estándar.

---

inscribed angle An angle whose vertex is on a circle and whose sides contain chords of the circle.

ángulo inscrito Ángulo cuyo vértice se encuentra sobre un círculo y cuyos lados contienen cuerdas del círculo.

---

inscribed circle A circle in which each side of the polygon is tangent to the circle.

círculo inscrito Círculo en el que cada lado del polígono es tangente al círculo.

---

inscribed polygon A polygon in which every vertex of the polygon lies on the circle.

polígono inscrito Polígono cuyos vértices se encuentran sobre el círculo.

---

intercepted arc An arc that consists of endpoints that lie on the sides of an inscribed angle and all the points of the circle between the endpoints.

arco abarcado Arco cuyos extremos se encuentran en los lados de un ángulo inscrito y consta de todos los puntos del círculo ubicados entre dichos extremos.

$\overset{\frown}{DF}$ is the intercepted arc.

Glossary/Glosario

interior angle An angle formed by two sides of a polygon with a common vertex.

ángulo interno Ángulo formado por dos lados de un polígono con un vértice común.

∠1 is an interior angle.

---

interior of a circle The set of all points inside a circle.

interior de un círculo Conjunto de todos los puntos que se encuentran dentro de un círculo.

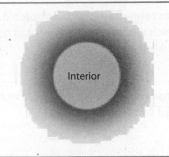

Interior

---

interior of an angle The set of all points between the sides of an angle.

interior de un ángulo Conjunto de todos los puntos entre los lados de un ángulo.

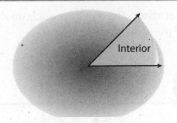

Interior

---

interior of a polygon The set of all points inside a polygon.

interior de un polígono Conjunto de todos los puntos que se encuentran dentro de un polígono.

Interior

---

inverse The statement formed by negating the hypothesis and conclusion of a conditional statement.

inverso Enunciado formado al negar la hipótesis y la conclusión de un enunciado condicional.

Statement: If $n + 1 = 3$, then $n = 2$.

Inverse: If $n + 1 \neq 3$, then $n \neq 2$.

---

inverse cosine The measure of an angle whose cosine ratio is known.

coseno inverso Medida de un ángulo cuya razón coseno es conocida.

If $\cos A = x$, then $\cos^{-1} x = m\angle A$.

---

inverse sine The measure of an angle whose sine ratio is known.

seno inverso Medida de un ángulo cuya razón seno es conocida.

If $\sin A = x$, then $\sin^{-1} x = m\angle A$.

---

inverse tangent The measure of an angle whose tangent ratio is known.

tangente inversa Medida de un ángulo cuya razón tangente es conocida.

If $\tan A = x$, then $\tan^{-1} x = m\angle A$.

---

irregular polygon A polygon that is not regular.

polígono irregular Polígono que no es regular.

Glossary/Glosario

Glossary/Glosario

isometry A transformation that does not change the size or shape of a figure.

isometría Transformación que no cambia el tamaño ni la forma de una figura.

Reflections, translations, and rotations are all examples of isometries.

---

isosceles trapezoid A trapezoid in which the legs are congruent but not parallel.

trapecio isósceles Trapecio cuyos lados no paralelos son congruentes.

---

isosceles triangle A triangle with at least two congruent sides.

triángulo isósceles Triángulo que tiene al menos dos lados congruentes.

---

iteration The repetitive application of the same rule.

iteración Aplicación repetitiva de la misma regla.v

J

joint relative frequency The ratio of the frequency in a particular category divided by the total number of data values.

frecuencia relativa conjunta La razón de la frecuencia en una determinada categoría dividida entre el número total de valores.

K

kite A quadrilateral with exactly two pairs of congruent consecutive sides.

cometa o papalote Cuadrilátero con exactamente dos pares de lados congruentes consecutivos.

Kite *ABCD*

L

lateral area The sum of the areas of the lateral faces of a prism or pyramid, or the area of the lateral surface of a cylinder or cone.

área lateral Suma de las áreas de las caras laterales de un prisma o pirámide, o área de la superficie lateral de un cilindro o cono.

12 cm

6 cm

8 cm

Lateral area = 4(6)(12) = 288 cm²

ENGLISH	SPANISH	EXAMPLES

lateral edge An edge of a prism or pyramid that is not an edge of a base.

arista lateral Arista de un prisma o pirámide que no es la arista de una base.

Right prism

---

lateral face A face of a prism or a pyramid that is not a base.

cara lateral Cara de un prisma o pirámide que no es la base.

Right prism

---

lateral surface The curved surface of a cylinder or cone.

superficie lateral Superficie curva de un cilindro o cono.

Right cylinder

---

leg of a right triangle One of the two sides of the right triangle that form the right angle.

cateto de un triángulo rectángulo Uno de los dos lados de un triángulo rectángulo que forman el ángulo recto.

---

leg of an isosceles triangle One of the two congruent sides of the isosceles triangle.

cateto de un triángulo isósceles Uno de los dos lados congruentes del triángulo isósceles.

---

legs of a trapezoid The sides of the trapezoid that are not the bases.

catetos de un trapecio Los lados del trapecio que no son las bases.

---

length The distance between the two endpoints of a segment.

longitud Distancia entre los dos extremos de un segmento.

$$AB = |a - b| = |b - a|$$

---

line An undefined term in geometry, a line is a straight path that has no thickness and extends forever.

línea Término indefinido en geometría; una línea es un trazo recto que no tiene grosor y se extiende infinitamente.

ENGLISH	SPANISH	EXAMPLES

line of symmetry A line that divides a plane figure into two congruent reflected halves.

eje de simetría Línea que divide una figura plana en dos mitades reflejas congruentes.

---

line segment *See* segment of a line.

segmento *Véase* segmento de recta.

---

line symmetry A figure that can be reflected across a line so that the image coincides with the preimage.

simetría axial Figura que puede reflejarse sobre una línea de forma tal que la imagen coincida con la imagen original.

---

linear pair A pair of adjacent angles whose noncommon sides are opposite rays.

par lineal Par de ángulos adyacentes cuyos lados no comunes son rayos opuestos.

∠3 and ∠4 form a linear pair.

M

major arc An arc of a circle whose points are on or in the exterior of a central angle.

arco mayor Arco de un círculo cuyos puntos están sobre un ángulo central o en su exterior.

$\overset{\frown}{ADC}$ is a major arc of the circle.

---

mapping An operation that matches each element of a set with another element, its image, in the same set.

correspondencia Operación que establece una correlación entre cada elemento de un conjunto con otro elemento, su imagen, en el mismo conjunto.

---

marginal relative frequency The sum of the joint relative frequencies in a row or column of a two-way table.

frecuencia relativa marginal La suma de las frecuencias relativas conjuntas en una fila o columna de una tabla de doble entrada.

---

measure of an angle Angles are measured in degrees. A degree is $\frac{1}{360}$ of a complete circle.

medida de un ángulo Los ángulos se miden en grados. Un grado es $\frac{1}{360}$ de un círculo completo.

$m\angle M = 26.8°$

ENGLISH	SPANISH	EXAMPLES
measure of a major arc The difference of 360° and the measure of the associated minor arc.	**medida de un arco mayor** Diferencia entre 360° y la medida del arco menor asociado.	$\text{m}\overset{\frown}{ADC} = 360° - x°$
measure of a minor arc The measure of its central angle.	**medida de un arco menor** Medida de su ángulo central.	$\text{m}\overset{\frown}{AC} = x°$
median of a triangle A segment whose endpoints are a vertex of the triangle and the midpoint of the opposite side.	**mediana de un triángulo** Segmento cuyos extremos son un vértice del triángulo y el punto medio del lado opuesto.	
midpoint The point that divides a segment into two congruent segments.	**punto medio** Punto que divide un segmento en dos segmentos congruentes.	B is the midpoint of $\overline{AC}$.
midsegment of a trapezoid The segment whose endpoints are the midpoints of the legs of the trapezoid.	**segmento medio de un trapecio** Segmento cuyos extremos son los puntos medios de los catetos del trapecio.	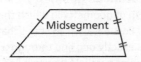
midsegment of a triangle A segment that joins the midpoints of two sides of the triangle.	**segmento medio de un triángulo** Segmento que une los puntos medios de dos lados del triángulo.	
minor arc An arc of a circle whose points are on or in the interior of a central angle.	**arco menor** Arco de un círculo cuyos puntos están sobre un ángulo central o en su interior.	$\overset{\frown}{AC}$ is a minor arc of the circle.
mutually exclusive events Two events are mutually exclusive if they cannot both occur in the same trial of an experiment.	**sucesos mutuamente excluyentes** Dos sucesos son mutuamente excluyentes si ambos no pueden ocurrir en la misma prueba de un experimento.	In the experiment of rolling a number cube, rolling a 3 and rolling an even number are mutually exclusive events.

Glossary/Glosario

Glossary/Glosario

N

net A diagram of the faces of a three-dimensional figure arranged in such a way that the diagram can be folded to form the three-dimensional figure.

plantilla Diagrama de las caras de una figura tridimensional que se puede plegar para formar la figura tridimensional.

10 m

6 m

10 m

6 m

***n*-gon** An *n*-sided polygon.

***n*-ágono** Polígono de *n* lados.

---

nonagon A nine-sided polygon.

nonágono Polígono de nueve lados.

---

noncollinear Points that do not lie on the same line.

no colineal Puntos que no se encuentran sobre la misma línea.

Points *A*, *B*, and *D* are not collinear.

---

non-Euclidean geometry A system of geometry in which the Parallel Postulate, which states that there is exactly one line through a given point parallel to a given line, does not hold.

geometría no euclidiana Sistema de geometría en el cual no se cumple el postulado de las paralelas, que establece que por un punto dado se puede trazar una única línea paralela a una línea dada.

In spherical geometry, there are no parallel lines. The sum of the angles in a triangle is always greater than 180°.

---

noncoplanar Points that do not lie on the same plane.

no coplanar Puntos que no se encuentran en el mismo plano.

T, *U*, *V*, and *S* are not coplanar.

O

oblique cone A cone whose axis is not perpendicular to the base.

cono oblicuo Cono cuyo eje no es perpendicular a la base.

---

oblique cylinder A cylinder whose axis is not perpendicular to the bases.

cilindro oblicuo Cilindro cuyo eje no es perpendicular a las bases.

ENGLISH	SPANISH	EXAMPLES
oblique prism A prism that has at least one nonrectangular lateral face.	**prisma oblicuo** Prisma que tiene por lo menos una cara lateral no rectangular.	
obtuse angle An angle that measures greater than 90° and less than 180°.	**ángulo obtuso** Ángulo que mide más de 90° y menos de 180°.	
obtuse triangle A triangle with one obtuse angle.	**triángulo obtusángulo** Triángulo con un ángulo obtuso.	
octagon An eight-sided polygon.	**octágono** Polígono de ocho lados.	
opposite rays Two rays that have a common endpoint and form a line.	**rayos opuestos** Dos rayos que tienen un extremo común y forman una línea.	$F \quad E \quad G$ $\overrightarrow{EF}$ and $\overrightarrow{EG}$ are opposite rays.
order of rotational symmetry The number of times a figure with rotational symmetry coincides with itself as it rotates 360°.	**orden de simetría de rotación** Cantidad de veces que una figura con simetría de rotación coincide consigo misma cuando rota 360°.	90° 90° 90° 90° Order of rotational symmetry: 4
orthocenter of a triangle The point of concurrency of the three altitudes of a triangle.	**ortocentro de un triángulo** Punto de intersección de las tres alturas de un triángulo.	P is the orthocenter. P
outcome A possible result of a probability experiment.	**resultado** Resultado posible de un experimento de probabilidad.	In the experiment of rolling a number cube, the possible outcomes are 1, 2, 3, 4, 5, and 6.
overlapping events Events that have one or more outcomes in common. Also called inclusive events.	**sucesos superpuestos** Sucesos que tienen uno o más resultados en común. También se denominan sucesos inclusivos.	Rolling an even number and rolling a prime number on a number cube are overlapping events because they both contain the outcome rolling a 2.

P

Glossary/Glosario

parabola The shape of the graph of a quadratic function. Also, the set of points equidistant from a point F, called the focus, and a line d, called the *directrix*.

parábola Forma de la gráfica de una función cuadrática. También, conjunto de puntos equidistantes de un punto F, denominado *foco*, y una línea d, denominada *directriz*.

---

parallel lines Lines in the same plane that do not intersect.

líneas paralelas Líneas rectas en el mismo plano que no se cruzan.

---

parallel planes Planes that do not intersect.

planos paralelos Planos que no se cruzan.

Plane *AEF* and plane *CGH* are parallel planes.

---

parallelogram A quadrilateral with two pairs of parallel sides.

paralelogramo Cuadrilátero con dos pares de lados paralelos.

---

pentagon A five-sided polygon.

diagrama Polígono de cinco lados.

---

perimeter The sum of the side lengths of a closed plane figure.

perímetro Suma de las longitudes de los lados de una figura plana cerrada.

Perimeter $= 18 + 6 + 18 + 6 = 48$ ft

---

permutation An arrangement of a group of objects in which order is important. The number of permutations of r objects from a group of n objects is denoted $_nP_r$.

permutación Arreglo de un grupo de objetos en el cual el orden es importante. El número de permutaciones de r objetos de un grupo de n objetos se expresa $_nP_r$.

For 4 objects A, B, C, and D, there are $_4P_2 = 12$ different permutations of 2 objects: AB, AC, AD, BC, BD, CD, BA, CA, DA, CB, DB, and DC.

---

perpendicular Intersecting to form 90° angles, denoted by ⊥.

perpendicular Que se cruza para formar ángulos de 90°, expresado por ⊥.

$m \perp n$

ENGLISH	SPANISH	EXAMPLES
perpendicular bisector of a segment A line perpendicular to a segment at the segment's midpoint.	**mediatriz de un segmento** Línea perpendicular a un segmento en el punto medio del segmento.	 ℓ is the perpendicular bisector of $\overline{AB}$.
perpendicular lines Lines that intersect at 90° angles.	**líneas perpendiculares** Líneas que se cruzan en ángulos de 90°.	 $m \perp n$
pi The ratio of the circumference of a circle to its diameter, denoted by the Greek letter π (pi). The value of π is irrational, often approximated by 3.14 or $\frac{22}{7}$.	**pi** Razón entre la circunferencia de un círculo y su diámetro, expresado por la letra griega π (pi). El valor de π es irracional y por lo general se aproxima a 3.14 ó $\frac{22}{7}$.	If a circle has a diameter of 5 inches and a circumference of C inches, then $\frac{C}{5} = \pi$, or $C = 5\pi$ inches, or about 15.7 inches.
plane An undefined term in geometry, it is a flat surface that has no thickness and extends forever.	**plano** Término indefinido en geometría; un plano es una superficie plana que no tiene grosor y se extiende infinitamente.	 plane R or plane ABC
plane symmetry A three-dimensional figure that can be divided into two congruent reflected halves by a plane has plane symmetry.	**simetría de plano** Una figura tridimensional que se puede dividir en dos mitades congruentes reflejadas por un plano tiene simetría de plano.	 Plane symmetry
Platonic solid One of the five regular polyhedra: a tetrahedron, a cube, an octahedron, a dodecahedron, or an icosahedron.	**sólido platónico** Uno de los cinco poliedros regulares: tetraedro, cubo, octaedro, dodecaedro o icosaedro.	
point An undefined term in geometry, it names a location and has no size.	**punto** Término indefinido de la geometría que denomina una ubicación y no tiene tamaño.	$P \bullet$ point P
point of concurrency A point where three or more lines coincide.	**punto de concurrencia** Punto donde se cruzan tres o más líneas.	

ENGLISH	SPANISH	EXAMPLES

point of tangency The point of intersection of a circle or sphere with a tangent line or plane.

punto de tangencia Punto de intersección de un círculo o esfera con una línea o plano tangente.

point-slope form
$y - y_1 = m(x - x_1)$, where m is the slope and (x_1, y_1) is a point on the line.

forma de punto y pendiente
$(y - y_1) = m(x - x_1)$, donde m es la pendiente y (x_1, y_1) es un punto en la línea.

polygon A closed plane figure formed by three or more segments such that each segment intersects exactly two other segments only at their endpoints and no two segments with a common endpoint are collinear.

polígono Figura plana cerrada formada por tres o más segmentos tal que cada segmento se cruza únicamente con otros dos segmentos sólo en sus extremos y ningún segmento con un extremo común a otro es colineal con éste.

polyhedron A closed three-dimensional figure formed by four or more polygons that intersect only at their edges.

poliedro Figura tridimensional cerrada formada por cuatro o más polígonos que se cruzan sólo en sus aristas.

postulate A statement that is accepted as true without proof. Also called an *axiom*.

postulado Enunciado que se acepta como verdadero sin demostración. También denominado *axioma*.

preimage The original figure in a transformation.

imagen original Figura original en una transformación.

primes Symbols used to label the image in a transformation.

apóstrofos Símbolos utilizados para identificar la imagen en una transformación.

$A'B'C'$

prism A polyhedron formed by two parallel congruent polygonal bases connected by lateral faces that are parallelograms.

prisma Poliedro formado por dos bases poligonales congruentes y paralelas conectadas por caras laterales que son paralelogramos.

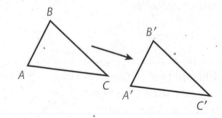

probability A number from 0 to 1 (or 0% to 100%) that is the measure of how likely an event is to occur.

probabilidad Número entre 0 y 1 (o entre 0% y 100%) que describe cuán probable es que ocurra un suceso.

A bag contains 3 red marbles and 4 blue marbles. The probability of randomly choosing a red marble is $\frac{3}{7}$.

ENGLISH	SPANISH	EXAMPLES
proof An argument that uses logic to show that a conclusion is true.	**demostración** Argumento que se vale de la lógica para probar que una conclusión es verdadera.	
proof by contradiction *See* indirect proof.	**demostración por contradicción** *Ver* demostración indirecta.	
pyramid A polyhedron formed by a polygonal base and triangular lateral faces that meet at a common vertex.	**pirámide** Poliedro formado por una base poligonal y caras laterales triangulares que se encuentran en un vértice común.	
Pythagorean triple A set of three nonzero whole numbers a, b, and c such that $a^2 + b^2 = c^2$.	**Tripleta de Pitágoras** Conjunto de tres números cabales distintos de cero a, b y c tal que $a^2 + b^2 = c^2$.	$\{3, 4, 5\}$ $3^2 + 4^2 = 5^2$

Q

ENGLISH	SPANISH	EXAMPLES
quadrilateral A four-sided polygon.	**cuadrilátero** Polígono de cuatro lados.	

R

ENGLISH	SPANISH	EXAMPLES
radial symmetry *See* rotational symmetry.	**simetría radial** *Ver* simetría de rotación.	
radian A unit of angle measure based on arc length. In a circle of radius r, if a central angle has a measure of 1 radian, then the length of the intercepted arc is r units. 2π radians $= 360°$ 1 radian $\approx 57°$	**radián** Unidad de medida de un ángulo basada en la longitud del arco. En un círculo de radio r, si un ángulo central mide 1 radián, entonces la longitud del arco abarcado es r unidades. 2π radians $= 360°$ 1 radian $\approx 57°$	
radius of a circle A segment whose endpoints are the center of a circle and a point on the circle; the distance from the center of a circle to any point on the circle.	**radio de un círculo** Segmento cuyos extremos son el centro y un punto de la circunferencia; distancia desde el centro de un círculo hasta cualquier punto de la circunferencia.	
radius of a sphere A segment whose endpoints are the center of a sphere and any point on the sphere; the distance from the center of a sphere to any point on the sphere.	**radio de una esfera** Segmento cuyos extremos son el centro de una esfera y cualquier punto sobre la esfera; distancia desde el centro de una esfera hasta cualquier punto sobre la esfera.	

Glossary/Glosario

ENGLISH	SPANISH	EXAMPLES
ray A part of a line that starts at an endpoint and extends forever in one direction.	**rayo** Parte de una línea que comienza en un extremo y se extiende infinitamente en una dirección.	 *D*
rectangle A quadrilateral with four right angles.	**rectángulo** Cuadrilátero con cuatro ángulos rectos.	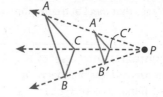
reduction A dilation with a scale factor greater than 0 but less than 1. In a reduction, the image is smaller than the preimage.	**reducción** Dilatación con un factor de escala mayor que 0 pero menor que 1. En una reducción, la imagen es más pequeña que la imagen original.	
reflection A transformation across a line, called the line of reflection, such that the line of reflection is the perpendicular bisector of each segment joining each point and its image.	**reflexión** Transformación sobre una línea, denominada la línea de reflexión. La línea de reflexión es la mediatriz de cada segmento que une un punto con su imagen.	
reflection symmetry *See* line symmetry.	**simetría de reflexión** *Ver* simetría axial.	
regular polygon A polygon that is both equilateral and equiangular.	**polígono regular** Polígono equilátero de ángulos iguales.	
regular polyhedron A polyhedron in which all faces are congruent regular polygons and the same number of faces meet at each vertex. *See also* Platonic solid.	**poliedro regular** Poliedro cuyas caras son todas polígonos regulares congruentes y en el que el mismo número de caras se encuentran en cada vértice. *Ver también* sólido platónico.	
regular pyramid A pyramid whose base is a regular polygon and whose lateral faces are congruent isosceles triangles.	**pirámide regular** Pirámide cuya base es un polígono regular y cuyas caras laterales son triángulos isósceles congruentes.	
remote interior angle An interior angle of a polygon that is not adjacent to the exterior angle.	**ángulo interno remoto** Ángulo interno de un polígono que no es adyacente al ángulo externo.	 The remote interior angles of ∠4 are ∠1 and ∠2.

Glossary/Glosario

ENGLISH	SPANISH	EXAMPLES
rhombus A quadrilateral with four congruent sides.	**rombo** Cuadrilátero con cuatro lados congruentes.	
right angle An angle that measures 90°.	**ángulo recto** Ángulo que mide 90°.	
right cone A cone whose axis is perpendicular to its base.	**cono recto** Cono cuyo eje es perpendicular a su base.	
right cylinder A cylinder whose axis is perpendicular to its bases.	**cilindro recto** Cilindro cuyo eje es perpendicular a sus bases.	
right prism A prism whose lateral faces are all rectangles.	**prisma recto** Prisma cuyas caras laterales son todas rectángulos.	
right triangle A triangle with one right angle.	**triángulo rectángulo** Triángulo con un ángulo recto.	
rigid motion *See* isometry.	**movimiento rígido** *Ver* isometría.	
rigid transformation A transformation that does not change the size or shape of a figure.	**transformación rígida** Transformación que no cambia el tamaño o la forma de una figura.	
rise The difference in the *y*-values of two points on a line.	**distancia vertical** Diferencia entre los valores de *y* de dos puntos de una línea.	For the points $(3, -1)$ and $(6, 5)$, the rise is $5 - (-1) = 6$.
rotation A transformation about a point *P*, also known as the center of rotation, such that each point and its image are the same distance from *P*. All of the angles with vertex *P* formed by a point and its image are congruent.	**rotación** Transformación sobre un punto *P*, también conocido como el centro de rotación, tal que cada punto y su imagen estén a la misma distancia de *P*. Todos los ángulos con vértice *P* formados por un punto y su imagen son congruentes.	

ENGLISH	SPANISH	EXAMPLES
rotational symmetry A figure that can be rotated about a point by an angle less than 360° so that the image coincides with the preimage has rotational symmetry.	**simetría de rotación** Una figura que puede rotarse alrededor de un punto en un ángulo menor de 360° de forma tal que la imagen coincide con la imagen original tiene simetría de rotación.	Order of rotational symmetry: 4
run The difference in the *x*-values of two points on a line.	**distancia horizontal** Diferencia entre los valores de *x* de dos puntos de una línea.	For the points $(3, -1)$ and $(6, 5)$, the run is $6 - 3 = 3$.

S

ENGLISH	SPANISH	EXAMPLES
same-side interior angles For two lines intersected by a transversal, a pair of angles that lie on the same side of the transversal and between the two lines.	**ángulos internos del mismo lado** Dadas dos líneas cortadas por una transversal, el par de ángulos ubicados en el mismo lado de la transversal y entre las dos líneas.	$\angle 2$ and $\angle 3$ are same-side interior angles.
sample space The set of all possible outcomes of a probability experiment.	**espacio muestral** Conjunto de todos los resultados posibles de un experimento de probabilidad.	In the experiment of rolling a number cube, the sample space is $\{1, 2, 3, 4, 5, 6\}$.
scale The ratio between two corresponding measurements.	**escala** Razón entre dos medidas correspondientes.	1 cm : 5 mi
scale drawing A drawing that uses a scale to represent an object as smaller or larger than the actual object.	**dibujo a escala** Dibujo que utiliza una escala para representar un objeto como más pequeño o más grande que el objeto original.	A blueprint is an example of a scale drawing.
scale factor The multiplier used on each dimension to change one figure into a similar figure.	**factor de escala** El multiplicador utilizado en cada dimensión para transformar una figura en una figura semejante.	Scale factor: 2
scale model A three-dimensional model that uses a scale to represent an object as smaller or larger than the actual object.	**modelo a escala** Modelo tridimensional que utiliza una escala para representar un objeto como más pequeño o más grande que el objeto real.	

Glossary/Glosario

ENGLISH	SPANISH	EXAMPLES
scalene triangle A triangle with no congruent sides.	**triángulo escaleno** Triángulo sin lados congruentes.	
secant of a circle A line that intersects a circle at two points.	**secante de un círculo** Línea que corta un círculo en dos puntos.	
secant of an angle In a right triangle, the ratio of the length of the hypotenuse to the length of the side adjacent to angle A. It is the reciprocal of the cosine function.	**secante de un ángulo** En un triángulo rectángulo, la razón entre la longitud de la hipotenusa y la longitud del cateto adyacente al ángulo A. Es la inversa de la función coseno.	$$\sec A = \frac{\text{hypotenuse}}{\text{adjacent}} = \frac{1}{\cos A}$$
secant segment A segment of a secant with at least one endpoint on the circle.	**segmento secante** Segmento de una secante que tiene al menos un extremo sobre el círculo.	$\overline{NM}$ is an external secant segment. $\overline{JK}$ is an internal secant segment.
sector of a circle A region inside a circle bounded by two radii of the circle and their intercepted arc.	**sector de un círculo** Región dentro de un círculo delimitado por dos radios del círculo y por su arco abarcado.	
segment bisector A line, ray, or segment that divides a segment into two congruent segments.	**bisectriz de un segmento** Línea, rayo o segmento que divide un segmento en dos segmentos congruentes.	
segment of a circle A region inside a circle bounded by a chord and an arc.	**segmento de un círculo** Región dentro de un círculo delimitada por una cuerda y un arco.	
segment of a line A part of a line consisting of two endpoints and all points between them.	**segmento de una línea** Parte de una línea que consiste en dos extremos y todos los puntos entre éstos.	

Glossary/Glosario

Glossary/Glosario

semicircle An arc of a circle whose endpoints lie on a diameter.

semicírculo Arco de un círculo cuyos extremos se encuentran sobre un diámetro.

set A collection of items called elements.

conjunto Grupo de componentes denominados elementos.

side of a polygon One of the segments that form a polygon.

lado de un polígono Uno de los segmentos que forman un polígono.

side of an angle One of the two rays that form an angle.

lado de un ángulo Uno de los dos rayos que forman un ángulo.

$\overrightarrow{AC}$ and $\overrightarrow{AB}$ are sides of $\angle CAB$.

similar Two figures are similar if they have the same shape but not necessarily the same size.

semejantes Dos figuras con la misma forma pero no necesariamente del mismo tamaño.

similar polygons Two polygons whose corresponding angles are congruent and whose corresponding side lengths are proportional.

polígonos semejantes Dos polígonos cuyos ángulos correspondientes son congruentes y cuyos lados correspondientes tienen longitudes proporcionales.

similarity ratio The ratio of two corresponding linear measurements in a pair of similar figures.

razón de semejanza Razón de dos medidas lineales correspondientes en un par de figuras semejantes.

Similarity ratio: $\dfrac{3.5}{2.1} = \dfrac{5}{3}$

similarity statement A statement that indicates that two polygons are similar by listing the vertices in the order of correspondence.

enunciado de semejanza Enunciado que indica que dos polígonos son semejantes enumerando los vértices en orden de correspondencia.

quadrilateral $ABCD \sim$ quadrilateral $EFGH$

similarity transformation A transformation that produces similar figures.

transformación de semejanza Una transformación que resulta en figuras semejantes.

Dilations are similarity transformations.

ENGLISH	SPANISH	EXAMPLES
simple event An event consisting of only one outcome.	**suceso simple** Suceso que contiene sólo un resultado.	In the experiment of rolling a number cube, the event consisting of the outcome 3 is a simple event.
sine In a right triangle, the ratio of the length of the leg opposite ∠A to the length of the hypotenuse.	**seno** En un triángulo rectángulo, razón entre la longitud del cateto opuesto a ∠A y la longitud de la hipotenusa.	$\sin A = \dfrac{\text{opposite}}{\text{hypotenuse}}$
skew lines Lines that are not coplanar.	**líneas oblicuas** Líneas que no son coplanares.	$\overleftrightarrow{AE}$ and $\overleftrightarrow{CD}$ are skew lines.
slide *See* translation.	**deslizamiento** *Ver* traslación.	
slope A measure of the steepness of a line. If (x_1, y_1) and (x_2, y_2) are any two points on the line, the slope of the line, known as m, is represented by the equation $m = \dfrac{y_2 - y_1}{x_2 - x_1}$.	**pendiente** Medida de la inclinación de una línea. Dados dos puntos (x_1, y_1) y (x_2, y_2) en una línea, la pendiente de la línea, denominada m, se representa con la ecuación $m = \dfrac{y_2 - y_1}{x_2 - x_1}$.	
slope-intercept form The slope-intercept form of a linear equation is $y = mx + b$, where m is the slope and b is the y-intercept.	**forma de pendiente-intersección** La forma de pendiente-intersección de una ecuación lineal es $y = mx + b$, donde m es la pendiente y b es la intersección con el eje y.	$y = -2x + 4$ The slope is -2. The y-intercept is 4.
solid A three-dimensional figure.	**cuerpo geométrico** Figura tridimensional.	
solving a triangle Using given measures to find unknown angle measures or side lengths of a triangle.	**resolución de un triángulo** Utilizar medidas dadas para hallar las medidas desconocidas de los ángulos o las longitudes de los lados de un triángulo.	
special right triangle A 45°–45°–90° triangle or a 30°–60°–90° triangle.	**triángulo rectángulo especial** Triángulo de 45°–45°–90° o triángulo de 30°–60°–90°.	

Glossary/Glosario

Glossary/Glosario

ENGLISH	SPANISH	EXAMPLES

sphere The set of points in space that are a fixed distance from a given point called the center of the sphere.

esfera Conjunto de puntos en el espacio que se encuentran a una distancia fija de un punto determinado denominado centro de la esfera.

---

square A quadrilateral with four congruent sides and four right angles.

cuadrado Cuadrilátero con cuatro lados congruentes y cuatro ángulos rectos.

---

straight angle A 180° angle.

ángulo llano Ángulo que mide 180°.

---

subset A set that is contained entirely within another set. Set B is a subset of set A if every element of B is contained in A, denoted $B \subset A$.

subconjunto Conjunto que se encuentra dentro de otro conjunto. El conjunto B es un subconjunto del conjunto A si todos los elementos de B son elementos de A; se expresa $B \subset A$.

The set of integers is a subset of the set of rational numbers.

---

supplementary angles Two angles whose measures have a sum of 180°.

ángulos suplementarios Dos ángulos cuyas medidas suman 180°.

∠3 and ∠4 are supplementary angles.

---

surface area The total area of all faces and curved surfaces of a three-dimensional figure.

área total Área total de todas las caras y superficies curvas de una figura tridimensional.

12 cm

6 cm

8 cm

Surface area $= 2(8)(12) + 2(8)(6) +$

$2(12)(6) = 432$ cm²

---

symmetry In the transformation of a figure such that the image coincides with the preimage, the image and preimage have symmetry.

simetría En la transformación de una figura tal que la imagen coincide con la imagen original, la imagen y la imagen original tienen simetría.

---

symmetry about an axis In the transformation of a figure such that there is a line about which a three-dimensional figure can be rotated by an angle greater than 0° and less than 360° so that the image coincides with the preimage, the image and preimage have symmetry about an axis.

simetría axial En la transformación de una figura tal que existe una línea sobre la cual se puede rotar una figura tridimensional a un ángulo mayor que 0° y menor que 360° de forma que la imagen coincida con la imagen original, la imagen y la imagen original tienen simetría axial.

T

tangent circles Two coplanar circles that intersect at exactly one point. If one circle is contained inside the other, they are *internally tangent*. If not, they are *externally tangent*.

círculos tangentes Dos círculos coplanares que se cruzan únicamente en un punto. Si un círculo contiene a otro, son *tangentes internamente*. De lo contrario, son *tangentes externamente*.

tangent of an angle In a right triangle, the ratio of the length of the leg opposite ∠*A* to the length of the leg adjacent to ∠*A*.

tangente de un ángulo En un triángulo rectángulo, razón entre la longitud del cateto opuesto a ∠*A* y la longitud del cateto adyacente a ∠*A*.

$$\tan A = \frac{\text{opposite}}{\text{adjacent}}$$

tangent segment A segment of a tangent with one endpoint on the circle.

segmento tangente Segmento de una tangente con un extremo en el círculo.

$\overline{BC}$ is a tangent segment.

tangent of a circle A line that is in the same plane as a circle and intersects the circle at exactly one point.

tangente de un círculo Línea que se encuentra en el mismo plano que un círculo y lo cruza únicamente en un punto.

terminal point of a vector The endpoint of a vector.

punto terminal de un vector Extremo de un vector.

tetrahedron A polyhedron with four faces. A regular tetrahedron has equilateral triangles as faces, with three faces meeting at each vertex.

tetraedro Poliedro con cuatro caras. Las caras de un tetraedro regular son triángulos equiláteros y cada vértice es compartido por tres caras.

theorem A statement that has been proven.

teorema Enunciado que ha sido demostrado.

Glossary/Glosario

ENGLISH	SPANISH	EXAMPLES
theoretical probability The ratio of the number of equally likely outcomes in an event to the total number of possible outcomes.	**probabilidad teórica** Razón entre el número de resultados igualmente probables de un suceso y el número total de resultados posibles.	In the experiment of rolling a number cube, the theoretical probability of rolling an odd number is $\frac{3}{6} = \frac{1}{2}$.
tick marks Marks used on a figure to indicate congruent segments.	**marcas "|"** Marcas utilizadas en una figura para indicar segmentos congruentes.	
transformation A change in the position, size, or shape of a figure or graph.	**transformación** Cambio en la posición, tamaño o forma de una figura o gráfica.	
translation A transformation that shifts or slides every point of a figure or graph the same distance in the same direction.	**traslación** Transformación en la que todos los puntos de una figura o gráfica se mueven la misma distancia en la misma dirección.	
transversal A line that intersects two coplanar lines at two different points.	**transversal** Línea que corta dos líneas coplanares en dos puntos diferentes.	
trapezoid A quadrilateral with at least one pair of parallel sides.	**trapecio** Cuadrilátero con al menos un par de lados paralelos.	
trial In probability, a single repetition or observation of an experiment.	**prueba** En probabilidad, una sola repetición u observación de un experimento.	In the experiment of rolling a number cube, each roll is one trial.
triangle A three-sided polygon.	**triángulo** Polígono de tres lados.	
triangle rigidity A property of triangles that states that if the side lengths of a triangle are fixed, the triangle can have only one shape.	**rigidez del triángulo** Propiedad de los triángulos que establece que, si las longitudes de los lados de un triángulo son fijas, el triángulo puede tener sólo una forma.	

ENGLISH	SPANISH	EXAMPLES

trigonometric ratio A ratio of two sides of a right triangle.

razón trigonométrica Razón entre dos lados de un triángulo rectángulo.

$$\sin A = \frac{a}{c}; \cos A = \frac{b}{c}; \tan A = \frac{a}{b}$$

---

trigonometry The study of the measurement of triangles and of trigonometric functions and their applications.

trigonometría Estudio de la medición de los triángulos y de las funciones trigonométricas y sus aplicaciones.

---

trisect To divide into three equal parts.

trisecar Dividir en tres partes iguales.

$\overline{AD}$ is trisected.

---

truth table A table that lists all possible combinations of truth values for a statement and its components.

tabla de verdad Tabla en la que se enumeran todas las combinaciones posibles de valores de verdad para un enunciado y sus componentes.

---

truth value A statement can have a truth value of true (T) or false (F).

valor de verdad Un enunciado puede tener un valor de verdad verdadero (V) o falso (F).

U

---

undefined term A basic figure that is not defined in terms of other figures. The undefined terms in geometry are point, line, and plane.

término indefinido Figura básica que no está definida en función de otras figuras. Los términos indefinidos en geometría son el punto, la línea y el plano.

---

union The union of two sets is the set of all elements that are in either set, denoted by ∪.

unión La unión de dos conjuntos es el conjunto de todos los elementos que se encuentran en ambos conjuntos, expresado por ∪.

$A = \{1, 2, 3, 4\}$

$B = \{1, 3, 5, 7, 9\}$

$A \cup B = \{1, 2, 3, 4, 5, 7, 9\}$

---

universal set The set of all elements in a particular context.

conjunto universal Conjunto de todos los elementos de un contexto determinado.

V

vector A quantity that has both magnitude and direction.

vector Cantidad que tiene magnitud y dirección.

Venn diagram A diagram used to show relationships between sets.

diagrama de Venn Diagrama utilizado para mostrar la relación entre conjuntos.

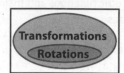

---

vertex angle of an isosceles triangle The angle formed by the legs of an isosceles triangle.

ángulo del vértice de un triángulo isósceles Ángulo formado por los catetos de un triángulo isósceles.

---

vertex of a cone The point opposite the base of the cone.

vértice de un cono Punto opuesto a la base del cono.

---

vertex of a parabola The highest or lowest point on the parabola.

vértice de una parábola Punto más alto o más bajo de una parábola.

---

vertex of a polygon The intersection of two sides of the polygon.

vértice de un polígono La intersección de dos lados del polígono.

A, B, C, D, and E are vertices of the polygon.

---

vertex of a pyramid The point opposite the base of the pyramid.

vértice de una pirámide Punto opuesto a la base de la pirámide.

---

vertex of a three-dimensional figure The point that is the intersection of three or more faces of the figure.

vértice de una figura tridimensional Punto que representa la intersección de tres o más caras de la figura.

Glossary/Glosario

ENGLISH	SPANISH	EXAMPLES
vertex of a triangle The intersection of two sides of the triangle.	**vértice de un triángulo** Intersección de dos lados del triángulo.	A, B, and C are vertices of △ABC.
vertex of an angle The common endpoint of the sides of the angle.	**vértice de un ángulo** Extremo común de los lados del ángulo.	A is the vertex of ∠CAB.
vertical angles The nonadjacent angles formed by two intersecting lines.	**ángulos opuestos por el vértice** Ángulos no adyacentes formados por dos rectas que se cruzan.	∠1 and ∠3 are vertical angles. ∠2 and ∠4 are vertical angles.
volume The number of nonoverlapping unit cubes of a given size that will exactly fill the interior of a three-dimensional figure.	**volumen** Cantidad de cubos unitarios no superpuestos de un determinado tamaño que llenan exactamente el interior de una figura tridimensional.	Volume = $(3)(4)(12) = 144$ ft³

X

x-axis The horizontal axis in a coordinate plane.	**eje x** Eje horizontal en un plano cartesiano.	

Y

y-axis The vertical axis in a coordinate plane.	**eje y** Eje vertical en un plano cartesiano.	

Index

Index locator numbers are in Module. Lesson form. For example, 2.1 indicates Module 2, Lesson 1 as listed in the Table of Contents.

Table of Measures

LENGTH

1 inch = 2.54 centimeters

1 meter = 39.37 inches

1 mile = 5,280 feet

1 mile = 1760 yards

1 mile = 1.609 kilometers

1 kilometer = 0.62 mile

MASS/WEIGHT

1 pound = 16 ounces

1 pound = 0.454 kilograms

1 kilogram = 2.2 pounds

1 ton = 2000 pounds

CAPACITY

1 cup = 8 fluid ounces

1 pint = 2 cups

1 quart = 2 pints

1 gallon = 4 quarts

1 gallon = 3.785 liters

1 liter = 0.264 gallons

1 liter = 1000 cubic centimeters

Symbols

≠	is not equal to	π	pi: (about 3.14)
≈	is approximately equal to	⊥	is perpendicular to
10^2	ten squared; ten to the second power	‖	is parallel to
		$\overleftrightarrow{AB}$	line AB
$2.\overline{6}$	repeating decimal 2.66666...	$\overrightarrow{AB}$	ray AB
$|-4|$	the absolute value of negative 4	$\overline{AB}$	line segment AB
$\sqrt{}$	square root	m∠A	measure of ∠A

Formulas

Triangle	$A = \frac{1}{2}bh$	Pythagorean Theorem	$a^2 + b^2 = c^2$
Parallelogram	$A = bh$	Quadratic Formula	$x = \frac{-b \pm \sqrt{b^2 - 4ac}}{2a}$
Circle	$A = \pi r^2$	Arithmetic Sequence	$a_n = a_1 + (n-1)d$
Circle	$C = \pi d$ or $C = 2\pi r$	Geometric Sequence	$a_n = a_1 r^{n-1}$
General Prisms	$V = Bh$	Geometric Series	$S_n = \frac{a_1 - a_1 r^n}{1-r}$ where $r \neq 1$
Cylinder	$V = \pi r^2 h$	Radians	$1\ radian = \frac{180}{\pi}\ degrees$
Sphere	$V = \frac{4}{3}\pi r^3$	Degrees	$1\ degree = \frac{\pi}{180}\ radians$
Cone	$V = \frac{1}{3}\pi r^2 h$	Exponential Growth/Decay	$A = A_0 e^{k(t - t_0)} + B_0$
Pyramid	$V = \frac{1}{3}Bh$		